Public Policy in Agriculture

In recent years, developed countries have formulated public policies in agriculture ranging from supporting rural life and farm income to promoting sustainability of food and fibre production.

Public Policy in Agriculture: Impact on Labor Supply and Household Income addresses the lack of empirical research in this area. It explores the impact of differing approaches to public policy through a series of international case studies, from the USA and Canada to South Korea, Norway, Slovenia, and Taiwan. At a time when much of the developed world has been experiencing budget deficits and policy-makers and the public in general have re-opened the debate on public expenditures in the agricultural sector, this is a timely volume.

Mishra, Viaggi, and Gomez y Paloma have written an authoritative guide to agricultural public policy that will serve as a reference for academics, researchers, students, and policy-makers.

Ashok K. Mishra is Kemper and Ethel Marley Foundation Chair in the Morrison School of Agribusiness at the WP Carey School of Business, Arizona State University, Tempe, USA.

Davide Viaggi is Professor at the Department of Agricultural Sciences of the University of Bologna, Italy.

Sergio Gomez y Paloma is senior researcher and scientific officer at the Joint Research Centre-Institute for Prospective Technological Studies (JRC-IPTS), European Commission, Sevilla, Spain.

Routledge Studies in Agricultural Economics
Series Editor: Ashok K. Mishra
Arizona State University, USA

1. Public Policy in Agriculture
Impact on Labor Supply and Household Income
Edited by Ashok K. Mishra, Davide Viaggi, and Sergio Gomez y Paloma

Public Policy in Agriculture

Impact on Labor Supply and Household Income

Edited by Ashok K. Mishra, Davide Viaggi, and Sergio Gomez y Paloma

Routledge
Taylor & Francis Group

LONDON AND NEW YORK

First published 2018
by Routledge

2 Park Square, Milton Park, Abingdon, Oxfordshire OX14 4RN
52 Vanderbilt Avenue, New York, NY 10017

Routledge is an imprint of the Taylor & Francis Group, an informa business

First issued in paperback 2019

British Library Cataloguing in Publication Data
A catalogue record for this book is available from the British Library

Library of Congress Cataloging-in-Publication Data
A catalog record for this book has been requested.

ISBN: 978-1-138-65212-5 (hbk)
ISBN: 978-0-367-87683-8 (pbk)

Typeset in Bembo Std
by diacriTech, Chennai

Contents

Figures

Tables

Contributors

Mary Clare Ahearn is retired from Economic Research Service, US Department of Agriculture. Currently she serves as the vice-chairman of Council on Food, Agricultural, and Resource Economics (C-FARE). Her primary areas of expertise are the economic well-being of farm operators and their households, the structure and the performance of the agricultural sector, and policies affecting structure and well-being. She also has experience in valuation of nonmarket goods and services and rural health care. She has authored numerous journal articles, book chapters, and co-edited books on farm costs and returns and related policy topics.

Walter J. Armbruster is President Emeritus, Farm Foundation in the United States. Currently he serves on the board of Council on Food, Agricultural and Resource Economics (C-FARE). Dr. Armbruster was the Editor of the Agricultural and Applied Economics Association's (AAEA) *Choices* magazine, and served as the Secretary-Treasurer of the International Association of Agricultural Economists (IAAE). He has authored numerous journal articles, book chapters, and other professional publications and co-edited books on a range of agricultural and related policy topics.

Ray Bollman retired from Statistics Canada and is currently a visiting professor at Brandon University. He has held a number of positions with Statistics Canada and the position of Chief of the Rural Research Group in Statistics Canada. He has served as President of the Canadian Association of Rural Studies and the Canadian Agricultural Economic Society. He was as a member of the founding committee of the Canadian Rural Revitalization Foundation and also a past chair of the OECD Working Party on Territorial Indicators. Ray was the founding editor of Statistics Canada's Rural and Small Town Canada Analysis Bulletins in 1998 and continued in this role up to his retirement.

Rembert De Blander is an applied econometrician at KU Leuven and Université catholique de Louvain. His main research interests lie in the field of applied (panel data) micro-econometrics; for example, the estimation of cost functions in order to study the effect of dairy quotas or the influence of biodiversity provision on the cost structure of farms.

Thomas Bournaris is an Assistant Professor in the Department of Agricultural Economics, Aristotle University of Thessaloniki. He received his BSc, MSc, and PhD in Agricultural Economics from the School of Agriculture, Aristotle University of Thessaloniki. His research interests are in agricultural economics, farm management and regional planning, impact assessment, sustainability, and efficiency. He has published papers in the *Journal of Environmental Management, Regional Studies, Journal of Policy Modeling,* and *Environmental Monitoring and Assessment.*

Mioara Borza has a PhD in Economics and is Lecturer in the Department of Accounting, Economic Information and Statistics, Faculty of Economics and Business Administration, Alexandru Ioan Cuza University of Iasi. Her interests in research are oriented to the most appropriate theoretical and practical approaches for an economic development in conditions of sustainability and eco-efficiency, in terms of rational consumption of resources, environmental protection, and social responsibility. All these issues are explored regarding agriculture and rural areas and environment.

Christopher Burns is an agricultural economist in the Farm Economy Branch of the Resource and Rural Economics Division of the USDA. His research evaluates how policy and economic factors influence farm household finances, farm structure, and farm production decisions. He also works on improving the missing data imputation methodology for the household section in the Agricultural Resource Management Survey (ARMS).

Hung-Hao Chang is a Professor in the Department of Agricultural Economics, National Taiwan University. He received his PhD from Cornell University. His research interests include agricultural and public policy analysis, food consumption and health, farm household economics, and applied microeconometrics. He was a visiting Scholar, University of California at Berkeley; Vice Secretary General, Rural Economics Society of Taiwan and Chair, International Cooperation Committee, Rural Economic Society of Taiwan.

Parthena Chatzinikolaou is a researcher in the Department of Agricultural Sciences, University of Bologna. She received her BSc and MSc in Agricultural Economics from the School of Agriculture at Aristotle University of Thessaloniki and her PhD from University of Bologna. Her research interests include agricultural economics, management of agricultural resources, and sustainability in agriculture. She has published papers in the *Journal of Policy Modeling, Land Use Policy, International Journal of Business Innovation and Research* and *New Medit.*

I-Chun Chen is a PhD student at the Department of Agricultural & Applied Economics, University of Wisconsin-Madison, US.

Pavel Ciaian is research officer at the European Commission (DG Joint Research Centre IPTS), Economics and Econometrics Research Institute (EERI), Slovak

Agricultural University (SAU), and the Catholic University of Leuven (LICOS), European Commission, JRC-IPTS, Edificio Expo 3 41092, Seville, Spain.

Alessandro Corsi is an Associate Professor of Agricultural Economics at the Department of Economics and Statistics "S. Cognetti de Martiis" of the University of Torino, Italy. His main recent research fields are agricultural labor markets and pluriactivity, and more specifically the economic behavior of family farms; wine economics, with special reference to the production choices of winegrowers; and the market of organic products and the functioning of Alternative Food Networks.

Jérémie Dong was a research assistant at the Earth and Life Institute of the Université Catholique de Louvain, Belgium, when this research was conducted. He has conducted analysis of farm productivity and household incomes, applying micro-econometrics to panel data.

Dusan Drabik is Assistant Professor, Department of Economics, Wageningen University & Research, Wageningen, Netherlands. He received his PhD from Cornell University, Ithaca, NY, USA. His expertise is in bio-based economy, agricultural economics, and agricultural policy.

Maria Espinosa is a researcher in the Microeconomic Analysis of EU agricultural holdings unit of Directorate-General (DG) Agriculture and Rural Development (European Commission), IPTS/JRC – European Commission Calle Inca de Garcilaso, 3, 41092 Sevilla (Spain). She holds a PhD in agricultural economics, using the choice experiments methodology to analyze farmers' participation in agri-environmental schemes.

Bruno Henry de Frahan is a Professor in the Earth and Life Institute of the Université Catholique de Louvain, Belgium. He conducts research in agricultural and trade policy using applied economic methods, in particular micro-econometrics and micro-simulations. In particular, he is currently interested in the farm income problem, agricultural risks and insurances, the reform of the Common Agricultural Policy, and non-tariff barriers in agricultural trade.

David Freshwater is Professor in the Department of Agricultural Economics, University of Kentucky, where he specializes in rural development, finance, and public policy. His current projects include Agricultural and Rural Finance Markets in Transition; Analyzing Industry-to-Occupation and Industry-to-Industry Dependencies and Linkages. His current research helps inform public policy and current issues in public policy.

Alexander Gocht, of the Institute of Farm Economics von Thünen Institute Federal Research Institute for Rural Areas, Forestry and Fisheries, Bundesallee, Germany, focuses his research on EU agricultural policy, farm and enterprise structure, and sustainability. He has worked extensively on the market impacts of changing agricultural policies and land and farmland rental markets.

Sergio Gomez y Paloma is an officer and researcher at the European Commission Joint Research Centre (JRC) and is graduated in Agricultural Sciences (Napoli University). Later he obtained a masters in Agribusiness (Milano, Catholic University), a DAA (Master) in Agricultural Development (Agro Paris Tech), and a PhD in Agricultural Economics (Bologna University). In 1990–1996 he was a lecturer at Roskilde Universitets center, Department of Economics and Planning, Denmark, where he was co-director of the European Master ESST (Society, Science, and Technology). He has been advisor to the EU Economic and Social Committee on EU/Middle East Economic Cooperation, Brussels (1992–1995), and 2011–2014 member of the Editorial Board of the *Applied Economics Perspectives and Policy* journal (Oxford University Press). He has published on agricultural economics, transition and development economics, and on efficiency and productivity issues. He is currently coordinating the EC-JRC teams Agri-Farm and Agri-Development, focusing on quantitative analysis of the farming sector in the EU, the Eurasian area and Sub-Saharan Africa.

Thomas Heckelei is Professor for Economic and Agricultural Policy, Institute for Food and Resource Economics (ILR), University of Bonn, Germany. His research interests include analysis of agricultural and environmental policies, agricultural sector and trade modelling, and Bayesian and applied econometrics.

Simon Jette-Nantel is an Assistant Professor in the Department of Agricultural Economics at the University of Wisconsin-River Falls and a farm management specialist with the University of Wisconsin Center for Dairy Profitability. His research interests revolve around farm structural changes and their impact on managerial needs, including changing financial and human resource management needs. His past research looked at the growing importance of off-farm income in farm households' decision-making and its potential impact on farm risk management decisions. He has a PhD in Agricultural Economics from the University of Kentucky.

Hyunjeong Joo is former PhD student in the Department of Agricultural Economics and Agribusiness, Louisiana State University, Baton Rouge, Louisiana. Her research interests include farm economics, agricultural policy, and land markets of South Korea.

d'Artis Kancs is a researcher at the European Commission (DG Joint Research Centre IPTS), Catholic University of Leuven (LICOS), and Economics and Econometrics Research Institute (EERI), European Commission, JRC, IPTS, Edificio Expo 3 41092, Seville, Spain.

Boštjan Kerbler is senior research associate, Institute of Urban Planning of the Republic of Slovenia.

Fedra Kiomourtzi belongs to the staff of the Lab of Agricultural Informatics of the School of Agriculture of Aristotle University of Thessaloniki. She has studied Business Administration. She has conducted research in national and European funded projects. She has published in the *Environmental Impact Assessment Review, New Medit, International Journal of Business Innovation and Research, International Journal of Business Information Systems*, in research series editions, and in international conference proceedings.

Jinsoon Lim is a doctoral student at the Morrison School of Agribusiness, Arizona State University. He previously worked for UNICEF and WFP and traveled in Asia and Africa to monitor and evaluate agricultural programs. He is also a CPA and certified plant protection engineer. His research interests include risk management, farm finance, and crop insurance. He earned a BS in Horticultural Science from Konkuk University and an MS in Agricultural, Environmental, and Development Economics from the Ohio State University.

Kamel Louhichi is senior researcher in the Agriculture and Life Sciences in the Economy Unit Institute for Prospective Technological Studies (IPTS) European Commission-Joint Research Centre (JRC) Edificio EXPO E-41092 Seville, Spain. He specializes in agricultural economics and environment, public policies analysis, biofuels, agricultural sector modelling, bio economic modelling, and mathematical programming.

Basil Manos is a Professor in the Department of Agricultural Economics, Aristotle University of Thessaloniki. He has studied mathematics, economics, operational research, and agricultural economics at Aristotle University and the London School of Economics. His research interests are in farm management and regional planning, impact assessment, sustainability, and efficiency. He has published papers in *Regional Studies, Journal of Policy Modeling, Journal of Environmental Planning and Management, Land Use Policy, Environmental Monitoring and Assessment,* and *the Journal of Environmental Management.*

Sandra Marquardt is a researcher at Johann Heinrich von Thünen-Institute of Farm Economics, Bundesallee, Braunschweig, Germany. She completed her studies of agricultural economics at the University of Hohenheim. Her work in the field of 'model-based policy impact assessment' focused on capturing sustainability aspects using the general equilibrium model MAGENT. She also works with the CAPRI modelling system to ensure a consistent accounting of emission and nutrient flows.

Maria I. Marshall is a Professor in the Department of Agricultural Economics, Purdue University. She received her PhD from Kansas State University. Her research focuses on small business development and family business management. Her small and family business research is focused on areas such as the resource exchange between the household and the business, family business management, and marketing.

Costică Mihai, PhD in Economics, is Associate Professor in the Department of Economics and International Relations, Faculty of Economics and Business Administration, Alexandru Ioan Cuza University of Iaşi (Romania). His main domains of research activity are Environmental Economics, Sustainable Development, and Agricultural Economics. He is research coordinator for the Laboratory of Studies and Analysis on Environmental Economics in CERNESIM Environmental Research Center and executive director of the Research Center in Aquaculture and Aquatic Ecology.

Ashok K. Mishra is Kemper and Ethel Marley Foundation Chair in Food Management, Morrison School of Agribusiness, W. P. Carey School of Business, at Arizona State University, USA, where he conducts research and teaching activities in public policy, finance, agribusiness, and food security. He has published more than 130 papers in peer-reviewed journals, 12 book chapters, and more than 190 presentations at national and international conferences. The quality of his research output has been recognized through several awards, most notably the Outstanding Journal Article award in the agricultural economics profession's premier journal, the *American Journal of Agricultural Economics*, as well as the Outstanding Journal Article award in the prestigious *Journal of Agricultural and Applied Economics*. He assumed a leadership role in the agricultural economics profession by serving as either an editor and/or associate editor for four journals in addition to service work for the American Agricultural Economics Association (AAEA). He has presented his work to non-academics such as the USDA Secretary; Organization of Economic Co-operation and Development (OECD); National Public Policy Education Committee; National Agricultural Research, Extension, Education, and Economics Advisory Board; and key policymakers from the Office of Management and Budget, Council of Economic Advisors. Mishra received a PhD in Economics from North Carolina State University in 1996. Previously he has held positions at Louisiana State University, and the Economic Research Service of the USDA. His international work is in collaboration with the International Food Policy Research Institute (IFPRI), the International Rice Research Institute (IRRI), the International Maize and Wheat Improvement Center (CIMMYT), and the International Crop Research Institute for the Semi-Arid Tropics (ICRISAT).

Klaus Mittenzwei is senior researcher at the Norwegian Agricultural Economics Research Institute (NILF), Oslo, Norway. He received his PhD from the Department of Economics and Resource Management, Norwegian University of Life Sciences. His work focuses on national and international agricultural policies.

Dimitre Nikolov is a Professor at the Institute of Agricultural Economics in Sofia, Bulgaria. He received his MSc in agricultural economics at the University of National and World Economy in Sofia. His research interests are in farm management and financing, impact policy assessment in agriculture, farm sustainability and efficiency, and innovation and risk management in agriculture. He has published papers in *Land Use Policy, Bulgarian Journal of Agricultural Economics and*

Management, Agricultural Finance Review, Agroeconomia Croatica, Bulgarian Journal of Agricultural Science, and *Tagungsband.*

Daniel Prager is a research economist at the USDA's Economic Research Service (ERS). Daniel's current research at ERS focuses on various aspects of farm household well-being, including trends in income and wealth, household income volatility, and access to health insurance. He also works on improving the imputation of missing values within the Agricultural Resource Management Survey (ARMS). Daniel received his PhD in Development Economics from the University of Wisconsin-Madison and his BA in economics from Columbia University.

Lilli Aline Schroeder is a researcher at the Johann Heinrich von Thünen-Institute of Farm Economics, Bundesallee, Braunschweig, Germany. She completed her studies of agricultural sciences at the University of Göttingen. At the Thünen-Institute of Farm Economics in Braunschweig, she is involved in validating the EU-wide modelling system CAPRI for policy impact assessments. She focusses mainly on environmental impacts of Rural Development (RD) measures and contributes with her work to policy advice and to further improve the simulation of RD measures in the CAPRI model.

Saleem Shaik is an Associate Professor in Agribusiness and Applied Economics at North Dakota State University. He received his PhD in Agricultural Economics from University of Nebraska, Lincoln. His current topics revolve around applied policy analyses and technology assessment, and efficiency/productivity using quantitative analytical tools, including econometrics, statistics, and mathematical programming. Current work includes areas of agriculture, production, finance, and institutional (farm program and crop insurance) issues.

Hugo Storm is a research fellow at the Chair of Economic and Agricultural Policy, Institute for Food and Resource Economics, University of Bonn, Germany. He received his PhD in agricultural economics from the University of Bonn. His research interest includes farm structural changes, programs payments, and farm-level spatial analysis.

Lih-Chyun Sun is an Associate Professor in the Department of Agricultural Economics, National Taiwan University, Taiwan.

Mihai Talmaciu is Associate Professor in the Department of Management, Marketing and Business Administration, Faculty of Economics and Business Administration, Alexandru Ioan Cuza University of Iasi and a Researcher in the Laboratory for environmental studies and economic analysis at the Study Center in Environmental Science for North-East Region, Iasi, Romania. His research domains of interests are regional and rural sustainable development, agricultural policy, agricultural cooperation, and sustainable development in tourism and services.

Davide Viaggi is a Professor in Agricultural Economics and Rural Appraisal at the University of Bologna, Italy. He graduated in Agricultural Sciences at the University of Bologna and got a PhD in Agricultural Economics and Policy at the University of Siena. His main research interests include agricultural policy evaluation, economics of innovation, economics of water use in agriculture, economics of agri-environmental schemes, environmental evaluation, farm management, and bio economy issues. In recent years he has especially worked on the design and impacts of the EU Common Agricultural Policy and on the issues connected to the provision on public goods by agriculture and forestry. He has participated in several EU-funded projects, among which he coordinated the FP7 projects CAP-IRE and CLAIM, and is now coordinating the H2020 project PROVIDE. Davide is author of about 400 publications, including some books and several articles on the main agricultural economics and environmental economics journals, and a number of conference papers. In the period 2012–2016 Davide was been Editor-in-Chief of the journal *Bio-based and Applied Economics*. Besides his academic activity, Davide is also an expert and consultant for the EU Commission, ministries, and local administration.

Renee D. Wiatt serves as the Family Business Management Specialist for the Department of Agricultural Economics at Purdue University, namely for the Purdue Initiative for Family Firms (PIFF). She works on extension and applied research in family business management and collaborates with partners such as centers focused on agriculture and families, Extension teams focused on agriculture and farm management, and researchers to develop funded programming focused on family business management. She is responsible for coordinating with producer associations to determine family business needs as well as conducting research and fund-raising focused on family businesses.

Acknowledgements

Any large project involves an equally large number of individuals, and this book is no exception. As editors of this volume we are grateful to a great number of people who collaborated with us, supported us and assisted us in the preparation of these chapters of the book, as well as the underlying activities that occurred behind them. The idea of this book came several years ago from a workshop held at the European Commission's Joint Research Centre (JRC) in Seville, Spain. That is the place where I first met my co-editors, Davide and Sergio. Over the years we became very good friends with similar educational attainment, backgrounds and research interests, though a continent apart. Secondly, we would like to thank the chapter writers themselves, who willingly and efficiently revised or prepared materials so that they could be utilized in this form. Thirdly, there are country research teams that organized and conducted studies in North America and Europe.

We would like to thank the Marley Foundation for their support of time spent on this book by Ashok Mishra. We sincerely appreciate the sacrifices made by our families, since the time spent putting this edited book together was time that would have otherwise been spent at home and with family members. Their sacrifice and understanding enabled the editors to spend the time required for this volume to become a reality.

Finally, the views expressed are purely those of the authors and may not in any circumstances be regarded as stating an official position of the European Commission, Economic Research Service of the US Department of Agriculture or of any other institution with which they are associated.

Ashok Mishra
Davide Viaggi
Sergio Gomez y Paloma

Chapter 1

Introduction

Ashok K. Mishra, Davide Viaggi, and Sergio Gomez y Paloma

Governments in most developed countries have a strong tendency to engage in policies supporting risk management in agriculture. For example, the US New Deal programs, brought about as a result of the Great Depression, greatly inflating the price of food, included commodity price supports, marketing order, production controls, import barriers, and crop insurance that was instituted to reduce income risk for farmers. The particular structures of the federal farm programs have changed over time, but the central planning philosophy behind them has changed little over the past eight decades in the United States and among other industrialized nations (e.g., the Common Agricultural Policy of the European Union). The public policies were initially designed to reduce income risk and support rural populations that were heavily involved in production agriculture—where the main source of income was farming and the majority of the population resided in the rural areas. Most farms were organized such that family members ran the farm, supplied most of the inputs, and earned most of the income from farming.

In today's farming, a farm's organization and operation are not straightforward. Public policy in agriculture has given way to larger farms. The average farm size in the United States is about 437 acres and about 30 acres in the EU, and they often specialize in cash grain production. Farmers and families have additional time that they can allocate to off-farm activities. The political economy of agriculture in developed countries in the 1970s (Buttel, 1982) described part-time farming as a response to increasing social and economic inequalities among farmers, which led many producers to seek off-farm employment. He explained that the movement of industrial jobs into rural areas provided more opportunities for members of farm households to acquire off-farm employment (Barkley, 1990). In addition, "the social and economic deterioration of these industrial cities has led many former urban dwellers to move to farms while continuing to hold off-farm employment" (Buttel, 1982: 293). Some were choosing to combine on-farm and off-farm work not only to diversify their income sources to reduce risk, but also for the lifestyle, such as for a hobby or for a rural residence; and the desire for profits was not the main goal (Barlett, 1986). As is the case in other developed countries, part-time farming became viewed as a persistent aspect of the structure and culture of agriculture (Buttel, 1982; Rosenfeld, 1985; Barlett, 1986; Gasson,

1986; Buttel et al., 1990; Fuller, 1990; Sachs, 1996; Kimhi, 2000). Buttel (1982) stated: "It is widely recognized that part-time farming in the United States tends to reflect a relatively stable or permanent combination of farm and non-farm work throughout most of the life cycle, instead of being a transitional status of entrance into and/or disengagement from farming" (p. 294). Similar trend has been noticed in the European Union—especially countries whose agriculture is driven by the Common Agricultural Policy (Benjamin and Kimhi, 2006).

In addition to government subsidies, farmers are also using other income risk management tools. These include futures and options, hedging and crop insurance. Additionally, many farmers are supplementing farm income from off-farm sources, such as working off the farm for wages or a salary. This is especially true for small farms, whose gross cash income is less than $250,000. Small farms account 91% of all farms and 23% of agricultural production. Small farms have a product mix distinctly different from that of larger farms: small commercial farms focus on commodities that do not necessarily require a full-time commitment of labor (Mishra et al., 2002). Therefore, small-farm households depend heavily on off-farm income—self-insurance strategy and the non-farm economy are important to them. As a result, the continuing evolution of production agriculture, government fiscal deficits, and changes in farms' families and structure raises a variety of issues to consider in developing policy for modern farms and rural households (Gardner, 2002).

In recent years, 85%–95% of farm household income has come from off-farm sources, including employment earnings, other business activities, and unearned income. The relative importance of off-farm income varies considerably from farm to farm, and declines as farm commodity sales increase (Mishra et al., 2002). However, even among the largest farming operations, 8% of farming operations with annual sales exceeding $250,000, off-farm income accounts for 24% of farm household income on average. For the 83% of US farming operations that have annual sales of $250,000 or less, off-farm income typically accounts for all but a negligible amount of farm household income.

Today the economic well-being of farm households not only depends on the income from farming but to a large extent an income from non-farm employment as well. The fact that nearly 80% of total household income originates from off-farm sources, with income from off-farm wages and salaries being the major contributor, is a case in point to the importance of these sources of income to farm households (Mishra et al., 2002). The closing of the income gap, which has materialized in recent years, has been attributed to the growth in the earnings from off-farm sources. To generate income, farmers and their families make decisions about whether to work on the farm, off the farm, or a combination of both, which has implications for income and wealth accumulation for households, food consumption and savings.

There are several problems with government support in agriculture. First, the federal subsidies for farm businesses are costly to taxpayers, and it damages the economy. Second, subsidies induce overproduction and inflate land prices in rural

America. The flow of subsidies and regulations from Washington, D.C., or Brussels, in the case of the European Union, hinders farmers from innovating, diversifying their land use, and taking other actions needed to prosper in a competitive global economy. Third, subsidies do not reach the targeted group. For example, almost 30% of agricultural subsidies go to the top 2% of farms and over 80% to the top 30%. In short, the design of such polices in agriculture has been skewed, and small farms have not received many benefits from these subsidy programs (Gardner, 2002).

Given this new paradigm, there has been conflicting evidence on the impact of public policy on labor allocation of farm families. For example, from a macroeconomic perspective, it has been found that public policies have no impact on migration of labor out of agriculture. But recently empirical evidence, in many developed economies, at the microeconomic level has found that public policies designed to support farm income have a negative impact on farming times and have increased off-farm labor supply of farm families. Such policies not only have an impact on labor allocation decisions but also affect farm inputs, such as farmland values, variable inputs, and the transfer of farm business. These effects are differentiated according to different policy instruments; for example, there is evidence in the EU that while investment subsidies have halted labor shedding on farms, changes in direct payments had no employment effects (Petrick and Zier, 2012). Other evidence suggest that while labor reallocation due to policy changes may be negligible for active farms, agricultural policies can strongly affect labor reallocation throughout the sector (Raggi et al., 2013).

Finally, despite the increased attention being paid to public policy in agriculture in developed countries in global trade, the World Trade Organization, academic and agricultural economics and economics literature, solid research on the consequences of public policy in agriculture is still quite limited. Specifically, the literature lacks a common source of information on assessing the impacts of public policy on labor allocation decisions, input usage, household income and food security as it relates to industrialized nations. For example, evidence from Canada, the United States, and European countries shows that off-farm labor supply has a larger impact on rural households' income, then it yields lessons that public policy in agriculture is not sound legislation—perhaps resulting in a deadweight loss to society in general. Additionally, income diversification via off-farm work is associated with higher incomes and food consumption (Reardon, Delgado, and Matlon, 1992). However, little is known about the association between off-farm work and farm household food expenditures among developed economies. This edited volumes intends to provide readers, with various backgrounds, information on policy interventions in the agricultural sector by the governments in developed economies and their consequences on labor allocation, land use, farmland valuation, environment, and farms' succession decisions.

This book has 19 chapters. Chapter 1 is devoted to establishing the agriculture policy of developed countries and introducing the idea of farm families taking off-farm jobs in order to supplement their income. It also speaks about how the off-farm jobs are usually taken by spouses and children, and the farmers who take extra jobs are often those who own small- to medium-sized farms, while large farm owners make enough from farm operations to turn a profit. Chapter 2 covers the drivers of agricultural policy, and how the policy is related to the globalization and technological advancement of agriculture. It then gives a description of how farm size affects policy and what subsidies the farm receives. Chapter 3 focuses on Bulgarian and Greek farms, and how public policy affects the farm based on a variety of factors, including former employment, gender, emigration and immigration, among other factors. The main focus in on social sustainability, and how farmers' social activities could drive how they are affected by policy.

Chapter 4 speaks about how rural structures affect farms and agricultural policy in Romania. The country has had a difficult time since the fall of the Communist Bloc, and it has been a troublesome transition to a market economy. Romanian society faces several challenges due to their reliance on maintaining the historical peasant culture as well as the population's obedience towards oppressive regimes. Chapter 5 provides specifics about how farms are defined in Canada. This is a very important distinction, due to the fact that how a farm is defined affects what subsidy it receives, and how much they receive. It also covers how subsidies and earnings are distributed amongst the farms and farmers. Chapter 6 discusses how agricultural policies in the United States affect household income for farmers and labor. It discusses how current policy is designed around reducing the risk in farming, and keeping the farmers in business through labor policies. Chapter 7 is about the rise of part-time farms in Canada. Part-time farms are rather ill-defined, but policy needs to include them as they begin to grow in number. These types of farms have to have special consideration, since part-time farm operators almost always have other jobs than on their farms. Chapter 8 is devoted to comparing farm incomes to non-farm incomes and how policy affects farm incomes. A main point is that farmers, while having an income level almost equal to the non-farm population, suffer more greatly from poverty and income disparity.

Chapter 9 focuses on farm policy in Norway, and how agricultural policy in that country is mainly devoted to exports and has a smaller production due to the geographic makeup of the country. The main idea is that since Norwegian agriculture is limited, Norwegian farmers are more likely to take off-farm jobs. Chapter 10 introduces the CAP, the Common Agriculture Policy, of the European Union. Recently there was a new method of distributing subsidies introduced, the Basic Payment Scheme. The chapter aims to quantify the changes in the total budget allocation and in the average decoupled unit payments under the post-2013 CAP, in comparison to the former CAP, and to assess to what extend the post-2013 CAP will reduce the intra and inter-MS (member states) disparities in the distribution of funds.

Chapter 11 expands on the CAP issues, focusing on the environmental efforts of the CAP, referred to as Greening. It features several economic models, showcasing how a shift away from the Greening would affect the CAP and farm incomes. Chapter 12 covers how farm policies are related to the real estate value of farms. It has several models, showing how policies affect farms, based on political parties and other variables. It also takes crop insurance into consideration, showing that crop insurance is one of the most important aspects of farm policy. Chapter 13 describes European land markets and how different institutions affect those markets. It establishes the different land classifications and how EU environmental regulations are related to the land markets. Chapter 14 provides a look at South Korean farms and how governmental subsidies affect the farmers through regression analysis. It focuses on farmland values and how they are affected by government subsidies, and how those subsidies are capitalized.

Transitioning a family business to the next generation often begins with naming a successor. Chapter 15 investigates the factors that lead farm business owners to name a successor for the business. This chapter shows sufficient levels of capital, intentions to sell or give the business to family members, regular discussion of goals, estate planning, the senior generation feeling prepared to hand down the business, the number of generations in management of the business, and the owner's years of experience all have an effect on a family business naming a successor.

The younger generation is not interested in the farming sector, and this has been noted by several developed countries in the European Union. Chapter 16 discusses the use of Common Agriculture Policy (CAP) in bringing back young people to farming sector. Specifically, the chapter analyzes the impacts of common agricultural policy on farm succession in Slovenia. The author shows that the EU's common agricultural policy has been effective in promoting the takeover of farms and their timely transfer to young successors. Chapter 17 discusses how elderly farmers in Taiwan are receiving pensions, and whether these pensions affect the younger adults in the family. It finds that the pension program increases young farmers working off farm, since their elderly relatives already receive support through the pension. Chapter 18 provides a review of current literature related to farm succession and inheritance, and the differences between the two. It also provides a brief discussion of the effects of a farmer designating an heir, rather than letting the farm pass out of the family. Finally, Chapter 19 provides concluding remarks.

References

Barkley, A. P. (1990) The determinants of the migration of labor out of agriculture in the United States, 1940–85. *American Journal of Agricultural Economics* 72(3): 567–573.

Barlett, Peggy F. (1986) Part-time farming: saving the farm or saving the life-style? *Rural Sociology* 51(3): 289–313.

Benjamin, C., and A. Kimhi (2006) Farm work, off-farm work, and hired farm labour: estimating a discrete-choice model of French farm couples' labour decisions. *European Review of Agricultural Economics* 33(2): 149–171.

Buttel, Fredrick H. (1982) The political economy of part-time farming. *GeoJournal* 6(4): 293–300.

Buttel, Fredrick H., Olaf F. Larson, and Gilbert N. Gillespie, Jr. (1990) *The Sociology of Agriculture*. New York: Greenwood Press.

Fuller, Anthony M. (1990) From part-time farming to pluriactivity: a decade of change in rural Europe. *Journal of Rural Studies* 6(4): 361–373.

Gardner, B. (2002) *American Agriculture in the Twentieth Century*. Cambridge, MA and London: Harvard University Press.

Gasson, Ruth. (1986) Part time farming strategy for survival? *Sociologia Ruralis* 26(3–4): 364–376.

Kimhi, A. (2000) Is part-time farming really a step in the way out of agriculture? *American Journal of Agricultural Economics* 82(1): 38–48.

Mishra, A. K., M. Morehart, H. El-Osta, J. Johnson, and J. Hopkins. (2002) Income, Wealth, and Well-Being of Farm Operator Households. Economic Research Service; USDA. Agricultural Economics Report No. 812. Washington, D.C.

Petrick, M., and P. Zier. (2012) Common agricultural policy effects on dynamic labour use in agriculture. *Food Policy* 37(6): 671–678.

Raggi M., L. Sardonini, and D. Viaggi. (2013) The effects of the common agricultural policy on exit strategies and land re-allocation. *Land Use Policy* 31: 114–125.

Reardon, T., C. Delgado, and P. Matlon. (1992) Determinants and effects of income diversification amongst farm households in Burkina Faso. *Journal of Development Studies* 28(3): 264–296.

Rosenfeld, Rachel. (1985) *Farm Women: Work, Farm, and Family in the United States*. Chapel Hill, NC: The University of North Carolina Press.

Sachs, Carolyn. (1996) *Gendered Fields: Rural Women, Agriculture, and Environment*. Boulder, CO: Westview Press.

Chapter 2

The relationship between farm families and the structure of agriculture

Mary Clare Ahearn and Walter J. Armbruster

The most basic and traditional way to describe the structure of an industry is by its number and size distribution of firms. Besides size distribution, an assortment of other indicators, such as level of specialization, are highly relevant to a consideration of industry structure. Furthermore, the topic of structure is generally invoked in the context of dynamics and the direction and speed of structural change (e.g., Dunne, Jensen, and Roberts, 2009). All these considerations are relevant in an evaluation of agricultural structure as well, but agriculture is unique among industries in the role played by farm families. Unlike other industries, agriculture is characterized, and even celebrated, as being family-dominated. Regardless of the stage of development, farm families continue to play a dominant role across countries in managing all aspects of farm production activities. The nature of that role has changed amidst the major drivers of structural change. In this chapter we will consider the major drivers of structural change, including policy, and the evolving role of farm households.

Fundamental drivers of structural change

Our description of the drivers of structural change in agriculture, follow those identified by Armbruster and Ahearn (2014). The two fundamental drivers of structural change are globalization and technological change. To a certain extent, similar trends are evident throughout most developed countries, and are increasingly evident in the emerging commercial farming sectors across Latin America, Africa and in other developing countries. The scale and speed of change varies depending upon domestic and trade policy, social systems and cultural preferences, but the key underlying drivers of change are rapidly and widely shared in today's global economy and interconnected world.

Globalization and trade policy

While most of the food consumed worldwide is produced locally, countries have relied on trade in agricultural commodities for centuries to supplement and complement their domestic production. During the last half century agricultural trade has grown around fivefold (FAO, 2015). While significant, it should also be noted that trade in agricultural and food products has grown at a slower rate than trade in manufactured goods. Agriculture has not been fully incorporated into the multilateral trade negotiations, which reduced the industrial tariffs. In addition, many developed countries have supported their domestic agricultural production, while developing countries have generally not. These variations in domestic support have altered the pace and balance of globalization. Another aspect of the globalization of agriculture has been the development of international food supply chains, which to some extent have replaced traditional trade structures with modern production and distribution systems, bolstered by changing consumer preferences.

The imports and exports of agricultural and food products tied to globalization puts a premium on efficient farm production to hold down costs of exports and to keep lower-cost imports from replacing U.S. production. Trade negotiations play an important role in determining the implications of globalization for U.S. domestic agricultural policy and products. Trade negotiations also establish guidelines for the types of food safety or other requirements countries may impose on product quality characteristics. It is critical that standards are not established which are designed primarily to create a barrier to imports from any single or a group of countries, which could offset productivity efficiency as a key determinant of trade flows. This is increasingly important amid concerns about food security for the burgeoning world population of poor consumers and a growing middle class demanding improved diets.

Technology adoption

One of the 17 Sustainability Development Goals released in 2015 by the United Nations addresses the need to improve food security of citizens through increased agricultural productivity (UN, 2015). The strategies identified for attaining that goal include investing in rural infrastructure, research, and extension; providing access to markets and marketing information; increasing crop and livestock genetic diversity; as well as eliminating trade-distorting policies.

Given the relatively fixed nature of arable land and projected population growth, investing in the multiple avenues for yield growth are critical. At least since Hayami and Ruttan (1971), development experts have recognized the importance of increasing agricultural productivity as key to improving a country's development outcomes. Technical change leads to higher levels of agricultural productivity as capital inputs are substituted for labor. Development proceeds as labor is transferred from the agricultural to the nonagricultural sectors. For example, researchers have found that in developing countries value added per worker in non-agricultural industries is four times as large as in agriculture (Gollin, Lagakos, and Waugh, 2014). Using the Food and Agricultural Organization (FAO) databases, Fuglie and Rada (2015) have estimated the sources of growth in global agricultural output over time (Figure 2.1). Improvements in productivity have increasingly been the major source of growth in output.

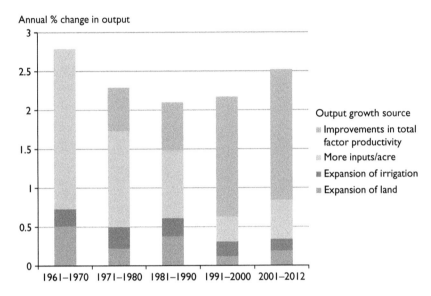

Figure 2.1 Sources of growth in global agricultural output, 1961–2012

Source: Fuglie and Rada, 2015.

Advances in technology adoption are made possible by public, and increasingly private, investments in research and extension. R&D leads to technology adoption that often replaces labor, and generally reduces costs and/or increases yields. For example, in the United States, the United States Department of Agriculture (USDA) Land-Grant University System provides basic research findings of the land grant universities—which were established under the Morrill Acts of 1862 and 1890—that are transferred to farmers by the university-based Cooperative Extension programs, authorized by the Smith-Lever Act of 1914. This collaborative system's success is recognized worldwide, and its structure is often mimicked with varying degrees of success. Estimates of U.S. productivity growth from 1948 to 2011 show agricultural output grew 1.49% per year, while aggregate input use increased only 0.07% annually. Positive growth in the farm sector was mainly due to 1.42% per year total factor productivity growth (Figure 2.2) (Wang et al., 2015).

Technology adoption is often accompanied by increasing farm size. The increasing size of farms tends to reduce cost of production because of efficiencies in machinery use, cost savings from purchases of larger quantities of inputs at volume discounts, and ability to obtain marketing efficiencies. Larger-size farms are often the early adopters of technology derived from research and development, either public or private, leading to increases in productivity. Cost-saving technologies create efficiencies such as those available from using GPS systems to guide planting and harvesting machinery, and to collect large amounts of site-specific data which

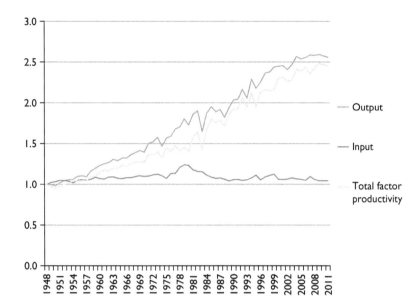

Figure 2.2 Indices of U.S. farm output, input, and total factor productivity, 1948–2011

Source: Wang et al., 2015.

facilitate decisions affecting input use, disease control strategies, and even crop choice. Investments in machinery and accompanying technology have increased significantly, as equipment has become larger and more sophisticated to accommodate an increasing scale of operations. The benefit to the producer purchasing such equipment is the efficiency with which planting and harvesting, as well as intermediate field operations, are carried out. The gains come in part from eliminating wasteful overlaps in planting, with accompanying savings in fertilizer and pesticide application costs, and in part from the decreased labor time and reduced fuel costs for field operations.

Agricultural policy

Agricultural policies vary across the globe, with the exception of the European Union, which shares a member-wide Common Agricultural Policy (CAP). While they differ greatly, policies can be grouped into those that emphasize several factors: market price support, reductions to costs of inputs and capital, reducing downside risk of revenue and income, direct payments to farmers, and payments for provision of public goods. The Organization for Economic Cooperation and Development (OECD) summarizes these policies annually for the OECD countries. The 2015 report summarizes the policies for the OECD countries, as well as for selected emerging economies (OECD, 2015). The 49 countries included in the 2015 report account for nearly 90% of global value added in agriculture. Collectively, they transferred approximately US$601 billion, as measured by the Producer Support Estimate (PSE), to agricultural producers through a variety of programs. Some progress has been made by countries to move away from policies that affect market prices and input subsidies to policies that do not affect the production decisions of farmers and thereby distort trade. While this has been occurring at different rates by various countries, the latest OECD report concludes that the emerging economies are moving in the opposite direction. Recent estimates of PSEs are provided in Table 2.1 for selected countries.

It is also important to note that, within a country, farmers are not supported in an equal fashion. As U.S. farm policy has developed since the 1930s, policies have grown from a relatively homogenous set that provided price support based on commodity production to a more complex set of policies that address a range of issues. The major share of support in the United States is from production-oriented agricultural policies that provide payment to major commodity producers based largely on production quantities. They include such programs as direct payments based on historical yields and acreage, countercyclical payments, loan deficiency payments, disaster assistance programs, or payments tied to conservation practices associated with production. Changes in policies over time are surely connected to changes in farming structure (Sumner, Alston, and Glauber, 2010), although clear causation is difficult to establish.

Tax policy

Tax policy involves a variety of provisions that impact how firms and households organize their finances to minimize their tax burden and therefore can have indirect impacts on farm structure. For example, tax policy affects the use of capital in

Table 2.1 Producer support estimates as a share of gross farm receipts, 2012–2014, select countries

Brazil	3.7%
Canada	11.2%
China	19.2%
European Union	19.2%
Norway	59.8%
South Korea	50.8%
United States	8.2%
OECD, average	17.9%

Source: OECD, 2015.

agriculture by the provisions associated with expensing of capital acquisition in the calculation of taxable income. Tax policy may also influence structural change by fostering growth in the number of small farms. While small farms earn little or nothing in cash income from farming, a key to understanding structural change and small farm survivability is to recognize the importance of the full range of returns to farming. Small farm households generally are full owners of their farmland for which values have historically, and especially recently, risen rapidly, providing owners with unrealized capital gains. The majority of farm families reside on their farm property, and many of the costs associated with the dwelling are included in farm business expenses, often resulting in farm losses for small farms.

Additional drivers of change in structure and organization

There are numerous other factors that may also drive change in farm size and structure. These include consumer food preferences, input costs, and risk management.

Consumer Food Preferences. Consumer food preferences and expectations are important drivers of change in products sold by retailers. Whether they are also major drivers of change in the size and structure of farms depends upon how consumer preferences influence new opportunities or create challenges for producers. A policy approach in the form of food safety regulations is one driver of change based on consumer preferences, which are not adequately provided by the market due to externalities associated with the lack of ability to readily observe unsafe conditions in food throughout the supply chain. On the other hand, retailers voluntarily establishing compliance standards for their supply-chain participants, all the way to the farm level in some cases, increasingly provide for consumer preferences for knowledge of food production methods.

Input Costs. Input costs may be affected by factors outside the control of agriculture and can also be important drivers of changing structure and size of farms. For example, the price of fuel, fertilizer, and debt financing are heavily influenced by factors outside of the agricultural sector. Rising costs of such inputs to agricultural production may diverge from prices of the resulting farm output in the short run, leading to financial failure of some farms, which are then sold, and thus contributing to changes in the structure of the sector.

Risk Management. Diversification of production to provide alternative sources of income is one element of risk management that has long been the mainstay of farms from smaller through larger operations. As the size of a farm increases, risk management becomes an ever more challenging element in determining its success or failure. Crop insurance, subsidized at the federal level, is especially utilized by major field crop producers, which tend to be larger than other farms, and is an example of one risk management tool that has gained in popularity in recent years. The most recent Farm Bill has moved policy support for agriculture to more emphasis on increased subsidies for crop insurance to replace direct payment to producers. This has encouraged more producers to adopt crop insurance as a risk management strategy.

An international look at farm size

A traditional approach to reflecting structural diversity, within and across countries, is the reporting of statistics focused on the size of holdings (Lowder, Skoet, and Singh, 2014). The structure of a country's agriculture has a significant impact on how farm families are connected to farm production. Notably, farm structure is relevant to choices about crop mix, the allocation of family labor, sources of family income, and land tenure and ownership.

Most commonly in developing countries, the size distribution of farms/holdings are reported in hectare classes. For example, it is common to define smallholders as those that operate on 2 hectares or less. In developed countries, the more common measure of economic size is based on the economic output of a farm reflecting the combined market value of the agricultural commodities produced. Though farm definitions vary across countries, it is estimated that there are approximately 570 million farms in the world. The majority of these are considered family farms, but vary greatly in size. Using the most recent data available from 111 countries where farm size data were available, Lowder, Skoet, and Singh (2014) were able to account for 460 million of the estimated 570 million farms. They report that 72% of the farms were less than 1 hectare (ha.). (Note: 1 hectare = 2.47 acres.) Another 12% were 1–2 ha.; 10% were 2–5 ha.; 3% were 5–10 ha.; 1% were 10–20 ha.; and only 2% were 20 ha. or more.

The size distribution, when measured by land area, varies greatly by country even for developed countries. Table 2.2 shows three very-aggregated groups of farms by size, labeled small (less than 10 acres), medium (about 10–250 acres), and large (about 250 or more acres). Approximately half of Canadian farms would be classified as large in this size classification, compared to one-quarter of U.S. farms and only 3% of European farms (EU-28). A major reason for this is the more dispersed geography of Canada, which limits the ability of small and medium farms to have access to nonfarm job opportunities, in addition to Canada's less inclusive definition of a farm, compared to the EU and the United States.

In the case of the European Union, tracking structural change is made more complicated by the accession of New Member States. For example, the number of

Table 2.2 Percent of farms by size and total farms, by country

	United States, 2012	Canada, 2011	EU-28, 2010
Small, %	11	6	67
Medium, %	65	44	30
Large, %	24	50	3
Total number of farms	21,09,303	2,05,730	122,48,000

Sources: Census of Agriculture and Eurostat Farm Structures Survey, USDA, NASS, 2014.
Note: Small = <10 acres (or 5 ha for EU) and Large is ≅ 250 acres (or 100 ha for EU).

Member States reflected in the Farm Structures Survey has changed from 9, to 15, to 27 to the current 28. As the EU expanded from 15 to 28 Member States, it went from 5.6 million to 12.2 million farms, and the number of small farms grew disproportionately. When size was harmonized and measured monetarily by the European Size Unit (ESU), rather than in land area, Ahearn and Effland (2009) reported that for 2007 the EU-15 had a smaller share of small farms and a larger share of midsized farms than the United States. The United States was found to have a larger share of large farms compared to the EU-15, as shown in the comparison of Table 2.2 based on statistics for the EU-28.

International year of the family farm

The year 2014 was declared as the International Year of the Family Farm (IYFF) and generated a significant amount of interest in defining a family farm and in characterizing different types of family farms. FAO convened an International Working Group on Family Farming (IWG-FF) to review definitions of family farms and provide guidelines to conduct similar reviews around the world. The IWG-FF reached a consensus on an "umbrella" concept. The IWG-FF recognized the importance of the following issues in defining a family farm: pluriactivity (i.e., off-farm sources of income), multifunctionality (i.e., recognizes the benefits other than agricultural production from farming), diversification, sustainability, food security, rural wage work, and community links. This is viewed as a paradigm shift among many international organizations and paves the way to replace previous policies that were exclusively compensatory, with a policy mix that is mainly aimed at promoting investment for developing family farm potential.

While there is no internationally agreed-upon definition of "family farm", various stakeholders have adopted definitions. According to Lowder, Skoet, and Singh (2014) the term is most commonly used in countries of Latin America and the Caribbean as well as in some developed countries, including the United States and some European countries. Many definitions of family farms intentionally focus on less affluent and/or small farms. The above-named authors found that the most common characteristic among the definitions was to specify that a member of the household owns, operates and/or manages the farm either in part or fully. Other less common characteristics in their review of family farm definitions was a specified minimum amount of labor provided by the family.

The IWG-FF defined a family farm as "an agricultural holding, which is managed and operated by a household and where farm labor is largely supplied by the household." As part of the International Year of the Family Farm, the FAO endorsed the IWG definition and offered the following, which encompasses both family management and reliance on family labor:

> Family Farming (which includes all family-based agricultural activities) is a means of organizing agricultural, forestry, fisheries, pastoral and aquaculture production which is managed and operated by a family and predominantly

reliant on family labor, including both women's and men's. The family and the farm are linked, co-evolve and combine economic, environmental, social and cultural functions.

The requirement that labor be predominantly provided by the family limits the scale of production, perhaps to a scale that is not economically efficient, and hence limits labeling family farms to smaller holdings. Because of this, it is unlikely that developed countries will adopt this limiting definition of a family farm. However, in recognition of the international celebration of family farms, some governmental statistical agencies did provide estimates of family farms based on the FAO definition. In Canada, the definition of a family farm is based on legal status/business structure of the farm business. It includes unincorporated farms and family corporations. In 2011, 97% of farms in Canada were classified as family farms (AGR, 2014). They accounted for 87% of gross farm receipts. The Canadian Agricultural Census collects information on whether or not wages were paid to non–family members, but does not collect data on the share of hours worked by non–family members. With this limitation in the ability to apply the U.N. definition, and assuming that any farm that hired labor would be classified as a nonfamily farm, it is estimated that 80% of Canadian farms are family farms and account for 43% of Canadian gross farm receipts.

In the United States, the current definition of a family farm, adopted in 2005, is based on the majority of family ownership of the farm assets by the principal operator of the farm. Though the definition varies, the results regarding family farms in the United States are very similar to the Canadian experience, i.e., within 2 percentage points. Approximately 98% of U.S. farms are classified as family farms, and they account for 85% of the value of production (USDA ERS, 2015b). Historically, the United States did not identify a particular group of farms as family farms because it was generally perceived that all farms were family farms. However, when a farm household program was developed in the Economic Research Service, USDA and micro-level data collected through the Farm Costs and Returns Survey (FCRS, the predecessor to the current Agricultural and Resource Management Survey (ARMS)), a pragmatic motivation to define a family farm emerged. In particular, it became clear that unless the operator and his or her family were closely tied to the farm business, it was unrealistic to expect the farm operator to share financial resources, including off-farm income, with the farm business. In other words, it was not tenable to ask a hired manager for his or her family income and characteristics and assume that this information had the same relevance to the management of a farm as it would for a family farm. Beginning with the 1988 FCRS, the family farm definition was established as farms other than those organized as cooperatives or nonfamily corporations, or when the operator reported not receiving any of the net income of the business (Ahearn, El-Osta, and Perry, 1993). In 2005, the current definition was modified to focus exclusively on family ownership of assets, rather than legal form of organization, but this change had little effect on the share of farms classified as family farms (USDA ERS, 2015b). Very similar to the situation in

Canada, nearly 80% of U.S. farms do not hire any labor. But, unlike the Canadian Census, the ARMS collects hours worked on U.S. farms by family and hired workers, therefore, the U.N. labor-based definition of a family farm could be quantified and it is estimated that 87% of farms meet this definition, accounting for 58% of the value of production.

Like Canada and the United States, the European Union does not use a family farm definition based on the majority of farm labor. However, Eurostat provided an estimate of family farms, based on the FAO definition (Eurostat, 2014). They reported, for 2010, that 96.9% of all farms in EU-28 countries were classified as family farms. These farms accounted for 67.3% of all land in farms. It is perhaps not surprising that there is a great deal of diversity among the 28 Member States in its use of family and hired labor on farms. Three countries accounted for nearly one-third of all farms and one-third of family farms—Romania, Italy, and Poland. Perhaps more surprisingly, nearly one-quarter of France's farms, known to have a relatively productive agricultural sector, use only hired labor.

Dimensions of the farm household and farm business connections in the U.S.

After peaking at 6.8 million farms in 1935, the number of U.S. farms declined until the 1970s. The 2012 Census of Agriculture reported 2.1 million farms. The current definition of a farm was adopted in the mid-1970s. It is a very inclusive definition and embraces farms operated by households that are retired or attracted to farming for reasons not primarily related to production, such as the rural lifestyle or investment opportunities. In addition, since the definition is dollar-based but not adjusted for changing price levels, it becomes more inclusive with each passing year as price levels change.

The number of total farms and the average acreage per farm has been very stable during recent decades. However, this stability in farm numbers masks significant structural change over the period. Figure 2.3 shows the number and percent of farms in different constant dollar sales classes for Census of Agriculture years 1997 through 2012 (Ahearn and Harris, 2014). During the period, both the number and the share of farms increased for those farms with less than $10,000 in gross sales, but most of that came from the very smallest farms, called "point farms". Point farms are those with sales less than $1,000 in gross sales, but normally expected to sell at least that amount of agricultural products. Most users of farm structure data are surprised to find that a large and growing share of U.S. farms have no sales, about 25% in a typical year.

The largest size class, here identified as those with sales of $1 million or more, also saw increases in their numbers and share, while the next largest class ($500,000 to $1 million) was relatively stable, with only minor declines. The largest declines were in the mid-sizes of $10,000 to $499,999 in sales, which went from 48% of all farms in 1997 to 36% of all farms in 2012.[1] This evidence of a declining middle is a continuation of an ongoing trend. Recently, there has been a renewed emphasis

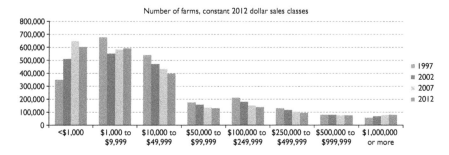

Figure 2.3 The very smallest and the very largest farms are increasing in numbers

Source: Censuses of Agriculture, sales adjusted by the Producer Price Index for farm products, USDA, NASS, 2014.

on extension activities directed towards the farms "of the middle", especially with respect to local food farms (Kirschenmann et al., 2014). The Agriculture of the Middle research and extension collaboration defines the middle as $50,000 to $500,000 in sales, but there is no consensus regarding what constitutes the middle among various data users.

At least two distinct forces drive the evolving structural changes of the U.S. farm sector. First, concentration in production is likely to continue as a result of the pressures to minimize costs and consumer prices and to provide products with attributes that are more tailored to the specific demands of consumers. Half of all agricultural products in 2012 were produced by 1.6% of U.S. farms (approximately 33,330) (USDA NASS, 2014). Second, the farm households that operate farms, and especially the small farms that dominate the farm sector in numbers, though not in farm output, will continue to require access to income from off-farm sources.

Off-farm work among farm families is not new. The Census of Agriculture has collected information on days worked off the farm by the principal operator since 1929 and, in 1935, provided a definition of part-time farming that included several elements, including hours worked and income earned. Though not a new phenomenon in agriculture, Figure 2.4 shows that multiple-job holding among farm families has only increased over time. While the importance of off-farm income and off-farm work as a permanent lifestyle choice for many farm households has been documented for some time, the magnitude of its importance nationally was not widely recognized until improved farm household surveys were conducted beginning with the USDA's 1988 Farm Operator Resource version, Farm Costs and Returns Survey (predecessor to the Agricultural Resource Management Survey). First among the contributions of the farm household surveys was the ability to debunk the view perpetuated by a set of highly constructed statistics that portrayed farm operator households as economically disadvantaged, on average, compared to nonfarm or all U.S. households.

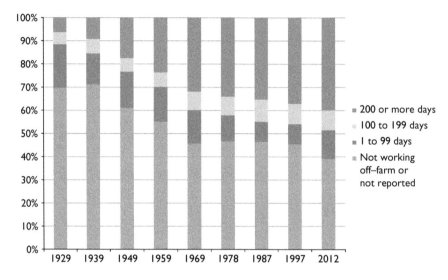

Figure 2.4 Days worked off-farm by principal farm operator, 1929–2012

Sources: Compiled in Ahearn and Lee (1991) for 1929–1982; USDA, NASS, thereafter.

The USDA, ERS typology of farms identifies three groups of family farms based on farm size (measured as gross cash income). The size breaks are at $350,000 and $1 million. In 2014, 90% of family farms were identified as small, operating 46% of farmland and accounting for 22% of the value of production (USDA ERS, 2015a). Because of the diversity of this large group of family farmers, they are further distinguished by the major occupation of the principal operator, who reports being retired from farming, having an off-farm major occupation, or farming as a major occupation. In 2014, half of the small farms indicated that the major occupation of the principal farm operator is a nonfarm occupation. Furthermore, in many of the households there is a spouse or other family member who has a nonfarm occupation.

Compared to the U.S. population, farm operator households have higher incomes and net worth, and are more likely to have health insurance. In other words, based on the major well-being indicators, farm operator households are a financially advantaged group. The prevalence of multiple jobholding among farm operators and other household members explains how farm families operating small farms—again, 90% of all farms—are able to generate cash income and have access to employment-based health insurance (Ahearn, El-Osta, and Mishra, 2013). However, access to off-farm income sources does not explain why a large share of farm families continue to farm and reside on farms when they lose money farming year-after-year. In other words, for these families, they seemingly pay to live on farms.

The paradox of this situation is that there are other returns that farm families consider when engaging and continuing in farming, in spite of continued farm losses. In part these can be explained by the advantages afforded farm families by tax policies, as mentioned previously. First of all, farm losses can be used to reduce taxable income from nonfarm sources. Second, a farm is not just a place of farm business, it is a farm residence, and many of the expenses associated with the farm dwelling can be covered by the farm business. Farms, and other businesses, are the beneficiary of tax regulations that reduce taxes, for example, through accelerated depreciation of capital items and reduced local property taxes. Third, a major source of returns to farm families is through unrealized capital gains on farm assets. These returns are significant, and investment in farm assets often offers a buffer to riskier nonfarm investments, particularly in light of the government farm income support and risk management programs. The prevalence of unrealized capital gains is behind the old saying that "a farmer lives poor and dies rich." Finally, a farm lifestyle is perceived by many as a preferred lifestyle and offers a family "psychic" income.

Tax policies and legal liability considerations also play a role in an emerging trend in the links between farm households and farm businesses. Some farms, usually large successful family farms, are organizing in complex ways that are difficult to track because they involve family ownership of different aspects of farm-related businesses. For example, some distinct businesses may provide various inputs, like farm machinery, to the farm production business as traditionally defined, and another business may be engaged in the first handling of the production, but all companies are owned by individuals related by blood or marriage. The complexity of the interconnected organization is motivated by the goal of careful tax management and risk management, in addition to profit maximization, from the farm household perspective. Unfortunately, these complex organizations are also difficult to track in traditional censuses and surveys because the universe of farms includes only the farm production business. However, the financial decisions make sense only from the perspective of the interconnected multiple businesses. Currently, progress in understanding the evolution of these complex forms of organization are best understood through the use of state-level farm records systems (Featherstone et al., 2011).

As mentioned, there are 2.1 million farms in the United States. Household economic well-being statistics are reported for the principal operator and his or her family operating family farms. Some of these farm households also rent out some of the land they own to other farmers—approximately 13% did in 2014 (USDA NASS, 2015). The land they rented out accounted for 20% of land rented out in 2014. But, it should also be noted that some households, while not included in the farm household population, are closely associated with farming because they own and rent out farmland they own to other farm operators. Some of these households even participate in government farm programs. In 2014, approximately 1.9 million "non-operating" landlords rented out farmland. Of the 1.4 million who were either individuals or in partnership, the majority (55%) had once been a farm operator.

Government farm programs

The United States has a long history of government involvement in agriculture, as is true for most developed nations. Most farm policies are defined in a so-called farm bill developed approximately every 5 years. The most recent is the Agricultural Act (AA) of 2014. The 2014 AA continued and expanded many of the programs established in the 2008 legislation. Provisions that often garner the most attention are those that involve direct payments to farmers and landlord, but the recent legislation also included significant development of the crop insurance programs, with subsidized premiums, that has been the subject of intense policy discussion. Benefits of traditional commodity programs, which generally target production and/or acreage, are received by midsized and large farms. This is also true for the class of conservation programs, termed working-lands programs, and the indemnities associated with subsidized crop insurance. On the other hand, the traditional conservation programs, like the Conservation Reserve Program, largely go to small farms, in terms of sales, because this program requires that land be set aside for conservation uses, like conserving native grasslands.

The farm bill also targets some provisions of farm commodity and conservation programs to individuals based on the demographic characteristics of operators. This policy approach differs from the historical, and still dominant, farm policies, which focus on commodities and acreage in terms of production. Beginning farmers are defined as farmers or ranchers who have operated a farm or ranch for 10 years or less. Other policy-targeted groups are sometimes referred to as "socially disadvantaged" farmers or "nontraditional" farmers; both these terms can be vague and problematic, as producers in these categories are likely not to view themselves by those labels any more than other producers. Farmers in this category have not necessarily experienced prejudices, although they have one or more of the personal characteristics, which places them in this category.

Still other policy initiatives have focused on loan programs and outreach assistance, including to diverse farmers. The USDA administers loan programs for beginning farmers (beginning with the 1992 Act) and the so-called 2501 program to provide outreach and technical assistance through the Socially Disadvantaged Farmers and Ranchers Program (beginning with the 2002 Act). The 2008 Act established the Beginning Farmer and Rancher Development Program to competitively fund training and outreach programs for beginning farmers; many of the awards have gone to support programs targeting beginning and diverse farmers. Moreover, the Farm Credit Act requires the Farm Credit System to have programs focused on young, beginning and small farmers.

Although farming is diverse in many ways, farming is one of the least diverse occupations in terms of demographics, with the dominant demographic being white males. Eighty percent of principal operators are white males, disproportionately older, and the large majority (84%) of these white male operators has been farming for 10 years or more. Beginning farmers are bringing more diversity to the farm sector. Beginning farmers are about 20% of the farm population, and with the exception of Black farmers, at least one-third of the principal operators of the targeted groups considered in this paper are beginning farmers. There are likely many factors explaining the somewhat higher diversity among beginning farmers; among those factors are the outreach policy initiatives authorized in the farm bills and administered by the USDA and the efforts of individual lending institutions.

The groups targeted in various farm programs generally have a much smaller farm size distribution than other farms. In particular, the targeted groups have a much smaller share of large farms. There is one notable exception to this generalization. Farms with a principal farm operator who is Asian are more likely to operate large farms. For example, where only 4% of all U.S. farms had sales of $500,000 or more, 9% of Asian-operated farms did. Also, note that Asian farmers generate these sales on small average acreage since they are likely to be engaged in production of high-value agricultural crops. Table 2.3 presents the distribution of farms by size of farm for the targeted groups and all farms for 2012. With the exception of Asian-operated farms, the remaining groups had from 31–47% of the farms in the sales class of $1,000 or less.

Many small farms are actually not interested in expanding. This is clear from both previous work on entry and exit of farms over time (e.g., Ahearn, Korb, and Yee, 2009) and research on small nonfarm business. Studying a sample of small nonfarm businesses, Hurst and Pugsley (2011) found that most small business owners report that they do not want to grow, but instead are motivated by other nonpecuniary benefits of small business ownerships. Recently, Katchova and Ahearn (2016) linked individual farms across the Censuses and explored how beginning farmers expanded over more than a decade and found that life cycle played a major role. Older beginning farmers were much less likely to expand than young beginning farmers.

While the Hispanic farmer population has historically had a younger age profile, that is changing, as Hispanic farmers who entered decades ago have successfully expanded their operations and have a relatively strong financial position. And, the dynamic is changing for the women farmer group, too, which historically was dominated by older-aged farmers, believed to be surviving spouses. For example, as the senior farmer population (65 years and older) has increased for all U.S. farmers and the targeted groups over the past 3 decades, the share of senior women has remained stable. This implies that a new cadre of women farmers is likely to be in need of access to credit, like never before.

All evidence indicates that Asian farmers are typical in terms of their age distribution but atypically successful in terms of their financial position. The opposite is true of Black farmers. The decline in their numbers seems to have stabilized, but an even smaller share of Black farmers is young and their farm incomes are very low. The large group of Black farmers with small commodity sales is finding a way to stay small, but be profitable. The prevalence of "fractionated" land ownership may prevent these operators from incurring debt and expanding to a size that generates greater farm income. Perhaps, the continued development of the local food supply chain in the South will result in new opportunities for this targeted group.

Table 2.3 Economic class of all farms and those targeted under government farm programs, 2012

Gross sales	All farms	Beginning <10 years current farm	Women principal operator	Hispanic principal operator	Black or african american	Native american	Asian	Hawaiian or other pacific	More than 1 race
Less than $1,000	27%	33%	42%	28%	34%	33%	12%	24%	29%
$1,000–$2,499	12%	16%	14%	15%	20%	15%	9%	16%	15%
$2,500–$4,999	10%	12%	11%	12%	15%	11%	7%	12%	13%
$5,000–$9,999	10%	11%	10%	11%	13%	11%	10%	13%	13%
$10,000–$24,999	12%	11%	10%	12%	10%	12%	14%	14%	13%
$25,000–$49,999	7%	6%	5%	7%	4%	6%	10%	7%	7%
$50,000–$99,999	7%	4%	3%	6%	2%	5%	10%	6%	4%
$100,000–$249,999	7%	4%	3%	5%	1%	4%	11%	4%	3%
$250,000–499,999	4%	2%	1%	2%	1%	2%	7%	2%	2%
$500,000–$999,999	2%	1%	1%	1%	0%	1%	5%	1%	1%
$1 million or more	1%	1%	0%	2%	0%	1%	5%	1%	1%
Total farms	21,28,982	5,93,109	2,37,819	50,592	29,090	15,494	8,375	983	7,661

Source: USDA, NASS, 2014.
Note: Some farms are in more than one category.

Finally, it should be mentioned that the nonfarm employment activity of farm operator households, especially of small farms, points to the importance of rural development policies. Employment growth in rural areas can provide alternative occupations or supplemental incomes for operators whose farms are too small to provide adequate family income.

Concluding comments

The structure of the farming sector in the United States and many other developed countries is reflected in the number and size distribution of farms, particularly those classified as family farms. Globalization and technology adoption are driving structural change, which varies by characteristics of individual country domestic policy, trade policy, the evolving role of farm households, and the socioeconomic system. While many developed countries have supported domestic agricultural production, most developing countries have not. More recently, international food supply chains have somewhat replaced agricultural standards for imported and exported products which were previously developed through trade negotiations.

Increasing concern about future food security worldwide necessitates investment in rural infrastructure research and extension, better access to markets, increasing crop and livestock genetic diversity, and eliminating trade distorting policies. Improving agriculture's productivity technology adoption is critical to the development outcomes for countries. But consumer food preferences, input costs and risk management strategies, among other factors, also impact changes in farm size and structure.

Agricultural policies vary by country, or, in the case of the European Union Common Agricultural Policy, are region-wide. While policies differ greatly they tend to emphasize market price support, reductions to costs of inputs and capital, limiting downside risk for revenue and income, direct payments to farmers, and payments for provision of public goods. Policy changes across time affect farm structure, and some progress has been made in movement away from those which affect market prices and input subsidies to policies that do not affect production decisions of farmers and thereby distort trade. This trend is critical to ensuring food security for the world's burgeoning population and increasing number of middle-class consumers.

Though farm definitions vary across countries, there are approximately 570,000,000 farms worldwide. The majority are considered family farms, which vary greatly in size, even within developed countries. Family farms often depend on off-farm income sources for family expenditures and may rely totally on family members for farm labor, but the larger operations typically also employ non–family members.

The current U.S. sales-based definition of a farm originated in the mid-1970s and is very inclusive, becoming more so each year as price levels change. While the total number of farms and their average acreage has been quite stable during recent decades, significant structural change has nonetheless occurred. The number and share of farms producing less than $10,000 in gross sales has increased, especially for the very smallest with less than $1,000 gross sales. The largest size class producing $1 million or more in gross sales has also seen increased numbers and share of production, and the next largest class producing over $500,000 in sales was relatively stable. However large declines occurred in the mid-sizes of farms grossing between $10,000 and $500,000 in sales, continuing an ongoing trend of a declining numbers of middle-size farms. The increasing concentration of production will likely continue in order to minimize production costs and consumer prices. Further, farm households, especially small farms that dominate the farm sector numbers, will continue to require access to off-farm sources of income.

Overall, U.S. farm operator households have higher incomes and net worth than the general population and are more likely to have health insurance. This indicates that they are generally a financially advantaged group. However, a large share of farm families continually lose money farming. The farm losses can be used to reduce taxable income from non-farm sources, the farm residence expenses may be covered by the farm business, and significant unrealized capital gains and investment in farm assets buffers risk, particularly given government farm income support and risk management programs in which many farms participate.

U.S. government farm programs have particularly targeted traditional commodity production, which benefits primarily midsized and large farms. The same is true for working-lands conservation programs and the indemnities associated with subsidized crop insurance. Traditional conservation program benefits largely go to smaller-sales farms and require land to be set aside into conserving uses rather than employed in crop production. The most recent farm policy includes programs that are targeted based on the demographic characteristics of operators.

Many small farms are not interested in expanding. Rural development policies are especially important for this and select other groups who are interested in staying small in their farm operations but need to supplement farm income to provide adequate family income.

Note

1 If changes in price levels were ignored, as is done in the publicly available trend data from NASS, it would appear as if there was an increase in the number of farms between $250,000 and $499,999, and especially $500,000–$1 million.

References

AGR (Agriculture and Agri-Food Canada). 2014. Family Farms in Canada: A Profile for the United Nations, FAO, International Year of the Family Farm. Unpublished presentation.

Ahearn, M. and A. Effland. 2009. "U.S. Farm Policy and Small Farms", Paper presented at the 111 EAAE-IAAE Seminar 'Small Farms: decline or persistence', University of Kent, Canterbury, UK, 26–27 June.

Ahearn, M., H. El-Osta, and A. Mishra. 2013. "Considerations in Work Choices of U.S. Farm Households: The Role of Health Insurance", Journal of Agriculture and Resource Economics 38(1): 19–33.

Ahearn, M., H. El-Osta, and J. Perry. 1993. "Economic Well-Being of Farm Operator Households, 1988–90", USDA, ERS, AER No. 666, Jan. 1993.

Ahearn, M. and V. Harris. 2014. "20-Year Evolution of Farm Structure Brings Sector Resilience". Presentation at the Agricultural and Applied Economics Association Meetings, Minneapolis, MN, July 27–29.

Ahearn, M.C., P. Korb, and J. Yee. 2009. "Producer Dynamics in Agriculture: Empirical Evidence." In *Producer Dynamics: New Evidence from Microdata,* ed. R. Dunne, J.B. Jensen, and M.J. Roberts. Chicago: The University of Chicago Press, pp. 369–94.

Ahearn, M. and J. Lee. 1991. "Multiple Job Holding among Farm Operator Households in the United States", Chapter 1 in Hallberg, Findeis, and Lass, (ed.), *Multiple Job-Holding among Farm Families.* Ames: Iowa State U. Press.

Armbruster W.J., and M.C. Ahearn. 2014. "Changing Structure and Organization of US Agriculture". In: Neal Van Alfen (ed.), *Encyclopedia of Agriculture and Food Systems,* Vol. 2, San Diego: Elsevier; pp. 201–219.

Dunne, T., J.B. Jensen, and M. Roberts. (eds.). 2009. *Producer Dynamics: New Evidence from Micro Data,* Chicago: University of Chicago Press.

Eurostat. 2014. Agricultural, Forestry, and Fishery Statistics 2014 edition. Luxemburg, doi: 10.2785/59171.

FAO (Food and Agriculture Organization). 2015. Statistical Pocketbook. World Food and Agriculture. United Nations. Available online: http://www.fao.org/3/a-i4691e.pdf.

Featherstone, A., M. Wood, K. Herbel, and M. Langemeier. 2011. Innovations Using Farm Records Systems. Presented at the Enhancing Data for Complex Agricultural Establishments conference, Niagara-on-the-Lake, Ontario, Canada, June.

Fuglie, K. and N. Rada. 2015. International Agricultural Productivity Data Product. ERS, USDA. Available online: http://www.ers.usda.gov/data-products/international-agricultural-productivity/documentation-and-methods.aspx.

Gollin, D., D. Lagakos, and M. Waugh. 2014. "The Agricultural Productivity Gap in Developing Countries". *Quarterly Journal of Economics* 129(2), 939–993.

Hayami, Y. and V. Ruttan. 1971. *Agricultural Development: An International Perspective.* Washington, D.C.: The Brookings Institution Press.

Hurst, E., and B.W. Pugsley. 2011. "What Do Small Businesses Do?" The Brookings Institution, Economic Studies Program. Brookings Papers on Economic Activity 43(2): 72–142.

Katchova, A. and M. Ahearn. (2016) "Dynamics of Farmland Ownership and Leasing: Implications for Young and Beginning Farmers", *Applied Economic Perspectives and Policy* 38(2): 334–350.

Kirschenmann, F., S. Stevenson, F. Buttel, T. Lyson, and M. Duffy. 2014. *Why Worry about the Agriculture of the Middle?* Agriculture of the Middle. Available online: http://www.agofthemiddle.org/

Lowder, S., J. Skoet, and S. Singh. 2014. What Do We Really Know about the Number and Distribution of Farms and Family Farms in the World? ESA Working Paper 14-02.

OECD (Organization for Economic Cooperation and Development). 2015. Agricultural Policy Monitoring and Evaluation. 2015. OECD Publishing, Paris. doi:10.1787/agr_pol-2015-en

Sumner, D.A., J.M. Alston, and J.W. Glauber. (2010). Evolution of the economics of agricultural policy. *American Journal of Agricultural Economics* 92(2), 403–423.

UN (United Nations). 2015. Transforming Our World: The 2030 Agenda for Sustainable Development. A/RES/70/1.

USDA ERS (United States Department of Agriculture, Economic Research Service). 2015a. America's Diverse Family Farms, 2015 Edition. EIB No. 146, December.

USDA ERS (United States Department of Agriculture, Economic Research Service). 2015b. Farm Household Well-Being Briefing Room. Glossary. Available online: http://ers.usda.gov/topics/farm-economy/farm-household-well-being/glossary.aspx.

USDA NASS (United States Department of Agriculture, National Agricultural Statistics Service). 2014. 2012 Census of Agriculture. United States Summary and State Data. Vol. 1, Geographic Area Series, Part 51, Feb.

USDA NASS (United States Department of Agriculture, National Agricultural Statistics Service). 2015. Farmland Ownership and Tenure: Results for the 2014 Tenure, Ownership, and Transition of Agricultural Land Survey. 2012 Census of Agriculture Highlights. ACH 12–27. September.

Wang, S.L., P. Heisey, D. Schimmelpfennig, and E. Ball. 2015. "Agricultural Productivity Growth in the United States: Measurement, Trends, and Drivers", USDA, ERS, ERR No. 189. July.

Chapter 3

Influence of CAP on social sustainability in Greek and Bulgarian rural areas

Dimitre Nikolov, Basil Manos, Parthena Chatzinikolaou, Thomas Bournaris, and Fedra Kiomourtzi

Introduction

A traditional argument connected to CAP is the issue of maintaining economically vital rural communities, particularly in disadvantaged regions where alternative income opportunities are limited. This issue is still a big driver of policy action in the poorest areas due to the decreasing prices of agricultural products and the difficulties of many farms. However, in the last decade, a full range of new issues have emerged. The maturing of population in rural areas raises the issue of "greying" society in connection to liveliness of rural areas and residential use of farms. Intra- and extra-EU migration has led to important changes in the agricultural labor market and in non-agricultural residential communities in rural areas. While particularly in southern Europe immigrant labor has brought a major contribution to economic survival of agriculture and created new opportunities for labor allocation outside farming for local families, it also has generated new social inclusion problems (Kasimis et al., 2003). This, together with the movement of populations outside towns, renews the issue of rural-urban interaction. The role of the household as the core of the independent farm is changing with the increasing labor opportunities for the youth, and this also changes the profile of gender issues in rural areas. Gender issues are a typical aspect of the agriculture labor division. Though it may be argued that they have a strong social rather than biological foundation (Shortall, 2002), they are attached to both technology changes and modes of governance and social vision (Prugl, 2004). Altogether, these strong changes ask for a revision of problems connected with the management of social capital and social inclusion. On the one hand, exclusion is an issue with a long story in rural areas, though the study of mechanisms and the relations with policy have been for a long time insufficient in spite of their relevance (Shucksmith and Chapman, 1998; Shortall, 2004). On the other, social capital, individual skills and knowledge is an increasing factor in productivity and competitiveness, particularly in an enlarged and liberalized economy. Interactions with policy are not always straightforward, but certainly important (Winter, 1997). New perspectives in rural development include consideration of local as well as EU wide issues. For example, the international cooperation between rural areas reveals an increasing connectivity within and outside the EU (Ray, 2001).

In the context of the research project entitled CAP-IRE (Assessing the multiple Impacts of the Common Agricultural Policy on Rural Economies), which is a European FP7 funded project, there was an attempt to assess multiple impacts of the CAP in 11 European rural areas, including Greek and Bulgarian case study areas. The objective of this chapter is to make a comparison between Greek and Bulgarian rural areas by measuring social sustainability indicators. This chapter focuses on the effects of household behavior on social sustainability in terms of changes in employment, gender, migration and social capital. In order to study and measure these impacts, we studied a number of indicators relating to economic data, but also employment, social cohesion, social inclusion and demographic changes. The necessary data was collected through a household survey, which included a questionnaire, submitted to a large sample of farm households in the European Union countries. We have selected some questions of this questionnaire, which focus on the social indicators that we have chosen to compare the two European Union rural areas.

Social sustainability

Social sustainability is "one of the three legs of the sustainability stool" (the other two are environmental and economic): each leg needs the support of the other two. There is general agreement that the different dimensions of sustainable development have not been equally prioritized by policy makers within the sustainability discourse (Drakakis-Smith, 1995). There is limited literature that focuses on social sustainability to the extent that a comprehensive study of this concept is still missing. A recent study by the OECD (2001) points out that social sustainability is currently dealt with in connection to the social implication of environmental politics rather than as an equally constitutive component of sustainable development.

As a result, there have been very few attempts to define social sustainability as an independent dimension of sustainable development. Each author or policy maker derives their own definition according to specific criteria, making a generalized definition difficult to achieve. For example, from a sociological standpoint (Littig and Griessler, 2005) define social sustainability as a quality of societies. It signifies the nature-society relationships, mediated by work, as well as relationships within the society. Social sustainability is given, if work within a society and the related institutional arrangements satisfy an extended set of human needs and are shaped in a way that nature and its reproductive capabilities are preserved over a long period of time and the normative claims of social justice, human dignity and participation are fulfilled.

In recent years, social sustainability has also become an important component of the mainstream political discourse of governments, which has attempted to identify the issues involved with this concept. A report by the European Panel on Sustainable

Development (EPSD, 2004) points out that the Lisbon European Council in 2000 launched the inaugural idea of a social dimension as an integral part of the sustainable development model. An entire section of the Lisbon conclusions covered four main dimensions of social sustainability. These included the following:

- A commitment to enhance education, especially in relation to the new skills required for the "knowledge-intensive" economy
- Revamping employment policy so as to create "more and better jobs"
- Modernizing social protection to accommodate the many challenges faced by welfare states, to "make work pay" and to promote equality;
- The development of a strategy to counter poverty and social exclusion by "promoting social inclusion" (EPSD, 2004: 18)

Along similar lines, Omann and Spangenberg (2002) contend that social sustainability focuses on the personal assets like education, skills, experience, consumption, income and employment and comprises every citizen's right to actively participate in his/her society as an essential element. Thus, in their analysis, access to societal resources is a key element of social sustainability.

These attempts to identify the main elements of social sustainability highlight that a coherent and comprehensive theoretical framework for a fully integrated approach to sustainability is still lacking from the literature, and it is unlikely that one could be developed in the near future. This is due to the multifaceted nature of the concept of sustainability that amalgamates social, environmental and economic matters into a new independent entity.

Social sustainability indicators

Indicators are fundamental instruments to measure the progress toward social sustainability. Indicators linked to surveys and questionnaires are an essential part of the sustainability assessment and implementation process because they reflect people's perceptions of rural areas where they live. Further, the choice of indicators should depend on local circumstances and the needs and priorities of local people. The use of such indicators is a clear step toward more inclusion and representativeness that acknowledges place-specific conditions and the importance of subjective values at the policy-making level. However, it can be argued that it poses methodological problems related to the aggregation and comparison of the value of the indicators.

The first major step toward the identification of sustainability indicators can be traced back to Agenda 21, a blueprint of action to be taken toward the achievement of sustainability launched at the UN Conference on Environment and Development (Earth Summit) at Rio de Janeiro (UN, 1992). The UN Commission on Sustainable Development (UNCSD) developed and tested, in 22 countries, a set of 134 indicators in the categories of society, economies, environment and institutions with methodology sheets for each indicator (UN, 2001). This set was subsequently revised twice and finalized in 2006 and consists of a set of 50 core indicators, which are part of a larger set of 98 indicators of sustainable development.

Despite that a significant emphasis is given to social sustainability in community development policies, there exists only a handful of tools for its assessment, let alone for its promotion. Indeed, several indicators have been developed for the measurement of the different components of social capital, but these have been deployed only to design community surveys at the local level or used as proxies to deduct the level of social capital of countries from available national statistics. This indicates that more empirical work needs to be done on social capital tools if the promotion of this concept is to be included in social sustainability policies.

Since the initial attempt by the UNCSD, a plethora of sustainability indicators have been developed. EUROSTAT also uses many indicators in order to describe social sustainability by measuring social phenomena such as demographic changes, employment, social cohesion, social inclusion and social capital. Data constraints loom large in a regional study, and "subject to availability" turns out to be a significant caveat. Many of the indicators we might like to track are simply not available by region. The list of the proposed social indicators shows the indicators, which are in practice examined, reflecting the balance between the ideal and the constraints of data availability. EUROSTAT has data availability for many of the main social indicators in all CAP-IRE case study areas. For these reasons we propose to use social indicators defined by EUROSTAT in order to describe the social dimension.

Areas of study and data

A household survey was carried out in order to collect empirical information about present and future trends of changes in farms and the effects of the CAP and its reform on such changes. The data for this chapter came from the results of this survey for the 11 case study areas of the CAP-IRE Project (2013). The regions that we analyze and compare in this chapter are Macedonia-Thrace in Greece and the South-East Planning Region in Bulgaria. The rest case study areas are Emilia-Romagna in Italy, Noord-Holland in Netherlands, Podlaskie in Poland, North East Scotland in United Kingdom, Andalusia in Spain, Centre and Midi-Pyrenees in France, Lahn-Dill-District and Ostprignitz-Ruppin in Germany.

The region "Macedonia and Thrace" is located at the northern part of Greece. This region has about 2 million inhabitants, 20% of the total population of Greece. The biggest city is Thessaloniki, with about 1.2 million inhabitants. The study region is divided into 3 provinces – those of West Macedonia, Central Macedonia, and East Macedonia and Thrace – and 16 prefectures. The west and north part of the region is covered by mountains, between which is the famous Olympus. The south part of the region is coast. Many tourists visit the region during the winter (for skiing and agritourism) and the summer (for the nice coasts), offering a good income. The region has also important industry, mainly steel, textile, chemicals and petroleum products, energy units and food industries. The agricultural area of the total region is 1,384,700 ha, 40.6% of which is irrigated. Main crops in the region are cotton, sugar beets, trees (peaches, apples and pears) corn, hard wheat and tobacco. The study region has a strong integration between agricultural and industrial system, with the creation of a relevant agri-food system. It is to some extent concentrated around big cities, where the agricultural production is specialized in specific productions.

The South-East Planning Region in Bulgaria covers an area of 14,600 sq. km, 13% of the area of Bulgaria. It consists of three administrative districts – Bourgas, Sliven and Yambol. The population is about 782,000 inhabitants, about the 10% of the population in the country. The geographical location of the South-Eastern Region, with its broad outlet on the Black Sea, and the long boundary with Turkey is of strategic significance. The region is one of the richest in Bulgaria in biological diversity and natural old forests, providing opportunities for development of specialized tourism and recreation in the inside of the region. The main economic sectors in the region are tourism, agriculture and industry. The main industrial sectors are food and drinks production, textiles, petrochemical products, and wood processing. The agriculture produces the 18.8% of the regional GDP and uses the 6% of the employment. The main productions are grapes, fruit, corn, and cattle breeding. Fishery and aquaculture are present along the coastline. Water resources are limited and unevenly distributed, which necessitates using them wisely; if not managed effectively, they may turn into an obstacle for agricultural development. The climatic conditions, diverse landscape (including along the Black Sea coast) and the generous availability of spas and curative mud are favorable conditions for tourism development. The region has rich cultural heritage whose protection and maintenance requires more efforts than are presently made.

The survey included a questionnaire submitted to a large sample of farm households and requested information related to both farm and non-farm activities. The sample was 300 farm households from Macedonia-Thrace in Greece and 273 farm households in the South-East Planning Region in Bulgaria.

EUROSTAT uses many indicators in order to describe social sustainability by measuring social phenomena such as demographic changes, employment, social cohesion, social inclusion and social capital. We used the main social indicators defined by EUROSTAT in order to estimate the social sustainability. The used social indicators are the indicators, which are in practice examined, that reflect the balance between the ideal and the constraints of data availability. We have selected a number of questions from this questionnaire, which consists of the social indicators on which are based the identification of trends of changes in employment, gender, migration and social capital in rural areas in Greece and Bulgaria. The selected social indicators are presented in Table 3.1.

Table 3.1 Proposed social indicators

K1	Members of household working on the agricultural holding full-time
K2	Members of household working on the agricultural holding part-time
K3	Off-farm activities
K4	Lifelong learning (education level of the respondent)
K5	Lifelong learning (formal agricultural Education)
K6	Percentage of total household revenue from farming
K7	Members of a sports club, recreation or other social organization
K8	Members of the farmers union or other farming pressure group
K9	Members of a nature conservation organization or environmental organization
K10	Using Internet for buying production means
K11	Using Internet for selling products
K12	Household members younger than 18
K13	Early school leavers
K14	Household members older than 65
K15	Male members of household
K16	Female members of household
K17	Household members 18–65
K18	Full-time male employees
K19	Part-time male employees
K20	Full-time female employees
K21	Part-time female employees
K22	Employees who are citizens from other EU countries
K23	Employees who are citizens from non-EU countries
K24	Long-term unemployment

Source: Authors' survey

Results for social sustainability indicators

The next table (Table 3.2) contains the results for K1 and K2 indicators, the agricultural holdings that have at least one family member working on the farm full-time or part-time. The differences are statistically significant ($\alpha = 0.0001$). All the

Table 3.2 Family members working on the farm

	Macedonia-Thrace (GR)	South-East Planning Region (BG)	Average (11 CSAs)
Full-time	100%	89.4%	**82.5%**
Part-time	57.7%	39.2%	**48.6%**

$\alpha = 0.0001$

Source: Authors' survey

agricultural holdings in Macedonia-Thrace (GR) have family members working on the farm full-time, and more than the half of them (58%) have family members working part-time. Additionally, in the South-East Planning Region (BG) most of the agricultural holdings (89%) have family members working full-time and 39% have family members working part-time. We can observe that both regions have higher rates than the average (83%) for family members working full-time, but only Macedonia-Thrace (GR) has a higher rate than the average in family members working part-time.

Figure 3.1 shows the results for K3 indicator, the agricultural holdings doing any activity different from crop cultivation and animal rearing. The rate of the agricultural holdings doing other gainful activities of all the case study areas is 20%. In both regions the rates are lower than the average. More specifically, in the South-East Planning Region (BG) 14% and in Macedonia-Thrace (GR) 12% of the agricultural holdings do other gainful activities.

In the next table (Table 3.3) and in Figure 3.2 we can see the results for the K4 and K13 indicators, the education level of the respondent and the rates of early school leavers. The differences are statistically significant ($\alpha = 0.0001$). Regarding the high education level of the respondents, the indicator contents are the respondents that have upper secondary education, post-secondary education, and the first stage of tertiary education or second stage of tertiary education.

In all case study areas, more than the half of the respondents (67%) has a high education level, and in the South-East Planning Region (BG), where the rates are much higher than the average, most of the respondents (92%) are highly educated. On the other hand, in Macedonia-Thrace (GR) only 22% of the respondents have a high education level.

As regards the early school leavers, the indicator contents show the respondents that have only primary or secondary education. In all case study areas, less than 35% of the respondents are low-educated. Moreover, in the South-East Planning Region (BG) the rates are lower than the average, and more specifically, there are only 8% early school leavers. On the other hand, Macedonia-Thrace (GR) has the higher percentage in early school leavers, and the rate is much higher than the average, because 78% of the respondents have primary or secondary education.

Figure 3.3 shows the agricultural holdings that have at least one member with formal agricultural education (K5 indicator). As we can observe, in all case study areas, more than the half the agricultural holdings (57%) have at least one member

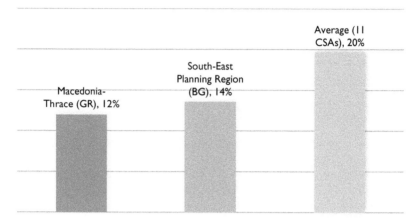

Figure 3.1 Activities different from farming

Source: Authors' survey

Table 3.3 Education level

	Macedonia-Thrace (GR)	South-East Planning Region (BG)	Average (11 CSAs)
None and primary (elementary school)	37.7%	2.9%	**14.8%**
Lower and secondary (primary school)	40.7%	4.8%	**18.2%**
Upper secondary education (high school)	17.0%	64.7%	**33.7%**
Post-secondary, non-tertiary education (professionalizing master)	3.0%	2.6%	**20.0%**
First stage of tertiary education (degree)	1.7%	25.0%	**11.5%**
Second stage of tertiary education (PhD)	0.0%	0.0%	**0.5%**

$\alpha = 0.0001$

Source: Authors' survey

with formal agricultural education. The rates for both regions are slightly lower than the average. More specifically, 47% and 45% of the agricultural holdings have at least one member with formal agricultural education in Macedonia-Thrace (GR) and in the South-East Planning Region (BG), respectively.

The next table (Table 3.4) shows the percentage of total household gross revenue that comes from farming (K6 indicator). The differences are statistically

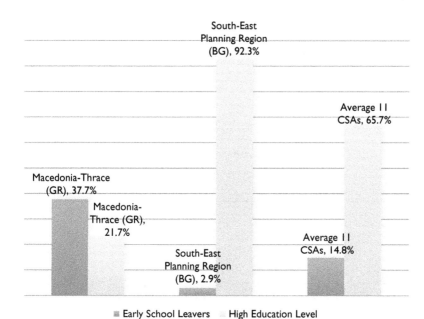

Figure 3.2 Education level

Source: Authors' survey

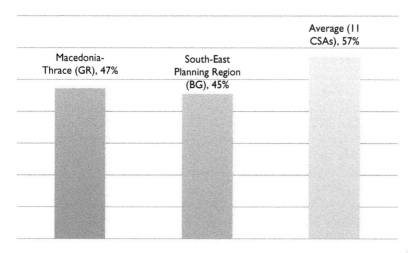

Figure 3.3 Formal agricultural education

Source: Authors' survey

Table 3.4 Percentage of total household gross revenue that comes from farming

Indicators	Macedonia-Thrace (GR)	South-East Planning Region (BG)	Average (11 CSAs)
< 10%	1.0%	1.9%	**11.7%**
10–29%	0.3%	5.5%	**9.5%**
30–49%	4.0%	17.9%	**11.0%**
50–69%	14.7%	20.1%	**15.0%**
70–89%	26.7%	21.6%	**14.9%**
> 89%	53.3%	31.9%	**35.1%**

$\alpha = 0.0001$

Source: Authors' survey

significant. ($\alpha = 0.0001$). In all case study areas, in 22% of the agricultural holdings less than 30% of the total revenue comes from farming, and in about 10% of the agricultural holdings 30–49% of the total household revenue is coming from farming, where in the rest of them more than 50% of the of the total revenue comes from farming.

In Macedonia-Thrace (GR), in about all the farm households more than 50% of the total household revenue is coming from farming, and more specifically in more the half of them, more than 89% of the total revenue comes from farming. Moreover, in the South-East Planning Region (BG), in only 8% of the agricultural holdings less than 30% of the total revenue comes from farming, in about 18% of the agricultural holdings 30–49% of the total household revenue is coming from farming, where in the rest of them more than 50% of the of the total revenue comes from farming.

Figure 3.4 shows the agricultural holdings that have at least one family member who is a member of any Social Network (K7-K8-K9 indicators). More than 30% of the agricultural holdings in all case study areas are members in a sports club, recreation or other social organization, more than half (54%) of the agricultural holdings are members in the farmers union or any other farming pressure group, but only 9% of the agricultural holdings are members in a nature conservation organization or other environmental organization.

In Macedonia-Thrace the rates are slightly lower than the average, where 23% of the agricultural holdings are members of a sports club, recreation or other social organization, more than the half (53%) of the agricultural holdings are members in the farmers union or any other farming pressure group and only 2% of the agricultural holdings are members in a nature conservation organization or other environmental organization. In the South-East Planning Region (BG) the rates are also lower than the average, where more than 20% of the agricultural holdings are members in the farmers union or any other farming pressure group, but less

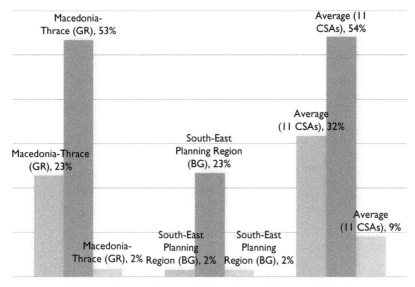

Figure 3.4 Members of any social network

than 2% of the agricultural holdings are members in a sports club, recreation or other social organization, or in a nature conservation organization or other environmental organization.

The next table and figure indicate the agricultural holdings that have at least one employee (male or female) working on the farm (K18, K19, K20 and K21 indicators). As we can observe, both regions have higher rates than the average in all indicators. In Macedonia–Thrace (GR) 32% of the agricultural holdings have male employees working full-time, and more than the half of them (57%) have male employees working part-time. Moreover, in the South–East Planning Region (BG) the half of the agricultural holdings (52%), have male employees working full-time and 30% of them have male employees working part-time. The rates for all case study areas are lower, where less than 30% of the agricultural holdings have male employees working full- or part-time (Table 3.5). As regards female employees (Figure 3.5), the rates for all case study areas are lower: Only 6% of the agricultural holdings in all case study areas have female employees working full-time. Also, in Macedonia–Thrace (GR), where the rates are lower than the average, 3% of the agricultural holdings have female employees working full-time. Curiously, in the South–East Planning Region (BG), the rate is much higher than the average, because more than 20% of the agricultural holdings have female employees working full-time.

Table 3.5 Male employees working on the farm

Indicators	Macedonia-Thrace (GR)	South-East Planning Region (BG)	Average (11 CSA's)
Male full-time	32.0%	52.4%	**21.6%**
Male part-time	57.3%	29.5%	**27.0%**

α = 0.0001

Source: Authors' survey

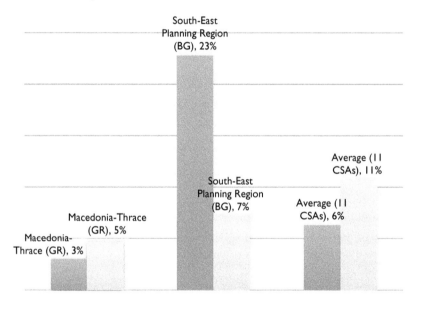

Female – full time   Female – part time

Figure 3.5 Female employees working on the farm

Source: Authors' survey

Moreover, 11% of the agricultural holdings in all case study areas have female employees working part-time, 5% of the agricultural holdings in Macedonia-Thrace (GR) have female employees working full- or part-time, and 7% of them in the South–East Planning Region (BG) have female employees working part-time.

The average of agricultural holdings using the Internet for buying production means in all case study areas is 17%. In Macedonia-Thrace (GR) the rate is lower than the average, where only 8% of the holdings used the Internet for buying production means. On the other hand, the South–East Planning Region (BG) has a higher rate than the average, because more than 25% of agricultural holdings use the Internet for buying production means.

Regarding the agricultural holdings using the Internet for selling products, the rates are lower for all case study areas. The average of the agricultural holdings using the Internet for selling products of all case study areas is only 8%, where in Macedonia-Thrace (GR) only 3% of the agricultural holdings use the Internet for selling products. On the other hand, the South-East Planning Region (BG) has a much higher rate than the average, where 20% of the agricultural holdings are using the Internet for selling products.

As regards the maturing of population, in all case study areas, 13% of the household members are older than 65 years (Table 3.6). In both regions the rates are lower than the average. More specifically, in the South-East Planning Region (BG) 10% of the household members are older than 65 and in Macedonia-Thrace (GR) only 5% of the household members and are older than 65. Furthermore, 23% of the household members are younger than 18 years in all case study areas, but the rates in both regions are lower than the average. More specifically, in Macedonia-Thrace (GR) only 16% of the household members are younger than 18, and finally, in the South-East Planning Region (BG) only 17% of the household members are younger than 18.

Both regions have higher rates of long-term unemployment in households than the average. More specifically, in Macedonia-Thrace (GR) the long-term unemployment rate is 4.3%. Additionally, in the South-East Planning Region the long-term unemployment rate is 3.9%. On the other hand, the average of long-term unemployed of all the case study areas is less than 3%.

The agricultural holdings that have at least one foreign employee working on the farm (K22, K23 indicators) are another issue. Macedonia-Thrace (GR) has higher rates than the average, and more specifically, 13% of the agricultural holdings have foreign employees from other EU countries, but 64% have foreign employees from non-EU countries. The average for all case study areas is lower, where less than 10% of the agricultural holdings have foreign employees from other EU countries or

Table 3.6 Household member composition

Indicators	Macedonia-Thrace (GR)	South-East Planning Region (BG)	Average (11 CSA's)
Members >18	15.8%	16.8%	**22.9%**
Members <65	5.3%	9.7%	**12.9%**
Members 18–65	77.9%	73.5%	**64.2%**
Male members	50.5%	51.4%	**52.5%**
Female members	49.5%	48.6%	**47.5%**

$\alpha = 0.0001$

Source: Authors' survey

from non-EU countries. On the other hand, we can observe that in the South-East Planning Region (BG) none of the agricultural holdings have foreign employees from other EU countries or from non-EU countries.

Conclusions

The main idea of this chapter is to make a comparison between a Greek and a Bulgarian rural area in terms of social sustainability indicators. This chapter also compares the two rural areas with the average of the eleven European Union rural areas.

The data show that the problem of low educational attainments of the respondents is particularly relevant for rural areas, where also the problem of low agricultural education is common in case study areas with many early school leavers. The low educational level of most of the rural population causes a low employment rate and, consequently, may decrease the income, which in turn negatively affects the chance of receiving high-quality education. Only in some case study areas is the employment rate very high. This may be partly explained by poor employment opportunities in many rural areas. The employment rate provides a different picture in the breakdown by gender, showing that in all case study areas the female employment rate is generally lower than the male one. This difference may be explained by two facts: (1) the participation of women in education is lower than that of men in all the case study areas covered by the study, and (2) a large number of young women are still discouraged from entering the labor market.

The long-term unemployment rate is quite high in Macedonia-Thrace (GR) and the South East Planning Region (BG), signaling that many people risk being caught in an "unemployment trap." The risk of being long-term unemployed is especially high for people with low educational attainment.

As regards the implications of ageing of the labor market in rural areas, people aged 65 and over represent less than 10% of the population in Macedonia-Thrace (GR) and the South-East Planning Region (BG). This may reveal, not only an unfavorable demographic trend, which may reduce local labor supply in the next few years, but can also pose a risk for the future sustainability of social protection systems.

The diffusion of Internet use for buying productions means or for selling products is in general considered as a tool for stimulating economic development in rural areas and improving the functioning of economic activity and labor market. Internet usage is high in the South-East Planning Region (BG), while it is still very low in Macedonia-Thrace (GR).

An important element characterizing rural areas is that of accessibility to and participation in any social institution, especially nature conservation organizations or other environmental organizations. The rates are quite higher concerning the participation to sports clubs, recreation or other social organizations. Moreover, in all case study areas, more than the half the households are members in farmers unions or other farming pressure groups.

Diversified sources of income may indeed reduce the risk among farmers. The diffusion of very small or even semi-subsistence farms is a matter of serious concern, because in Macedonia-Thrace (GR) and the South-East Planning Region (BG), less than 15% of farmers are no longer interested only in production of raw materials for agro-business but also in other activities such as agro-tourism, environment protection, transmission of traditional knowledge (such as processing of traditional products) to new generations, all of which provide openings for urban populations to participate in activities linked to eco-tourism (Nikolov et al, 2015).

With regard to immigrant employments, research has shown that the rates of migrants from outside the EU are much higher than the rates of migrants from other EU countries, in all case study areas. However, the higher rates shown in areas where economic sectors are characterized by strong seasonality and involve less-qualified people are relevant. This is mainly the case of Macedonia-Thrace (GR), once a traditional emigration area, which has become a destination for a large number of immigrants during the last 15 years.

The aim of this chapter is not the assessment of developed, developing and underdeveloped areas, but a comparison made among the 24 selected social indicators, and it does not necessarily mean that these areas follow a path of social sustainability decline. This analysis permits to point out some specific problems that characterize rural areas and determine specific problems for the rural population. This set of problems includes several difficulties linked to demography, remoteness, education, and to some special features of the labor market.

References

CAP-IRE (2013). *Assessing the Multiple Impacts of the Common Agricultural Policies (CAP) on Rural Economies (CAP-IRE)*, available at http://cordis.europa.eu/publication/rcn/14738_en.html.

Drakakis-Smith D. (1995). Third World Cities: Sustainable Urban Development, *Urban Studies* 32, Nos. 4–5.

EPSD (European Panel on Sustainable Development) (2004). From here to Sustainability – Is the Lisbon/Goteborg Agenda Delivering?, EPSD Report No 1, 2004-12-01, available at http://www.gmv.chalmers.se/epsd/index.htm

Kasimis C., Papadopoulos. G., Zacopoulou E. (2003). Migrance in Rural Greece. *Sociologia Ruralis* 43 (2): 168–184.

Littig B. & Griessler E. (2005). Social Sustainability: A Catchword between Political Pragmatism and Social Theory, *International Journal of Sustainable Development*, 8, 1 (2): 65–80.

Nikolov D., Anastasova-Chopeva M., Radev T., and Borisov P. (2015) State and Prospects for Development of Small Farms. Sofia, Bulgaria: Avangard Prima, pp. 77–81.

OECD (2001). Analytic Report on Sustainable Development SG/SD(2001)1-14, OECD, Paris.

Omann I. and Spangenberg J.H., (2002). Assessing Social Sustainability. The Social Dimension of Sustainability in a Socio-Economic Scenario, paper presented at the 7th Biennial Conference of the International Society for Ecological Economics in Sousse (Tunisia), 6–9 March 2002.

Prugl E. (2004). Gender Orders in German Agriculture: From the Patriarchal Welfare State to Liberal Environmentalism. *Sociologia Ruralis* 44 (4): 350–372.

Ray C. (2001). Transnational Co-operation Between Rural Areas: Elements of a Political Economy of EU Rural Development. *Sociologia Ruralis* 41 (3): 280–295.

Shortall S. (2002). Gendered Agriculture and Rural Restructuring: A Case Study of Northern Ireland. *Sociologia Ruralis* 42 (2): 161–172.

Shortall S. (2004). Social or Economics Goals, Civic Inclusion or Exclusion? An Analysis of Rural Development Theory and Practice. *Sociologia Ruralis* 44 (1): 110–123.

Shucksmith M., Chapman P. (1998). Rural Development and Social Exclusion. *Sociologia Ruralis* 38 (2): 225–242.

Winter M. (1997). New Policies and New Skills: Agricultural Change and Technology Transfer. *Sociologia Ruralis* 37 (3): 364–381.

Chapter 4

The evolving patterns of rural structures under the impact of public policies in Romania

Costică Mihai, Mihai Talmaciu, and Mioara Borza

The rural environment is characterized by processes and phenomena that intertwine economics with social aspects, modernism with traditionalism, as well as politics with the natural environment. This complex relationship represents the basis of our analysis regarding the establishment of rural development strategies and policies. Such elements need to be centred on humans and their social environment, and aspects such as natural, financial, material and cultural potential need to be involved and capitalized with a focus on increasing welfare and quality of life. Man represents the pivot around which policies and strategies need to be created so that natural resources can be mobilized and directed towards the goal of reaching a high level of welfare. Such programmes need to be based on traditional economic and service sectors, which represent the cultural heritage of peasantry. Starting from these, solutions must be identified to insure the development and modernization of rural organizations while maintaining/preserving the time-honored inheritance of the rural population.

Challenges faced by the rural society of Romania during the transition to a market economy

The rural society and peasant culture represent a foundation for the Romanian people, having withstood the test of time as well as the repeated attempts by previous political regimes (both capitalist and communist) to destroy or alter these elements (Knight 2010). From a wider Romanian perspective, the rural environment is traditionally regarded as being the least modern component of society, with strong signs of underdevelopment (Micu 2010). However, its importance is suggested by Samuel Huntington (1968), who states that he who rules the countryside, rules the country. The fact that the rural environment represents the most important component of Romanian society is suggested both by its geographical coverage, 87.1% of the country's surface area, as well as its significant involvement of the population, 47.2% of the total population (Eurostat 2015).

The rural society shows a high level of conservativism and inertia, being the place where "numerous events take place, but little evolution, where changes occur, but development does not" (Mungiu-Pippidi 2010). While urban societies are occasionally focused on reforms, rural areas have always shown a tendency towards stagnation. Traditionally, the remarkable resistance to change and progress seen in rural areas can be explained by two causal factors (Mungiu-Pippidi 2010):

- Peasant culture – peasants were described by twentieth-century anthropologists as being passive, collectivistic, envious, fatalistic and untrusting individuals, and politicians have regarded them as a final obstacle in the path of social and economic progress.
- Obedience towards oppressive regimes – in some studies, peasants were described as victims who complied, but did not fully agree, except as voluntary contributors in the conservative order of things.

The evolution of the Romanian rural environment was marked by historical events that led to political regime changes and, implicitly, alterations in public policies regarding rural organizations that had a significant impact on peasant culture and the values of villagers, affecting the economic and social systems in their entirety. The major issues that affect the rural areas of Romania (mainly underdevelopment and with a low quality of life) result from the dual rift faced by the rural society of Romania:

- The abolishment of private property after 1945 and the implementation of collectivistic agrarian and social relationships.
- The restructuring of rural organizations based on capitalistic principles after 1989, with the restoration of private land ownership and of the dignity of Romanian peasants.

The last 25 years of evolution in Romanian agriculture have seen several transformations with regard to legislation and property rights. The first draft of the land fund (Law 18/1991) was intended to have a dual impact with regard to the restitution of agricultural lands: the restoration of property rights to former owners who were expropriated after the first communist government came to power on March 6, 1945, but also the restoration of private usage rights for people whose land was administered by the state as part of cooperatives and state farms. Thus, almost all agricultural companies and cooperatives that existed before 1989 were dissolved, marking the start of the long "odyssey" of small-scale and inefficient farming that sought mainly to provide self-sustenance.

Romanian views regarding agriculture are different from European ones. In Romania, it is considered that this sector should consist mainly from large- and very large-scale farms that would ensure high efficiency. In spite of this view, the reality is that agricultural lands are extremely fragmented.

Table 4.1 shows that, even though the very small farms (below 2 hectares) are by far the most numerous, their total surface is small compared to the other categories.

Table 4.1 Number of farms in Romania by size, 2013

	Less than 2 ha	2–4.9 ha	5–9.9 ha	10–19.9 ha	20–29.9 ha	30–49.9 ha	50–99.9 ha	Over 100 ha
Number	2,589,920	691,260	193,870	45,650	10,260	8,470	7,260	13,080
Total surface	1,848,060	2,298,250	1,389,240	719,090	274,820	387,330	570,170	7,168,940

Source: Eurostat 2015

The situation in the case of family farms has not changed significantly, in spite of the fact that, over the last few years, large investments have been made in rural development.

The reasons for this persistent underdevelopment of Romanian agriculture stem from the main issues which the rural economy and agriculture industry have faced:

- The lack of vision and coherence of public policies
- The lack of stability of legal and institutional frameworks (combined with the weak implementation of regulations)
- The dichotomy between large (industrial) farms and small (peasant) farms
- The persistence of poverty and the aging of the population
- The difficulties caused by bureaucracy and financing possibilities
- The disparities that exist in the import/export relationships with other European countries
- The presence of specific negative effects on the natural environment in rural areas.

After Romania joined the European Union, a large number of small family farms (under 1 hectare) ware no longer financed as a result of decisions made by Romanian governmental authorities as part of the negotiations with the EU. This measure was meant to discourage the persistence of this category of farmers and to determine them to form associations or to transfer their property rights towards other categories. However, by the end of 2013, it seems that the effects are not the ones that were desired, as many of these small farms have continued to exist. By analysing this "persistence in inefficiency," some characteristics can be deduced with regard to the role and impact of these small farmsteads on the rural society of Romania:

1   *The meaning of land ownership for the Romanian peasant.* Ever since the first farmland allotments towards peasants that took place as part of the reforms implemented by Alexandru, Ioan, Cuza in 1964, property rights gained a significant role in peasant families, being transmitted with great care to their descendants. Land became an indicator of wealth and individual significance at the local level.
2   *The importance of land use for individuals.* For long periods of time, the rural population has been involved primarily in agricultural activities that involved

work in the fields. As a result, most workers in this sector became specialized in working the land, regardless of its ownership. Although, during the communist years, the consolidation of land use and the development of the industrial sector led to a part of the population becoming specialized in other activities, the collapse of the Romanian economy after 1989 caused farmers to return to their traditional occupations.

3   *The role of land in insuring existential and food security for many families that lack other means of subsistence.* The sustenance of numerous rural families is strongly connected to the harvests generated by land use, regardless of its surface. Even if small-scale farming is inefficient and depends on natural factors, by assessing the overall context of their existence – the absence of other economic sectors or means of subsistence – it can be stated that farmlands represent an essential existential factor for a large proportion of the rural population. In the post-1989 period, the rural landscape of Romania has crossed some periods of tension and of hesitant evolution. Over 20 years needed to pass before the first positive results of national and European rural development policies began to emerge. Up to the year 2000, public policies had an unfavorable impact on the rural environment, resulting in the loss of large portions of the assets of the Romanian agricultural sector.

Overall, with regard to the issues that impact the rural environment in Romania, a clear classification can be observed, such as economic and financial issues, strategic issues, social issues, environmental problems and international cooperation problems. The main focus has been on economic issues related to agricultural and food production, followed by the social and international cooperation issues, while aspects such as the protection of environmental factors have been practically overlooked or regarded as being of low priority.

Evolution of rural organizations under the impact of public policies

Public policies and economic organizations

Agriculture remains the base occupation for residents of rural areas, even if it is no longer regarded as an engine for economic growth or the central component of the Romanian economy. After the fall of the communist regime in 1989, the foundations of the current agricultural system were laid. This sector of the economy is labor-intensive, but it is undercapitalized, uses rudimentary or outdated technologies and generates low productivity.

One of the most ardent issues of the Romanian agricultural sector concerns its structure, namely the fragmented nature of farmlands, which does not allow companies to become major players in the marketplace. The average size of a Romanian farm has increased slowly from 2.3 hectares in the first half of the 1990s up to

3.59 hectares in 2013 (Eurostat 2015). Under these circumstances, the creation of added value and the entry of small farmsteads on the market remain problematic. Potential solutions to the structural problem involve the encouragement of associations to integrate small farmers on the market, the development of agricultural consultancy services (increased roles for agricultural chambers of commerce) and the institutionalization of the Romanian agriculture.

The current highly fragmented structure, in which 2.6 million small or subsistence farms are not eligible for the direct payments system (Luca 2009), is the result of a prolonged reform process started through the land fund law 18/1991. This piece of legislation provided only a partial solution for the issue of land retrocession and reinstatement of property rights by setting a maximum limit of 10 hectares and the reconstruction of the property on an area established by a commission – a procedure that generated numerous abuses and lawsuits. The completion of the land reform was made more difficult by an ambiguous and volatile legal environment. Thus, between 1991 and 2005, 11 legal acts (laws and governmental orders) were adopted in order to regulate land rights. Some of the most relevant include the following:

- Law 169/1997 – that allows former owners or their descendants to request up to 50 hectares of farmland and up to 30 hectares of forest areas per family
- Law 1/2000 – regarding the reconstruction of property rights on the same previous area, based on the principle "restitution in integrum"
- Law 400/2002 – regarding awarding ownership to thousands of individuals based on a set of 1945 lists that mentioned people who would receive farmlands as a result of the post-war agricultural reform
- Law 247/2005 – regarding the full restitution of forests and buildings associated with agricultural or forested lands outside of localities.

Another characteristic of the Romanian agriculture is the dichotomy between:

- small-scale agriculture aimed at self-sustenance and subsistence – 3.475 million farms with less than 10 hectares of land (of which 2.6 million under 1 hectare), representing 97.62% of all farms and covering only 37.7% (5.535 million hectares) of the total agricultural land surface (Eurostat 2015); and
- large-scale, market-oriented agriculture – 13.08 thousand entities, representing 0.37% of the total number of farms and covering 48.92% (7.168 million hectares) of the total agricultural land surface (Eurostat 2015).

Beyond these, a relatively insignificant segment of mid-sized farms exist (10–100 hectares of land) – 7,126 thousand entities, representing 2.01% of the total number and covering 13.3% (1.195 million hectares) of the total agricultural land surface (Eurostat 2015). Even though peasant farms are considered (by the Common Agricultural Policy) to be the backbone of agriculture in the EU member states,

Romanian governmental policies after 1990 sought to support mainly large farms that broke off from the former State Agricultural Enterprises (IASs). These companies received the largest share of the direct subsidies and enjoyed protection against external competition.

Out of the major issues that need to be resolved through rural development policies in Romania are the following:

- Support for non-agricultural sectors that can reduce the share that agriculture contributes to the GDP, which was around 7% in 2010 and 6% in 2012, compared to the 1.7% EU average in 2012 or 0.8% in the case of developed nations such as Germany (Burja 2014)
- Reduction of the workforce involved in agriculture: nearly 30.6% of the working population in 2010 was active in the agricultural sector, compared to the 5.2% EU average (Burja 2014)
- The structure of properties and the structure of the rural economy
- The size and productivity of Romanian farms
- The market focus and the competitiveness of farms
- Diversification of the rural economy.

It is necessary to implement policies and strategies that support the development of competitive production organizations, that increase the productivity of agricultural labor, that contribute to the increase of income and quality of life for rural families. It is necessary to create market-oriented, large-scale farms that use advanced and highly productive technologies and that have capital investment capabilities. The legal framework that favors the increase of farm sizes and the consolidation of lands has evolved slowly.

In order for farms to gain a relevant share of the market and become competitive in relation to companies from developed nations, it is necessary to adopt new work methods and advanced technologies. It is also imperative to provide practitioners with the complex knowledge and abilities that cannot be obtained based solely on practical experience. Thus, modern agriculture requires that farmers possess knowledge in the fields of biology, chemistry, biochemistry, agrotechnics, veterinary medicine, management, marketing, accounting, law etc. Even with specialized consultancy services available, they must have a basic familiarity and understanding of such disciplines by attending specialized schools or training programmes. In 2012, only 2.1% of Romanian farmers had basic agricultural training, 0.4% had full training, and 70.9% had only practical experience (Burja 2014).

With regard to subsidy policies, before Romania joined the EU, such support remained high, being directed mainly towards large-scale farms (given that the awarding of subsidies was 88% dependant on the level of production). From 2003 through 2005, the total support for agriculture in Romania was 6% of GDP far surpassing the average of the OECD countries (Knight 2010). The share of payments depending on land surface was only 4%, meaning that nearly all subsidies were awarded to large farms. A very small number of peasants received meagre payments and the majority of small farmers did not receive anything. Under these circumstances, the subsidy policies in the transition period (before joining the European Union) did not contribute to the modernization and adoption of new work methods and technologies within the large number of small- and medium-sized peasant farms. As a result, these were not able to become competitive in relation to the corresponding farms that existed in the other EU member states.

Diversification of rural economic structure

The Romanian rural environment presents a large variety in terms of human capital, the economic, social, cultural and natural environment. A major challenge for the Romanian rural space is the modernization of economic and social structures through the diversification of economic activities and creation of new jobs, so that the potential of human capital from rural areas may be turned to better use by attracting the significant redundancy of human resources employed in agriculture to the non-agricultural sectors. Economic growth and occupancy of human resources in rural areas are positively influenced by the favorability of natural resources, the surrounding environment quality, and the important human potential existing in the Romanian villages, but there are also many factors exerting a negative influence:

- The preponderant one-sector character of rural economy and the poor diversity of sectorial structures
- The demographic conditions unfavorable for development: the decrease of birth rates associated to the amplification of migration phenomenon that has led to the decline of the young population, the aging of the population and the narrowing of the base of age pyramid
- Inadequate infrastructures (access, buildings, communications, sanitary, educational, etc.) – some infrastructure categories completely lack and where they exist their quality is poor and their modernization level is precarious
- The low level of life quality
- The low level of human capital: low level of training, skills and knowledge, innovation and entrepreneurial initiatives
- Social capital and poorly developed institutions.

Although the specialists in development highlight the importance of entrepreneurship and innovation for the improvement of the welfare level in the rural environment, we may not imagine that all inhabitants of the Romanian villages may be potential entrepreneurs (Voicu & Radulescu 2003; Ignat 2012), especially whether we take into account the preponderantly conservative attitude of their large majority. One of the major obstacles lying in front of the development of the SMEs sector and the diversification of economic structure in the rural environment is the difficult access to funding, and the credit costs are still high. The territorial distribution of financial services is unfavorable to the economic environment from the rural regions, as they are less accessible to the enterprises from the rural environment.

Another obstacle in the way of development of rural entrepreneurship is the population's reduced entrepreneurial capacity, in the conditions in which people are old and the training level, skills and entrepreneurial abilities are totally inadequate.

Romania is facing a significant gap in terms of the diversification of the structure of rural economy as compared to the EU average values. The gap is even more significant if we look at the countries having advanced economies. The high weight of the tertiary sector in GDP or GVA is an attribute of a modern and developed economy. In case of Romania, it was only 46.5% in 2010, as compared to the EU country average of 64.6% (EC, DG AGRI 2013). The structural issues of the Romanian economy are reflected by the great weight of primary sector in GVA, about 6% in 2012 as compared to 1.7 % average of EU-27 (EC, DG AGRI 2013), or the high weight of occupation in the primary sector of 30.6%, as compared to the European average of 5.4% (EC, DG AGRI 2013).

The encouraging of entrepreneurial initiatives and the diversification of rural economy through the setting up of microenterprises, small and medium enterprises, might solve the structural problems on a social level. Thus, the weight of population employed in agriculture would reduce and the potential of the human resources from the rural environment might be turned to better use, hidden unemployment determined by the integral non-use of work time of the population employed in agriculture might dwindle and the inhabitants' income might increase and the life quality of the village inhabitants might improve. From the analysis of the situation of rural SMEs, we may affirm that they do not have the capacity to offer enough jobs for the population. Thus, from total SMEs having a non-agricultural profile at the national level existing in 2011, only 18.1% carried out their activity in the rural environment, their density per one thousand inhabitants being much smaller (9.64 SMEs/one thousand inhabitants) than the national average (23.66 SMEs/1,000 inhabitants) (INS TEMPO online).

Due to the slow rhythms and/or the incapacity of enterprises in the food industry to adapt to the European standards, and the deficiencies in terms of providing the supply chain with raw materials, after Romania's accession to the European Union their number reduced by 13%. In 2011 there were left 7,508 enterprises (about 1.6% of all companies in this industry), and 98% of them were SMEs (INS TEMPO online). At the same time, the weight of population employed in the food industry was 2.1% in 2011, as compared to the European average of 2.8% (Eurostat 2015). Another particularity of the Romanian economy is the high ratio between the population employed in agriculture and the population employed in the food industry, 12:1, as compared to EU average, where this ratio is 5:1 (EC, DG AGRI 2013).

In the context in which 70% of the production is exported primarily processed or unprocessed (Ministry of Agriculture and Rural Development, Directorate General for Rural Development, Management Authority for PNDR, 2013), this is an essential industry that may offer various possibilities for the efficient valorization of the diverse raw materials. The relatively low level of equipment and the old-fashioned technologies used in most units reflect the low level of labor productivity of this sector which, in 2010, was 78% below the European average (40,785 euros/person in the EU-27; 9,086.3 euros/person in Romania) (Eurostat 2015) and product quality. At the national level, there is a good potential, but yet untapped, for recognition and promotion of the local brands by their inclusion in the EU quality schemata. Although there are 4,180 traditional products, in 2013 only one product was recognized and protected at the community level. After 2007, through the accessing of European-specific funds, a series of new viable units was created, answering the community market requirements. The sector still needs support, however, especially for modernization and retechnologization, in parallel with structuring and organization of agro-food networks.

Another aspect contravening the idea of diversification of the economic structure of rural Romania is the severe compression of social economy in the rural regions, reflected by the considerable reduction of the number of service workshops and arts and craft units. Despite all the cooperative past of Romanian agriculture during the communist regime, it has been unanimously acknowledged that at present, the cooperative sector is poorly developed as compared to the other EU member states. Thus, the number of cooperative units in agriculture was reduced almost by half in the period 2005–2010 (Management Authority for PNDR, 2013). Unlike the cooperative units from other advanced European countries, the Romanian cooperative units in agriculture are mostly active in the field of agricultural production and less in fields complementary to agriculture, such as processing and marketing. An alternative for the diversification of the economy is the practice of some traditional activities (crafts, craftsmanship) either by craftsmen working on their own or by persons organized in associations and cooperative units. Out of the total number of existing cooperative units in 2010 (2017 units), 42.5% were arts and crafts cooperative units (Management Authority for PNDR, 2013).

As compared to other states where support policies for the development of rural economy were efficient and oriented towards the promotion of the national interest, in the case of Romania, the internal agro-food markets were exposed to a higher pressure determined by the abundance of imports of agro-food products from countries where production was effectively supported by the state policies. Moreover, the national enterprises that specialized in exports of agro-food products and were very active before 1989 have collapsed or diminished much of their activity. In this context, we remind the negative influence of the state policies on taxes and fees paid by the small entrepreneurs from the agro-food sector. The lack of regulations and enforcement of market regulations to support the internal agro-food production is largely due to IMF refusal to accept the Market Law, and to the lack of insistence and argumentation with convincing factors from the part of national representatives at the level of agricultural sector (Dona 2008).

Public policies and social structures

As an effect of the development policies adopted in the second half of the past century and in the 25 years of the post-communist period, Romania is facing now major issues relating to the social structures from the rural environment.

Thus, during the communist regime, as an effect of the industrialization and "socialist transformation of agriculture" policy, a high decline of the rural population was registered following the migration from the rural regions to the urban ones, and on the cultural level many of the secular trades and traditions of the inhabitants of the Romanian villages were lost. Due to dispossession of the right of property, the new class of agricultural proletarians took the place of the former farmers from the interwar period. That way, generations of peasants were lost as they were uprooted and moved to the urban areas; many of the skills and knowledge acquired for centuries through the practicing of agriculture were also lost, as they were not transmitted to the next generations (Knight 2010). Many of the traditional practices and agricultural ideas were affected as well, such as the terms "collectivization" and "cooperative," which acquired negative connotations in the minds of many Romanians. The second issue of development in the interwar period was the introduction of a competitive system of large farms of industrial size that were meant to replace the peasant farms and the peasants in society.

After 1990, following the decline of may industrial sectors, the direction of migratory flows reversed from the urban regions to the rural ones, from non-agricultural sectors to agriculture. Former workers in the enterprises which closed their gates came back to the rural area and became farmers, but they had to start from square one as amateur farmers, without the necessary skills that they would have inherited from their ancestors. Thus, in this period, agriculture has had an important role on the social level, namely of a branch that absorbed individuals, created jobs and ensured the subsistence of human resources laid off by the other sectors. Furthermore, the demographic environment of the rural area was strongly altered by the mass migration of the qualified young population towards other European countries, a phenomenon that has amplified after Romania's accession to the EU. The demographic indicators relating to the Romanian rural areas reflect the negative aspects regarding the population and the social environment.

A characteristic of the demographic environment in the rural region is the aging of the population, with implications for Romanian agriculture due to the very high number of old farmers. In 2010, about 60.4% of farmers were over age 55 and only 7.3% were people under age 35 (EC, DG AGRI 2013). Farmers' qualification level is also extremely reduced. Only 2.5% of all farm managers have agricultural training, as compared to the EU-27 average of 29.1% (EC, DG AGRI 2013). This situation has caused problems at the economic level, namely the slow pace of renewal and modernization of agriculture due to being stuck with the obsolete technologies; work methods having a poor productivity; the failure to apply some modern management methods; the weak level of specialized knowledge, skills and capacities; and the slow rhythm of technology and know-how transfer.

In Romania, there are great disparities in terms of the income level between the residency environments determined by the limited access of population to better-paid jobs in the non-agricultural sectors. Thus, in 2011, the average income per household in the rural environment was 503 euros, as compared to the average income in the urban area, which was 621 euros/household (Management

Authority for PNDR 2013). In these conditions, the weight of population exposed to the poverty risk or social exclusion risk is quite high, namely 54.2% of the entire population (Management Authority for PNDR 2013). An important segment of rural population showing a high risk of poverty and social exclusion is the Roma population. Thus, the total disposable income of the Roma households is three times less than that of the population in general.

The education level of the rural population has improved after 1990, but at a slower pace than in the urban environment. This aspect is tightly connected to the low level of income of the rural inhabitants, limiting the access of the young population to a higher training level. An unfavorable aspect for the provision of qualified human resources in agriculture is the continuous reduction in the last decade of the number of agricultural high schools, accompanied by the descending trend of the numbers of graduates from these high schools (from 2511 graduates in 2005 to 2328 in 2011) (Management Authority for PNDR 2013). The low attractiveness of the work in agriculture due to the inadequate work conditions and the decrease of the number of graduates from agricultural schools are factors that have contributed to the poor enrollment of farmers in continuous training activities, Romania being among the weakest performers among the 27 countries in 2012, namely 0.5% of the entire rural population as compared to the EU-27 average of 6.6% (EC, DG AGRI 2013).

As for the use of the human resource in agriculture, though statistics report a huge number and percentage of individuals employed, almost implausibly, the analysis of employment characteristics is more suggestive: full-time, part-time, unemployed people, workforce performances, etc. Thus, of the entire agricultural population, only 11.38% are employees (Eurostat 2015); the rest are landowners, farmers and members of their families. Agriculture is not a trade in itself for many people, but only an alternative for survival or obtaining some supplementary income. Thus, about 33.6% of the employed population works part-time (Burja 2014). Another particularity is the high number of women within the entire employed population as compared to other European countries.

The seasonal character of agricultural work creates some temporary migratory flows from emerging economies to developed ones. In these conditions, adequate policies of social inclusion are necessary so as to offer specific ways of employment and social security in the rural areas, to develop some skills that may offer employment opportunities by which the negative effects of seasonality of work in agriculture might be overcome. Following the development of the secondary and tertiary sector from the last decade, some part of the active population from the rural environment has been attracted to the urban areas. Thus, in 2012, the active population in the urban environment was 3.3% higher than that in the rural environment (41.6%) (Eurostat 2015), a fact highlighting the need for development of the non-agricultural activities in the rural areas. Despite the fact that the active population from the rural environment has registered a slight decreasing trend due to dwindling of birth rates and the aging of the rural population, in Romanian villages there is a huge potential workforce, which, in the absence of some alternative employment opportunities, is employed, to a high extent, in subsistence and semi-subsistence agriculture.

Following the trend of employment rate at national level, in the rural areas the employment rate for the age group 15–64 has known a decreasing trend in the period 2005–2012, from 61.6% to 60.2% (EC, DG AGRI 2013). At the same time, we may notice a continuous decrease of the amount of individuals employed in agriculture for the same period. In terms of territory, there are significant gaps relating to the structure of employed population: there are still counties where the amount of the population employed in agriculture reaches 40% of the entire population and rural localities where industry or the tertiary sector have minimum values, and agriculture represents more than 80% of all jobs (Management Authority for PNDR 2013). As for the professional statute of the persons employed in agriculture, in 2012, about 89% of the total were freelancers and non-remunerated familial workers, a low amount being represented by the employed workforce (Eurostat 2015).

In 2012, the rural unemployment rate was 5%, maintaining below the national average of 7% and the EU-27 average of 10%. (EC, DG AGRI 2013) The more reduced rate of unemployment in the rural environment associated with the higher rate of employment in agriculture masks the hidden unemployment determined by the failure to integrally use work-time. Among the social categories in the rural environment that are most exposed to the unemployment risk are the youth, aged between 15 and 24 years (EC, DG AGRI 2013). The weight of unemployed persons of this category has increased significantly from 13.9% in 2005 to 15.9% in 2012. At the same time, the long-term unemployment rate in the rural environment was 3.2% of the rural active population in 2012 (EC, DG AGRI 2013).

A major issue having a deeply negative impact on the development of rural economy and life quality in the rural environment is the lack, insufficiency or precarious state and poor quality of infrastructures. The network of modernized county and communal roads represents only 10.6% from the national infrastructure. Out of 31,639 km of communal roads, 48% are causeways, and 29% are dirt roads, which are unusable sometimes during the rainy seasons (Management Authority for PNDR 2013). Despite that in recent years there has been some progress, the access of the rural population to the water distribution networks and sewage networks is still extremely limited. In 2012, 13.6% of the rural localities were connected to the drinking water supply network (Management Authority for PNDR 2013).

A vital aspect for the favorable evolution of the economy and rural environment is related to community development, regarded as the basis for the public policies specific to the rural environment supporting and accentuating the participation of citizens in the economy and progress of society, and increasing their capacity to be more active and directly involved in community life, since these are ways of social-economic development of the rural space and communities. At present, the rural citizens are among the poorest social categories in Romania, with a low level of life quality and reduced employment opportunities. The community development in the rural environment as an essential condition for its progress is in direct correlation with the evolution of rural economy and the progress of the agricultural sector being understood as a complex formative process meant to provide the conditions for economic and social progress for the entire community and to contribute to increased life quality. The essence of the community development process is associated with social innovation, which means a change of attitude, mentality and initiative of the community members.

Public policies and the environment

As result of public policies adopted after 1990, the intensity of economic activities was permanently reduced, with favorable effects on the environment. In the same time, due to the lack of some coherent environmental protection policies, phenomenon of irrational exploitation of environmental factors were manifested – for the economic goals – and some processes of degradation for the quality of natural environmental components. Although the Romanian natural environment is characterized by a proper conservation of its natural resources (water, soil, biodiversity) and its traditional landscapes, they are continuously exposed to various factors of pressure specific for the anthropogenic environment, which determines the degradation phenomenon and resulting quality reduction.

The used agricultural area has decreased continuously after 1990. In 2005–2010 it dropped by 4.3% (from 13.9 million hectares to 13.3 million) (Eurostat 2015). Regarding the land's exploitation, in 2010 the largest percentage (61.1%) was exploited intensively, compared with 38.9% (Eurostat 2015) of extensive exploitation, less aggressive for the environment. The surfaces exploited in organic systems were insignificant (only 2.3% in 2012) (Eurostat 2015). The percentage is rising compared to 2007 by about 35%. In this context it is necessary to adopt some policies and practices that lead to limiting the decline of the used agricultural area, to preserve and protect the quality of soil resources, to increase the forested areas (mainly through forestation of agricultural lands exposed to degradation phenomenon and improper agricultural use) and reduce the unused areas.

The quality and productivity of Romanian agricultural land is satisfactory, as most lands fit in grades 2 and 3 of creditworthiness. But they are endangered by intensification of some degradation phenomenon: 47% of lands are exposed to erosion risk, 48% to drought risk, 25% to temporary excess water risk, 50% with low content in humus, 42% with low content in phosphorus, 23% are affected by acidity, 44% are exposed to secondary compaction risk and 14% to primary compaction risk (Management Authority for PNDR 2013). The diminution of risk factors' effects can be achieved through policies that will encourage the implementation of specific measures for soil protection in high-risk areas and develop the services of information, training and consultancy for farmers.

The favorable effect of forests on conservation and protection of environmental factors (air, water, soil, biodiversity) is well known. The national forest surface is well below the EU average, respectively 31.3% compared to 42.4% – the EU average in 2012 (Eurostat 2015). During 2005 to 2012 a diminution was registered of about

10,000 hectares, and in 2013 was increased with 9,356 ha (according to National Institute of Statistics). Of the total forest area (6,538 million hectares and 280,000 hectares of virgin forests), 53.3% are forests with special protection functions: 43% soil protection, 31% water protection, 11% recreational functions, 10% scientific functions and 5% protection against climatic and industrial factors. Approximately 40.97% of the forest area (2.76 million hectares) is found in the sites of "Nature 2000" (Management Authority for PNDR 2013), which favors the application of sustainable development principles into their administration and makes it possible to find solutions that permit the development of economic activities consistent with biodiversity protection.

Romania has a great diversity of habitats, natural, and agricultural ecosystems (forests, water etc.), which determines the necessity of adopting some practices of sustainable management, which should confer to agricultural land, forest, and wetlands an economic and environmental high value. In the case of agricultural lands, the encouragement of traditional agriculture practices (extensive) can contribute to the reduction of agriculture's impact on the environment. In the same time, the harmonization and adaptation of new and modern technologies with traditional agriculture can contribute to improving economic and environmental performances of small and medium farms (traditional) and will favor agricultural production and conserve the biodiversity and quality of natural habitats.

The extensive character of an important part of Romanian agriculture is reflected by reduction of agricultural input's utilization of agro-chemical types and high labor consumption associated with low energy consumption. Thus, in 2010, for 71.5% (about 30.6% more than European average) of the agricultural area, the chemicalization level was much reduced: 22.5% was at a medium level and only 6% of surface area was at a high level of chemicalization (EC, DG AGRI 2013). The advantage of smaller quantities of chemical administration per unit area can be eliminated by limited agro-techniques' knowledge of small farmers and by their irrational and uneven utilization, but is possible to occur the risk of pollution with nutrients and other agrochemicals in some areas. Thus, by irrational use of chemicals in 2005–2010, there was registered a surplus of nitrogen balance by about 6.8 kg/ha and a deficit of phosphorus with −1.3 kg/ha (EC, DG AGRI 2013).

The total energy consumption in agriculture and forestry has registered a rising trend in 2007–2011 (from 260 kTOE to 433 kTOE), but the utilization level of renewable energy is very low (1.7% of total renewable energy production comes from agriculture, compared with 10.6% in the EU-27, in 2010). A positive aspect is the increase by 8.8% of renewable energy produced in agriculture in 2007–2011 (Management Authority for PNDR 2013). In this context it is a low emission of greenhouse gases from agriculture and other rural activities. The GHG emissions from agriculture decreased by 6.4% (18,941.5 Gg CO_2 equivalents) in 2011, compared to 20,236.9 Gg (CO_2 equivalents) in 2007 (EC, DG AGRI 2013).

Common agricultural policy contribution to the development of the Romanian rural area

Effects of the common agricultural policy in the pre-adhesion period

The development of rural space and economy is a priority of European policies, and the interest for this orientation has a higher level of visibility for countries coming from the ex-communist bloc. The Romanian rural economy, strong but sensitive and affected by various types of crises that occurred periodically during the transition period from a centralized to a market economy, is in a relaunch process under the stimulus of European and national policies and strategies to reinforce the agricultural component as a basic contributor to the economic relaunch.

The first significant programme which has had the capacity to bring together the political and strategic intentions and measures for improving the socio-economic conditions of the Romanian rural area was the National Programme for Rural Development, one of the basic tools of post-accession phase, especially regarding the capacity to attract financing from the European Agricultural Fund for Rural Development. The responsible evaluators of the programme have accentuated the necessity of agriculture development through domestic production support, including the traditional and organic production, the development of micro-enterprises, the stimulation of small businesses initiative and the encouragement of innovation and retechnologization in the agricultural sector.

The expected results from the National Rural Development Programme are summarized as follows (Donna 2008):

- Increasing the number of projects that follow, to develop and reinforce the main objectives of National Plan for Agriculture and Rural Development
- Redirecting and focusing the bilateral relations based on mutual interest objectives established with member states
- Increasing the capacity of private co-financing, public and internal.

At the base of SAPARD Programme implementation in Romania was the National Plan for Agriculture and Rural Development, which has classified the Romanian priorities for the rural development areas on the following four directions:

1   Improvement of access to markets and competitiveness of agricultural processed products
2   Improvement of infrastructures for rural development and agriculture
3   Development of rural economy
4   Development of human resources.

We consider that the European Union had an essential role in this change fairly recently, because the actions that determine the functionality of Romanian rural economy have produced the beginning of favorable change. The newly created relationships are observed on multiple levels: rural-urban, national-international, sectors and activity domains, institutional-inter-institutional, etc.

The LEADER (*Liaison Entre Actions de Développement de l'Économique Rurale*, or "Links between the rural economy and development actions") approach can address, in the light of its specificity, an equilibrated development of rural areas. The involving of local activists to the development of areas where they operate will contribute to the development of local governance and to a dynamic development supported by a local strategy conducted, implemented and managed by representatives of Local Action Groups (LAG). In the year 2012, the territory covered by the LAGs was about 142,267 km^2, and membership accounted for 30% of the total population (6,770,589 inhabitants).

The national policies and funding programmes available for supporting the rural economic development are circumscribed in a complex set of proposals and appropriate measures (PACT Foundation, 2012):

1   Configuration of a mechanism to elaborate the public policies that consider the following requirements: be participatory, be based on real studies and statistical data and be periodically subjected to a review process
2   Increasing the level and quality of education in the rural area by elaboration of some systems and subsidy measures that lead to elevation of educational level in rural area and lifelong training and alternative or non-formal education
3   Participative development of policies and measures adapted to the real needs manifested by different target groups, through their contribution and active participation
4   A better connection of funding programmes to the rural communities needs in order to access easily the funds allocated for rural areas, so to implement projects that will respond to priorities and are based on local resources
5   Information about the existence of certain financial services and simplifying the access to these by elimination or reduction of bureaucratic actions
6   Inventory, with aim to valorize as more efficient the local resources.

On 31 July 2007, Romania ceased the process of signing the contracts with the final beneficiaries of SAPARD (Special Access Programme for Agricultural and Rural Development), and the total amount contracted was 1,131,853,787, 75 Euro for a number of 4,746 contracts signed. On 31 December 2009, total contracted value was 1,023,409,304, 60 Euro for a number of 4,451 projects. The decrease by 9.58% compared to contracted value and by 6.22% compared to number of approved projects is due to cancellation of some projects.

Common agricultural policy and its effects in 2007–2013

When put into action of Common Agricultural Policy has encountered a real resilience in terms of the objectives achievement, especially regarding the efficiency of agricultural activities and lands unification. However, it must take into consideration that in Romania, the level of subsidy has begun, according to negotiations, from 25% in 2007, increasing by 5% in the next years until 2010 and by 10% after this year, following that until 2016 the subsidies percentage will be equal to that of European countries (EU-15) (Table 4.2).

This lower funding compared to other states has led to a perpetuation of competitive backwardness of Romanian agriculture, especially performed in small and medium farms. In addition, the fixation of the threshold of 1 hectare in order to receive subsidies excluded more than 2.74 million holdings in 2012 from these subsidies, therefore sentencing these farms to developing only subsistence activities (Otiman 2012).

It can be noted, therefore, that the subsidies of Common Agricultural Policy for 2007–2013 have been oriented especially to rural development and, by direct payments, have benefited especially medium and large farms that range in size between 100 and 500 hectares; in 2008, those farms received over 51% of the total subsidies (Luca 2009). However, the vitality of agriculture and Romanian rural areas cannot be achieved without a substantial participation of small and medium farms (20–100 ha) in the economic and social life of the village. Encouraging the initiation of such farms, especially on the basis of programmes such as "Farmer" or "Life Annuity" (national aid accepted by the European Union), could lead to an increase in their number and to an increase of productivity in these farms.

If the impact of these subsidies continues to be limited, small farms cannot benefit from the maximum support of the Common Agricultural Policy, as indicated by the small percentage of Romanian small-farm subsidies compared to those of other European countries. At the level of subsidy amounts available for rural development, the situation is completely different, with Romania benefiting, like other eastern European countries, by significant amounts for infrastructure development and rural facilities. The orientation funds for the adduction systems for water and sanitation, social and cultural educational institutions, and transport infrastructure are important opportunities for the Romanian rural economy.

Table 4.2 Alignment of Romanian subsidies to the level of UE-15 countries

Year	2007	2008	2009	2010	2011	2012	2013	2014	2015	2016
Percentage of Romanian subsidies compared to UE-15	25	30	35	40	50	60	70	80	90	100

Source: European Commission, 2004

New stipulations of common agricultural policy for Romania

Based on the experience and results from 2007–2013, the European Union countries focused their efforts to sustain the three major directions of action: food security, environment and economic growth in rural areas. In this sense, the specific objectives of the new programme for financial support of Common Agricultural Policy are, primarily, connected to improvement the quality of rural activities, namely increasing the competitiveness of European agriculture on global and national level, conserving diversity for agricultural production systems of EU countries, adapting the agricultural production to new environmental challenges in connection with climate change and natural resources protection.

To achieve these objectives, the financial allocation proposed is 373 billion euros, of which for Romania are provided funds of 17.5 billion euros. These funds are with 3.7 million more than the budget for 2007–2013 (13.8 billion euros). Although the funds for Romania have increased for the Pillar II–Rural Development, they have overall dropped by 13.5% (Lile 2015). To ensure *food security*, European farmers, including the Romanians, are protected against prices' volatility, providing them with funding levels that consolidate their position along food chains. This protection *supports the rural development* in order to sustain the young farmers and rural entrepreneurship. For Romania, a novelty compared to the 2007–2013 period, it is represented by supporting the small farmers through a simplified scheme designed to increase their access to financing and reduce the administrative burdens related to these payments. The direction focused on ecology and competitiveness in agriculture is an important component of the new programme that supports the sustainable agriculture and introduces the new in agriculture through stimulation of research and development.

Conclusion

The impact of national and European policies on the Romanian agriculture and the rural environment has varied in intensity and effect over time, especially in the post-1989 era. During Romania's transition to a market economy, these effects were mainly observed in the rural society and economy. Even if significant efforts have been made to increase the competitiveness of Romanian agricultural entities, small farms (surface less than 1 hectare) were not able to access these financing programmes and could not be consolidated into more efficient medium and large enterprises. This means that Romanian agriculture is still dominated by obsolete and conservative practices that lack efficiency and are not market oriented. The agricultural population, which represents a significant part in the active population of Romania, is affected by the issue of an aging workforce. The lack of employment opportunities in the industrial and service sectors has virtually locked a large proportion of this workforce in small individual farms aimed at subsistence.

From an environmental perspective, given that most farms use large volumes of labor force but little equipment and other specific materials, Romania shows a relatively low level of pollution and degradation of soil and other environmental components. Still, the lack of rationality and the heterogeneous use of farmlands can have negative effects on the public goods generated by agricultural ecosystems in Romania. The increase in financing included in the Common Agricultural Policy, especially with regard to rural development, has encouraged growth both in terms of rural infrastructure and in the diversification of activities in the rural landscape. The 2014–2020 period maintains the major financing lines for rural development, but also supports environmental aspects and the implementation of fundamental research results in agricultural and other rural practices. The agricultural sector in Romania currently shows significant gaps compared to other EU member states. However, the experience gained over the previous time periods with regard to public mechanism interventions, as well as the continued policy support for the development of agriculture and other activities, are generating positive and sustainable results that provide support to the hopes of economic development in the Romanian rural landscape.

References

Burja, V. (2014). Some Aspects of Employment in Romanian Agriculture, Annales Universitatis Apulensis Series Oeconomica, vol. 1, issue 16.
Dona, I. (2008). *Dezvoltare rurală*, USAMV Publisher, Bucureşti.
EC, DG AGRI (European Commission, Directorate General for Agriculture and Rural Development) (2013). Rural development in the EU statistical and economic information, Report 3013, European Union 2013, http://ec.europa.eu/agriculture/statistics/rural-development/2013/full-text_en.pdf, accessed on 4 Sept. 2015.
Eurostat (2015). European Commission, http://ec.europa.eu/eurostat/data/database, accessed 4 Sept. 2015.
Huntington, S. (1968). *Political Order in Changing Societies*, Yale University Press, London, p. 292.
Ignat, R. (2012). Premises and Challenges of Entrepreneurship in Romanian Rural Areas, *Economia Seria Management*, vol. 15, issue 2, ASE, Bucarest.
INS TEMPO Online (2015), Institutul Naţional de Statistică, Bucureşti, www.http://statistici.insse.ro/shop/, accessed on 4 Sept. 2015.
Knight, D. K. (2010). *Romania and the Common Agricultural Policy: The Future of Small Scale Romanian Farming in Europe*, Eco Ruralis, with the support of Terre Humaine Foundation, http://sar.org.ro/wp-content/uploads/2013/01/Romania-and-the-Common-Agricultural-Policy.pdf, accessed on 21 Sept. 2015.
Luca, L. (2009). *Two Extremes Don't Make One Right: Romania and the Reform of the Common Agricultural Policy of the EU*, Romanian Center for European Policies, Soros Fundation for Romania, Bucarest.
Lile, R., Stanciu, S., Martin, S., Meszlényi, R. (2015). Common Agricultural Policy for the Period 2014–2020: A Solution for Agricultural Management. *Journal of Economics and Business Research*, Volume 21, No. 2, pp. 134–144.
Micu, C. (2010). *Development of the Rural Problem in Romania: An Interpretative Frame*, Acta Universitatis Danubius, "Danubius" University Galaţi.
Ministry of Agriculture and Rural Development. (2011). The Management Authority for the SAPARD Programme. Final Report concerning the implementation of SAPARD Programme in Romania, June 2011. http://old.madr.ro/pages/dezvoltare_rurala/sapard/raport-final-implementare-raport-sapard-ro.pdf, accessed on 16 Sept. 2015.

Ministry of Agriculture and Rural Development, Management Authority for PNDR (2013). Analiza socio-economică în perspectiva dezvoltării rurale 2014–2020, http://www.madr.ro/docs/dezvoltare-rurala/programare-2014-2020/analiza-dezvoltarii-rurale-agricultura-iulie-2013.pdf, accessed on 15 Aug. 2015.

Ministry of Agriculture and Rural Development, Management Authority for PNDR (2014). Raport anual de progrese privind implementarea programului național de dezvoltare rurală în România în anul 2013, http://www.madr.ro/docs/dezvoltare-rurala/raport-anual/Raport-anual-de-progrese-PNDR-2013.pdf, accessed on 15 Aug. 2015.

Mungiu-Pippidi, A. (2010). *A Tale of Two Villages: Coerced Modernization in East European Countryside*: Central European University Press, Budapest.

Otiman, P. I. (2012). *Agricultural Economics and Rural Development*, New Series, Year IX, no. 1, pp. 3–24.

PACT Foundation (2012). Community development in the rural area, chapter in the White Chart of NGOs from Romania, PACT Foundation (Partnership for Community Action and Transformation), www.oot.ro/cdownloads/files/file_c1dfb23d0da116.pdf, accessed on 16 Sept. 2015.

Voicu, R., Radulescu, C. V. (2003). *Managementul unitatilor agroalimentare*, Editura ASE, Bucuresti.

Chapter 5

Households associated with agricultural holdings

Selected socio-economic dimensions

Ray Bollman

Introduction

The socio-economic situation of family farms and farming families remains an on-going public concern, and hence a public policy concern, in most countries. The objective of this chapter is to review the nexus of family farms and farming families in Canada. One interesting question, at least in a Canadian context, is, Who wants data on off-farm income of operators (and the household members) of households associated with an agricultural holding?[1] The first item to clarify is that people, not farms, have off-farm income. "Farms" do not have off-farm income. It is conceptually incorrect to talk about the off-farm income of farms. We can talk about the off-farm income of only individuals or families (or households). Then, we must focus upon the question, What is the decision that will be improved with data on the off-farm income of farmers or farming families? We offer some guesses. Our *first guess*, regarding data on the off-farm income of farming families, follows from the objective of the European Common Agricultural Policy, which is to provide a fair standard living for farming families.[2] A socially acceptable standard living implies being above the low-income cut-off. This is a family (or household) concept. Thus, the question is, Is the farmer residing in a family (or household) with total income (from all sources) above the low-income cut-off: yes or no. This would appear to be the first reason for tabulating and analyzing the data on the income of the family of a farmer.

Our *second guess*, regarding data on the off-farm earnings of farmers, would respond to the question, Is the return to labour of the farmer acceptable or appropriate? Thus, we want data on the labour earnings of the farmer from farm and off-farm work to compare to the labour earnings of individuals in other occupations/industries. *Another guess* regarding data on the off-farm income of farmers is a response to the issue where agricultural market analysts wish to determine the elasticity of the supply response of agricultural commodities to changes in price, and the analysts may wish to determine if the elasticity differs for farms operated by full-time farmers versus farms operated by operators with a significant share of time allocated to off-farm work (or, perhaps, individuals with a large share of their income from pensions or investments).

A *good guess* regarding the existence and continuation of off-farm work by members of households associated with agricultural holdings is that off-farm work is a risk-reducing strategy for the household. This was certainly possible in the days when a 10% or 20% swing in the gross revenue of a "commercial" farm could be covered by the off-farm work by one household member. However, today, the gross revenues of "commercial" farms are much bigger such that the off-farm work of more than one family member would be needed to cover a 20% swing in gross revenue. Arguably, the era has ended for the situation when off-farm work by a family member would "stabilize" the household income for households associated with a commercial farm. Perhaps a *better guess* regarding data on the off-farm income of farmers (and maybe farming families) is that since farmers will (sometimes) sign loan agreements to use some off-farm income to repay the farm loan, then some lenders will loan money to farms/farmers on the basis of the off-farm income. Thus, to understand investment decisions of farms/ farmers, it may be necessary to know the availability of off-farm income (because some lenders will grant a farm loan to a non-viable farm *if* the operator agrees to use off-farm income to repay the loan). However, this may be ancient history. I think that, nowadays, a full-time off-farm job would repay only a relatively small farm loan. A *weak guess* concerns the links to rural development policy.

The implications of rural development policy (which may be defined as public policy investments to create rural jobs) for the well-being of households associated with agricultural holdings goes back to at least 1972, when Smith and Martin (1972) noted, "The rural economy is more important to farmers than farmers are to the rural economy." Policy analysts who anticipated declining policy support for farms were pondering the potential role for rural development to create off-farm jobs for members of farming families in the scenario where a decline in farm subsidization made some farms unable to support a farming family. This was one impetus for early investigations on the impact of the off-farm labour market on the well-being of households associated with an agricultural holding.

In 1971, the off-farm income of census-farm operator households was essentially equal to the net farm income of the farming sector (Statistics Canada, 1973). This was an eye-opener for policy analysts at the time even though earlier estimates had shown a significant level of off-farm income in 1958 (Fitzpatrick and Parker, 1965; Fitzpatrick, 1967). Thus, off-farm work by farmers has always been part of the experience of many households associated with agricultural holdings. Rural development (specifically, the creation of non-farm jobs) is important for the well being of a significant share of households associated with an agricultural holding.

An aside: inter-relationships between agriculture policy and rural development

As an aside, we might note other considerations regarding the inter-relationships between agriculture policy and rural development? In fact, there is only a weak linkage from agricultural policy to rural development. First, across OECD countries, only 53% of policy support for agriculture goes to predominantly rural regions (Bollman, 2006). The remaining support for agriculture goes to intermediate and predominantly urban regions. Second, for the agricultural policy support that does arrive in predominantly rural regions, it is received by only 9% of residents of the predominantly rural region. This is a weak linkage from agricultural policy to rural development. However, there is another way to look at the contribution of agricultural holdings to rural development. About 18% of households associated with a census-farm are also operating a non-farm business and thus represent a source of entrepreneurship for the creation of rural non-farm jobs (Bollman, 1998). Vogel and Bollman (2012) have estimated the contribution of these "farm portfolio entrepreneurs" to rural employment.

The rhetoric of "farms"

One initial objective of this chapter was to review the problems that arise from the observation that agricultural data systems need to estimate the total supply of agricultural production in order to generate estimates of GDP in agriculture, for data on expected supply entering marketing channels, the data for estimating per food consumption in each country, etc. A basic building block of these agricultural data systems is a Census of Agriculture that attempts to cover all agricultural production. The data are obtained by identifying census-farms[3] and by enumerating the operator[4] of the census-farm. The statistical agency then publishes the count of the number of agricultural holdings and uses the word "farm" to describe the unit of observation (i.e. the agricultural holding). I do not think anyone from the Minister of Agriculture to the preschool student singing "Ole MacDonald Had a Farm" would label many (and arguably most) of these agricultural holdings to be a farm.

Typology of farmers versus a typology of farms

Colleagues in Statistics Canada have followed the lead of colleagues in Agriculture and Agra-Food Canada and colleagues in the Economics Research Service of the United States Department of Agriculture by mixing farm characteristics and operator (and family characteristics) in a so-called typology of "farms" (Statistics Canada, 2008b). The interesting feature of this typology is the personification of farms. Farms are labelled as being senior and are classified as "pension" farms. Farms are enjoying life and are classified as "lifestyle" farms. Farms are "in poverty" and are classified as "low-income" farms. However, two points are to be noted:

- First, of course, farms do not receive pensions and farms do not have a lifestyle and farms cannot be living in "straitened circumstances." Only individuals or families can get a pension or enjoy a lifestyle or live in "straitened circumstances."
- Second, the individuals / families with these characteristics may be expected to be associated with any size of agricultural holding.

Thus, it would appear useful to develop a typology of agricultural holdings and, independently, to develop a typology of individuals/families associated with agricultural holdings. Then, it would appear useful to cross-tabulate the typology of agricultural holdings and the typology of individuals/families in order to understand the following:

a   The structure of agricultural holdings associated with the characteristics of individuals/families
b   The structure of individuals/families associated with the characteristics of agricultural holdings

One framework would simply be a classification of whether the agricultural holding is a farm (yes versus no) cross-classified by whether the individual is a farmer (or whether the family is a farming family) (yes versus no) (Table 5.1).

Table 5.1 Proposed farmer and farms typology

Proposed Typology of "Real" Farmers versus "Real" Farms

		Is this business a farm?	
		No	**Yes**
Is this person a farmer?	**No**	"Unreal" farmer on an "Unreal" farm	"Unreal" farmer on a "Real" farm
	Yes	"Real" farmer on an "Unreal" farm	"Real" farmer on a "Real" farm

Is this person a farmer?

One option: Does the person classify him/herself on the Census or Labour Force Survey as having "farming" as the major occupation?

Another option: Does this person have net farm income as the major source of income (i.e., where the absolute value of net farm income is greater than the absolute value of total income from all sources)? This is problematic as revenue of incorporated farms does not flow to individuals as net farm income and thus does not appear as net farm income on the Census or on the Survey of Labour and Income Dynamics.

Is this business a farm?

One option: Picking up on the anecdote that "my last husband was a golfer", one might define a business as a farm if the level of expenditures were greater than the annual golf fees at a nearby golf course. If the level of expenditures exceeds this level, then the person would be expected to manage the enterprise as a business so that the losses would be restricted to the level of the golf fees of the previous husband.

Another option: Would an enterprise of this size be expected to generate a level of net farm income that would meet the low-income cut-off for a family of four (because the 1969 Task Force on Agriculture (Canada, 1969) defined a "viable" farm as an enterprise that can meet the living expenses of the farming family)?

As noted in the footnotes to the simple classification in Table 5.1, there are various ways

a   to classify agricultural holdings as "farms" or "non-farms" (and the choice will depend upon the analytic objective being pursued); and, there are various ways

b   to classify an individual as a "farmer" or as a "non-farmer" (or a family as a "farming family" or a "non-farming" family) (and again the choice will depend upon the analytic objective being pursued).

If the objective is to understand the on-farm versus off-farm labour allocation of individuals and families associated with an agricultural holding, then we might suggest the following:

•   Agricultural holdings might be classified according to their expected capacity to generate an income to meet the minimum income requirements of a farming individual or a farming faming. Operators or operator families associated with a farm business smaller than this threshold may be expected to face a "demand" from within the family to search for non-agricultural earnings to bolster family income.

•   Individuals/families might be classified by their actual supply of labour to farming versus non-farm occupations. (For one example, see Clemenson and Bollman, 1985.)

For this classification, we have chosen to classify operators, rather than families. Thus, the threshold of gross farm revenue to be "viable" is the level anticipated to generate a net farm income (plus cash wages received from the farm) to meet the low income cut-off for a single rural individual. Using these criteria, the average structure for the 1971 to 2006 period is that 33% of Canadian census-farm operators may be classified as "real" farmers on "real" farms (Table 5.2). Specifically, these are operators associated with a census-farm with gross farm revenue over the "viability" threshold and the operator reports farming as the major occupation. Importantly, this structure has essentially been the same since 1971 (see Table 5 in Bollman, 2009).

Given this calculation, the major, perhaps obvious, point is that there is not a one-to-one mapping between whether the individual is a "farmer" and whether the operation is a "farm." Among operators who are "farmers" (i.e. operators who claim "farming" is their major occupation), 50% operate "viable" farms (which, in this table, would be anticipated to generate the minimum standard of living for a single rural individual) and 50% are operating "non-viable" farms (Table 5.2). Among "viable" farms, two-thirds of the operators are "farmers" (i.e. with farming as their major occupation) and one-third of the operators of "viable" farms do not report "farming" as their major occupation. Thus, a significant share of operators of "viable" farms do not report, "farming" as their major occupation. The main point is that "real farmers" operate both "unreal farms" and "real farms." Also, "real farms" are operated by "real farmers" and "unreal farmers." There is not a large overlap of "real farmers" and "real farms."

Table 5.2 Distribution of census-farm operators by main occupation and by association with "viable[1]" or "non-viable[1]" census-farms, Canada, average over the 1971 to 2006 census periods

Main occupation of the operator[2] of a census-farm	Number of operators (average over the 1971 to 2006 census years)			As a percent of the operators in each year (row percent)			As a percent of the operators in each farm size class (column percent)			As a percent of all operators (average over the 1971 to 2006 census years)		
	"Non-viable[1]" Census-farms (below the threshold for a single rural individual)	"Viable[1]" Census-farms (equal to or above the threshold for a single rural individual)	All Census-farms	"Non-viable[1]" Census-farms (below the threshold for a single rural individual)	"Viable[1]" Census-farms (equal to or above the threshold for a single rural individual)	All Census-farms	"Non-viable[1]" Census-farms (below the threshold for a single rural individual)	"Viable[1]" Census-farms (equal to or above the threshold for a single rural individual)	All Census-farms	"Non-viable[1]" Census-farms (below the threshold for a single rural individual)	"Viable[1]" Census-farms (equal to or above the threshold for a single rural individual)	All census-farms
Operators[2] with a non-farming occupation	90,802	14,054	104,856	87	13	100	49	13	35	30	5	35
Operators[2] with a farming occupation	96,005	97,411	193,416	50	50	100	51	87	65	32	33	65
All operators[2]	186,807	111,465	298,272	63	37	100	100	100	100	63	37	100

[1] A "viable" farm in this table is a census-farm with gross revenue anticipated to generate a net farm income above the low income cut-off for one rural individual. This follows the recommendation in Canada. (1969) **Canadian agriculture in the seventies: Report of the Federal Task Force on Agriculture** (Ottawa: Canada Department of Agriculture).

[2] Operators in this table refer only to operators with a major occupation stated, with some hours of work "last week" and with some weeks worked "last year." Operators of non-family incorporated census-farms and "other" census-farms (such as institutional farms, co-operative farms, Hutterite Colonies, etc.) are excluded.

*Since 1991, each census-farm may report more than one operator.

Source: Statistics Canada. Agriculture-Population Linkage database. 1971–2006.

Thus, to understand farms, it would appear better to design a typology of farms. To understand farmers (or farming families), it would appear better to design a typology of farmers. Only then would it seem profitable to cross tabulate the two typologies to see the interrelationship between the typology of operators of agricultural holdings and the typology of agricultural holdings. To emphasize, the major point is that being a "farmer" is not a one-to-one match with the agricultural holding being a "farm." Consequently, analysts dealing with issues relating to the agricultural holding (stability of farming income, rates of returns to farming resources, etc.) should focus on the agricultural holding – and perhaps the focus should be only on holdings that are "farms." Similarly, analysts dealing with issues relating to individuals operating the holding (human capital attributes of the individual, whether the individual lives in a household with total income below a low income cut-off) should focus on the individual – and perhaps the analyst should focus only on individuals who are "farmers."

One conceptualization of "the agricultural population"

Harrison and Cloutier (1995) offered a useful, in my view, typology of individuals associated with agricultural holdings. They identified three ways that individuals may be associated with agricultural holdings: operators of census-farms (390,575 individuals); individuals with some net farm income (477,630 individuals); and individuals with a farm-related occupation (501,530 individuals) (Figure 5.1). They assigned the term "classic farmer" to the 202,360 individuals who reported being a census-farm operator with some net farm income and with a farm-related occupation being the major occupation (Harrison and Cloutier, 1995, p. 7). The remaining 559,940 (762,200 minus 202,360) individuals were associated with agricultural holdings but not meet the threshold of being a "classic farmer."

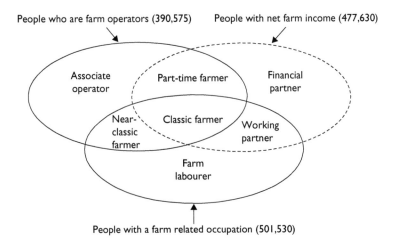

Figure 5.1 Farming population and farmer classification, Canada

Understanding household earnings: Patterns and change over time

When we look at the distribution of income by source for all households with a census-farm operator present, we see the well-known pattern: (a) unincorporated net farm income is a small share of the total household income; and (b) over time, this share has decreased (see Figure 5.1 in Bollman, 2009). To understand these patterns, a number of factors should be taken into consideration:

1   What is the impact of changes in the way that farm earnings are paid to household members?
2   What is the distribution of households according to the size of the farm business with which they are associated? How has this distribution changed over time?
3   What is the impact of an increase in participation of females in the "formal" (or "measured") labour force?

How farm earnings are received by household members

Over time in Canada, the share of census-farms that are incorporated has been increasing over time. In 2001, family incorporated census-farms represented 12% of all census-farms but contributed 34% of aggregate gross revenue of census-farms (see Table 1 in Bollman, 2009). In Canada, in each of census data and survey data and tax-filer data, each member of a household reports the income received from each source. The only identifiable farm income source is unincorporated net farm income. However, for an individual associated with a farm that is incorporated, this individual would receive earnings from the incorporated farm as (a) wages and salaries (which would include management fees), and/or (b) dividends (which are a component of "investment income").

As shown by Ehrensaft and Bollman (1992) and Fuller and Bollman (1992) for the 1986 Agriculture-Population Linkage,[5] the analytic conclusions may be misleading if analysts fail to adjust their data for this feature of income reporting. Misleading conclusions were shown to be most likely for households associated with larger farms, as these holdings are more likely to flow some farm earnings to household members as "farm wages." Also, larger holdings are more likely to be incorporated – and thus the only way for individuals to receive farm earnings is as wages or dividends. Using the data available from the Agriculture-Population Linkage,[6] we follow Ehrensaft and Bollman (1992) and use an algorithm that uses the information from the Census of Agriculture questionnaire on "wages paid to family members" to estimate the portion of wages and salaries received by household members that may be designated as "agricultural earnings." This calculation is applied to all census-farm operator households (whether associated with unincorporated or incorporated farms). A similar calculation is made to estimate the portion of investment income received by household members that may be designated as "agricultural investment income." See Ehrensaft and Bollman (1992) for details of this calculation.

With the estimation of household "agricultural (labour and capital) earnings" and "non-agricultural (labour and capital) earnings," we see that among all households with a census-farm operator present, that the share of household income from "agricultural earnings" varied between 26% and 33% of total household income over the 1986 to 2001 period[7] (see Figure 2 in Bollman, 2009). The bottom line, when we consider all households with a census-farm operator present, is as follows:

a   Using the data "as reported" (see Figure 1 in Bollman, 2009), the share of household income coming from "net farm income" declined from 24% in 1986 to 17% in 2001, a decline of 7 percentage points.

b   Using the "estimated" data on "agricultural earnings" and "non-agricultural earnings" (see Figure 2 in Bollman, 2009), the share of household income coming from "agricultural earnings" declined from 33% in 1986 to 26% in 2001, a decline of 7 percentage points.

c   Thus, the "estimated" data appear to reflect the same trend as the "reported" data but the estimated labour and capital earnings show a 9 percentage point higher share of census-farm operator family income being derived from the agricultural holding.

One factor to note in Figures 1 and 2 in Bollman (2009) is the (albeit relatively small) increase in the share of household income derived from non-earned income. Non-earned income includes government social transfer payments (Old Age Security pension, Guaranteed Income Supplement, Canada Pension Plan and Quebec Pension Plan benefits, Employment Insurance benefits, Canada Child Tax benefits and "other" income from government sources) plus "other" income (retirement pensions, superannuation and annuities and 'other' money income, such as alimony, bursaries, etc.). In 1971, non-earned income represented 9% of the income of households with a census-farm operator present and this doubled to 18% in 2006.

Structure of agricultural holdings by business size

To understand the inter-relationship between the source of income of households associated with an agricultural holding and the size of the farm business, we develop a classification of agricultural holdings according to their anticipated capacity to provide a minimum level of living for household members. Households associated with agricultural holdings below this threshold would be expected to report non-agricultural earnings to provide adequate household income. We adopt the definition of a "viable farm" from the 1969 report of the federal task force on agriculture (Canada Department of Agriculture, 1969), which indicated a "viable farm" would be a farm able to provide a minimum level of living for a farming family.[8] As a proxy for this "minimum level of living for a farming family," we have selected the Statistics Canada low-income cut-off for a rural family of four (Statistics Canada, 2008a). In order to estimate the size of an agricultural holding that would be expected to be "viable," we use the ratio of realized net farm income (plus the wages paid to family members which is treated as a farming expense in the farm accounts) per dollar of gross farm revenue as published by Statistics Canada (annual) to estimate the level of gross farm revenue that would be anticipated to generate a level of net farm income to meet the low-income cut-off. We show four size classes of gross farm revenue for agricultural holdings:

1   Holdings with less than one-half of the gross farm revenue to be "viable"
2   Holdings with 50% to 99% of the level of gross farm revenue to be "viable"
3   Holdings with 100% to 149% of the level of gross farm revenue to be "viable"
4   Holdings with 150% or more of the level of gross farm revenue to be "viable".

   The important finding from this classification is that there has been virtually no change in the structure of agricultural holdings according their anticipated capacity to generate net farm income above the low income cut-off (see Figure 4 in Bollman, 2009). Since 1971, about 80% of census-farm operator households have been associated with an agricultural holding that is "non-viable." Specifically, these holdings would not be anticipated to generate a level of net farm income that met the Statistics Canada low income cut-off for a family of four. Thus, we would suggest that it is not a change in the structure of agricultural holdings over time that is driving the change in structure of household income.
   Among the 80% of households associated with agricultural holdings anticipated to generate a net farm revenue less than the low income cut-off for a rural family of four, non-agricultural earnings would be expected to be relatively higher – and agricultural earnings would be expected to be a relatively lower share of household total labour and capital earnings. When we calculate our "estimated agricultural labour and capital earnings," we see that (a) The larger the farm, the higher the share of household labour and capital earnings that is estimated to be agricultural earnings (see Figure 6 in Bollman, 2009); and (b) although there is a drop in this share over time, for households associated the larger farms, estimated agricultural labour and capital earnings in 2006 represented 59% of household earnings (compared to the 24% generated by unincorporated net farm income as shown for these households in Figure 5 in Bollman, 2009). Thus,

1   using an "estimated agricultural labour and capital earnings" shows that households associated with "viable" farms appear to generate at least one-half of their earnings from the farm (see Figure 6 in Bollman, 2009);
2   but this share has been declining (somewhat) for households associated with each size of farm; and
3   no relationship is expected nor evident for the majority of households (60% in 1986 and 68% in 2008) associated with farms with gross revenue less than 50% of the threshold to be "viable."

Perhaps it is not surprising that households associated with a "viable" farm are now generating about one-half of their earnings from the farm. This simply suggests that about one-half of the earnings of the household is being generated by someone else who is not farming.

Increasing labour force participation rates of women

One important contributing factor to the change in the mix of earnings over time in all Canadian households is the increasing participation of women in the (formal or measured) labour market. The contribution to total household income by the "wife" in the household with an operator present has increased from between 7% and 12% in 1971 to between 31% and 37% in 2006 (see Figure 7 in Bollman, 2009). This share and the increase in share are similar for all census-farm operator households, regardless of the size of the associated farm business. To summarize our review of patterns and change in household earnings of census-farm operator households:

1 Our "estimated labour and capital earnings" is an improvement over simply using the data according to the way it was collected.
2 There has been no change in the structure of census-farm operator households in terms of their association with agricultural holdings anticipated to generate agricultural earnings above the low income cut-off.
3 Thus, it would appear that a changing farm structure is not driving a decline in the share of household earnings that is generated from the agricultural holding.
4 Agricultural earnings, as a percent of total household earnings, are declining for households associated with each size of farm business.
5 The contribution to household income by the "wife" has increased in a similar fashion for households associated with each size of farm business.
6 Thus, it would appear that the increase in the labour force participation by women in census-farm operator households is part of the explanation for an increase in the share of household earnings generated from non-farm earnings.

Regional patterns

Contrary to expectations, the incidence of off-farm work by census-farm operators is higher for operators who are further from a larger urban centre (Alasia et al., 2008). One advantage of the Agriculture-Population Linkage is that a large sample size (one-fifth of all census-farm operator households) provides considerable geographic detail. The multivariate analysis by Alasia et al. (2008) held constant farm variables, operator variables and household variables to determine the independent impact of distance from a city on the probability of the operator participating in off-farm work.

Here, we use simple tabulations to discuss the household share of earnings that are generated by the farm across the urban-to-rural gradient.[9] First, we note that the recent decline in the share of census-farm operator households associated with "viable" farms has occurred in each type of region (see Figure 8 and Table 2 in Bollman, 2009). A slightly higher share of census-farm operator households are associated with "viable" farms in small city metro regions. Second, among households associated with "viable" farms, there is no difference across regions in terms of the share of household earnings generated from agricultural earnings (see Figure 9 and Table 2 in Bollman, 2009). A comparison of two maps may be instructive. Map 1 (in Bollman, 2009) refers to households associated with a census-farm in 2001 with gross revenue less than $250,000.[10] We show "non-agricultural (labour and capital) earnings" (labelled as "income from non-agricultural employment") as a percent of total household income. For all census-farm operator households in 2001, this represents 26% of total household income (see Figure 2 in Bollman, 2009). Map 1 shows that in marginal agricultural areas (essentially areas on the agricultural<>forestry interface), "if" one is enumerated to be operating a "non-viable" census-farm, then non-farm employment is key. After acquiring non-farm employment, then some residents are enumerated to be operating a census-farm with gross revenue less than $250,000. In addition, if one is operating a census-farm with gross revenue less than $250,000 in the vicinity of Ottawa, Toronto, Edmonton or Vancouver, again non-farm employment provides, on average, more than 60% of total household income. Map 2 (in Bollman, 2009) refers to households on "viable" census-farms. In almost all regions, if the census-farm generates gross revenue of $250,000 or more, then "non-agricultural employment" income is less than 47% (and typically less than 35%) of total household income.

Labour supply generated by census-farm operator households

As noted above, if one-half of the earnings of the household associated with an agricultural holding is derived from the farm, then one-half is being generated by other household members who are working elsewhere. Following the algorithm used by Bollman and Smith (1986), we see that members of census-farm operator households supplied an estimated 1 billion hours of labour to farm and non-farm occupations (see Table 6 in Bollman, 2009). Since 1991, 74% of the labour supplied by census-farm operator households has been provided by an operator (see Figure 10 in Bollman, 2009). These operators may be male or female and they may have "farming" or "non-farming" as their major occupation. Nevertheless, the share of household labour generated by individuals listed as an operator of a census-farm has been 74% of total household labour since 1991.

The share of household labour that was supplied by operators and allocated to a "farming" occupation was 50% from 1971 to 2001 (and fell to 46% in 2006) (see Figure 11 in Bollman, 2009). Operator labour allocated to non-farm occupations increased from 13% in 1971 to 28% in 2006. Part was due to a 7 percentage point jump in 1991 when more than one operator could be listed for each census-farm. The share of household labour supplied by non-operators to non-farm occupations has been essentially constant (varying between 16% and 19% between 1981 and 2006). The 8 percentage point decline in the allocation of labour by non-operators to a farming occupation in 1991 is due to the change in the classification to allow more than one operator be identified for each census-farm. Since 1971, the share of labour supplied by females in census-farm operator households has increased from 20% to 33% in 2006 (see Figure 12 in Bollman, 2009). Since 1991, the share has been relatively constant, in the range of 30% to 33%.

Although the allocation of household labour to non-farm jobs by both females and males has increased, the greatest increase has been by females. In 1971, 8% of household labour was a female working in a non-farm job (see Figure 13 in Bollman, 2009). By 2006, females working in non-farm jobs represented 22% of household labour. The increase by males has not been as great. In 1971, males working in a non-farm job represented 20% of household labour – and this increased to 26% of household labour in 2006. The declining share of household labour allocated to a farming occupation is entirely due to the declining share supplied by males – down from 61% of household total labour in 1971 to 41% in 2006. The female allocation of labour to a farming occupation has not changed – fluctuating between 9% and 13% of total household labour over this period.

By rearranging the above results and consistent with the ongoing change in the structure of earnings when all census-farm operators are considered, we see a decline in the share of census-farm operator household labour allocated to a farming occupation. In 1971, 73% of household labour was allocated to a farming occupation, and this has declined to 52% in 2006 (see Figure 14 in Bollman, 2009). Above, we noted that females were increasing their share of household earnings – and this was associated with in increase in non-farm earnings within census-farm operator households. Here, again, the increase in labour supplied by household members is, largely, by females with non-farming occupations.

Typology of households by farm and non-farm work patterns

Above, we were classifying individuals according to their major occupation. Here, we offer a typology of households according to the following factors:

a   Whether the main occupation of the "husband" is farming or non-farming.
b   Whether the main occupation of the "wife" is farming or non-farming.
c   A significant share of households are classified as "other." These are cases where there is no husband-wife couple in the household or where there is more than one husband-wife couple in the household. Also, cases where the "husband" has no stated occupation (including retired "husbands") are also classified as "other" households.

In 2006, the three largest groups were as follows:

- 64,285 census-farm operator households (27%) reported both the "husband" and the "wife" to have a non-farm occupation (Figure 15 in Bollman, 2009). There has been little change since 1991.
- 56,780 census-farm operator households (24%) reported the "husband" with a farming occupation and the "wife" with a non-farm occupation. There has been little change since 1986.
- 44,455 census-farm operator households (18%) were classified as "other" households. Again, there has been little change since 1986.

In 1971, the largest group was 89,080 census-farm operator households (25%) that were classified as "husband" with a farming occupation and "wife" with no occupation stated. This group declined to 13,640 (6%) in 2006.

In 1991, the largest group was 72,315 census-farm operator households (25%) that were classified with both the "husband" and the "wife" reporting farming as the major occupation. This group declined to 40,690 households (17%) in 2006.

Since 1981, the number of census-farm operator households with the "husband" with a non-farm occupation and the "wife" with a farming occupation has been relatively small (varying between 6,350 and 9,200 households) (about 4% of all census-farm operator households).

The share of "husbands" with farming as their major occupation has remained relatively constant for the entire 1971 to 2006 period (the lower three groups in Figure 16 in Bollman, 2009). The share declined from 55% in 1971 to 46% in 2006. Among these households with the "husband" with a farming occupation, the share of households with the wife also with a farming occupation varied between 16% and 25% – recording 17% of all census-farm operator households in 2006. The share with the "wife" with no stated occupation declined and the share with the wife with a non-farming occupation increased steadily over this period. The other side of this coin is that the share of "husbands" with a non-farm occupation was also relatively stable – increasing from 29% in 1971 to 35% in 2006. If we rearrange the groups in Figure 16 (in Bollman, 2009) to group the occupational classification of the "wife" in the lower three groups in the chart, Figure 17 (in Bollman, 2009) shows (more clearly) the increase in the share of households with the "wife" with a non-farm occupation (the lower two groups in Figure 17 in Bollman, 2009) – from 15% in 1971 to 51% in 2006.

Finally, we replicate Figure 16 (in Bollman, 2009) for only households associated with a "viable" farm. Not surprisingly, a very small share of census-farm operator husband-wife households show a "husband" with the major occupation to be non-farming (see Figure 18 in Bollman, 2009) (varying between a low of 6% in 1986 and a high of 11% in 2006). (This should not be confused with the classification of individuals presented in Table 4 in Bollman, 2009.) In 2006, 75% of the households associated with a "viable" farm reported a "husband" with a farming occupation. We continue with the focus on households associated with "viable" farms. For these households, if the "husband" reports farming as the major occupation, then we see that agricultural (labour and capital) earnings represent over 50% of total household earnings (Figure 19 in Bollman, 2009). The share contributed by agricultural earnings has declined somewhat over time. However, for households associated with "viable" farms and for households with the major occupation of the "husband" being "non-farming," agricultural earnings are a lower share of household earnings (generally less than 50%) and there is no discernable trend over time. Interestingly, among households associated with "viable" farms, for households with the "husband" with a farming occupation, the average household income (in constant $2005) from all sources ranged over the 1986 to 2006 period between $60,000 and $80,000 (Figure 20 in Bollman, 2009). The range was between $80,000 and $120,000 for households with the "husband" with a non-farming occupation. In these households, there is a "viable" farm generating earnings and a "husband" working in a non-farming occupation. For reference, the average Canadian household income from all sources was $69,548.

The angst of the succession of the family farm

The vast majority of census-farms in Canada are "family farms" (Bollman, 2005). The succession of the family farm to the next generation has remained as a topic of discussion since at least WW2, and it is now easier for the male son of a farming family to take over the family farm. This is because the number of sons per farming family has decreased over time (Figure 2 in Bollman, 2005). Specifically, when we look at individuals born between June 2, 1936, and June 1, 1941 (first column in Figure 2), and who were living on a census-farm when they were 10 to 14 years of age, we see that the number of individuals in this age cohort (or birth cohort) who were census-farm operators when they were 30 to 34 years of age was 16% of the number of kids. Thus, only 16% of farm kids "graduated" to be a census-farm operator by age 30 to 34. However, for individuals born from June 2, 1961, to June 1, 1966, we see that almost double (30%) "graduated" to become a census-farm operator. We acknowledge that daughters are now receiving equal attention in the discussion of the succession of the family farm, and thus the discussion deserves some reconstruction.

Our observation on the changing demographics of family families is one part of the discussion regarding "How hard is it to enter farming?" At least until recently,[11] there was a constant ratio between the average industrial wage rate and the price of an acre of land. Thus, there was no change over time in the acres that one could purchase when working at the average industrial wage rate. Of course, the acres required to have a "viable" farm has continued to increase. However, the difficulty facing a farm kid who wanted to take over the family farm has certainly been reduced simply by the reduction in the number of kids per farming family.

Where do the family farmer and the farming family fit into Canadian agricultural policy?

Agricultural policy in Canada is essentially focussed on the production of commodities. The Minister of Agriculture is essentially the minister of agriculture commodity production. There is certainly rhetoric and a significant flow of funds to agricultural holdings (i.e. those with significant commodity production) in order to stabilize the rate of return on farm assets as an incentive to keep resources invested in agriculture during short-run downturns. By design, the programs are not intended to provide longer-run "support" to any set of farm resources. Of course, the exception is the long-run view of keeping resources in the sectors with supply management (milk, eggs, and poultry meat). Agricultural policy certainly has rhetoric regarding the support for the family farm and support for the farming family. After all, individuals associated with farming constitute a significant portion (perhaps up to one-third) of the voters in some constituencies. Given the obvious (to me, at least) fact that agricultural policy is focussed on the efficient production of agricultural commodities (with stabilization insurance programs designed to keep resources in agriculture during short-run fluctuations), it is surprising to find ongoing discussions suggesting that smaller farms or poorer farmers are not receiving their "fair" share of agricultural policy. Admittedly, this discussion appears more often in the US agricultural policy debate. Few studies in Canada have estimated the distribution of agricultural policy payouts by size of farm or by size of household income (one example is Bollman, 1989).

There was one recent agricultural program with a family focus – the Canadian Farm Families Options Program (Agriculture and Agri-Food Canada, 2006). It was a two-year pilot program which helped farmers and their families improve their income prospects, while enabling them to access services to gain knowledge, develop new skills, and invest in strategic planning and management activities. Only individual farmers and farm families whose total income from all sources was below a specific threshold were eligible to apply. This program died a natural death. There was virtually no support from most farmer organizations because it appeared to be a "welfare" program. Farmers would support programs targeted at their business because it was not a welfare program but farmers would not support a welfare program for farmers. Anecdotal evidence is that this program was very helpful for eligible farmers and farming families in improving their planning and management capacity for either continuing in farming or transitioning to a non-farm career. The Canadian Farm Families Options Program was a "canary in the coal mine" that confirmed that organizations representing farmers did not want nor expect programs based on economic need (in this case, income from all sources below a given threshold).

One hypothesis in policy discussions is that public policy has induced members of farming households to work off the farm. The competing hypothesis is that public policy has induced rural residents with non-farm jobs to acquire an agricultural holding, and they thus become enumerated as operating an agricultural holding in subsequent surveys or censuses of agricultural holdings. In Canada, the general case is that agricultural land is taxed at a relatively lower rate. Thus, there is an incentive for rural dwellers to operate an agricultural holding that meets the minimum requirements to trigger a lower rate of property taxes on the agricultural land. This is one example where public policy may encourage the observation of off-farm work by households with an operator of an agricultural holding. Also, in the federal income tax system, so-called part-time farmers (as described in Section 31 of the income tax act) are allowed to write off farm losses up to a specified level. Some of these tax filers are building a viable farm enterprise by using off-farm income to finance their investments in their expected-to-be-viable farm enterprise. Other tax filers simply continue to report a negative net farm income every year (up to the allowable loss), and the expenditures are more likely a contribution to their rural lifestyle than they are a contribution to productive farm investments. This is an example where public policy triggers an observed statistical association, suggesting "public policy has induced members of farming households to work off the farm." There may be an increase in the off-farm work by operators of census-farms but perhaps no increase in their non-farm work.

Some analysts have documented the increase in the incidence of off-farm work by operators of census-farms. First, the incidence of off-farm work by operators of census-farms in Canada has varied since 1941 (within the range of 35% to 45%). However, part, if not most, of any increase in off-farm work by the operators of census-farms appears to be partly due to the movement of work to an off-farm site that was formerly done on the farm. We developed a rough methodology to approximate the size and the change in non-farm work performed by operators of Canadian census-farms since the beginning of the farm accounts in 1926: specifically, how much time has been allocated to the production of fuel (e.g. oats for horses), the production of traction power (e.g. horses), the production of fertilizer (e.g. manure), the preparation of the farm accounts, etc. Today, all of these non-farm activities generally take place off the farm. Our estimates suggest that on-farm "non-farm" activity declined in Canada up to the 1990s (Bollman, 2013). Those working off-farm are working more hours. Thus, "off-farm activity" has increased (somewhat) since 1941. However, our overall estimate of "non-farm" work by operators of Canadian census-farms is a decline up to the 1990s and an increase since then. Thus, we suggest that a discussion of the historical trends in off-farm work needs to refocus to a discussion of the trends in "non-farm" work – some of which occurs on the agricultural holding

Is part-time farming efficient?

Another policy issue that reoccurs is the question, Is part-time farming less efficient or more efficient? Interestingly, the analysis has always considered whether off-farm work by the operator "causes" the farm operation to be inefficient. First, farmers, not farms, participate in off-farm work. Therefore, the question is whether it is efficient for the operator to allocate part of his/her time to farming and to allocate another part to an off-farm job? This is different from the question of whether part-time farms[12] are efficient. Thus, it would seem that the better way to ask the question is, How does the total return to the labour of the farmer vary according to the mix of on-farm work and off-farm work? One study showed that full-time off-farm work generates a higher return to operator labour than a 50:50 split of labour to off-farm and to on-farm work. Similarly, full-time on-farm work generates a higher return to operator labour than a 50:50 split of labour between on-farm and off-farm work. Thus, it appears that part-time farming is *not* an efficient allocation of the time of the farmer (Bollman, 1991). As noted, there has been a relatively stable incidence of off-farm work by operators of census-farms since 1941(within the range of 35% to 45%). There is little evidence that off-farm work, or part-time farming, is part of the ladder toward the operation of a full-time or commercial farm (Bollman, 1981; Bollman and Steeves, 1982).

Do young(er) operators have an agricultural-related post-secondary education?

Farm production technology is continuously becoming more complex. An analysis of Agriculture-Population Linkage data has shown that the level of educational attainment of the operator is associated with more productive farms (Furtan et al., 1979). Here we assess the share of younger operators who have completed some agriculture-related post-secondary education.[13] We designate "under 45 years of age" to be "younger" as, on a net basis, there is an increase in the number of census-farm operators up to age 45 (see Figure 21 in Bollman, 2009). In the older age groups, more operators leave than enter the sector. Among younger operators, the share of operators associated with "viable" farms who report some "agricultural-related" post-secondary education ranges from a high of 42% in the province of Quebec to a low of 15% in the province of British Columbia (see Figure 22 in Bollman, 2009). These data are displayed by province because, in Canada, education is a provincial jurisdiction. Thus, one way to interpret these data is that the post-secondary institutions providing "agricultural-related" post-secondary education have doubled the market share of younger operators in some provinces compared to other provinces.[14]

Summary

Farming families and family farms remain a policy focus in Canada. In this chapter, we have highlighted selected topics to understand various aspects of the nexus between family farms and farming families. An estimated "agriculture labour and capital earnings" shows that, during the 1990s, agricultural earnings were about 30% of total earnings for the average household associated with an agricultural holding. Households associated with larger agricultural holdings are more likely to have members reporting wages from their incorporated farms, and thus our estimated "agriculture labour and capital earnings" presents a more accurate view of the role of the agricultural holding in generating income for the household.

The distribution of agricultural holdings, according to the capacity to provide a net farm income above the Canadian low income cut-off, has not changed over time. In other words, the share of "non-viable" census-farms has not increased. Thus, it would appear that the persistence in the structure of agricultural holdings is not driving the change over time in the source of earnings of households associated with an agricultural holding. Estimated agricultural labour and capital earnings, as a percent of total household earnings, has declined for households associated with agricultural holdings in each size class of farm business. One major ongoing feature during the study period was the increase in the number of females in the "measured" labour force. Within census-farm operator households, more women were being "measured" in the labour force and most of these women were working in non-farm occupations.

Males in census-farm operator households have shown some shift in labour supply from a farm occupation to non-farm occupations – but most of the shift in the labour supplied by census-farm operator households has been by women. Thus, for census-farm operator households, most of the increase in earnings from non-farm sources is due to the increased participation of women in non-agricultural jobs. A typology of "farmers" cross-tabulated with a typology of "farms" indicates that there is not a one-to-one mapping of whether the operator is a "farmer" (with farming being the major occupation) and whether the agricultural holding is a "farm" (with gross revenue above the threshold anticipated to generate a net farm income above the Canadian low-income cut-off). To understand farm issues such as the variability of farm income or the rate of return to resources invested in farming, it would seem preferable to use farm variables to build a typology. To understand farmer issues such as the human capital of farmers or whether the farmer lives in a household with income below the low-income cut-off, it would seem preferable to use farmer variables to build a typology.

Related observations suggest the following:

• Although there may be an increase in the off-farm work by census-farm operators, this may be (almost) entirely due to the shift of non-farm work from the farm to an off-farm location. Thus, the participation of census-farm operators in non-farm work appears not to have changed (much) over time.

• Part-time farmers, with half of their earnings from farming and half their earnings from off the farm, generate less total earnings. Thus, given their fixed human capital resource, they generate a higher return (i.e. are more efficient) if they work full-time on the farm or full-time off the farm.

• A relatively small share of young census-farm operators has attained any agriculture-related post-secondary education. The share differs by province and suggests that post-secondary institutions in some provinces need to increase their presence in this market.

Notes

1 These considerations were triggered by numerous observations by farm leaders who observed that no one asks for the non-teacher income of a teacher (or the teacher's family) and no one asks for the income of an auto worker when not at the assembly plant, etc.

2 In Canada, the farming family income from all sources of farming families reached the level of income of non-farm families in 1973 (Bollman and Smith, 1987) and has stayed above the level of income of non-farm families since that time. This conclusion holds for three types of farming families: a family with one individual reporting unincorporated net farm income, a family with one individual who is self-employed with an agricultural occupation and a family with one individual with net farm income being the major source of income. Note, however, that in 1981 the incidence of low income (13%) was smaller for families on smaller farms (due to the role of off-farm income) but the incidence was greater (21%) for families on mid-sized farms (in the third quartile of gross farm revenue) due the situation that the farm was too big to allow the operator to work off-farm but the farm was not big enough to generate a "viable" level of net farm income.

3 In Canada, a census-farm is any agricultural holding with agricultural products for sale (or potentially for sale). In Canada, 36% of census-farms had gross revenue of less than $10,000 in 2011, compared to the United States, where 75% of census-farms had gross revenue less than $10,000 in 2012. (See also Oliveira et al., 1995).

4 The operator is identified as the person responsible for the day-to-day operation of the agricultural holding for the simple reason that this person will be most familiar with the answers to the questions on the census questionnaire.

5 Canada has had, since 1971, a unique database that includes the characteristics of family farms and the characteristics of farming families. This database is constructed by a micro-record linkage of the Census of Agriculture questionnaire and the Census of Population questionnaire for the household for each operator of an agricultural holding (see also Keita, 2004). This "Agriculture-Population Linkage" database exists for the census years of 1971, 1981, 1986, 1991, 1996, 2001 and 2006. In 2011, there was a micro-record linkage of the Census of Agriculture questionnaire and the questionnaire for the National Household Survey. This is one database that provides a "common source of information for policy analysts." For more information see Bollman (2009), Shaw (1979), Statistics Canada (1975a–1975d, 1976a, and 1976b), and Statistics Canada (http://www.statcan.gc.ca/pub/95-633-x/2007000/6500075-eng.htm). (For the 2011 linkage of the Census of Agriculture and the National Household Survey, see Statistics Canada (http://www.statcan.gc.ca/eng/ca2011/index).

Other databases provide less comprehensive data, but at more frequent intervals. For information on the Farm Financial Survey, see Statistics Canada (http://www5.statcan.gc.ca/olc-cel/olc.action?objId=21F0008X&objType=2&lang=en&limit=0) and for information on the farm tax-filer data program, see Statistics Canada Whole Farm Database (http://www5.statcan.gc.ca/olc-cel/olc.action?objId=21F0005G&objType=2&lang=en&limit=0). Statistics Canada's Labour Force Survey provides monthly data on the labour allocation of individuals to each industry sector and for each occupation group for the main job of an individual (and selected information for a secondary job). A special tabulation would be able to generate data on the labour allocation of everyone in the household where one or more individuals are associated with the agricultural sector.

6 All tabulations in this paper concerning the Agriculture-Population Linkage exclude households associated with widely held or non-family corporate farms or farms with "other" types of legal organization (institutional farms, co-operative farms, Hutterite Colonies, etc.). In 2001, these holdings represented 2% of all census-farms and contributed 13% of aggregate gross farm revenue.

7 The income data for the 2006 Census of Population were assembled with a different methodology and the results, particular for unincorporated net farm income and for unincorporated net non-farm business income, are not comparable with previous years (Statistics Canada, 2008d).
8 "'Viable farm', if it means anything, means a farm which, with current management, produces an income greater than the poverty level of income" (Canada, 1969, p. 21).
9 The urban-to-rural gradient is implemented by using the USDA "Beale codes" as applied to Canada by Ehrensaft and Beeman (1992).
10 Essentially, these are "non-viable" farms (Canada, 1969) as our calculation for the gross farm revenue threshold for a "viable" farm in 2001 was $217,414.
11 Recently, land prices have spiked thanks to a spike in grain prices in 2012 and a nosedive in interest rates.
12 A "part-time farm" may be considered an agricultural holding that requires less than 12 months of labour by the operator.
13 "Agriculture-related fields of study include the following groups in the Classification of Instructional Programs (Statistics Canada, 2007): 01 – Agriculture, agricultural operations and related sciences (including all "sub" categories); 13.1301 – Agricultural teacher education; 14.0301 – Agricultural / biological engineering and bioengineering; 26.03 – Botany / plant biology (including all "sub" categories); 26.07– Zoology / animal biology (including all "sub" categories); 26.08 – Genetics (including all "sub" categories); 47.06 – Vehicle maintenance and repair technologies (including all "sub" categories); and 51.25 –Veterinary biomedical and clinical sciences (including all "sub" categories).
14 These inter-provincial differences persist over time. A time series is not presented here, as the coding for "major field of study" changed in 2006 and a concordance is not possible with the earlier coding. However, using the coding available in earlier Agriculture-Population Linkage databases does generate similar findings.

References

Agriculture and Agra-Food Canada. (2006) *Canadian Farm Family Options Program* (Ottawa: Agriculture and Agra-Food Canada) (http://publications.gc.ca/collections/collection_2009/agr/A118-7-2006E.pdf).

Alasia, Alessandro, Alfons Weersink, Ray D. Bollman, John Cranfield (2008) "Off-farm labour decision of Canadian farm operators: Urbanization effects and rural labour market linkages," *Journal of Rural Studies* 25, pp. 12–24. (http://dx.doi.org/10.1016/j.jrurstud.2008.04.002).

Bollman, Ray D. (1979) *Off-farm Work by Farmers* (Ottawa: Census Analytic Study, Statistics Canada, Catalogue no. 99–756).

Bollman, Ray D. (1981) "Changes at the Urban–rural Interface: The Contribution of Off-farm Work by Farmers" in Margot A. Bellamy and Bruce L. Greenshields (ed.), *The Rural Challenge*: Contributed Papers read at the 17th International Conference of Agricultural Economists (Aldershot, England: Gower) (http://ageconsearch.umn.edu/handle/197102).

Bollman, Ray D. (1989) "Who Receives Farm Government Payments?" *Canadian Journal of Agricultural Economics*, Vol. 37, No. 3 (November), pp. 351–378.

Bollman, Ray D. (1991) "Efficiency Aspects of Part-time Farming" in M. C. Hallberg, Jill L. Findeis and Daniel A. Lass *Multiple Jobholding among Farm Families* (Ames: Iowa State University Press), pp. 112–139.

Bollman, Ray D. (1998) "Agricultural Statistics for Rural Development." In Holland, Theresa E. and Van den Broecke, Marcel P.R. (ed.) *Agricultural Statistics 2000: An International Conference on Agricultural Statistics* (Voorburg, The Netherlands: International Statistical Institute), pp. 29–41. Also published as *Agricultural Statistics for Rural Development*. (Ottawa:

Statistics Canada, Agriculture and Rural Working Paper No. 49, Cat. No. 21-601-MIE, 2001). (www.statcan.ca/cgi-bin/downpub/listpub.cgi?catno=21-601-MIE).

Bollman, Ray D. (2005) Family Farms and Farming Families: The Overlap of Two Institutions, Paper presented to the EAAE Seminar on Institutional Units in Agriculture, Wye Campus of Imperial College, Ashford, Kent, UK, April 9–10 (http://ageconsearch.umn.edu/handle/24440).

Bollman, Ray D. (2006) "The Demographic Overlap of Agriculture and the Rural Economy: Implications for the Coherence of Agricultural and Rural Policies," Chapter 3 in Dimitris Diakosavvas (ed.) *Coherence of Agricultural and Rural Development Policies* (Paris: OECD), pp. 95–112. {Also published as Bollman, Ray D. (2007). *The Demographic Overlap of Agriculture and Rural* (Ottawa: Statistics Canada, Agriculture and Rural Working Paper, Catalogue no. 21-601-MIE). (http://www.publications.gc.ca/Collection/Statcan/21-601-MIE/21-601-MIE2006081.pdf).

Bollman, Ray D. (2009) Households associated with agricultural holdings: Selected socio-economic dimensions. Paper prepared for presentation to the Second Meeting of the Wye City Group on Statistics on Rural Development and Agriculture Household Income, June 11–12, Rome, Italy (http://www.fao.org/search/en/?cx=018170620143701104933%3Aqq82jsfba7w&q=wye&cof=FORID%3A9&siteurl=www.fao.org%2Fhome%2Fen%2F&ref=&ss=456j104000j3).

Bollman, Ray D. (2013) "Pluriactivité: A retro-prospective," Presentation to Rural Transformations in Troubled Times: A Policy Decade in Review – The 10th Anniversary Conference of the International Comparative Rural Policy Seminar, Bertinoro, Italy, June 22–23 (https://www.brandonu.ca/rdi/files/2011/02/Bollman-2013-ICRPS-pluriactivity-Jun22.pdf).

Bollman, Ray D. and Pamela Smith. (1986) "Integration of Canadian Farm and Off-farm Markets and the Off-farm Work of Farm Women, Men, and Children," Chapter 15 in G. S. Basran and David A. Hay (1988) *The Political Economy of Agriculture in Western Canada* (Toronto: Garamond Press), pp. 185–202.

Bollman, Ray D. and Pamela Smith. (1987) "The Changing Role of Off-farm Income in Canada." *Proceedings of the Canadian Agricultural Outlook Conference* (December).

Bollman, Ray D. and Allan D. Steeves. (1982) "The Stocks and Flows of Canadian Census-farm Operators over the Period 1966–1976," *The Canadian Review of Sociology and Anthropology*, Vol. 19, No. 4 (November), pp. 576–590.

Canada Department of Agriculture. (1969) *Canadian agriculture in the seventies: Report of the Federal Task Force on Agriculture* (Ottawa: Canada Department of Agriculture)

Clemenson, Heather A. and Ray D. Bollman (1985) "A Profile of Managers of Agricultural Resources," Paper presented to the International Conference: Management of Rural Resources: Problems and Policies', University of Guelph, July 14-20. Published as « Les agriculteurs canadiens des années 1980 », *Cahiers de recherche sociologique*, Vol. 5, No. 1 (Printemps, 1987), pp. 79–102.

Ehrensaft, Philip and Jennifer Beeman. (1992) "Distance and diversity in nonmetropolitan economies," Chapter 9 in Ray D. Bollman (ed.) *Rural and Small Town Canada* (Toronto: Thompson Educational Publishing), pp. 193–224.

Ehrensaft, Philip and Ray D. Bollman. (1992) *The Microdynamics and Farm Family Economics of Structural Change in Agriculture* (Ottawa: Statistics Canada, Agriculture Division, Working Paper No. 16) (www.statcan.gc.ca/cgi-bin/downpub/listpub.cgi?catno=21-601-mie).

Fitzpatrick, John M. (1967) *1958 Farm Survey Report No. 2: Farm and Farm Family Income, Farm Expenditures and Resources in Canadian Agriculture* (Ottawa: Dominion Bureau of Statistics, Catalogue no. 21-509).

Fitzpatrick, John M. and C.V. Parker (1965) "Distribution of Income in Canadian Agriculture," *Canadian Journal of Agricultural Economics*, Vol. XIII, No. 2, pp. 47–64.

Fuller, A. M. and Ray D. Bollman. (1992) "Farm Family Linkages to the Non-farm Sector: The Role of Off-Farm Income of Farm Families," Chapter 11 in Ray D. Bollman (ed.). *Rural and Small Town Canada* (Toronto: Thompson Educational Publishing).

Furtan, W. H. and Ray D. Bollman (1979) "Returns to Operator Education in Saskatchewan," *American Journal of Agricultural Economics*, Vol. 61, Number 2 (May), pp. 318–321.

Harrison, Rick and Sylvain Cloutier. (1995) *People in Canadian Agriculture* (Ottawa: Statistics Canada, Catalogue no. 21–523).

Keita, Naman. (2004) *Improving Cost-Effectiveness and Relevance of Agricultural Censuses in Africa: Linking Population and Agricultural Censuses* (Ghana: FAO Regional Office for Africa, Working Paper No. 30).

Oliveira, Vic, Leslie Whitener and Ray D. Bollman (1995) "Farm Structure Data: A Canada–U.S. Comparative Review," *Canadian Journal of Agricultural Economics (Special Issue on Farms, Farming Families and Farming Communities)*, pp. 29–46.

Shaw, Paul (1979) *Canada's Farm Population: Analysis of Income and Related Characteristics* (Ottawa: Statistics Canada, Census Analytic Study, Catalogue no. 99–750).

Smith, Arthur H. and William E. Martin. (1972) "Socioeconomic Behavior of Cattle Ranchers, with Implications for Rural Community Development in the West," *American Journal of Agricultural Economics* (May), pp. 217–225.

Statistics Canada. (1973) "Off-farm Income," *Quarterly Bulletin of Agricultural Statistics* (July-September), Vol. 66, No. 3 (Catalogue No. 21–003).

Statistics Canada. (1975a) *Basic Socio-economic Characteristics of Farm Operators: Canada and Provinces* (Ottawa: Statistics Canada, 1971 Census of Canada, Vol IV – Part 4 (Bulletin 4.4 – 1), Catalogue no. 96–712)

Statistics Canada. (1975b) *Cross-classified Socio-economic Characteristics of Farm Operators* (Ottawa: Statistics Canada, 1971 Census of Canada, Vol IV – Part 4 (Bulletin 4.4 – 2), Catalogue no. 96–713).

Statistics Canada. (1975c) *Cross-classified Socio-economic Characteristics of Farm Operators with Off-farm Employment and Income: Canada, the Provinces and the Regions* (Ottawa: Statistics Canada, 1971 Census of Canada, Vol IV – Part 4 (Bulletin 4.4 – 3), Catalogue no. 96–714).

Statistics Canada. (1975d) *Cross-classified Socio-economic Characteristics of Farm Operators' Families: Canada and Provinces* (Ottawa: Statistics Canada, 1971 Census of Canada, Vol IV – Part 5 (Bulletin 4.5 – 1), Catalogue no. 96–715).

Statistics Canada. (1976a) *Cross-classified Socio-economic Characteristics of Farm Operators' Households: Canada and Provinces* (Ottawa: Statistics Canada, 1971 Census of Canada, Vol IV – Part 5 (Bulletin 4.5 – 2), Catalogue no. 96–716).

Statistics Canada. (1976b) *Cross-classified Socio-economic Characteristics of Farm Operators' Dwelling Facilities: Canada* (Ottawa: Statistics Canada, 1971 Census of Canada, Vol IV – Part 5 (Bulletin 4.5 – 3), Catalogue no. 96–717).

Statistics Canada. (1976c) *Farm Operators by Economic Class showing such characteristics as Sex, Age, Income, Schooling and Off-farm Employment* (Ottawa: Statistics Canada, 1971 Census of Canada, Catalogue no. 96–734).

Statistics Canada. (2003) *Agriculture-Population Linkage Data for the 2001 Census* (Ottawa: Statistics Canada, Catalogue no. 95F0303). (http://www.statcan.gc.ca/bsolc/olc-cel/olc-cel?catno=95F0303XIE&lang=eng).

Statistics Canada. (2007) *2006 Census Dictionary* (Ottawa: Statistics Canada, Catalogue no. 92-566) (http://www12.statcan.gc.ca/english/census06/reference/dictionary/index.cfm).

Statistics Canada. (2008a) *Low Income Cut-offs for 2006 and Low Income Measures for 2005* (Ottawa: Statistics Canada, Income Research Paper Series No. 004, Catalogue no. 75F0002MIE).

Statistics Canada. (2008b) *Statistics on Income of Farm Families: 2005* (Ottawa: Statistics Canada, Catalogue no. 21-207) (http://www.statcan.gc.ca/bsolc/olc-cel/olc-cel?catno=21-207-X&chropg=1&lang=eng).

Statistics Canada. (2008c) *Agriculture-Population Linkage Data for the 2006 Census* (Ottawa: Statistics Canada, Catalogue No. 95-633) (http://www.statcan.gc.ca/bsolc/olc-cel/olc-cel?catno=95-633-X&lang=eng).

Statistics Canada. (2008d) *Break in the Agriculture-Population Linkage net farm income data series* (Ottawa: Statistics Canada, Catalogue no. 95-633) (http://www.statcan.gc.ca/pub/95-633-x/2007000/6500081-eng.htm).

Statistics Canada. (annual) *Net Farm Income: Agriculture Economic Statistics* (Ottawa: Statistics Canada, Catalogue no. 21-010) (www.statcan.gc.ca/bsolc/english/bsolc?catno=21-010-XIE).

United Nations. (1947) *United Nations Studies of Census Methods. Collation of Results of Population and Agricultural Census, No. 1* (New York: United Nations).

Vogel, Stephen and Ray D. Bollman. (2012) *Farm Portfolio Entrepreneurship and Its Importance in the Rural Economy: A Canadian and U.S. Comparison*. Presentation to the 59th Annual North American Meetings of the Regional Science Association International, Ottawa, Ontario, November 7–10.

Whitener, Leslie, Ray D. Bollman and Fu Lai Tung. (1995) "Trends and Patterns in Farm Structural Change: A Canada–U.S. Comparison," *Canadian Journal of Agricultural Economics (Special Issue on Farms, Farm Families and Farming Communities)*, pp. 15–28.

Chapter 6

The effects of U.S. agricultural policies on farm household income and labor

Daniel Prager and Christopher Burns

Introduction

Over the last century, the productivity of American agriculture has increased dramatically. More food and fiber are being produced today than at any time in history (Wang et al., 2015). This has been made possible through large-scale gains in labor and land productivity; fewer farmers are working today than in decades past, while the amount of cultivated land has remained constant since the 1980s. This increase in productivity is attributable to major changes in the technology used to produce agricultural commodities. It has also fundamentally changed the structure of U.S. farms. While over 2 million family farms still exist in the United States, an increasing amount of production is taking place on larger farms.

Accordingly, there have been major changes in the structure of farm households; today the typical farmer relies substantially on off-farm income. In addition, due to changing priorities of the U.S. federal government, there have been large shifts in the size, scope, and purpose of government agricultural policy. Farm legislation in the early 20th century was aimed at supporting prices and controlling the supply of agricultural products at a time when most production was done on small farms that relied heavily on farm income. Today, agricultural policies are designed to help farms mitigate revenue and price risk through less distortionary programs, such as crop insurance and margin protection programs. This chapter will explore how the confluence of federal agricultural policies and the changing structure of the farm have affected farm household income and labor allocation.

Brief history of the U.S. farm economy

Since before the country's founding, American agriculture has held a pivotal place in the national economy. In 1930, it accounted for 7.7% of U.S. GDP and employed over 20 million people across 6.3 million farms (and associated enterprises), or roughly one-fifth of the working U.S. population. (NASS, 1930; Dimitri et al., 2005) Since then, the size of the sector has declined to slightly more than 3 million farm operators on 2.05 million farms, according to the most recent Agricultural Census in 2012. Currently, the output of farms—$177 billion in 2014—accounts for about 1% of

U.S. GDP (Bureau of Economic Analysis, 2015). As the ratio of capital to labor used on farms has shifted towards the former, economies of scale have pushed costs down in many farms. At the same time, many households own small farming operations which are not their primary source of income. More production is taking place on larger farms and the structure of farm households has changed accordingly.

In addition to becoming larger, farms have become increasingly specialized: in 1900, each farm produced an average of over 5 commodities; by 1992, this number had fallen to under 2 commodities per farm (Dimitri et al., 2005). Farm programs can play a key role in both increasing and stabilizing the income of these farm operations. Farm households also employ other means of stabilizing their earnings and consumption, including working off-farm, consuming their on-farm production, and saving during good years. As with families throughout the United States, farm households are increasingly smaller. Farm households have decreased from 5.2 people per household at the turn of the last century to just 2.1 people in households today (across the United States, the decrease was from 4.6 to 2.6 people per household) (Gardner, 2002). Consequently, household labor on farms has been supplanted by hired labor and augmented by new technologies (Figure 6.1).

Technology changes and farm household labor

Animal power was the dominant technology in U.S. agriculture until the early 20th century. In 1930 U.S. farms had approximately 18.7 million horses and mules, but only 920,000 tractors (Dimitri et al., 2005). The invention and adoption of the

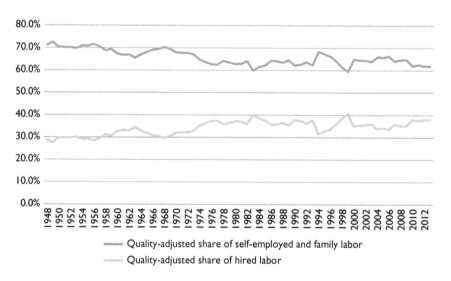

Figure 6.1 The share of total self-employed and family labor hours, 1948–2013

Source: USDA, Economic Research Service, *Agricultural Productivity in the United States*, data product, 2016.

gasoline-powered farm tractor replaced millions of mules and horses, with 86% of farms reporting a tractor by 1950. The growth in use of tractors led to tremendous gains in productivity and labor-hours saved, allowing farmers to accomplish tasks such as pulling, plowing, planting, and harvesting in dramatically less time. For example, in 1900 the average farmer spent 147 hours to produce 100 bushels of corn, but by the mid-1980s this had been reduced to 3 hours (Gardner, 2002).

Further technological advances such as hybrid seeds, the mechanical cow-milker, and the cotton-picker, combined with inexpensive chemical fertilizers and pesticides, led to a dramatic increase in yields and farm output. U.S. agricultural output nearly tripled between 1948 and 2013 (Figure 6.2), growing at an average annual rate of 1.52% (USDA ERS 2016). During the same period total labor hours from hired and self-employed/ family labor declined substantially, with a larger decline in self-employed/family labor. These trends reflect both the impact of laborsaving technology on labor demand and better job opportunities in off-farm labor markets during this period. The effect of higher wages in manufacturing and other nonfarm industries led to a migration of labor off the farm following the end of WWII (Gardner, 2002).

Another feature of laborsaving technologies is they encourage farms to become specialized, as they often require large fixed capital investments. Thus, the adoption of productivity-enhancing technology by U.S. farms has also contributed to a rise in the share of hired labor used on the farm relative to self-employed/family labor. As farms adopted these technologies, they grew in size in order to achieve the necessary

Figure 6.2 Total quality-adjusted U.S. agricultural output and labor input (hours worked): 1948–2013

Source: USDA, Economic Research Service, *Agricultural Productivity in the United States*, data product, 2016.

output levels to achieve the lowest per-unit costs. The result has been significant growth in the number of large farms (MacDonald, Hoppe, and Korb, 2013).

History of government agricultural policy

Until the 1930s, U.S. farm legislation was not focused directly on supporting farm income or creating a farm safety net. Instead, policies were more focused on generating government revenue, supporting domestic prices through import or export tariffs, and encouraging the purchase and cultivation of agricultural land. Beginning with legislation passed in the 1860s, the United States started to build a strong foundation for expanding agricultural production, increasing productivity, and raising farm incomes. In 1862, the Morrill Act established land-grant universities for the purpose of agricultural and mechanical arts, while the Homestead Act of the same year encouraged farming by giving 160 acres to settlers who worked the land for five years. The Department of Agriculture was established in the same year. The Hatch Act of 1887 provided grants for agricultural research, leading to a system of state agricultural extension services.

The early 20th century saw farm incomes boom due to high commodity prices caused by shortages created by World War I (this period is known as the "golden era" of U.S. agriculture). However, these economic conditions disappeared in the 1920s as European agricultural production returned to normal levels, decreasing export demand for U.S. agricultural products. Large surpluses in farm commodities quickly led to lower farm incomes, and the situation grew more severe with the economic crash of 1929. In response to this economic crisis, the New Deal would bring the first significant farm legislation aimed at raising farm incomes and stabilizing commodity prices (Effland, 2000).

The economic distress caused by the Great Depression galvanized political support not only for new policies for boosting the general economy, but also for a new set of agricultural policies aimed at supporting prices and incomes. While prior farm legislation had attempted to raise prices and incomes by controlling supplies, these programs were not effective. The continued persistence of low farm incomes and low commodity prices (i.e. "the farm problem") led to several large government programs as a part of the New Deal.

Commodity programs

The first farm bill, the Agricultural Adjustment Act (AAA) of 1933, was designed to set floors below which commodity prices would not fall, while also providing supply controls and income supports. The goal was to raise farm incomes up to "parity" with earlier high-income years (1910–1914). The mechanism for supporting prices was to dramatically reduce the supply for staple commodities. Mandatory price supports were established for corn, wheat, and cotton in the Agricultural Adjustment Act of 1938 (Effland, 2000). This legislation also incorporated the Commodity Credit Corporation (CCC) with the goal of stabilizing farm income and prices.

The CCC is authorized to make loans, purchases, and payments to farmers in order to maintain balanced and adequate supplies of agricultural commodities.[1]

While each successive farm bill has added or changed programs to adapt to the economic conditions of the time, the combination of price supports and supply management were the essential mechanisms of federal farm policy until the end of the 20th century. A recurring theme of each successive farm bill has been more voluntary production controls and greater market orientation for price supports. For example, the Food and Agricultural Act of 1965 was the first legislation to make production controls voluntary for wheat, feed grains, and upland cotton. It also abandoned the "parity" goals for farm income in favor a system of income support ("deficiency payments") to farmers for lower support prices.

By the 1980s commodity programs were designed more for income stabilization than for supply controls. This trend towards less distortionary programs that allowed farmers more flexibility in planting decisions continued with the 1996 farm bill (FAIR Act). This act replaced price support and supply control programs with a program that paid farmers based on their historical production of specific commodities on a fixed number of acres (termed "base acres"). Because the base acres and yields were fixed, these payments were decoupled from current market conditions and consequently less distortionary. This bill also had a second tier of payments that were made on current output when market prices were below support price levels, known as loan rates.

The most recent farm bill (the Agricultural Act of 2014) brought the end of direct payments for specific commodities and moved the farm safety net towards risk management, mainly through price and revenue loss insurance for specific crops. (A number of transitional programs were introduced to soften the blow for producers reliant on direct payments.) By managing the downside risk of agriculture, this legislation aims to protect producers while reducing the historical distortionary policies in commodity markets.

Land conservation

Soil and land conservation programs have been a part of U.S. agriculture policy since the Soil Conservation and Domestic Allotment Act of 1936. Two decades later, the Agricultural Act of 1956 established the Soil Bank program, which introduced the conservation reserve and authorized short- and long-term removal of land from production, with annual rental payments made to farmers. This program removed highly erodible land from agricultural production and established native or other permanent vegetable cover in an effort to combat erosion.

Land conservation and acreage idling played a large role in supply control mechanisms of U.S. agricultural policy until the 1980s. While supply management fell out of favor as a policy tool for price stabilization, the 1985 farm bill established the Conservation Reserve Program (CRP). This program encourages farmers to convert highly erodible land or other environmentally sensitive acreage to vegetative cover for a period of time (usually ten years). More recent farm legislation has added programs that incentivize farmers to protect farmland currently under production, as well as protecting vulnerable grasslands, wetlands, and other natural resources.

Crop insurance

The federal crop insurance program has become the major policy tool for the farm safety net over the last two decades. As opposed to policies designed to support prices or control commodity supplies, crop insurance is designed to insure farmers against yield and price losses. Federal crop insurance dates back to the Agricultural Adjustment Act of 1938, when Congress established the Federal Crop Insurance Corporation (FCIC). However, risk management using crop insurance was limited in scope until 1980, largely due to low farmer participation rates and high program costs. In 1980, Congress expanded crop insurance into a national program that covered the majority of cropland under cultivation. Another significant reform was the Federal Crop Insurance Reform and Department of Agriculture Reorganization Act of 1994. This legislation supplemented crop insurance program with a new catastrophic coverage level (CAT) and stipulated that producers must purchase coverage at the CAT levels or above to participate in commodity, conservation, and loan programs.

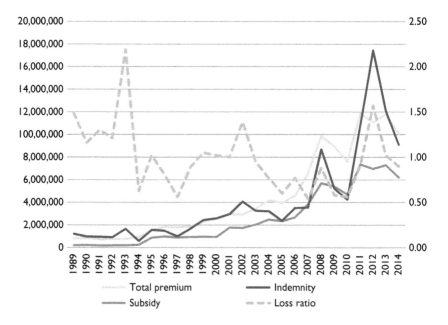

Figure 6.3 Insurance subsidies, 1989–2014

Source: Risk Management Agency.

Table 6.1 Direct government payments to farms, 1933–2015

	1933–1939	1940–1949	1950–1959	1960–1969	1970–1979	1980–1989	1990–1995	1996–2001	2002–2007	2008–2013	2014–2015
Total direct government payments, yearly average (billions of 2009 dollars)	$5.3	$5.6	$3.0	$12.3	$7.8	$14.8	$13.9	$19.5	$17.3	$11.2	$9.7
Percent allocated to:											
Commodity programs	8%	–	4%	77%	84%	65%	34%	–1%	–	–	–
Production flexibility contract payments	–	–	–	–	–	–	21%	35%	4%	–	–
Loan deficiency payments and marketing loan gains	–	–	–	–	–	–	8%	24%	13%	1%	2%
Fixed direct payments	–	–	–	–	–	–	–	–	29%	41%	0%

(continued)

Table 6.1 Direct government payments to farms, 1933–2015 (continued)

	1933–1939	1940–1949	1950–1959	1960–1969	1970–1979	1980–1989	1990–1995	1996–2001	2002–2007	2008–2013	2014–2015
Counter-cyclical payments	–	–	–	–	–	–	–	–	14%	3%	–
Price Loss Coverage (PLC) and Agricultural Risk Coverage (ARC)	–	–	–	-	–	–	–	–	–	–	26%
Supplemental and ad hoc disaster assistance	–	–	–	–	–	–	10%	29%	10%	14%	30%
Conservation	41%	58%	47%	9%	9%	7%	17%	11%	16%	29%	34%
Miscellaneous programs*	51%	42%	49%	13%	8%	28%	10%	3%	14%	11%	7%

*Includes Tobacco Transition Payments, Cotton Transition Assistance Program, Milk Income Loss Coverage, Peanut Quota Buyout Payments, Certificate Exchange Gains, and Average Crop Revenue Election Program (ACRE).

Source: USDA, ERS Farm Income and Wealth Statistics.

Participation increased substantially following the 1994 farm bill, with almost two-thirds of total planted acreage of field crops insured by 1998. As shown in Figure 6.3, total premiums, subsidies, and indemnities for federal crop insurance have risen dramatically since the mid-1990s.[2] From 1996 to 2012, total insurance premiums increased from $2 to $12 million, and total insurance subsidies increased from $1 to $7 million over the same period. Insurance indemnities have also increased dramatically, peaking in 2012 when a large drought negatively affected much of the Midwest corn and soybean crop.

The latest farm bill (2014) made two significant additions to previous legislation with the price loss coverage (PLC) and agricultural risk coverage (ARC) programs for specific crops. The former pays farmers an indemnity if prices fall below a specified reference point. The ARC program is based on revenue benchmarks (i.e. combination of yield and price benchmarks), and has both an individual and county version available for specific crops.

To summarize, government programs have changed significantly over time, moving from distortionary policies intended to control supply and support prices, to policies based on decoupled payments and insuring farm businesses against price and revenue risk. Table 6.1 breaks out these various agricultural programs, showing how the distribution of direct payments to farms has shifted from 1933 to 2014.

What does farm household income look like today?

Many modern farm households are diversified enterprises with multiple sources of income. Recent data collected through the Agricultural Resource Management Survey (ARMS) paint a complex picture of the farm household. Just as there are many types of farm enterprises, likewise there exist many classes of associated households. The majority of farm households rely quite heavily on off-farm sources of income. In recent years, as farm production has become increasingly concentrated in large farms, the median farm household earned slightly negative on-farm income; all of their income was derived from off-farm sources. This is especially true of farms with low sales volumes. Yet, even for larger farm households, off-farm income remains an important component of household income. Farm household income has increased steadily over the past few decades, surpassing median U.S. household income in 1998. In 2014, farm households earned $80,620 in total household income, an increase of 50% from a decade earlier. However, farm households experience considerably larger year-to-year variations in income. All U.S. households experience a loss of one-half their income at an annual rate of 9%. Comparatively, two-thirds of households operating large farms do. This is driven by fluctuations in prices and yields, in addition to choices made by farmers about the amount of acres to farm or the size of their livestock herd.

Along with income that has outpaced the national average in recent years, farm households are increasingly comprised of households with large amounts of assets. In 2014, the last year for which data are available, only 2.7% of farm households had assets below the median wealth of all U.S. households ($82,500). This high level of wealth is due in significant part to a sharp increase in farmland values in the early part of the

21st century. As farms have become large and specialized, operators and spouses nevertheless engage in off-farm employment. In general, household members work off-farm based on the amount of time available (after completing their on-farm responsibilities) and on the market opportunities for off-farm income. Across all farms in the United States, farm households earned a median of $70,000 in off-farm income. Though not all households received income from all sources, Figure 6.4 shows the average percentage received across categories. Wages constituted about 55% of off-farm income, while unearned income (transfers, interest, dividends, and other income) represented about 30%. The final piece is nonfarm business income, which contributed 15% on average, though most farm households do not own a nonfarm business.

Farm typology

The Economic Research Service of the USDA classifies farm households into three types, based on the farm or ranch they operate (the ERS "collapsed typology," Hoppe and MacDonald, 2013): residence farms, where the principal operator is either primarily employed off-farm or is retired from farming; intermediate farms, where the primary occupation of the principal operator is farming, but the farm operation earns less than $350,000 in gross cash farm income; and commercial farms, those operations earning $350,000 or more in gross cash farm income.[3] Farm households identified with residence farms—those either retired from farming or with an off-farm occupation—earned the highest amount of off-farm income; however, off-farm income was important to both intermediate and commercial farms as well. Those households associated with intermediate farms earned positive average income ($4,000) from farming, but median household income from farming has remained close to zero. Intermediate farm households have been reliant on off-farm income, earning $56,400 from all off-farm sources in 2014. It is the commercial farm households—those operating farms with at least $350,000 in farm household—who derive a majority of their income from farming.

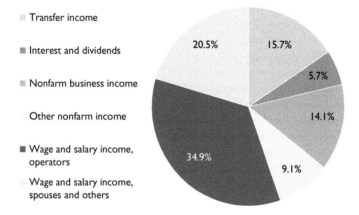

Figure 6.4 Sources of off-farm income, 2014

Source: Agricultural Resource Management Survey, 2014.

In fact, in 2014, only 37% of residence farm households earned positive farm income, yet these households earned only 7% of total household income from farming. Just over half (53%) of intermediate farm households earned positive farm income, which totaled 27% of these households' total income. Conversely, 86% of commercial farm households had a positive flow of income from their farming operation. This corresponded with 77% of their (much larger) household income. Though they received income more on-farm income than residence farm owners and more off-farm income than those operating commercial farms, intermediate farm households earned the lowest overall income, $65,000 in 2014. The median commercial farm household earned $108,000 in on-farm income, over three times the $29,000 earned from off-farm sources. As with residential farms, the total income of intermediate and commercial farm households over the last 20 years has increased substantially. Figure 6.5 shows the importance of farm and off-farm income to farm households over the period from 1996 to 2014.

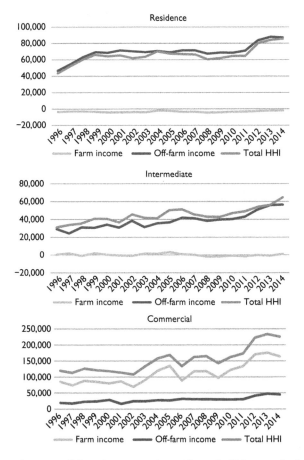

Figure 6.5 Farm income, off-farm income, and total household income by farm typology, 1996–2014

Source: Agricultural Resource Management Survey, 1996–2014.

Government payments at the farm level

Payments to farms from the federal government constitute an important part of farm income, and can be split into two main categories: government payments and crop insurance subsidies. Government payments are comprised of three groups: commodity payments, both direct and countercyclical; conservation payments, and other forms of payments (including transition payments). Crop insurance subsidies, described above, constitute a direct transfer of income to farms, but one which does not show up on the farm's income statement. Analysis of government payments to farms shows that the average payment has varied considerably over the period from 1996 to 2014, with payments peaking in 2001. Figure 6.6 shows the overall level of

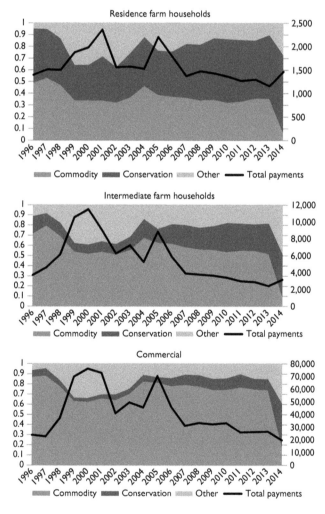

Figure 6.6 Government payments by type and farm typology, 1996–2014

Source: Agricultural Resource Management Survey, 1996–2014.

payments for commercial, intermediate, and residence farms, as well as the average amount of government payments (for farms which received payments). Residence farms receive both the lowest level of total payments, but the highest amount of payments from conservation programs. In the 18-year period ending in 2014, residence farms received about $1,500 per year from commodity, conservation, and other payments. Because residence farms spend the least amount of time working on their operations, and have the lowest amount of acreage under production, they receive only a relatively small amount of direct and countercyclical payments. Residence farm households received a large bulk of their income from conservation payments. In the last decade conservation payments constituted half of their total government payments.

While intermediate and commercial farms reported receiving significant conservation payments as well, these households received more than half of their total payments from commodity programs. The size of farm subsidies scales with the size of the farm operation and is larger for farms that produce certain program commodities, such as corn, wheat, or soybeans. Intermediate farms (those with a gross cash income of less than $350,000) received government payments of about $5,500 per year, while commercial farms received payments of $36,100 per year. The visible falloff in direct payments in 2014 shows presages the change in farm programs towards price-based mechanisms introduced with the most recent farm bill.

Income volatility

Farm income is highly variable, and this variability can affect household welfare, as well as production choices and environmental quality. Farm households receive income from both on and off-farm sources. The amount of on-farm income earned by the household depends on the production of the farm operation, but also on the overall supply and demand for farm products, which determine the market price. A crop or livestock farm cannot quickly or easily change the set of commodities they produce and therefore are highly susceptible to fluctuations in the market price, as well as to droughts, floods, pests, disease, and other factors which can damage a crop or diminish a herd. Risk adverse operators strive to maximize their income in any one year while also maintaining a steady stream of income for years to come.

Mishra et al. (2002) examined the well-being of U.S. farm households using traditional measures such as total household income, but also farm household wealth and expenditures. The authors found that while farm business income is considerably variable, farm household income is relatively stable. Using cross-sectional data from the ARMS, they found that off-farm income played a larger role in total household income in 1999 than in 1993, a trend which has continued into the 21st century. Consequently, the farm business played a smaller role as a source of income, and thus in determining household well-being.

A recent analysis of farm households used panel data to look at the volatility on the same farm over two years between 1996 and 2013.[4] While farm household income is more volatile than U.S. household income, the authors found that household income volatility for commercial farms has decreased by about 0.8% per year since 1996. Off-farm income volatility has decreased by about 1.8% over the same period. Principal operators who are older or had a higher level of education were also found to have less income volatility. A calculation of the certainty equivalent of direct payments and crop insurance showed that countercyclical payments are preferable to direct payments for risk adverse farm households.[5] Crop insurance was even better: that each dollar of crop insurance indemnities received was worth $1.38 to the household, on average. Government payments played an important role in reducing income volatility for the household (Key et al., 2017).

Farm household labor

In a farm household, many factors influence the allocation of labor, including the amount of labor needed for the farming operation, the skill set of household members, and off-farm labor opportunities. In 2013, over three-fourths of farm households had a household member who received a wage or salary from off-farm employment. For many households, the amount of labor available for off-farm activities is inversely correlated with the demands of the farm operation. Many operations, especially those producing livestock, require significant, recurrent time investments to run. Across all farm households in 2013, farm operator worked an average of 18 hours per week off-farm, with spouses adding 13 hours.[6] However, only 47% of operators and 46% of spouses reported working off-farm and these households reported median off-farm work of 40 hours per week. Residence farm households were the most likely to have off-farm work, with 64% of farm operators working off-farm. Conversely, only one-quarter of intermediate and commercial farm households reported working any hours off-farm and, when they did so, these operators worked fewer hours per week at the median (28 and 27 hours, respectively).

The demands of a farm operation have significant implications for the labor structure of the household. The average on- and off-farm labor allocation of operators and spouses is listed in Table 6.2. On one extreme, dairy operations require the principal operator (or other farm worker) to milk cows multiple times a day and often restrict or eliminate the opportunity for off-farm work. In 2013, dairy operators worked an average of 68.9 hours per week on the farm, with the spouse contributing an additional 26.6 hours per week. Only 13% of dairy farm operators and 31% of spouses worked any hours off-farm throughout the course of the year. In contrast, beef cattle and general livestock operators may let their animals feed or graze unattended. Over half of beef cattle operators were employed off-farm in 2013, working more hours when they did. In the subset of farms where the operator or spouse worked off-farm, the households of dairy operators earned just $55,000 from off-farm labor, as compared to $115,000 for the households operating beef cattle farms.

Although commercial farm operators worked off-farm less than residence farm operators, they earned more a higher wage for their efforts. Delving into the off-farm occupations of farm operators can help explain why. A modern

Table 6.2 Operator and spouse hours (on- and off-farm), 2013

	Operator (on-farm)	Spouse (on-farm)	Operator (off-farm)	Spouse (off-farm)
Dairy	38.8	12.0	14.3	17.8
Rice, tobacco, cotton, peanuts	44.8	10.4	9.8	14.3
Cash grain	17.3	8.3	17.8	15.3
Hogs	27.5	13.7	15.9	14.9
Poultry	24.2	10.0	19.8	16.9
High value crops	33.2	10.8	24.8	20.9
Beef cattle	32.1	17.3	15.2	15.2
General livestock	68.9	26.6	3.3	10.6
Other field crops	22.1	12.9	20.1	18.5

Source: Agricultural Resource Management Survey, 2013.

farm operation is typically a complex and multifaceted business requiring skills in supervision, purchasing, sales, and marketing, in addition to managing the farm operation. Farm operators, therefore, often have skills applicable to other types of endeavors. The 2010 ARMS collected information on the type of occupation farmers pursue in off-farm employment. It found that over third of farm operators and spouses worked in management and professional occupations. As compared with all nonmetropolitan area workers, farm households were more likely to work in management or services and less likely to work in sales or office support. The highest percentage of operators working in management and professional operations were those either with a college degree or those operating large farms (Brown and Weber, 2013)

Farm household wealth

Two major trends have shaped in the increase in farm household wealth over the past two decades: an increase in the income of farm households (described above) and the large-scale rise in farmland value over that period. A large portion of the total value of farm and nonfarm assets of farm households is captured in real estate holdings. The primary dwelling of roughly half of all residence households and two-thirds of all intermediate and commercial households is owned by the farm operation. About 80% of total farm assets and almost one-third of nonfarm assets are in real estate (including both land and structures). Since 1970, the value of farmland real estate—this major source of wealth for farm households has grown from an inflation-adjusted value of roughly $850 dollars per acre to over $2,700 per acre in 2014.

In 2014, the average U.S. households had a median wealth of $82,500, while the average farm household had a median wealth of $873,000, over ten times that amount. The majority of large farm operations hold farmland or other real estate, and even smaller farms own much of their equipment. As with farm income, the wealth of farm households varies depending on type of farm. Because they produce less, the median residence farm households own fewer farm assets ($328,000) than non-farm assets ($410,000). Conversely, intermediate farms own slightly more farm assets ($572,000) than nonfarm assets ($362,000), and commercial farm households, with over $350,000 in *annual* gross cash farm income, hold over four-fifths of their assets in their farm operation ($2.5 million) with the rest in nonfarm assets ($447,000).

This considerable wealth has accumulated steadily over the last two decades. Concomitant with the increase in farmland real estate, average household net worth increased by over 50% since 2004. Across all farm households, total household net worth—farm and nonfarm assets less farm and nonfarm debt—totaled nearly $900,000 in 2004. It has grown steadily, at an average rate of 5% per year, to $1.47 million in 2014. Nonfarm assets have grown at a much faster rate. Between 2004 and 2014,[7] the median farm household saw their nonfarm assets more than double, to just over $400,000 in 2014, while farm assets increased just over $20,000 to $440,000. For residence farms this disparity has been more striking. Median nonfarm assets for residence farms were $158,000 in 2004. This has grown to $410,000 in 2014. Across that time period, farm assets have remained roughly constant. Commercial farms have seen a similar trend in their nonfarm assets, but farm assets have increased by nearly a million dollars from $1.6 million in 2004 to $2.5 million in 2014.

Conclusion

Since the Agricultural Adjustment Act of 1933, support programs have been created to raise the level of farm income, reduce price and income risks, and close the gap between farm and nonfarm incomes. These programs have changed significantly over time, moving from distortionary policies intended to control supply and support prices, to policies based around decoupled payments and risk management (i.e. crop insurance). The wellbeing of farm households and their sources of income have also changed dramatically. In the 1930s, most farm households relied on the farm business as their primary source of income and were significantly poorer than the average nonfarm household. In contrast, today most farm households are dependent on off-farm sources of income and have considerably higher levels of net worth and total household income than nonfarm households.

The 2014 Farm Bill ushered in a new regime in farm support programs: rather than giving individual operators direct payments, farmers are eligible for subsidized insurance programs or transitional payments to ease the shift from subsidized commodity production. In addition to having a more stabilizing effect on income generation, these payments are less distortionary and more likely to be in line with WTO obligations (Glauber and Westhoff, 2015). The effect of these farm programs, however, must be considered in the context of the current production environment, where an increasing percentage of production is taking place on fewer, larger farms while many farm households pursue off-farm activities as the main source of their income.

The twin goals of government programs are increasingly land conservation (of idle or working lands) and the stabilization of farm revenues. Smaller farms operated by households with significant off-farm income often participate in the former. Households earning the majority of their income from the farming benefit more from the latter, and their operations should benefit from the fact that that many new programs will pay out when the farm economy as a whole is doing poorly. While these programs will not entirely offset the recent declines in net farm income they are likely to contribute to better welfare of affected households.

Notes

1 For example, the CCC can provide interim financing at harvest time for farmers by offering them a marketing assistance loan for covered commodities. In return the farmer must pledge his commodity as collateral, but can return the loan amount plus interest if the commodity price rises above the loan rate. He is then free to sell his commodity on the open market.
2 We note that although the FCIC is administered by the Risk Management Agency, crop insurance is sold and serviced through private insurance companies. The operating costs for these companies and the insurance premiums for farmers are subsidized by the government.
3 All comparisons of income and wealth used in this chapter have been adjusted to 2014 dollars using the GDP price deflator, available from the St. Louis Federal Reserve. <<Provide Reserve's website URL?>>Farms were classified as residence, intermediate, or commercial according to whether their gross cash farm income was above or below $350,000 in 2014 dollars.
4 This study used an analysis of farm households which were surveyed two times between 1996 and 2013. Although the sample is not representative of the overall farm population, it is statistically similar to a random sample of commercial farm households.
5 The certainty equivalent is certain amount a household would be equally happy receiving, as compared to the risky income source. In this study, a relative risk-averse coefficient of 2.0 was used, corresponding with a "moderately" risk-averse household.
6 Across all farms in 2013, about 12% of farm households reported a female as the operator. However, women operators were disproportionately concentrated in residence and intermediate farms. In commercial farms, only 3% of farms had a female operator.
7 In 2004, ARMS began disaggregated collection of off-farm household assets and debt, allowing a more accurate comparison to 2014 values.

References

Brown, Jason and Jeremy G. Weber. The off-farm occupations of U.S. farm operators and their spouses. U.S. Department of Agriculture, Economic Research Service. EIB-117. 2013. Available online at: https://www.ers.usda.gov/publications/pub-details/?pubid=43792.

Bureau of Economic Analysis (BEA), Gross-Domestic-Product-(GDP)-by-Industry Data. 2015. Available online at: http://www.bea.gov/industry/gdpbyind_data.htm

Dimitri, Carolyn, Anne B. W. Effland, and Neilson C. Conklin. The 20th century transformation of U.S. agriculture and farm policy. Vol. 3. Washington, DC, USA: U.S. Department of Agriculture, Economic Research Service, 2005.

Effland, Anne B. W. "U.S. farm policy: The first 200 years." *Agricultural Outlook* 269 (2000): 21–25.

Gardner, Bruce L. *American agriculture in the twentieth century: How it flourished and what it cost.* Harvard University Press, 2002.

Glauber, Joseph W. and Patrick Westhoff. "The 2014 Farm Bill and the WTO." *American Journal of Agricultural Economics* (2015) 97 (5):1287–1297.

Hoppe, Robert A. and James M. MacDonald. Updating the ERS Farm Typology. U.S. Department of Agriculture, Economic Research Service, 2013.

Key, Nigel, Daniel Prager, and Christopher Burns. Farm household income volatility: an analysis using panel data from a national survey, Economic Research Report No. 226. Economic Research Service. February 2017.

MacDonald, James M., Robert A. Hoppe, and Penni Korb. Farm size and the organization of U.S. crop farming. U.S. Department of Agriculture, Economic Research Service, 2013.

Mishra, Ashok K., Hisham S. El-Osta, Mitchell J. Morehart, James D. Johnson, and Jeffrey W. Hopkins. Income, wealth, and the economic well-being of farm households. Washington, DC, USA: U.S. Department of Agriculture, Economic Research Service, AER No. 812, 2002.

NASS (National Agricultural Statistics Service), USDA Census of Agricultural 1930. U.S. Department of Agriculture, 1930. Available online at: http://agcensus.mannlib.cornell.edu/AgCensus/censusParts.do?year=1930).

Wang, Sun Ling, Paul Heisey, David Schimmelpfennig, and Eldon Ball. Agricultural productivity growth in the United States: Measurement, trends, and drivers. Economic Research Report No. 89. Economic Research Service, 2015. Available online at: https://www.ers.usda.gov/publications/pub-details/?pubid=45390

Chapter 7

Part-time farms in Canada

Changing concepts and changing policy

David Freshwater and Simon Jette-Nantel

Introduction

In virtually all OECD member countries off-farm, earned income exceeds net farm income for most farm households (Jones, Moreddu and Kumagai, 2009). This phenomenon is true for most farms in all size classes, except the very largest farms in terms of sales. But even for these farms off-farm income is often a non-trivial share of household income. In Canada, as Bollman notes, part-time farming has a long history, going back to the early French settlements of the 16th century (Bollman, 1982). From this long-run perspective the idea of the "full-time family farm," where the household allocates the vast majority of its labor to the farm enterprise, is a historical aberration, even though it has been the basis of Canadian agricultural policy during the last 80 years.

In a general sense the decision to become a part-time farmer can be seen as reflecting four broad forces. The first is the underlying technology of agriculture that determines how much labor is required to produce some quantity of specific farm commodities and what level of investment in land and machinery is required to be technically efficient in doing so. The second is the opportunity cost of being a full-time farmer that is driven by the number of available off-farm opportunities and the relative income each opportunity offers. The third reflects the aspirations of the farm household in terms of their lifestyle and how the members, including the operator, want to jointly allocate their labor. Finally, government policy can play some role in facilitating or impeding part-time status by how support programs for agriculture are structured, including differences in eligibility and levels of support for full- and part-time operators.

The definition of a part-time farm is imprecise. In the majority of the literature it reflects the allocation of a significant amount of the primary operator's working time to some other form of employment beyond the home farm. The essence of the concept is that farm labor and off-farm labor are substitute activities. An operator engaging in off-farm work recognizes opportunity costs that are not relevant for the full-time farmer. To a lesser extent off-farm work by other members of the operator's household is also considered to constitute off-farm activity, but this is typically seen as a less central issue. For the balance of the chapter, unless otherwise noted, the focus will be on the labor allocation decision of the primary operator.

Part-time farm operators in Canada

Alasia and Bollman (2009) identified two key trends in Canadian agriculture several years ago. The first was that the number of farm operators has declined over time – a 16% fall between 1991 and 2006 – and the second was the share of farms with a part-time operator has increased over time, a 9% increase over the same interval (2009, p. 1). More recently, between 2006 and 2011 the number of farm operators fell another 10%, but the share of part-time operators also declined from 48.4% to 46.9%, suggesting that the growth in the share of operator off-farm employment may have stopped. Perhaps this reversal is only an aberration, reflecting the Great Recession of 2008–2010 – a period of time when conditions in farming were favorable while conditions in the rest of the economy that offer the opportunities for off-farm employment were poor. Or, it may suggest that the structure of agriculture has reached some sort of equilibrium, with just under half of all farms having part-time operators.

Typically, an important factor in discussions of Canadian agriculture is a recognition of the dual structure of farming between eastern and western Canada (Drummond, Anderson and Kerr, 1962; Fowke, 1946; Schmitz, Furtan and Bayliss, 2002). Opportunities and incentives vary considerably between the east and west regions. In eastern Canada, composed of Ontario, Quebec and the Atlantic provinces, the structure of agriculture is different than it is in western Canada, which is primarily the three Prairie Provinces of Manitoba, Saskatchewan and Alberta. As a result, Canada has long had a two-part agricultural policy that protects smaller farms in the east, which mainly serve a domestic market, and a more export-focused agricultural policy in the west.

Farm settlement took place earlier in the east and was based mainly on small farms due to topography, technology and pre-Confederation land allocation mechanisms. The climate and topography allowed a wide range of crops to be produced, as well as most livestock species. Population density was relatively high, and over time rural settlements diversified beyond being only farm market towns and added manufacturing, first powered by water and then electricity. Local and within province markets absorbed a large share of production. These conditions facilitated both opportunities for off-farm income, and created incentives, due to the preponderance of small farms (Lattimer, 1927). By contrast, western Canada was settled as a central element of a national development strategy of encouraging immigrants to homestead relatively large farms to populate a large and somewhat homogeneous western territory (Fowke, 1946). Climatic conditions restricted the range of crops, and the local rural settlement structure was typically determined by the maximum distances farmers could transport grain to elevators. Most rural communities did not develop beyond a role as agricultural service centers. International commodity markets have always been the primary destination for most production. Consequently, the combination of large and relatively isolated farms and limited nearby opportunities for off-farm employment historically resulted in fewer part-time farmers.

Agricultural policy in Canada is further complicated by the sharing of responsibility between the federal government in Ottawa and the provinces. Ontario and Quebec have both been large enough with diversified economies to engage in constructing their own supplemental policies for agriculture. Also, since agriculture in these provinces is mainly oriented to internal markets, there has been less concern with international competitiveness. More recently, Alberta has also introduced supplemental policies as its revenues from oil production provided more provincial funds. However, beef and grains and oilseed production dominate Alberta agriculture, and, as these are export-oriented commodities, support has been more complex.

Part-time farming has been a part of this conflict, especially when it is seen as reducing farm productivity and international competitiveness, especially in western Canada. But it has also been a central issue in struggles in some provinces, especially Quebec, to preserve both full-time family farms and keep farm incomes high enough to discourage off-farm work (OECD, 2010). Table 7.1 shows the evolution of farm operator numbers and the role of part-time farming for operators between 1991 and 2011 for Canada and for the five provinces where agriculture is most significant, both in terms of land use and value of output. In all cases the trends identified by Alasia and Bollman are clear, but there is significant variability among the provinces, reflecting a different distribution of commodities, differences in policy and differences in off-farm employment opportunities.

Table 7.1 Farm operators Canada and selected provinces: total number and those with off-farm employment, census years 1991–2011

		1991	1996	2001	2006	2011
Canada	Total	390,870	385,605	346,200	327,060	293,925
	Work off-farm	145,005	176,215	154,225	158,260	137,740
	Percent	37.1%	45.7%	44.5%	48.4%	46.9%
Quebec	Total	53,355	53,155	47,385	45,470	43,920
	Work off-farm	13,875	17,115	14,390	15,125	15,640
	Percent	26.0%	32.2%	30.4%	33.3%	35.6%
Ontario	Total	100,910	96,935	85,015	82,410	74,840
	Work off-farm	40,605	45,805	38,655	40,860	35,770
	Percent	40.2%	47.3%	45.5%	49.6%	47.8%

(continued)

Table 7.1 Farm operators Canada and selected provinces: total number and those with off-farm employment, census years 1991–2011 *(continued)*

		1991	*1996*	*2001*	*2006*	*2011*
Manitoba	Total	34,780	33,255	28,800	26,625	22,315
	Work off-farm	12,280	14,940	13,165	12,695	10,305
	Percent	35.3%	44.9%	45.7%	47.7%	46.2%
Saskatchewan	Total	78,025	72,930	66,275	59,185	49,475
	Work off-farm	27,465	32,190	28,745	28,595	22,830
	Percent	35.2%	44.1%	43.4%	48.3%	46.1%
Alberta	Total	81,420	82,455	76,195	71,660	62,050
	Work off-farm	32,665	41,005	37,475	39,105	32,245
	Percent	40.1%	49.7%	49.2%	54.6%	52.0%

Two obvious outliers are Quebec and Alberta. Between 1961 and 2011 the share of operators with off-farm activity increased the most in Alberta, and remains the least in Quebec. In Alberta the combination of oil fueled growth that increased the availability of off-farm income and the high share of beef production, typically the most common enterprise for small farms, created a 12% increase in the share of farm operators working off the farm between 1991 and 2011. In Quebec a combination of a high proportion of farms being dairy enterprises and strong support to maintain medium-size full-time family farms by the provincial government kept the share of off-farm employment about 12% below the level in Ontario in 2011. Other than Quebec, off-farm operator employment grew, the least in Ontario, by about 7% (but this is from the highest initial share in 1991). In Manitoba and Saskatchewan the share of operators with off-farm labor increased by about 11%, slightly more than the national growth rate of 10%.

Clearly the simple idea of a dual structure is no longer useful for understanding part-time farming in Canada. Farms in the west remain: larger, more exposed to international competition, and their operators have fewer opportunities for nearby off-farm jobs than is the case in central Canada. Yet, by 2011 three of the five selected provinces have similar shares of operators with off-farm labor, and the two outliers,

Alberta and Quebec, have levels of off farm activity that are inconsistent with the core hypothesis of the Canadian dual structure of agriculture model.

Figures 7.1 and 7.2 reproduce results from Jette-Nantel, Freshwater, Beaulieu and Katchova (2011) for various farm sales classes[1] (see Table 7.2 for sales class definitions). Figure 7.1 shows that about 60% of all operators in the data set had off-farm employment income, and that as farm sales increase the percentage of operators with off-farm income declines, from about 87% for hobby/pension farms to about 40% for very large commercial farms. Results for incorporated farms can be considered an anomaly because corporations typically pay operators a salary. Strikingly, average off-farm income is higher for operators of very large commercial farms than is the case for large, and for small and medium, commercial farms. Average operator off-farm income is highest for hobby/pension farms at about $53,000, but is second highest for very large commercial farms at about $19,000, which is close to the average for all farms.

Figure 7.2 provides information on the distribution of the share of off-farm income in total operator net income within each sales class by reporting median income and income at the 75th and 90th percentiles for each class. These high percentile results provide a sense of upper bounds for the role of off-farm income across different sales classes. For these high-percentile operators, farming may well be an ancillary endeavor, but the farm can be large. For all farms the median share

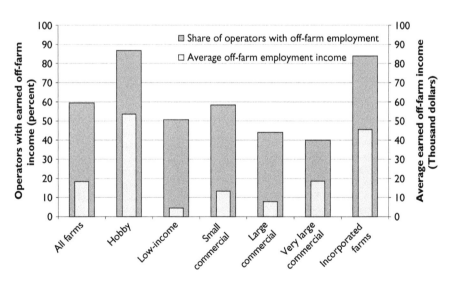

Figure 7.1 Share of operators with off-farm income and average off-farm income, by farm typology, Canada, 2001–2006 averages

Source: Statistics Canada, Whole farm database.

Table 7.2 Statistics Canada farm typology

Non-commercial

Hobby/pension	Includes all farms which earned on average less than $50,000 in annual farm market revenues, and more than $50,000 in annual total off-farm income, while maintaining an average total operator income[1] above $25,000.
Low-income	Includes farms which earned on average less than $25,000 in total income annually, and generated less than $50,000 in annual farm market revenues.

Commercial[2]

Small	Farms with average farm market revenues of less than $100,000/yr
Large	Farms with average farm market revenues between $100,000/yr and $500,000/yr
Very large	Farms with average farm market revenues of more than $500,000/yr

[1]Total operator income includes off-farm income from all sources and net farm income, including program payments.

[2]Small and medium farms are classified as commercial only if they are excluded from non-commercial categories.

Note: All criteria are evaluated based on the 2001 to 2006 averages.

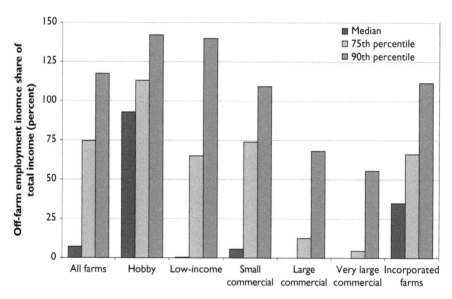

Figure 7.2 Off-farm employment income as a share of total income, by farm typology, Canada, 2001–2006 averages

Source: Statistics Canada, Whole farm database.

of operator off-farm earned income is less than 10%, and the median value is essentially 0% for large and very large commercial farms, where the majority of farm operators do not have earned off-farm income, and for those that do, average earnings are low relative to net farm income. For small commercial farms the median share of earned off-farm income is slightly less than the median for all farms. For hobby/pension farms the median share is about 90% of all income.

For the one in four farms in the 75th percentile in each class, off-farm earned income can be important. For hobby/pension farms it is about 115% of all operator income, due to negative net farm income, while for small and medium commercial farms it is about 75% of total operator income. For large and very large commercial farms the share of income from off-farm employment is less than 10% in the 75th percentile. For the 90th percentile – the one in ten farms in the category with the highest off-farm earnings – we see that off-farm earned income exceeds 50% of total operator income in all categories, and in farms smaller than large commercial it exceeds 100% of total income, which requires that these farms mostly have negative net farm income over the 2001–2006 interval.

More generally, research on off-farm income in Canada largely finds the same results as in other developed countries. As already noted, operators are more likely to engage in off-farm employment if they operate a small farm; engage in the production of commodities that are more compatible with off-farm work, for example cow-calf but not dairy; have higher levels of education; are younger; have less experience farming and have a working spouse (Alasia et al., 2009; Alasia and Bollman, 2009; Bollman, 1979; Bollman, 1982; Howard and Swidinsky, 2000; Shaw, 1979; Swidinsky, Howard and Weersink, 1998).

Over time the degree of sophistication in the analysis has increased from simple descriptive statistics of national averages based on data from a single point in time to econometric models based on richer data sets, including linked micro data files. These allow a richer set of questions to be asked, particularly, how do patterns of off-farm labor vary by geography? Recall that the dual structure of agriculture is at its heart a geographic phenomenon, reflecting both differences in agronomic conditions and how geography shapes, settlement patterns, transportation networks and industrial location decisions. On this basis, one might expect, a priori, a difference between the rate of off-farm employment between central Canada and the Prairies. However, Figure 7.1 shows this is now not the case.

Both Alasia et al. and Jette-Nantel et al. examine geographic patterns of the intensity of off-farm operator employment at a sub-provincial level. In both cases the initial hypothesis is that proximity to larger local labor markets should increase the rate of off-farm employment. One might expect a greater availability of jobs, but there is a greater likelihood that people with a primary occupation outside agriculture might decide to start a part-time farm, and that higher land values in close proximity to an urban agglomeration might limit the size of farms and necessitate off-farm employment.

Alasia et al. conclude the opposite effect is found – farm operators more distant from a large urban agglomeration are more likely to work off-farm than are similar operators close to the urban center (p. 25) – while Jette-Nantel et al. find the hypothesized effect. The two studies use different data sets: 2001 Census of Agriculture for Alasia et al. and the Longitudinal Tax-Filer Data Base from 2001 to 2006 for Jette-Nantel et al. Alasia et al. use all farms, while Jette-Nantel et al. eliminate farms with less than $10,000 in sales. However, for their analysis of the effect of distance Alasia et al. restrict the data to include only farms with less than $250,000 in sales. Econometric models differ, with Alasia et al. using a one-stage probit model and Jette Nantel et al. using a two-stage approach with a first-stage probit model and second-stage OLS regression. However, both studies use a similar geography based on Statistics Canada classifications. Clearly, this is more than a bit disconcerting, because there would seem to be strong theoretical support for the null hypothesis, but at the same time the analysis of Alasia et al. also seems sound.

Theories of part-time farming

In North America the conceptual literature on part time farming goes back at least to the 1930s (Salter and Diehl, 1940), and theories about the motivation for seeking off-farm income have evolved through time. At least five distinct theories now exist. The first and oldest is that off-farm income is a transition mechanism, for beginning farmers to achieve full-time status and for older full-time farmers to transition to retirement. The second model, commonly used by agricultural economists, sees off-farm income as providing an opportunity for supplemental income to the farm household. The main difference from the transition model is that part-time status is no longer a temporary phenomenon, but reflects a decision by the operator to spread labor across multiple activities. The third approach is parallel to the supplemental income model in that it too sees off-farm income as a long-term action, but it employs a different rationale. This approach is common in the rural sociology literature and can be characterized as a necessity decision. It focuses on the growing inequality among farms, where a small number of large farms control an increasing share of land, production and income (Buttel, 1982). All operators are assumed to desire to be full-time farmers, but the majority of farmers have enterprises that are too small to achieve this status and are forced to seek off-farm employment to meet family and farm income requirements. A fourth perspective can be thought of as a rural development approach. Here off-farm employment is a mechanism that links farming to the rest of the rural economy. Part-time farming is seen as part of the evolution of rural regions from a dependence on agriculture to a more diversified economic structure. The idea of multiple job-holding is central to this approach, as it is a way for individuals and households to combine a number of seasonal or part-time occupations into the equivalent of a full-time job. The final theory sees part-time farming as a risk management strategy. It differs from the second model in that the main rationale is not supplemental income per se, but risk reduction. It rests upon the existence of a weak positive to weak negative correlation between agricultural returns and other sources of income that leads to a blend of farm and off-farm income, reducing total income variability.

As the share of farm operators engaged in off-farm employment has increased through time, the range of motivations for their decision has increased. And, at the same time, underlying conditions in production agriculture have changed as have the nature of government policies. The result is a far more complex set of behaviors that complicate both the structure of agriculture and the effectiveness of agricultural policy.

Off-farm income as a transition mechanism

While part-time farming has always been a part of Canadian agriculture, especially in Atlantic Canada, it was not seen as contributing to progress in farming until quite recently. In the post–World War II era, Canadian agricultural policy focused on increasing efficiency through mechanization and scientific farming, and on encouraging farm consolidation. The objective was to reduce farm numbers and increase output, which was consistent with the rapid decline in farm numbers between 1950 and the mid 1970s. In this context larger specialized farms that fully employed all the time of the operator and a significant portion of time of the household were seen as desirable. While small, diversified farms remained numerous, there was an expectation that they would steadily shrink in number and that production would be dominated by commercial, full-time enterprises. Policy at the time was designed to support full-time farms through a mix of commodity-based programs that implicitly favored larger farms, and export promotion programs, including transport subsidies. In 1970 Crown and Heady published a book that argued for the end of commodity programs in Canada and their replacement with direct income support. However, the authors envisioned a two-part program, a part that that would stabilize income for commercial farms and a second part that would encourage sub-commercial-scale farmers to exit the sector through a series of transition payments (p. 109).

A logical consequence of this philosophy was that part-time farming became to be seen as a transition mechanism, either for entrants who wanted to achieve full-time status or for older farmers who wanted a phased transition to retirement. There was little sense that part-time status was either viable or desirable as a long-run behavior. At the time the Canadian Federation of Agriculture, the largest farm organization in Canada, held as a policy plank that only full-time farmers should receive access to government programs. Bollman (1979) provided the basic model for the process, and it became a common element in subsequent studies of farm entry and exit (Cavazzani and Fuller, 1982; Kimhi, 2000; Sumner, 1982).

More recently, the idea that all farmers want to be full time has become less tenable, as off-farm income has come to dominate the income of the majority of farm households and the share of small farms in total farm numbers has not decreased. This does not mean that operator part-time farming is not a transition mechanism, but it does suggest that additional rationales are required.

Off-farm income as an opportunity to supplement farm income

In the agricultural economics profession for some time the leading perspective on the role of off-farm labor has been that it serves as a supplement to farm income. All but the very largest farms in Canada and the United States now generate the majority of their household income from off-farm sources. These include income farm operator labor, family labor and investment income. For many farms the share of operator labor allocated to on-farm work is less than for off-farm work (Kimhi and Bollman, 1999). Further, while the traditional perspective on operator labor is that it results in employee wages, a significant share of farm operators in Canada and other countries also have supplemental business income from a non-farm enterprise. In some cases these are farm-related businesses, including repair shops, agrotourism enterprises or food processing, but in other cases they can be unrelated enterprises, such as a restaurant, a construction company or a law firm (Carter, 1998; Alsos, Ljunggren and Pettersen, 2003).

One consequence of the increased specialization of farming is the possibility to reap economies of scale (Veeman and Gray, 2009). When farms produced multiple commodities, the fragmented labor demands limited the scope for taking advantage of scale possibilities. Specialization is the standard explanation for the increase in average farm size. However, specialization has benefits for small farms in that it reduces the required labor commitment to the farm by the operator, and this opens the possibility for off-farm employment. As the incidence of off-farm employment has increased for small and larger farms, the difference between them is typically not whether the operator has off-farm earnings but the degree of time commitment to each kind of employment.

Technological change and farms producing a smaller number of commodities have resulted in surplus labor, at least in parts of the year. This, combined with the broadening of the rural economy to create more numerous and a greater variety of opportunities for off-farm work, has contributed to more farms having off-farm income. Even in regions where large volumes of agricultural production are produced, such as the US Midwest or Southern Ontario, agriculture is only a small share of regional GDP and farms of all sizes have considerable amounts of off-farm income.

As a result, instead of small farms disappearing in Canada, as was projected by Crown and Heady in the 1970s, they have actually increased as a share of all farms. For the smallest farms (sales less than $50,000), the motive for farming is unlikely to be maximizing net farm income. Many of these farms generate less than $10,000 in sales, and most report negative net farm income in any year. Instead, the function of the farm is to provide a lifestyle and a tax shield. This of course implies the existence of an alternative source of household income, including from the operator. But even for intermediate-size farms, with sales between $50,000 and $250,000, net farm income alone is unlikely to result in a standard of living that corresponds to the median household income in Canada, so supplemental earnings are required.

Off-farm income as a necessity

The literature in rural sociology on off-farm employment is extensive, but it largely follows a different path in explaining its function. Rural sociologists have largely adopted a Marxist perspective on agricultural change in the 20th century (Lobao and Meyer, 2001). Ideas initiated by Fuguitt in 1959 underpin much of the work. His article argues that part-time farming results from both a push – an inability to earn enough on the farm – and a pull: greater opportunities for income and job satisfaction from off-farm activity. But instead of off-farm employment being mainly seen as an opportunity to expand income, the rural sociology literature sees it as the consequence of being unable to operate a large-enough enterprise to be a full time farmer. The result is a form of class struggle between wealthy capitalist large farms and a disadvantaged class of small-farm operators who are forced to seek wage labor to survive. Because these farmers are in a weak bargaining position in the wage economy, they typically find only low-wage employment, which leads to a persistent poverty trap.

This second category of farmers is seen as being particularly disadvantaged by the industrialization of agriculture and the "technology treadmill" that requires continuous investment to remain profitable. Because they lack the resources to adapt to market pressures, they are faced with either giving up their farm or taking on supplemental off-farm work to maintain their existence as farmers. The analysis has been elaborated to identify differences between farm operators with better formal education, better farm income and better social status who engage in off-farm employment because of pull factors and less-educated, limited resource farmers who are pushed into off-farm employment by low farm incomes (Buttel, 1982). Geography also plays a role in this process as farmers closer to urban areas, for example in southern Ontario, are considered to have more opportunities than those in more remote and less densely settled areas, for example the Prairie provinces.

It is this idea of off-farm work as a necessity and a diversion from the goal of full-time farming (Cavazzani and Fuller, 1982) that differentiates the sociological approach from the opportunity approach favored by agricultural economists. The approach takes as a given that farm owners' objectives are to be a full-time farmers. In the United States this literature tends to reference the idea of the "Jeffersonian yeoman farmer" who is seen as a foundation element of American democracy. In Canada the virtue of a full-time farming has roots in the National Policy of the late 19th and early 20th centuries where families were encouraged to homestead the western territory. More recently, the literature in Canada follows the form of a class struggle between capitalists, who act to concentrate farm resources in their hands, and a proletariat, made up of quasi-peasant small land-holders (Freidman, 1978; McMichael, 2009).

In its most modern form the sociological analysis of part-time farming is an integral part of the World Food System critique that opposes global trade agreements, the increasing influence of multinational corporations on agriculture, and the loss of traditional agricultural systems (van der Ploeg, 2006). In contrast, the idea of local food and sustainable agriculture based on small family farms is promoted as being more environmentally and socially desirable and better connecting farming to a broader rural society (Marsden, 2006; Sundkvist, Milestad and Jansson, 2005; Lamine, 2015).

Off-farm income as a bridge between agriculture and rural development

A fourth perspective on part-time farming comes from the literature that connects agricultural policy to rural development policy in the OECD countries (OECD, 2006; Pezzini, 2001). The idea has two parts. First, in Canada, as in other OECD countries, post–World War II farm households still made up the majority of the rural population and had a lower standard of living than the urban population. In this context, support for agricultural development by governments would implicitly support rural development, since farmers dominated the rural population. As late as 1979 in Canada, rural development policy was still conceived in terms of programs to address marginal farm families (McMillan and Winter, 1979). But, even by then, farmers had become a small share of the rural population, and many farm households were already more dependent on off-farm income than farm income. Hence, the second part. With these changes the quality of life of rural people in OECD countries, including farm households, largely now hinged on the ability to improve the quality of non-farm employment opportunities. While rural development policy had in the past been synonymous with agricultural policy, this was no longer the case (Freshwater, 1997).

As farm numbers began to decline, the average size of farms increased and farmers became less reliant on local businesses for inputs and other purchases. The initial concern was that this would lead to decline in rural communities (Lobao and Meyer, 2001). From this perspective, rural communities had existed largely to serve as market towns for surrounding farms. And, in those regions where farming dominated the local economy, consolidation did lead to decline. In much of western Canada and the United States, small towns shrank and some disappeared (Stabler and Olfert, 1994; Debertin and Goetz, 1996). However, in regions where farming was only a relatively small part of the local economy, the impact of farm consolidation on the region was smaller. And, in some of these regions growth in nonfarm firms led to increased opportunities for part-time farming that reduced the pressure for farm consolidation.

Off-farm income as a risk management strategy

Unlike the idea that off-farm income provides a way to supplement the level of farm operator or household income, the focus of this theory is off-farm income as a way to reduce variability in income. For a risk-averse individual, the decision to engage in off-farm employment may be beneficial, even if the new level of income is lower on average than could be achieved by full-time faming. This would be true if the perceived benefit from the reduction in total income variability from diversifying income sources was large enough to offset the loss of farm income. Consequently, this theory moves beyond the idea of the traditional "farm problem" with its focus on low incomes and suggests that even farmers who earn an adequate but variable income from their farm enterprise may wish to consider allocating some labor to non-farm employment.

The logic parallels the shift in focus of agricultural policy in North America, first by Canada in the 1980s, and then by the USA with the 2014 Farm Bill, to insurance-based programs as the primary form of support for farmers. The logic of these programs is that farm income is highly variable, and this leads to lower investment by risk-averse farmers than is socially desirable and hence to higher food costs for consumers. Provision of public insurance can shift this risk and improve social welfare. However, were this the case, farmers would be happy to purchase insurance at an actuarially fair price or perhaps with a modest subsidy. But farm insurance programs in both Canada and the United States, and in other countries, require large premium subsidies before farmers buy them (*Economist*, 2015).

This behavior suggests that either farmers are not risk averse, which seems unlikely, or the perceived value of the insurance programs is not high enough to justify paying an actuarially fair price. Two explanations for the latter perspective can be identified. The first is that most farm households have already found a way to manage variability in farm income by engaging in off-farm employment, which is only weakly correlated with the variability in farm income. This makes government-provided insurance redundant and only valuable if it is subsidized to the point that it becomes mostly an income-transfer mechanism. The second explanation is that, at least in the case of Canada, lags in receiving reimbursement when a loss occurs are both long enough and unpredictable enough that much of the insurance benefit is lost (Kimura and Anton, 2011).

Evidence of the latter situation comes from Kimura and Anton (2011) and Uzea, Poon, Sparling and Weersink (2013). Both papers employ simulation models to assess whether Canada's farm revenue insurance program – AgriStability – actually provides a strong insurance function. Payments from the program can take up to two years to arrive after the loss occurs (OECD, 2009). In both instances the models, calibrated using farm data for Saskatchewan (Kumura and Anton, 2011) and farm data from Ontario (Uzea et al., 2013), suggest that farmers receive income enhancement benefits from AgriStability but little benefit in the form of risk mitigation, largely due to payment lags. By contrast, crop insurance in Canada has detectable risk mitigation effects because payments are received in a timely manner (Kimura and Anton, p. 7; Uzea et al., p. 9).

Canadian farm policy and part-time farming

In this section, the evolution of Canadian farm policy is reviewed with a focus on how changing conditions in agriculture and in agricultural policy influenced the formation of part-time farms. The intent is to show that a simultaneous or endogenous relationship exists among underlying conditions in farming (technologies and market opportunities), the structure of agriculture (labor allocation of operators, farm size distribution and commodity mix) and farm policy (support mechanisms). Each of the three shapes the others and is in turn shaped by them. Part-time farming exists in part because conditions in agriculture allow it, or perhaps require it, to exist, and because policy has either supported its existence or has not effectively discouraged it. In turn, the existence of part-time farms influences how agriculture and farm policy evolve. Figure 7.3 provides a timeline that links the evolution of Canadian farm policy to the evolution of the five theories of why part-time farms exist.

As noted earlier, part-time farming existed in Canada before Confederation in 1867, so it precedes Canadian farm policy (Fowke, 1946). It may well have been more common than full-time farming in the early colonial period, when agriculture was not a major factor in local economies. In the period before Confederation, farming was an incidental activity compared to the fur trade, timber harvesting and fishing, all of which were major activities that provided materials to the parent countries (Innis, 1956a). Farming played a role in ensuring the security of settlements by providing a supplemental food supply, but there was little encouragement of settlers to take up farming.

Shortly after Confederation in 1867, the Canadian government introduced the National Policy to build strong east-west ties and bring the western territory into the country. A major part of this policy was the settlement of the Prairies through land grants and support for immigrants who would take up farming. This policy continued through the 1920s, although it largely was complete by the beginning of the First World War (Stewart, 1955). Virtually all these farms fully occupied all available family labor as they brought native prairie into grain production. As the west was settled the grain economy became a major source of national income and exports (Innis, 1956b). While part-time farms continued to exist, especially in eastern Canada, they accounted for declining share of production and an even smaller share of exports.

The Great Depression led to a fundamental reshaping of agricultural policy away from expansion to support for farmers experiencing a financial crisis, and in western Canada natural disaster in the form of drought. At this point in time the national government assumed virtually full responsibility for agriculture with the acquiescence of the provinces. Policies to support commodity prices, relocate farmers from the most damaged areas and introduce new conservation practices continued until the start of the Second World War in 1939, when the agriculture sector recovered (Drummond, Anderson and Kerr, 1966). Strong export demand continued after the war and full-time Canadian farmers, particularly in the west, were encouraged to increase production by mechanizing, specializing and expanding in size.

Only as the rate of farm exit slowed and it became apparent that small farms were not going to disappear did the idea of part-time farming become an issue. At first, it was seen as a barrier to consolidation and progress and as a source of inefficiency. While this perspective never completely disappeared, the idea of off-farm income as a transition mechanism became more common, reflecting the increased cost of becoming a young farmer (van Vliet, 1967).

Farming Environment	Full-Time/Part-Time Status
Colonial Era	**1600s**
Focus on export of fish, fur and timber	Farming largely part-time activity
Farming largely supplemental source of food	
Majority of population in Atlantic provinces	**1760s**
Increased settlement in Upper Canada	Farming more likely to be main
More focus on expanding agriculture to supply growing towns and for export to USA	occupation
Confederation	**1867**
National Policy becomes effective with growth in manufacturing in central provinces and new settlers in Western territory	**1890s**
Expansion of agricultural production-growth in wheat exports	In central provinces possibility to be a full time or part-time farm, in Western territory focus is on full-time family farms
Beginning of dual structure of agriculture east focus is on domestic market, west on export market	
Great Depression	**1930s**
Farm numbers and population peak in 1931	Full time farms in Western Canada
Farm economy collapses	hit especially hard
Federal government introduces support for agriculture	
Provinces allow more federal intervention	
Post WWII	**1950s**
Initial growth in farm exports	Focus on full-time farmer
Support for farm consolidation, mechanization and specialization	expectation that small farms will largely disappear
Period of weakening farm income	Part-time farming as a transition strategy
Growing questions about viability of Canadian agriculture	
Increasing provincial support for farming in larger, richer provinces	**1960s**
Modern Era	**1970s**
Slowing of farm exits and recognition that small farms are not disappearing	Part-time farming as income supplement either out of necessity
Growing international conflicts over support for agriculture	or as an opportunity
New focus on balanced growth and regional development, including rural areas	Expansion of part time farming beyond only small farms
Efforts to end farming in most marginal territory	**1980s**
	Part-time farming as part of a multiple job holding strategy driven by off-farm
Increasing number of bilateral and multilateral trade agreements	employment on small farms
	Steady growth in number of part-time operators
Trade disputes with US become common	
Recognition that small farms have strong household income	**1990s**
New focus for agricultural policy risk management	Increasing recognition that part-time farming is a risk management strategy that can compete with, or complement, government insurance
High degree of farm income volatility	
Frequent change in risk management mechanisms	**present**
Farmers require high levels of premium subsidy to participate in programs	Majority of farms part-time but majority of production from full-time farms

Figure 7.3 Timeline of Canadian agriculture and theories of part-time farming

When economic conditions deteriorated in the 1960s, the focus remained on full-time farms and on ways to support their income. However, at this time it became clear that part-time farming was a growing phenomenon that could not be explained solely as a transition mechanism. As the share of farm income coming from small farms steadily declined, the parallel ideas of opportunity and necessity emerged as a way to explain the persistence of this growing share of farms. At the same time, many rural regions were experiencing economic diversification that led to farming being only one part of their economy. At the same time, other rural regions, many of which depended on marginal agriculture, experienced chronic poverty that was not alleviated by traditional farm policy. The result was the recognition that a broader rural development approach was needed both to stimulate economic growth in rural regions and to alleviate poverty.

The last stage in the process came with the shift in Canadian agricultural policy to a whole-farm risk-management approach in the 1980s. Multiple factors drove this shift, but the role of off-farm income was not part of the deliberation. Once again, support programs assumed that farm income was by far the dominant source of farm household income, and that income stabilization could only be achieved by some form of insurance program. Although farm diversification could also provide greater stability, the shift to specialization as a way to increase productivity had gone so far that a return to farms with a large number of enterprises was not seen as feasible. Off-farm employment was not considered at all.

Conclusion

Since the 1980s the Canadian government, along with several provinces, have gone through multiple iterations of income stabilization programs (OECD, 2009). Over time, the cost share paid by farmers has declined, while the share of farm operators engaged in off-farm employment has increased. If the "farm problem" is now defined as income volatility, both stabilization programs and off-farm income can reduce volatility, but the latter approach is not consistent with longstanding belief in Canada that full-time farms are the best mechanism for improving productivity and exports. This belief has led policy makers to ignore the role of improved off-farm income and part-time farming as ways to improve farm income. Certainly the share of operators of large farms with off-farm employment is smaller than for small farms, but about 40% of operators of very large farms report off-farm earned income, and the average amount is not inconsequential.

Further, even with the existing suite of income stabilization programs there is a fairly high incidence of negative net farm income across all farm size classes in Canada. Recent AAFC analysis suggests that between 2003 and 2012 18% of farms with sales in excess of $1 million had negative net farm income in 5 or more years of the 10-year period (AAFC, 2014). Similarly, 29% of farms in the $100,000 to $249,999 sales class had 5 or more years of negative net farm income. Arguably, farms in these categories are supposed to be the best protected by stabilization programs, and might be expected to follow profit-maximizing behavior. But given these shares of farms with persistent negative net farm income, we suggest that perhaps off-farm employment can play a useful role in stabilizing total farm operator and household incomes.

Finally, it is important to recognize that there are multiple motives for allocating operator labor to off-farm employment. The five theories co-exist, and for some farms several of them may be relevant. Agriculture is part of broader social and economic forces that are reshaping both work and how families organize themselves. While opportunity costs remain an important means for understanding the allocation of labor between farm and off-farm work time, there can be other factors, including not only risk management, but also social and personal benefits from being in a different environment.

Note

1 These results come from tax-filer data that consist of farm operator tax records for farms that were in existence in both 2006 and 2001, and had gross farm revenue of $10,000 or more in 2006. The data set has a significantly smaller number of operators than is reported in the 2006 Census because it excludes farms that commenced operation between 2001 and 2006, as well as excluding the large group of small farms with revenue less than $10,000.

References

AAFC (Agriculture and Agri-Food Canada) (2014) *Farm income, financial conditions and government assistance data book.* AAFC: Ottawa.

Alasia, A. and Bollman, R. (2009) Off-farm work by farmers: *The implications of rural labor markets.* Catalogue no. 21-006-X, Statistics Canada: Rural and Small Town Canada Analysis Bulletin 8:1.

Alasia, A., Weersink, A., Bollman, R. and Cranfield, J. (2009) Off-farm labour decision of Canadian farm operators: Urbanization effects and rural labour market linkages. *Journal of Rural Studies* 25:1 pp. 12–24.

Alsos, G. A., Ljunnggren, E. and Pettersen, L.T. (2003) Farm-based entrepreneurs: What triggers the start-up of new business activities? *Journal of Small Business and Enterprise Development* 10:4 pp. 435–443.

Bollman, R. (1979) Off-farm work by farmers: An application of the kinked demand curve for labour. *Canadian Journal of Agricultural Economics.* 27:1 pp. 37–60.

Bollman, R. (1982) Part time farming in Canada: Issues and non-issues. *GeoJournal* 6:4 pp. 313–322.

Buttel, F. (1982) The political economy of part-time farming. *GeoJournal* 6:4 pp. 293–300.

Carter, S. (1998) Portfolio entrepreneurship in the farm sector: indigenous growth in rural areas. *Entrepreneurship and Regional Development* 10:1 pp. 17–32.

Cavazzani, A. and Fuller, A. M. (1982) International perspectives on part-time farming: A review. *GeoJournal* 6:4 pp. 283–389.

Crown, R. H. and Heady, E. O. (1970) *Policy integration in Canadian agriculture.* Iowa State University Press, Ames: Iowa.

Debertin, D. and Goetz, S. (1996) Rural population decline in the 1980s: impacts farm structure and federal farm programs. *American Journal of Agricultural Economics* 78:3 pp. 517–529.

Drummond, W. M., W. J. Anderson and T. C. Kerr (1966) *A Review of Agricultural Policy in Canada.* Agricultural Economics Research Council of Canada: Ottawa.

Economist, The. (2015) Milking taxpayers. *The Economist*, Feb 14, 2015.

Fowke, V, (1946) *Canadian agricultural policy: The historical pattern.* University of Toronto Press. Toronto: Ontario.

Freshwater, D. (1997) Farm production policy versus rural life policy. *American Journal of Agricultural Economics* 79:5 pp. 1515–1524.

Friedman, H. (1978) World markets, state and family farm: Social bases of household production an era of wage labor. *Comparative Studies in Social History* 20:4 pp. 545–586i.

Fuguitt, G. (1959) Part-time farming and the push-pull hypothesis. *American Journal of Sociology* 64:4 pp. 375–379.

Howard, W. and Swidinsky, M. (2000) Estimating the off-farm labor supply in Canada. *Canadian Journal of Agricultural Economics* 48:1 pp. 1–14.

Innis, Harold (1956a) Changing structure of the Canadian market, in Innes, M. (ed.) *Essays in Canadian economic history*, University of Toronto Press: Toronto.

Innis, Harold (1956b) The wheat economy, in Innes, M. (ed.) *Essays in Canadian Economic history*, University of Toronto Press: Toronto.

Jette-Nantel, S. Freshwater, D., Beaulieu, M. and Katchova, A. (2011) Farm income variability and off-farm diversification in Canadian agriculture. *Agri-Finance Review* 71:3 pp. 329–346.

Jones, D., Moreddu, C. and Kumagai, T. (2009) *The role of agriculture and farm household diversification in the rural economy: evidence and initial policy implications.* OECD Publishing: Paris.

Kimhi, A. (2000) Is part-time farming really a step in the way out of agriculture? *American Journal of Agricultural Economics* 82: 1 pp. 38–48.

Kimhi, A. and Bollman, R. D. (1999) Family farm dynamics in Canada and Israel: the case of farm exits. *Agricultural Economics* 21:1 pp. 69–79.

Kumura, S. and Anton, J. (2011) Farm income stabilization and risk management: some lessons from Agristability program in Canada. Paper presented at the 2011 European Association of Agricultural Economists Congress, Zurich Switzerland. Available Dec. 11, 2016 http://ageconsearch.umn.edu/bitstream/114755/2/Kimura_Shingo_387.pdf

Lamine, C. (2015) Agrifood systems: Reconnecting agriculture food and the environment. *Sociologia Ruralis* 55:1 pp. 41–61.

Lattimer, J. E. (1927) Canadian farming since Confederation. *Journal of Farm Economics* 9:3 pp. 361–367.

Lobao, L. and Meyer, K. (2001) The great agricultural transition: Crisis change and social consequences of twentieth century US farming. *Annual Review of Sociology* 27 pp. 103–124.

Marsden, T. (2006) The road towards sustainable rural development: Issues of theory policy and practice in a European context, in Cloke, P., Marsden, T. and Mooney, P. (eds.) *Handbook of Rural Studies.* Sage Publications: London pp. 201–212.

McMichael, P (2009) A food regime genealogy. *Journal of Peasant Studies* 36:1 pp. 139–169.

McMillan, J. A. and Winter, G. R. (1979) Income improvement versus efficiency in Canadian rural development programs. Paper presented at the 17th conference of the International Association of Agricultural Economists, Banff, Alberta. Available Dec. 11, 2016 https://ideas.repec.org/p/ags/iaae79/182399.html

OECD (2006) *Coherence of agricultural and rural development policies.* OECD Publishing: Paris.

OECD (2009) *Managing risk in agriculture: a holistic approach.* OECD Publishing: Paris.

OECD (2010) *OECD Rural Policy Review: Quebec, Canada.* OECD Publishing: Paris

Pezzini, M. (2001) Rural policy lessons from OECD countries. *International Regional Science Review* 24:1 pp. 134–145.

Salter, L. A., and Diehl, L. D. (1940) Part-time farming research. *Journal of Farm Economics* 22:3 pp. 581–600.

Schmitz, A., Furtan, H. and Baylis, K. (2002) *Agricultural policy, agribusiness and rent-seeking behaviour.* University of Toronto Press. Toronto: Ontario.

Shaw, P. (1979) Canadian farm and non-farm family incomes. *American Journal of Agricultural Economics.* 61:4 pp. 676–682.

Stabler, J. and Olfert R. (1994) Saskatchewan's rural communities in an urbanizing world. *Rural Development Perspectives* 9:2 pp. 21–28.

Stewart, A. (1955) Changes in the relative position of agriculture in the Canadian economy and the resulting policy implications. *Canadian Journal of Agricultural Economics* 3:2 pp. 1–14.

Sumner, D. (1982) The off-farm labor supply of farmers. *American Journal of Agricultural Economics* 64:3 pp. 499–509.

Sundkvist, A., Milestad R. and Jansson, A. M. (2005) On the importance of tightening feedback loops for sustainable development of food systems. *Food Policy* 30:2 pp. 224–239.

Swidinsky, M., Howard, W. and Weersink, A. (1998) Off-farm work by Canadian farm operators: An overview of structure and mobility patterns. Working Paper # 38, Agriculture Division, Statistics Canada. Catalogue no. 21-601-MIE98038.

Uzea, N., Poon, K., Sparling, D. and Weersink, A. (2014) Farm support payments and risk balancing: implications for financial riskiness of Canadian farms. *Canadian Journal of Agricultural Economics* 62:4 pp. 595–618.

van der Ploeg, J. D. (2006) Agricultural production in crisis, in Cloke, P., Marsden, T. and Mooney, P. (eds.) *Handbook of rural studies*. Sage Publications: London pp. 258–277.

van Vliet, H. (1967) Canadian approaches to rural poverty. *Journal of Farm Economics* 49:5 pp. 1209–1224.

Veeman, T. and Gray, R. (2009) Agricultural production and productivity in Canada. *Choices* 24:4. Available December 11, 2016: http://www.choicesmagazine.org/magazine/article.php?article=92

Chapter 8

Farm household incomes in OECD member countries over the last 30 years of public support

Bruno Henry de Frahan, Jérémie Dong, and Rembert De Blander

Farm household incomes in OECD member countries over the last 30 years of public support

At a time when policy makers in many developed countries still continue to justify farm support on the basis of relatively low and unstable farm incomes, this chapter examines first to what extent incomes of farm households are performing on average compared with those of non-farm households in several Organisation for Economic Co-operation and Development (OECD) member countries over the last 30 years. It then compares income distribution and poverty between the farm and non-farm communities. Among the three broad areas of concern with respect to agricultural policy (Hill, 1996), this chapter concentrates on the so-called parity issue (farmers are rewarded comparably with otherwise occupied individuals) and on the poverty issue (low-income prevalence is greater among farm families).[1] Because of the lack of appropriate panel dataset, it leaves aside the no less important instability issue (do farmers face more severe temporal income variations). This chapter starts to briefly review the farm problem in the next section and then proceeds to the parity and poverty analysis in the following sections.

The farm income problem in the literature

Low and unstable farm income has continuously been used to rationalise public support to farming in many developed countries. For instance, in the United States (U.S.), large-scale interventions to control farm supplies and increase farm prices began with the Agricultural Adjustment Act of 1933 in an attempt to raise the level of farm income and close the income gap between farm and non-farm households (Gardner, 1992; El-Osta *et al.*, 2007). Such government interventions subsequently took a permanent twist with the Agricultural Act of 1949. Today, the budget of the U.S. 2014 Farm Bill for the so-called farm safety net that contains the commodities and crop insurance titles aiming at shielding farmers against sharp fluctuations in commodity prices as well as crop failures and prices decline is planned at US$134.2 billion for the budgetary period, or about US$13.4 billion per year. This is a sum that corresponds to 14 per cent of the total outlays of the 2014 Farm Bill, but 68 per cent of the outlays without the food stamps and nutrition programmes.

In the European Union (EU), one of the five objectives of the Common Agricultural Policy (CAP) in the 1957 Treaty of Rome (Article 39) establishing the European Economic Community (EEC), subsequently repeated in the 2010 Consolidated Version of the Treaty on the Functioning of the EU is "to ensure a fair standard of living for the agricultural community, in particular by the increasing of the individual earnings of persons engaged in agriculture". This specific objective has been carried forward into subsequent European legislation. In this context, the budget of the 2014–20 CAP financial framework is divided into two pillars, of which the first is mainly dedicated to support farm incomes and limit their variability.[2] It is planned at €317.2 billion for the budgetary period, or about €45 billion per year, a sum that corresponds to 76 per cent of the combined budget of the two pillars of the CAP.

Likewise, OECD's (2004, p. 1) policy brief clearly summarises the (apparent) issues: "Improving the income situation of farm households remains a prominent objective of agricultural policies in many OECD countries". Whereas additional concerns came to the attention of policy makers in the last 20 years such as environmental protection, food safety and quality, animal welfare and rural economy viability, government programmes in the name of supporting and stabilising farm income still consume large sums of public money.

Despite the above justifications, evidence accumulated during the 1970s and 1980s (Gardner, 1992) dismisses the prevalence of low average incomes among farmers in the U.S. since the second half of the 1960s.[3] Thereafter, using data from the Agricultural Resource Management Survey (ARMS) of the USDA and the Survey of the Consumer Finances (SCF), Mishra et al. (2002) not only confirm that average incomes are similar for farm and non-farm households but also show that average wealth for farm households exceeds that of non-farm households in the U.S. for 1999. Using the same data, Katchova (2008) estimates that average household incomes are not significantly different when they are compared between commercial farms (those with sales greater than US$250,000) and non-farm entrepreneurs as well as between intermediate farms (those with sales lower than US$250,000) and wage-earning non-farm households in the U.S. for 2004. Similarly, using here the Integrated Public Use Microdata Series, Peake and Marshall (2009) find no significant differences between household income levels of farm and non-farm entrepreneurs in the U.S. for 2005. In terms of self-employment income, however, they show that the farm self-employed have a significant higher level of income than the non-farm self-employed.

In Canada, results from the tax-filer database reported in Hill (2012) suggest that farm households with gross farm revenues greater than Cdn$10,000 have on average an income similar to the all-households income average since the early 1970s. Results from the Farm Financial Survey database indicate that average household incomes of farmers with gross farm revenues greater than Cdn$10,000 come at or close to the all-households income average in 2001 for most of the provinces except Manitoba (Hill, 2012).

In Australia, results from a 3-year survey from 1989/90 to 1991/91 reported in Hill (2012) show that farm households have on average an income that is 89 per cent of the average household income. Results from the survey of Income and Housing Costs also reported in Hill (2012) indicate that farm households have, on average, an income that is about 90 per cent of the average income of households having no member employed in agriculture in 2011.

Less empirical evidence is available for other developed countries. Scattered national statistics collected by the Statistics Office of the European Communities (EUROSTAT, 2002) between 1972 and 1999 suggest that farm households have on average an income close to or higher than other households in most of the 15 EU member states. According to Hill (Agra CEAS, 2007), "the fragmentary evidence that is available [at the EU level] suggests that, far from being a disadvantaged sector of society, EU farm households as a group have relatively high incomes compared to the rest of society" and are of even higher wealth. In addition, an OECD (2003, p. 3) study also confirms that, "in most OECD member countries, farm households enjoy, on average, income levels that are close to those in the rest of the society". In sum, these empirical results do not suggest that farm households, as a group, have low average incomes in most OECD member countries.

The above general income studies, however, make an abstraction of two key issues. First, sub-sectors involved in the production of "homogeneous, high volume, bulk commodities and a few major perishables and non-food products" might be particularly vulnerable (Bonnen and Schweikhardt, 1998, p. 5). In a related aspect, Hill (1999) also pinpoints that some types of farm activities which are relatively labour-demanding and exacting in timeliness, such as dairy farming, may impose constraints on farm households in complementing their income from off-farm sources even when their incomes from farming might be satisfactory. Second, would the disappearance of the farm income problem either in the U.S., the EU or other OECD member countries, still prevail in the absence of government intervention? Gardner (1992), for instance, questions estimates from past studies that have evaluated the effects of policies on farm income. He outlines the difficulties in correctly estimating the structural effect of farm programmes on income, particularly when these programmes have varied so much through time.

To what extent do income distribution and low-income incidence differ between the farm households and non-farm households? These are relevant research questions for gearing future policy. In that respect, Gardner (2000) reports that both income inequality and poverty continue to fall among U.S. farm families during the 1970–90 period to the point that the poverty rate for farm households falls below the poverty rate for non-farm households by 1990. In addition, Mishra et al. (2002) report that the income distribution is slightly more concentrated among farm households compared to non-farm households in 1997. Katchova (2008) shows that income inequalities are similar for farm and non-farm households but slightly higher for intermediate farms compared to wage-earning non-farm households and commercial farms compared to non-farm entrepreneurs in 2004 for the U.S.

The use of the Canadian tax-filer database shows that poverty incidence among farm families dramatically declined in the 1970s to stabilise just above 2 per cent of the overall poverty line in the mid-1980s (Hill, 2012). The analysis of the Canadian Longitudinal Administrative Databank indicates that a minority, 14 per cent of farm households, suffer chronic low incomes between 1998 and 2007 (Hill, 2012).

From various microeconomic studies from EU member states in the 1990s, Hill (2000) concludes that income disparities among farm households are wider than among households in general, implying that, with an adequate average income among farm households, a greater proportion of poor households might be found among farm households. Another OECD (2001) study concludes that income inequality and low-income incidence and intensity are greater among farm households than among other households in most of the 14 OECD member countries for which data are available from the mid-1980s to the mid-1990s. The same study warns that these findings may, however, be affected by underestimating farm household incomes because incomes in kind and asset values are not accounted for and incomes from self-employment, including from farming, may be under-reported in household income surveys.

Plausible causes of the prevalence of low farm incomes in the U.S. until the early 1960s have been proposed in the literature on the farm problem. A review of these causes by Gardner (1992) distinguishes three complementary frameworks of potential explanations. The first framework corresponds to the basic farm problem model that focuses on commodity market conditions. The second framework examines factor market conditions to explain an earning disequilibrium between the farm and non-farm sectors. The third framework considers the compensating differential for skill differences and non-pecuniary aspects of farming to explain low farm relative to non-farm earnings. To understand the growth in incomes of farm households relative to non-farm households that prevailed in the U.S. since the 1940s, Gardner (2002) focuses on adjustments in the labour market with increasing economic integration between the farm and the non-farm sectors, in particular migration off farms and non-farm sources of income for households remaining on farms. He finds that labour-market integration is by far the predominant factor in the improvement of economic condition of low-income farm households between 1960 and 1980 in the U.S., instead of specifically agricultural variables such as government payments, agricultural productivity growth or farm-size growth.

Bonnen and Schweikhardt (1998) further develop these first two explanatory frameworks, while adding an historical perspective to them. They also strongly argue that the fragmentation of the farm sector into many diverse sub-sectors, which have their own economic peculiarities and market structures, should be considered when addressing the whole question of the economic vulnerability of commercial farming. According to them, focusing on the farm sector aggregate supply function to explain the economic vulnerability of the farm sector as a whole has become obsolete. They recommend that any macroeconomic analysis of the performance of the farming sector require a consistent underlying microeconomic framework.

Assessing the extent of low farm income is fraught with many measurement and accounting difficulties (see Gardner, 1992). Low farm income has generally been evaluated by comparing the average income of farm households to the average income of non-farm households at the country level using a combination of individual farm account data, household income survey data and sector-level aggregated income data. When income comparisons do exist, for example, from USDA (2015), EUROSTAT (1999 and 2002) and OECD (1999 and 2003), they are sensitive to the sources of information, the methods of estimation, and the definitions of incomes and farm households versus non-farm households that are used. These difficulties may also explain why factors identified in the economic literature, for example in Gardner (1992), which may result in low farm incomes, have never been tested systematically across different years and countries using empirical data. The conclusion of the OECD (2003, p. 33) study acknowledges "the absence of adequate information on the income situation of farm households" for properly designing and implementing income policies that are still prominent in most OECD member countries.

This chapter therefore aims to fill this gap by using meaningful income comparisons between farm and non-farm households for ten developed countries over a period covering the last 30 years. The next section of this chapter compares the average income levels of farm households to those of non-farm households by using the same harmonised database for years and countries for which data are available and applying consistently the same definitions of household categories across the ten selected countries over the 30-year period. The third section compares indicators of income distribution and poverty between farm households and non-farm households. The last section concludes with some general policy implications.

Comparisons of farm and non-farm household income levels

Both comparative and statistical analyses use the microeconomic database from the *Luxembourg Income Study* (LIS). This dataset contains socio-demographic, expenditure and income data that are collected at the household level through national household-based budget surveys. Using this microeconomic database that is harmonised across households, years and countries, has the great advantage that the same source of information for household incomes and characteristics is used to make comparisons across household categories, years and countries meaningful. Household data also allows the examination of the incidence and intensity of low income. From this database, we use the disposal household income net of taxes and subsidies to measure household income. This net disposable income of a household is then adjusted to account for its size and composition using an equivalence elasticity of 0.55 that corresponds to the power by which the needs of a household increase as the household size increases (see Förster, 1994). This measurement of personal incomes better reflects the standard of living of the farm community than the income of farm self-employment, since it includes all sources of income of the household, which is greatly relevant for most farm households. In addition, it also allows a comparison with the standard of living of households outside the farm community. This approach is advocated by Offutt (2002) and also implemented by the USDA.

In contrast, the European Commission prefers to calculate the reward of farming activities per work unit of family labour and compares it to the wages and salaries in the total economy per work unit of labour. This approach introduces two biases. First, it disregards any other incomes that can be nevertheless particularly important for the economic well-being of a majority of farm families. Second, it compares different sorts of rewards: rewards of farming activities that include some rewards to family-owned land and capital in addition to rewards to family's labour, on one hand, and rewards to employment labour only, on the other hand. The European Commission (2011, p. 8) defends its approach in a footnote of an annex on the basis that it

> focuses on farms and the agricultural sector as unit of analysis, not on agricul-
> tural households. The reason for this is that the objectives of the CAP are linked
> to the operation, competitiveness and performance of the sector/farm as an
> economic unit and not the economic survival of a household. ... Furthermore,
> there is little available data on incomes at the farm household level that could
> be used for analysis.

We nevertheless believe, as do others (Hill, 1996, 1999; OECD, 2003, 2004), that the European Commission uses an ambiguous approach to approximate the "standard of living for the agricultural community" and compare it to the non-agricultural community. Not collecting and analysing data on incomes at the farm household level neither is a sensible justification for a yearly budget of about €45 billion, dedicated to farm income support. The EU Court of Auditors has challenged the income assessment method of the European Commission and concluded that EUROSTAT does not have a satisfactory means to assess the CAP's objective of achieving a fair standard of living of the agricultural community (Court of Auditors, 2004).

In this chapter, the distinction between farm and non-farm households is made according to the source of the household's net disposable incomes. We follow the OECD (2001) 'narrow' definition of a farm household as that in which the household's farm self-employment income is equal or greater than half its factor incomes.[4] This OECD 'narrow' definition closely matches the EUROSTAT (1995) definition of an agricultural household as being one where more than half the income of the head of household comes from farming (Hill, 1995). We also follow the OECD (2001) counterpart definition of a non-farm household as that in which the household's farm self-employment income is lower than half its factor incomes.

We could use the OECD 'broad' definition of a farm household as that in which the household's farm self-employment income is not zero and the counterpart definition of a non-farm household as that in which the household's farm self-employment income is null. But, we decided not to use this OECD broad defini-tion in our main data analysis because we would have included farm households whose livelihoods do not mainly depend on farming.[5]

We could narrow down this category of non-farm households to those households whose non-farm self-employment income is greater than half their factor incomes to compare two categories of households whose self-employment activities contribute for at least half their factor incomes, so that compensation for business risk and return to business fixed assets are considered in both farm and non-farm household categories. We, however, do not use this definition of non-farm self-employed households because self-employment incomes tend to be under-reported unevenly across countries for income-tax reasons. Although farm self-employment incomes could also be under-reported, we prefer to rely on income composition to distinguish between farm and non-farm households because using instead the occupation or the industry of the reference person of the household also reported in the LIS database is more likely to raise problems in cross-country comparisons.

The use of income composition to distinguish between farm and non-farm households is likely to under-report farm households that have accidently low farm self-employment income compared with their other incomes, while their long-term livelihoods actually depend on farming. To assess the extent of this under-representation, one possibility is to measure correlations among different categories of households defined according to their income composition, occupation and industry. Another possibility is a sensitivity analysis on the threshold of the household's farm self-employment income with respect to its factor incomes defining whether the household is a farm or non-farm household.

From the LIS database, average incomes and indicators of low income and inequality are calculated for farm and non-farm households for OECD member countries that have at least 4 survey years of data in the database with a minimum of 40 farm households identified according to the OECD 'narrow' definition per survey wave to limit the risk that sampling errors affect the statistical results too much. Applying these selection criteria, 62 years of data survey covering ten OECD member countries are used for the comparisons of income levels.[6] Canada and the U.S. have the longest time series available, spanning from early 1970 to late 2000. Australia and Hungary have the shortest time series available from early 1990s to mid-2005. After the middle of 1990s, national household-based budget surveys from some European countries (for example, Germany, Italy, the Netherlands, Poland and the United Kingdom) have ceased to distinguish self-employment incomes obtained by farming from those generated by other activities.

Tables 8.1, 8.2 and 8.3 report the sample sizes of farm and non-farm households identified according to the OECD 'narrow' definition of a farm household as well as the mean and standard deviation of their total adjusted net disposable income by country and survey wave.[7] Larger sample sizes of farm households are found for Canada, Finland and the U.S. while smaller sample sizes are found for Australia, Italy and Luxembourg. The adjusted net disposable household incomes reported in the three Tables are deflated using the 2005 base Consumer Price Index from the OECD and converted into U.S. dollars using the Purchasing-Power Parity (PPP) exchange rate for household actual consumption from the OECD.[8]

Table 8.1 Sample size and real net disposable household income (US$/year) for Australia, Canada, and the United States

Country	Wave	Sample Size (%)			Real Net Disposable Household Income (US$/year)[a] Mean (standard deviation)		
		Farm hh[b]	Non-Farm hh[c]	All hh	Farm hh[b]	Non-Farm hh[c]	All hh
Australia	**1989**	239	14,211	14,450	22,503.33	19,957.17	19,999.28
		(0.95%)	(99.05%)	(100.00%)	(14,777.44)	(12,880.45)	(12,917.60)
	1995	82	6737	6819	13,061.07	18,502.08	18,436.65
		(0.95%)	(99.05%)	(100.00%)	(21,393.54)	(12,676.17)	(12,827.39)
	2001	83	6703	6786	13,807.23	20,536.94	20,454.63
		(0.95%)	(99.05%)	(100.00%)	(15,949.94)	(14,010.40)	(14,053.89)
	2003	97	10.113	10,210	17,213.54	20,605.57	20,573.34
		(0.95%)	(99.05%)	(100.00%)	(14,963.86)	(14,429.04)	(14,437.21)
	Total	501	37,764	38.265	16,646.29	19,900.44	19,865.98
		(0.95%)	(99.05%)	(100.00%)	(16,771.20)	(13,499.02)	(13,559.02)
Canada	**1971**	920	25,007	25,927	13,524.22	20,320.35	20,079.20
		(3.55%)	(96.45%)	(100.00%)	(12,510.88)	(14,114.59)	(14,116.70)
	1975	862	25,707	26,569	17,860.37	17,757.07	17,760.42
		(3.24%)	(96.76%)	(100.00%)	(16,165.74)	(10,755.88)	(10,972.91)
	1981	531	14,605	15,136	26,192.68	23,656.11	23,745.10
		(3.51%)	(96.49%)	(100.00%)	(23,281.41)	(13,940.84)	(14,378.00)
	1987	310	10,689	10,999	19,757.87	21,049.57	21,013.16
		(2.82%)	(97.18%)	(100.00%)	(14,241.01)	(11,959.58)	(12,030.95)

(continued)

Table 8.1 Sample size and real net disposable household income (US$/year) for Australia, Canada, and the United States (continued)

Country	Wave	Sample Size (%)			Real Net Disposable Household Income (US$/year)[a] Mean (standard deviation)		
		Farm hh[b]	Non-Farm hh[c]	All hh	Farm hh[b]	Non-Farm hh[c]	All hh
Canada	**1991**	384 (1.92%)	19,651 (98.08%)	20,035 (100.00%)	17,700.51 (13,504.92)	21,437.98 (12,332.51)	21,366.34 (12,366.28)
	1994	554 (1.48%)	36,921 (98.52%)	37,475 (100.00%)	19,086.68 (13,467.83)	22,676.35 (13,198.80)	22,623.28 (13,209.74)
	1997	544 (1.61%)	33,299 (98.39%)	33,843 (100.00%)	21,752.49 (18,823.41)	22,572.69 (14,535.71)	22,559.50 (14,614.59)
	1998	469 (1.50%)	30,749 (98.50%)	31,218 (100.00%)	16,973.27 (13,010.64)	23,702.99 (15,876.76)	23,601.89 (15,858.52)
	2000	413 (1.43%)	28,557 (98.57%)	28,970 (100.00%)	16,640.48 (12,687.80)	23,908.39 (16,234.33)	23,804.78 (16,211.96)
	2004	381 (1.37%)	27,439 (98.63%)	27,820 (100.00%)	20,878.66 (17,703.73)	25,912.48 (17,103.72)	25,843.54 (17,121.75)
	2007	279 (1.09%)	25,344 (98.91%)	25,623 (100.00%)	21,754.39 (16,282.23)	28,825.79 (23,022.59)	28,748.79 (22,971.35)
	Total	5647 (1.99%)	27,7968 (98.01%)	28,3615 (100.00%)	19,283.78 (15,699.36)	22,892.71 (15,389.19)	22,831.45 (15,437.75)

Real Net Disposable Household Income (US$/year)[a]

		Sample Size (%)			Mean (standard deviation)		
Country	Wave	Farm hh[b]	Non-Farm hh[c]	All hh	Farm hh[b]	Non-Farm hh[c]	All hh
United States	**1974**	604	10,871	11,475	29,218.18	23,924.92	24,203.54
		(5.26%)	(94.74%)	(100.00%)	(23,794.56)	(15,869.73)	(16,423.85)
	1979	231	14,130	14,361	22,778.66	24,327.87	24,302.95
		(1.61%)	(98.39%)	(100.00%)	(16,670.95)	(14,438.67)	(14,477.94)
	1986	97	11,517	11,614	16,795.45	26,355.05	26,275.21
		(0.84%)	(99.16%)	(100.00%)	(16,199.24)	(17,490.19)	(17,500.80)
	1991	429	58,609	59,038	20,065.74	26,030.19	25,986.84
		(0.73%)	(99.27%)	(100.00%)	(15,483.75)	(17,683.83)	(17,675.97)
	1994	366	56,507	56,873	21,759.81	26,958.99	26,925.54
		(0.64%)	(99.36%)	(100.00%)	(18,792.07)	(19,969.88)	(19,966.70)
	1997	280	50,040	50,320	23,739.48	29,232.10	29,201.54
		(0.56%)	(99.44%)	(100.00%)	(24,229.17)	(26,190.81)	(26,183.27)
	2000	240	49,393	49,633	40,204.04	30,429.12	30,476.38
		(0.48%)	(99.52%)	(100.00%)	(49,160.28)	(25,655.01)	(25,828.16)
	2004	373	76,074	76,447	31,217.20	30,696.72	30,699.26
		(0.49%)	(99.51%)	(100.00%)	(29,160.54)	(27,360.96)	(27,369.85)

(continued)

Table 8.1 Sample size and real net disposable household income (US$/year) for Australia, Canada, and the United States (continued)

| Country | Wave | Sample Size (%) | | | Real Net Disposable Household Income (US$/year)[a] | | |
| | | Farm hh[b] | Non-Farm hh[c] | All hh | Mean (standard deviation) | | |
					Farm hh[b]	Non-Farm hh[c]	All hh
United States	**2007**	333	75,539	75,872	33,810.24	31,613.55	31,623.19
		(0.44%)	(99.56%)	(100.00%)	(29,543.13)	(28,120.48)	(28,127.05)
	2010	308	74,880	75,188	38,512.24	30,254.67	30,288.49
		(0.41%)	(99.59%)	(100.00%)	(48,085.80)	(26,300.53)	(26,431.12)
	Total	3261	47,7560	48,0821	27,810.10	27,982.32	27,998.29
		(0.68%)	(99.32%)	(100.00%)	(27,111.95)	(21,908.01)	(21,998.47)

[a] Adjusted net disposable incomes deflated by the 2005 base Consumer Price Index from the OECD and converted into U.S. dollars by the Purchasing-Power Parity exchange rate for household actual consumption from the OECD.
[b] Farm household (hh) defined according to the 'narrow' definition (see p. 129).
[c] Non-farm household (hh) defined according to the 'narrow' definition of a farm household (see p. 129).

Source: LIS.

Table 8.2 Sample size and real net disposable household income (US$/year)[a] for France, Ireland, Italy, and Luxembourg

Country	Wave	Sample Size (%)			Real Net Disposable Household Income (US$/year)[a] Mean (standard deviation)		
		Farm hh[b]	Non-Farm hh[c]	All hh	Farm hh[b]	Non-Farm hh[c]	All hh
France	1978	1446 (13.78%)	9044 (86.22%)	10,490 (100.00%)	18,630.16 (18,408.86)	21,779.55 (18,262.83)	21,345.42 (18,314.36)
	1984	273 (2.36%)	11,302 (97.64%)	11,575 (100.00%)	8088.90 (4958.82)	14,715.70 (9418.92)	14,559.40 (9392.16)
	1989	260 (3.00%)	8418 (97.00%)	8678 (100.00%)	11,706.46 (7771.19)	15,691.86 (10,342.24)	15,572.45 (10,296.66)
	1994	203 (1.80%)	11,091 (98.20%)	11,294 (100.00%)	14,563.79 (9907.69)	18,534.83 (12,972.77)	18,463.45 (12,934.52)
	2005	474 (4.63%)	9766 (95.37%)	10,240 (100.00%)	15,125.48 (7944.68)	22,008.42 (13,785.76)	21,689.81 (13,647.59)
	Total	2656 (5.08%)	49,621 (94.92%)	52,277 (100.00%)	13,622.96 (9798.25)	18,546.07 (12,956.50)	18,326.11 (12,917.06)
Ireland	1987	395 (11.99%)	2899 (88.01%)	3294 (100.00%)	10,889.19 (13,279.94)	13,907.75 (9824.33)	13,545.78 (10,344.21)
	1994	336 (10.53%)	2856 (89.47%)	3192 (100.00%)	21,440.67 (18,027.84)	18,409.39 (26,770.79)	18,728.47 (26,003.79)
	1995	290 (10.25%)	2540 (89.75%)	2830 (100.00%)	23,398.75 (16,336.73)	18,740.93 (38,048.40)	19,218.23 (36,449.14)
	1996	259 (9.80%)	2383 (90.20%)	2642 (100.00%)	21,649.23 (12,767.23)	19,659.04 (51,390.56)	19,854.14 (48,972.08)

(continued)

Table 8.2 Sample size and real net disposable household income (US$/year) for France, Ireland, Italy, and Luxembourg (continued)

Country	Wave	Sample Size (%)			Real Net Disposable Household Income (US$/year)[a] Mean (standard deviation)		
		Farm hh[b]	Non-Farm hh[c]	All hh	Farm hh[b]	Non-Farm hh[c]	All hh
Ireland	**2004**	265 (4.36%)	5815 (95.64%)	6080 (100.00%)	17,734.50 (10,003.12)	21,559.92 (18,770.65)	21,393.19 (18,491.44)
	2007	261 (4.98%)	4980 (95.02%)	5241 (100.00%)	19,754.42 (12,031.99)	23,433.75 (18,876.64)	23,250.52 (18,611.90)
	2010	136 (3.15%)	4186 (96.85%)	4322 (100.00%)	20,217.6 (14,877.16)	22,953.73 (14,766.04)	22,867.63 (14,775.54)
	Total	1942 (7.04%)	25,659 (92.96%)	27,601 (100.00%)	16,234.81 (11,328.02)	17,179.30 (21,668.09)	17,161.36 (21,092.04)
Italy	**1987**	129 (1.61%)	7898 (98.39%)	8027 (100.00%)	21,003.35 (21,592.84)	22,778.55 (16,680.81)	22,750.02 (16,770.89)
	1989	132 (1.60%)	8142 (98.40%)	8274 (100.00%)	16,158.93 (9080.52)	21,081.15 (14,363.80)	21,002.63 (14,307.79)
	1991	118 (1.44%)	8070 (98.56%)	8188 (100.00%)	18,536.27 (10,629.44)	19,425.81 (12,322.72)	19,412.99 (12,299.87)
	1993	85 (1.05%)	8004 (98.95%)	8089 (100.00%)	15,301.4 (11,959.48)	17,917.47 (13,005.90)	17,889.98 (12,997.40)
	1995	91 (1.12%)	8044 (98.88%)	8135 (100.00%)	16,010.25 (22,787.25)	16,605.78 (12,331.75)	16,599.12 (12,494.80)

Country	Wave	Sample Size (%)			Real Net Disposable Household Income (US$/year)[a]		
					Mean (standard deviation)		
		Farm hh[b]	Non-Farm hh[c]	All hh	Farm hh[b]	Non-Farm hh[c]	All hh
Italy	Total	555	40,158	40,713	17,402.04	19,561.75	19,530.95
		(1.36%)	(98.64%)	(100.00%)	(15,209.91)	(13,741.00)	(13,774.15)
Luxembourg	1985	54	1958	2012	20,888.28	17,222.93	17,321.31
		(2.68%)	(97.32%)	(100.00%)	(11,663.28)	(7584.28)	(7740.34)
	1991	48	1909	1957	31,999.29	28,343.41	28,433.08
		(2.45%)	(97.55%)	(100.00%)	(18,454.36)	(14,742.06)	(14,849.18)
	1994	42	1771	1813	29,901.30	28,605.73	28,635.74
		(2.32%)	(97.68%)	(100.00%)	(10,008.33)	(13,632.10)	(13,558.43)
	2007	56	3697	3753	39,161.72	33,373.22	33,459.59
		(1.49%)	(98.51%)	(100.00%)	(27,280.78)	(28,445.50)	(28,433.64)
	2010	124	5340	5464	31,518.80	31,435.45	31,437.34
		(2.27%)	(97.73%)	(100.00%)	(32,639.51)	(19,376.17)	(19,771.21)
	Total	354	20,682	21,036	30,693.88	27,796.15	27,857.41
		(1.68%)	(98.32%)	(100.00%)	(20,009.25)	(16,756.02)	(16,870.56)

[a] Adjusted net disposable incomes deflated by the 2005 base Consumer Price Index from the OECD and converted into U.S. dollars by the Purchasing-Power Parity exchange rate for household actual consumption from the OECD.

[b] Farm household (hh) defined according to the 'narrow' definition (see p. 129).

[c] Non-farm household (hh) defined according to the 'narrow' definition of a farm household (see p. 129).

Source: LIS.

Table 8.3 Sample size and real net disposable household income (US$/year) for Finland, Hungary, and Norway

Country	Wave	Sample Size (%)			Real Net Disposable Household Income (US$/year)[a] Mean (standard deviation)		
		Farm hh[b]	Non-Farm hh[c]	All hh	Farm hh[b]	Non-Farm hh[c]	All hh
Finland	1991	843	10,906	11,749	14,091.41	16,859.95	16,661.31
		(7.18%)	(92.82%)	(100.00%)	(7370.44)	(7772.97)	(7777.37)
	1995	910	8352	9262	15,813.39	15,513.21	15,542.70
		(9.83%)	(90.17%)	(100.00%)	(8686.70)	(8438.53)	(8463.23)
	2000	1164	9259	10,423	19,855	20,432.39	20,367.91
		(11.17%)	(88.83%)	(100.00%)	(11,953.73)	(34,906.11)	(33,141.09)
	2004	867	10,362	11,229	21,968.39	22,042.49	22,036.77
		(7.72%)	(92.28%)	(100.00%)	(15,676.60)	(26,554.58)	(25,877.62)
	2007	382	10,090	10,472	24,150.36	25,234.10	25,194.57
		(3.65%)	(96.35%)	(100.00%)	(11,619.04)	(18,498.29)	(18,293.62)
	2010	284	9067	9351	23,579.22	25,375.45	25,320.89
		(3.04%)	(96.96%)	(100.00%)	(11,578.00)	(27,129.25)	(26,791.66)
	Total	4450	58,036	62,486	19,909.63	20,909.60	20,854.03
		(7.12%)	(92.88%)	(100.00%)	(11,147.42)	(20,549.96)	(20,057.43)
Hungary	1991	43	1976	2019	34,405.63	40,207.56	40,083.99
		(2.13%)	(97.87%)	(100.00%)	(14,023.52)	(26,744.54)	(26,548.53)
	1994	309	1629	1938	15,279.50	23,883.59	22,511.73
		(15.94%)	(84.06%)	(100.00%)	(7974.48)	(19,240.23)	(18,198.10)
	1999	491	1436	1927	7198.24	10,346.01	9543.95
		(25.48%)	(74.52%)	(100.00%)	(3475.03)	(6798.91)	(6276.58)

		Sample Size (%)			Real Net Disposable Household Income (US$/year)[a] Mean (standard deviation)		
Country	Wave	Farm hh[b]	Non-Farm hh[c]	All hh	Farm hh[b]	Non-Farm hh[c]	All hh
Hungary	**2005**	200	1835	2035	7003.54	9588.46	9334.42
		(9.83%)	(90.17%)	(100.00%)	(2557.01)	(7284.92)	(7005.99)
	Total	1043	6876	7919	15,971.73	21,006.41	20,368.52
		(13.17%)	(86.83%)	(100.00%)	(7007.51)	(15,017.15)	(14,507.30)
Norway	**1986**	145	4830	4975	34,954.72	20,778.94	21,192.11
		(1.64%)	(98.36%)	(100.00%)	(17,250.48)	(9071.62)	(9705.55)
	1991	640	7433	8073	22,331.59	22,712.74	22,682.52
		(1.64%)	(98.36%)	(100.00%)	(9127.71)	(13,063.04)	(12,795.29)
	1995	317	9810	10,127	22,308	24,145.42	24,087.9
		(1.64%)	(98.36%)	(100.00%)	(9407.93)	(18,974.41)	(18,751.58)
	2000	323	12,596	12,919	24,084.75	26,999.98	26,927.09
		(1.64%)	(98.36%)	(100.00%)	(11,584.17)	(31,825.41)	(31,481.48)
	2004	215	12,916	13,131	26,263.14	28,728.95	28,688.58
		(1.64%)	(98.36%)	(100.00%)	(16,121.94)	(88,360.17)	(87,658.47)
	Total	1640	47,585	49,225	25,988.44	24,673.21	24,715.64
		(1.64%)	(98.36%)	(100.00%)	(12,698.45)	(32,258.93)	(32,078.47)

[a] Adjusted net disposable incomes deflated by the 2005 base Consumer Price Index from the OECD and converted into U.S. dollars by the Purchasing-Power Parity exchange rate for household actual consumption from the OECD.

[b] Farm household (hh) defined according to the 'narrow' definition (see p. 129).

[c] Non-farm household (hh) defined according to the 'narrow' definition of a farm household (see p. 129).

Source: LIS.

Figures 8.1, 8.2 and 8.3 show the ratios of the average income of farm households, narrowly defined, to the average income of non-farm households for the selected countries and survey years with their approximate 95 per cent confidence intervals. For Australia, Canada and the U.S., average farm household income from 1971 to 2010 in Figure 8.1 fluctuates between 65 per cent and 132 per cent of the average non-farm household income, where the largest fluctuation is observed for the U.S. Among the 25 farm household income ratios, 12 are significantly lower than the parity level of 100 per cent. This is more the situation for Canada (7 over 11 income ratios) than for Australia (1 over 4 income ratios) and the U.S. (4 over 10 income ratios).

Among these 25 income ratios, four are significantly lower than 80 per cent of the parity level (1971, 1998, and 2000 for Canada, and 1986 for the U.S.). For Canada and Australia, after the fall in the farm household income ratio in the 1980s and the 1990s respectively, there follows a period during which the income ratio improves, reaching about 80 per cent of the parity level in the 2000s. For the U.S., fluctuations of the farm household income ratio in the 1970s and 1980s reflect the boom and the bust of farming during that period, dipping clearly during the mid-1980s farm crisis. The farm household income ratio has stayed above the parity level since 2000.

Compared to the series of farm household income ratios provided by the USDA (2015), this LIS-based series gives a parallel picture of the development of the farm household income ratio, despite using a broad definition of farm households for the former series and a narrow definition for the latter series.[9] We know that incomes from off-farm activities tend to stabilise and even raise the whole incomes of farm households (Mishra *et al.*, 2002). These new series of farm household income ratios nevertheless support the conclusion already reached in Gardner (1992) for the U.S., namely that farm household incomes (in these three countries) are not chronically low on average.

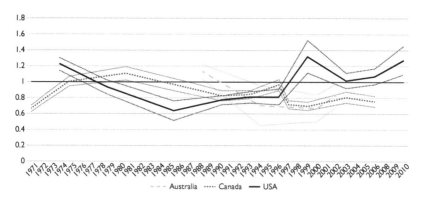

Figure 8.1 Mean ratio of the real net disposable farm household income to the real cash disposable non-farm household income with 95% confidence interval, AU, CA, US

Source: LIS.

For the seven European countries reported in this chapter, average farm household incomes from 1978 to 2010 in Figures 8.2 and 8.3 also fluctuate but to a lesser extent than for the three preceding non-European countries that tend to be more exposed to international markets. The largest fluctuations are observed for Norway, Ireland and France before the mid-1995 period. Among the 37 farm household income ratios, 16 are significantly lower than the parity level of 100 per cent. For France and Hungary, *all* reported income ratios are significantly lower than the parity ratio. To a lesser extent, unfavourable incomes also prevail in some years for Ireland (3 over 7 income ratios), Norway (2 over 5 income ratios), Finland (1 over 6 income ratios) and Italy (1 over 5 income ratios) but never for Luxembourg. Among these 37 income ratios, five farm household income ratios are significantly lower than 80 per cent of the parity level (1984 and 2005 for France, and 1994, 1999 and 2005 for Hungary). The income situation of farm households is therefore less favourable for France and Hungary than for the other five European countries. It is certainly not an unfavourable income situation for Finland, Luxembourg and Norway. The income situation for both Ireland and Hungary improved in the 2000s, but that improvement still needs to be confirmed with more recent observations, while the income situation for Italy is unsettled since the Italian time-series does not rely on many observations and stops in 1995. From the mid-1990s, there is a noticeable stabilisation of the incomes of the farm households with respect to non-farm households that might be attributable to the income stabilisation effect of the successive reforms of the CAP since 1992 that progressively switch the system of price interventions to a system of direct payments. It would be instructive to confirm whether this phenomenon also applies to Italy after 1995.

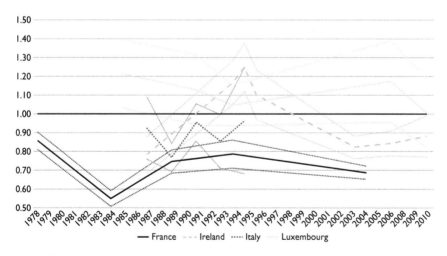

Figure 8.2 Mean ratio of the real net disposable farm household income to the real cash disposable non-farm household income with 95% confidence interval, FR, IR, IT, LU

Source: LIS.

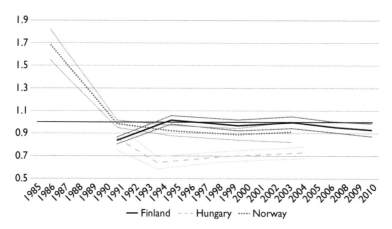

Figure 8.3 Mean ratio of the real net disposable farm household income to the real net disposable non-farm household income with 95% confidence interval, FI, HU, NO

Source: LIS.

Income studies reported in Hill (2012) tend to picture an income situation that is not as unfavourable for farm households in France, Italy and Ireland. The Institut National de la Statistique et des Etudes Economiques's (INSEE) study shows that the disposable income of French farm households per consumer unit is on average 3 per cent higher than the disposable income of all households in 1997 and 15 per cent lower in 2003. For Italy, the Salvioni and Colazilli (2005) study shows that the equivalent disposable income of Italian farm households is on average at or above the disposable income of all households between 1995 and 2002. For Ireland, the Central Statistics Office's (CSO's) study shows that the disposable income of Irish farm households is on average 5 per cent lower than the disposable income of all households in 2004. Of course, differences in the definition of a farm household, the measurement of disposable income and the sampling method may explain differences in those income comparisons. These updated series of farm household income ratios calculated from the LIS database and complemented with these three reported income studies confirm that farm household incomes for most of these seven European countries are not chronically low on average with, however, some reservation for France and Hungary.[10] It is therefore an empirical question to verify this conclusion for other European countries.[11]

Hypothetical explanations for the low income of farm households for some years or countries are several. It can be due to unfavourable commodity or factor market conditions. It can also result from an earning disequilibrium between the farm and non-farm labour markets that can be attributable to adjustment costs in labour movement in the short run, to skill and age differences, non-pecuniary preferences for farming or other non-comparabilities between farm and non-farm people in the long run, and also from problems in measuring incomes. But, in advanced, well-integrated economies like the OECD member countries, a more plausible source of explanations of income differences involves differences in income-earning capacity as a result of age, gender and skills of people, as well as the non-wages aspects related to the employment (Gardner, 1992).

In 1993 and 1999 for the U.S., Mishra *et al.* (2002) identify the stage at which farm operators are in their life cycle, i.e., their age, as the dominant factor influencing the level and sources of farm household incomes. They also identify farm type and size, operator education, farm tenure, and household size as other contributing factors. In 2001 for the U.S., El-Osta *et al.* (2007) confirm that the education level of the primary operator and farm tenure determine farm household prosperity. They also identify the education level of the spouse, ethnicity, location, succession plan, as well as contractual arrangements for purchasing inputs or selling products as other factors of household prosperity. In 2004 for the U.S., Katchova (2008) shows that a greater involvement with business activities is associated with higher economic well-being for farm households. Stages in the life cycle or demographic factors also impact the economic well-being of farm households in the study of Katchova (2008). For 2005, Peake and Marshall (2009) confirm the importance of several household and demographic factors for explaining the economic well-being of farm households, in particular the presence of a spouse and the education level of the household head. From reviewing several microeconomic studies, Hill (1999) assembles characteristics associated with the farm household income: the type and the size of farm, the extent of non-farm incomes, the age of the household head, and the peculiarity of the surveyed years. From those empirical studies, we can sum up that a combination of household (age, education, location) and farm (type, size, tenure, contracts) characteristics seems to explain so far the economic well-being of farm households in both the U.S. and Europe.

Our own preliminary analysis indeed shows a positive correlation between the farm household income ratios and the education level of the household head in the U.S. (0.78 for high level of education), Finland (0.67 and 0.49 for high and medium levels of education respectively), France (0.67 and 0.54 for high and medium levels of education respectively) and Italy (0.13 and 0.41 for high and medium levels of education), but not in Canada (−0.57 and −0.11 for high and medium levels of education) and Ireland (−0.25 and −0.09 for high and medium levels of education). It is inconclusive for the other four countries.

This accumulated evidence is a sign of a mature sector that is not anymore handicapped by a chronic low-income problem. Accordingly, objectives, instruments and expenses of agricultural policy in developed countries need to be revised in depth.

Comparisons of farm and non-farm household income distributions

The distribution of farm household incomes is now measured and compared to the distribution of non-farm household incomes using the narrow definitions of farm and non-farm households. Three indicators of income distribution are calculated for each household category, survey year and country: the Gini income distribution index, the low-income rate and the low-income gap. As in the OECD (2001) report, the low-income threshold is defined relatively as 50 per cent of the yearly median income of all households in the sample for each country and year. This relative approach also facilitates cross-country comparisons. The two poverty indicators are calculated from the same survey years that contain a minimum of 30 identified low-income farm households. The ratios of one particular indicator for farm households to the same indicator for non-farm households are then calculated and compared through the available observed period across countries. We, however, focus more on the income distribution index in reporting results.

The Gini index is defined in percentage as twice the area between the line of perfect equality and the Lorenz curve.[12] It is a measure of inequality of the income distribution. For Australia, Canada and the U.S., incomes are generally less equally distributed among farm households than non-farm households. From 1974 to 2010, there is, however, a discernible trend since 2004 for the U.S. towards similar income inequality among farm and non-farm households. This move into similar income distributions may reflect the increasing role of off-farm sources of income in determining the economic well-being of farm households for the U.S. (Mishra *et al.*, 2002).

In 2004, Katchova (2008) shows that income inequalities tend to rise with the involvement of the U.S. households, be it farm or non-farm households, in business activities. From rural residence farm households, through intermediate farm households, to commercial farm households, the Gini coefficient rises from 0.50 through 0.60 to 0.73. When these three Gini coefficients are compared to non-farm households without businesses (Gini of 0.48) and with businesses (Gini of 0.61), then the gap in income inequalities between farm and non-farm households closes down. These comparisons suggest that income inequalities of farm households should be compared to non-farm households that are also involved in self-employment income-generating activities, rather than to all non-farm households, as done in this chapter.

For European countries, the picture is more complex in terms of inequality. Finland and Italy have on average Gini indices that are about 20 per cent superior among farm households than among non-farm households. France and Ireland have on average Gini ratios that are less than 10 per cent superior among farm households than among non-farm households. These farm versus non-farm households Gini ratios tend to rise for Italy between the mid-1980s and the mid-1990s but to decline for Ireland between the mid-1980s and the mid-2000s. In contrast, Luxembourg and Norway have on average Gini indices that are similar among farm households and non-farm households. These farm versus non-farm households Gini ratios tend to decline for Luxembourg between the mid-1980s and the mid-1990s, and for Norway between the mid-1980s and the mid-2000s. For Hungary, Gini indices are on average lower among farm households than among non-farm households. In sum, except for these last three European countries, inequality in the income distribution is higher among farm households than among non-farm households.

From various microeconomic studies, Hill (1999) proposes different explanations to income inequality among farm households. First, he notices that lowest total incomes are not necessarily associated with the smallest farms, those that generate the smallest incomes from farming, but with larger farms that are too large to be operated on a part-time basis but too small to generate an adequate income from farming. Second, incomes from off-farm activities narrow down the income disparity that can be observed from farming only. Third, some types of labour-demanding farming, like dairying, are not conducive to take advantage of off-farm sources of incomes. Fourth, access to off-farm employment opportunities may be limited in some regions. Fifth, low total incomes in one year for some farm households may be just transitory. The transitory nature of some farm household incomes that results from year-specific farming conditions can indeed cause an overestimation of the disparity in total incomes among farm households, which could be avoided by using a panel dataset where available.

That the income distribution is moving towards a similar income inequality among both categories of households for Ireland, Luxembourg, Norway and the U.S. calls for a decomposition of income inequality by source of income to measure the contribution of the different sources of income to overall income inequality and determine which particular source contributes to income inequality (Adams, 1991). We hypothesise here that incomes from farming contribute relatively more to income inequality among farm households. We also suspect that the distribution of increasing farm direct payments since 1993 in the European Union as a result of the CAP reforms contributes in aggravating income inequality among farm households because those payments are concentrated on some farm households (OECD, 2001). For example, the Gini index of those payments calculated by Henry de Frahan and De Blander (2010) is 0.50 for Belgium in 2006, implying that 50 per cent of those payments are concentrated on the 20 per cent of the farm households that benefit from the highest payments. The Gini index of those payments is even higher at the EU level than in Belgium: 0.74 in 2006, implying that 76 per cent of those payments are concentrated on 20 per cent of the farm households that benefit from the highest payments (European Commission, 2008).

We calculate the ratios of the low-income rate (LIR) for farm households narrowly defined to the LIR for non-farm households across years for nine out of the ten countries. The LIR measures the cumulative proportion of households within the population below the low-income reference. It is a measure of the incidence of low income. Except for some countries and years, the incidence of low income is in general much higher among farm households than non-farm households. The farm to non-farm LIR ratios, however, vary widely across countries and years, making it difficult to discern a pattern. For the U.S., the farm low-income rate is generally above the non-farm low-income rate since 1979, with the highest difference in 1986 in the aftermath of the mid-1980s farm financial crisis. Compared to the U.S., the farm low-income rate for Australia, Canada and most European countries is generally much higher than the non-farm low-income rate.[13] The INSEE study reported in Hill (2012) confirms that the poverty incidence is about the double among French farm households than among non-farm households in 1997 and 2003. Even when the average incomes of farm households are close to or higher than the average incomes of non-farm households, the incidence of low income tends to be higher among farm households than among non-farm households except for the U.S. in 1974, Ireland in 1994, 1995 and 1996 and Norway in 1986.

We also calculate the ratios of the low-income gap (LIG) for farm households narrowly defined to the LIG for non-farm households for the same nine countries. The LIG measures the difference between the average income of the low-income households and the low-income reference, as a percentage of that low-income reference. It is a measure of the intensity of low income. For the U.S., the farm low-income gap is generally above the non-farm low-income gap since 1979, with the highest difference again in 1986 in the aftermath of the mid-1980s farm financial crisis. Compared to the U.S., the farm low-income gap for Canada is generally about the same magnitude with respect to the non-farm low-income rate but, for Australia, it is much higher than the non-farm low-income rate. For most European countries, the intensity of low-income rate is generally much higher among farm-households than among non-farm households except for Luxembourg and Norway. Their relative intensity of low income is, however, generally lower than their relative incidence of low income. This suggests that even if there are relatively more poor households among the farm households than among the non-farm households, poverty level among farm households on average is relatively less acute than poverty level among non-farm households on average. This is particularly the case for Finland, France and Italy. The relative intensity of low income of farm households may in some cases be higher than their relative incidence of low income, such as for Ireland. This suggests that poverty level among farm households on average is more acute than poverty level among non-farm households on average.

In summary, all three indicators of income distribution show that, except for a few countries or years, the incidence and the intensity of low income as well as the income disparity are often much higher among farm households than non-farm households for the OECD member countries for which data of farm household incomes are available. These comparisons of income distributions between the farm and non-farm communities confirm the conclusion reached in the OECD (2001) report. The incidence of low income and the disparity in incomes are most often higher among farm households than among non-farm households within the same country. For Ireland, Luxembourg, Norway and the U.S., the income distributions among farm households and non-farm households are, however, moving towards a similar pattern.

This implies that public policy to alleviate low incomes needs to be targeted to the permanent low-income group of farm households. The continuation of a general support would just exacerbate the already large income disparity among farm households. Therefore, to paraphrase Hill (2000), to deal with low incomes among farm households that essentially constitute a social concern, a social policy is most likely to be more adequate.

Conclusions and policy implications

Our times-series income analysis based on the *Luxembourg Income Study*'s data confirms that low income is not a chronic problem among farm households anymore in all of the ten surveyed OECD countries. At country level, average incomes of farm households are close or greater to those of non-farm households in most of the surveyed OECD countries since the 1970s. It is, however, not clear whether some countries, like France and Hungary, are still facing some recurrent low incomes. This possibility calls for further investigation. One direction would be to extend the time-series of farm and non-farm household incomes to more recent years. Another one would be to examine the influence of earning capacity factors such as differentials in age, gender, education, other skills, location, and even some peculiar conditions of the regional labour market that might explain such recurrent income differences. Farm type, size and location may also have some specific influence.

Large fluctuations in the relative average incomes of farm households from survey year to survey year are observed for some countries, in particular for the U.S., Australia and Canada and, to a lesser extent, for France and Ireland. At the same time, there is a noticeable stabilisation in the relative average incomes of farm households for some other countries since the mid-1990s, in particular for Finland, Hungary and Norway. It would be then instructive to examine if this relative income stabilisation persists for more recent years and starts to apply for France, Italy, Ireland and Luxembourg with the increasing direct payments of the successive CAP reforms. There is, however, a greater income inequality and poverty among farm households than among non-farm households, except for a few countries like Luxembourg and Norway and, more recently, for Ireland and the U.S. The question of the permanent nature of this greater income inequality poverty among farm households calls for an additional investigation that requires the availability of a household panel database. Decomposing income inequality by source of income to identify the contribution of each different income source to the overall income inequality would be instructive and feasible with the LIS database.

Limits to this income analysis are several. First, because the definition of a farm household rests on its income composition, farm households that experience a transitory low farm income with respect to their non-farm income are not anymore reported as farm households generating biases in the average total income level as well as in total income distribution. Second, because the LIS database may underreport income from the farming activity as well as from other self-employment activities, relative average incomes of farm households may be biased downwards and relative poverty of farm households may be biased upwards, while relative income distribution of farm households may be less subject to this measurement error if this error equally applies to the two groups of farm and non-farm households. Third, because either income from the farming activity is not reported separately from the other self-employment activities in the LIS database, making it impossible to distinguish farm and non-farm households, or the number of identified farm households is too small for statistical representativeness, the time-series that is left may become too short for some countries. Fourth, because the LIS database does not report farm structural characteristics, it is impossible to explain income from farming or even income from other activities with the help of those characteristics. It is, however, possible to test with an Oaxaca's (1973) counter-factual decomposition whether some differences in household and socio-demographic characteristics such as age, gender, ethnicity, education and location that are available in the LIS database may have some explanatory power in income level. Fifth, because the LIS database is not a panel database with repeating identified households, it is impossible to ascertain whether calculated income distribution and poverty are more than just transitory. Finally, not considering wealth as in Mishra *et al.* (2002) and Katchova (2008), this income analysis provides a partial picture of the economic well-being of farm households with respect to non-farm households.

There can be several policy implications. Because of lack of space, we limit ourselves to the most evident implication that mainstream policy-makers and other stakeholders continue to overlook, despite the accumulated evidence. If the general agricultural policy aim still consists of actually closing the income gap between farm and non-farm households, specific objectives can be derived in this logical sequence: (i) to define and identify low-income farm households, (ii) to determine factors that cause their low-income situation, (iii) to orient legislation and funds for mitigating those constraints, and (iv) eventually to rely on a social safety net for those low-income farm households that are definitely trapped into poverty. Instruments would then be drawn from a mix of social and fiscal policy, employment and retirement policy, education and training policy, research and development policy, credit and insurance policy, market and communication policy, environmental and recreational policy, and rural and infrastructure policy. Many of those instruments would need to be targeted specifically to low-income farm households, relying on a means test to determine their eligibility for public assistance. But, most likely, the urgent task consists of organising the collection and analysis of microeconomic farm household data on income composition and hypothetical factors that may characterise and explain their total income situation. Could this outlined policy implication be considered in the next U.S. Agricultural Act or EU CAP reform is still to be seen? Otherwise, we might just as well suggest removing the main agricultural policy aim from the U.S. legislation and the Treaty on the Functioning of the EU for the sake of better consistency in the intervention logic framed towards the agricultural sector.

Notes

1 These three issues actually form the core of the farm problem, recurrently treated in the economics literature for decades (see Gardner, 1992; Bonnen and Schweikhardt, 1998).
2 The second pillar of the CAP is mainly dedicated to assist agricultural adjustment, protect rural environment and promote non-agricultural activities.

3 Thanks to data collected by the Economic Research Service (ERS) of the U.S. Department of Agriculture (USDA).

4 Factor incomes consist of gross wages and salaries, farm self-employment income, non-farm self-employment income and cash property income. The farm self-employment income corresponds to the profit from the unincorporated enterprise, including payments from government farm programmes, and is recorded gross of social insurance contributions and income taxes but net of operational expenses. Incomes in kind are not accounted for in the U.S. and Canada LIS samples. A household which has negative farm self-employment income is also included as a farm household when its factor incomes are also negative and its farm self-employment income is smaller than half the factor incomes. Otherwise, the household with negative farm self-employment income is considered as a non-farm household.

5 Following this 'broad' definition of a farm household would, however, include households whose farm self-employment income contributes marginally to their factor incomes. This OECD broad definition of what constitutes a farm household is close to the current USDA (2016) definition of farm operator households, which consist of households of the primary operators of family farms in which, according to the 2005 USDA definition, the majority of the farm business assets is owned by individuals related by blood, marriage or adoption and from which a minimum of US$1,000 of agricultural products is produced and sold or would normally have been sold during a year.

6 The ten selected countries include Australia, Canada, Finland, France, Hungary, Ireland, Italy, Luxembourg, Norway and the United States.

7 Medians of net disposable incomes may be a superior statistics than the average because of the likely distributional characteristics with few very high-income households raising the average well above the incomes of most households.

8 In the remainder of the text, "household income" refers to the real adjusted net disposable household income expressed in 2005 PPP U.S. dollars.

9 The correlation coefficient between the two U.S. income ratio series is 0.47 for the ten overlapping years from 1974 to 2010.

10 The differences in information sources and household definitions prevent the comparisons of these new series of farm household income ratios with those reported in EUROSTAT (2002).

11 When the 'broad' definition of a farm household is used, the income picture (not shown here) changes slightly. For Australia, Canada and the U.S., the farm household income ratios are higher and more stable than those calculated on the basis of a 'narrow' definition of a farm household. For three of the seven selected European countries (Finland, Ireland and Luxembourg), the farm household income ratios are slightly higher than those calculated on the basis of a narrow definition of a farm household. A more diversified source of incomes out of farming indeed tends to stabilise and increase the farm household incomes for a total of six countries out of the ten that are surveyed. That on average farm household incomes are not chronically low is even more evident for these ten OECD member countries when a broad definition of farm households is considered.

12 In economics, the Lorenz curve is a graph showing the cumulative share of income earned by the cumulative share of households from lower income. The Gini index can be calculated by the following formula (Förster, 1994): $G = \frac{2}{n^2 \bar{y}} \sum_{h=1}^{n} h \left(y_h - \bar{y} \right) \cdot 100$ where n represents the number of households in the population, y_h the income of the hth household ranked in ascending order by its subscript and $\bar{y}$ the average income.

13 Except for Ireland and Norway for some of the observed years.

References

Adams, R. (1991). "The Effects of International Remittances on Poverty, Inequality and Development in Rural Egypt", Washington, D.C., International Food Policy Research Institute, Research Report 86.

Agra CEAS. (2007). "Feasibility Study on the Implementation of Income of Agricultural Households Sector (IAHS) Statistics", Eurostat, Luxembourg.

Bonnen, J.T., Schweikhardt D.B. (1998). "The Future of U.S. Agricultural Policy: Reflections on the Disappearance of the "Farm Problem", *Review of Agricultural Economics*, **20**(1), 2–36.

Court of Auditors. (2004). "Special Report No 14/2003 on the measurement of farm incomes by the Commission Article 33(1)(b) of the EC Treaty, together with the Commission's replies", Official Journal of the European Union, 2004/C, 20.2.2004.

El-Osta, H.S., Mishra, A.K., Morehart, M.J. (2007). "Determinants of Economic Well-Being Among U.S. Farm Operator Households", *Agricultural Economics*, **36**, 291–304.

European Commission. (2008). "Direct payments distribution in the EU-25 after implementation of the 2003 CAP reform based on FADN data", European Commission, Directorate-General for Agriculture and Rural Development, Brussels, November 2008.

European Commission. (2011). "Impact Assessment: Common Agricultural Policy towards 2020", SEC (2011) 1153 final/2, Annexes 3A-D, European Commission, Brussels.

EUROSTAT. (1995). "Manual of the Total Income of Agricultural Households (Rev.1)", Theme 5 Series E. Statistics Office of the European Communities, Luxembourg.

EUROSTAT. (1999). "Incomes of agricultural households sector – 2001 report", Statistics Office of the European Communities, Luxembourg.

EUROSTAT. (2002). "Incomes of the agricultural households sector", Statistics Office of the European Communities, Luxembourg.

Förster, M.F. (1994). "Measurement of low incomes and poverty in a perspective of international comparisons", in OECD Labour Market and Social Policy Occasional paper, No. 14, Paris.

Gardner, B.L. (1992). "Changing Economic Perspectives on the Farm Problem", *Journal of Economic Literature*, **30**(1), 62–101.

Gardner, B.L. (2000). "Economic Growth and Low Incomes in Agriculture", *American Journal of Agricultural Economics*, **82**(5), 1059–1074.

Gardner, B.L. (2002). *American Agriculture in the Twentieth Century: How It Flourished and What It Cost*. Harvard University Press, Cambridge, Massachusetts, and London, England.

Henry de Frahan, B., De Blander, R. (2010). "La Politique Agricole Commune: horizon 2014", *Reflets et Perspectives de la vie économique*, XLIX, 2010/2-3, 137–156.

Hill, B. (1995). "Total Income of Agricultural Households: 1995 Report", Theme 5 Series D, Statistics Office of the European Communities, Luxembourg.

Hill, B. (1996). "Monitoring incomes of agricultural households within the EU's information system – new needs and new methods", *European Review of Agricultural Economics*, **23**, 27–48.

Hill, B. (1999). "Farm Household Incomes: Perceptions and Statistics", *Journal of Rural Studies*, **15**(3), 345–358.

Hill, B. (2000). "Agricultural incomes and the CAP", Institute of Economic Affairs, Oxford, UIK, June 2000.

Hill, B. (2012). *Farm Incomes, Wealth and Agricultural Policy: Filling the CAP's Core Information Gap*. CAB International, Oxfordshire, UK, 4th Edition.

Katchova, A. (2008). "A comparison of the Economic Well-Being of Farm and Nonfarm Households", *American Journal of Agricultural Economics*, **90**(3), 733–747.

Luxembourg Income Study (LIS) Database, "https://urldefense.proofpoint.com/v2/url?u=http-3A__www.lisdatacenter.org&d=DwMFaQ&c=AGbYxfJbXK67KfXyGqyv2Ejiz41FqQuZFk4A-1IxfAU&r=yGFUKi8jkGoQcN9x7LrJ7qETrl6Jspv24h8ztgKmeWQ&m=apRXaQOAnqtVI-NJ_Pwo2T84CRsoGE10UILZqaS9QV8&s=UhVINYe_vQ-0qw5acyfnnv2mZaOURI7aM3wKlF3nIPc&e=" http://www.lisdatacenter.org (Australia 1989–2003, Canada 1971–2007, Finland 1991–2010, France 1978–2005, Hungary 1991–2005, Ireland 1987–2010, Italy 1987–95, Luxembourg 1985–2010, Norway 1986–2004, USA 1974–2010). Luxembourg: LIS.

Mishra, A.K., El-Osta, H.S., Morehart, M.J., Johnson, J.D., Hopkins, J.W. (2002). *Income, Wealth, and the Economic Well-Being of Farm Households.* Washington DC: USDA Economic Research Service Agricultural Economic Report Number 812.

Oaxaca, R. (1973). "Male–female wage differentials in urban labor markets", *International Economic Review*, **14**, 693–709.

OECD. (1999). "Distributional Effects of Agricultural Support in Selected OECD Countries", AGR/CA/(99)8/FINAL, Organisation for Economic Co-operation and Development, Paris.

OECD. (2001). "Low Incomes in Agriculture in OECD Countries", AGR/CA/APM(2001)19/FINAL, Organisation for Economic Co-operation and Development, Paris.

OECD. (2003). "Farm Household Incomes: Issues and Policy Responses", Organisation for Economic Co-operation and Development, Paris.

OECD. (2004). "Policy Brief: Farm Household Incomes – Towards Better Informed Policies", Organisation for Economic Co-operation and Development, Paris.

Offutt, S. (2002). "The future of farm policy analysis: A household perspective. Presidential Address", *American Journal of Agricultural Economics*, **84**, 1189–1200.

Peake, W.O. and Marshall, M.I. (2009). "Has the 'Farm Problem' Disappeared? A Comparison of Household and Self-Employment Income Levels of the Farm and Nonfarm Self-Employed", Selected Paper for presentation at the Southern Agricultural Economics Association, Annual Meeting, Atlanta, Georgia, January 31–February 3, 2009.

Salvioni, C., Colazilli, G. (2005). "Redditi, consumi e ricchezza delle famiglie agricole e rurali italiane" In Basile, F., Cecchi, C. (editors). Proceedings of the Conference "Diritto all'alimentazione, agricoltura e sviluppo", Rome (16–18 September 2004), Franco Angeli, Italy.

USDA. (2015). "Farm Operators' Household Income Compared With U.S. Household Income", U.S. Department of Agriculture, Economic Research Service and National Agricultural Statistics Service, Agricultural Resource Management Survey and U.S. Census Bureau, Current Population Survey. Data as of November 24, 2015.

USDA. (2016). "Farm Household Well-Being – Glossary", U.S. Department of Agriculture, Economic Research Service, http://www.ers.usda.gov/topics/farm-economy/farm-household-well-being/glossary.aspx#farmoperatorhousehold February 2, 2016.

Chapter 9

Farm labor and farm income
Case study from Norway

Klaus Mittenzwei, Hugo Storm, and Thomas Heckelei

Introduction

Seeking the answer to the question of how farmers allocate their limited labor resources has a long tradition in the agricultural economics literature (Schultz 1990, Benjamin 1992). The role of off-farm income to close the income gap between farm households and non-farm households has been emphasized by various scholars (e.g. Schmitt 1989, Gardner 1992, Mishra et al. 2002). Ahearn et al. (2006) focus on the role of government subsidies on the allocation decision. This chapter contributes to this literature. In particular, we investigate the relationship of farmers' decisions to combine farm income with off-farm wage income and to what extent this affects their total household income. To this end, we combine taxpayer information and agricultural data at the farm household level to study labor decisions and the income of Norwegian farm households and compare with the income situation of all households. Using data of almost 40 000 farm households for the year 2009, we find that farm households obtain an income that is on average larger than that of all Norwegian households. However, there is a large variation. Descriptive statistical analysis looking at joint distributions of key structural variables, policy support and income at farm level provides unique information.

Empirical studies of farm households are often restricted to a sample of farms provided by farm accountancy databases. The data underlying the analysis in this chapter instead comprise the entire Norwegian farm population, including detailed information on on-farm production activities as well as specific information on various sources for farm and off-farm income at the household level. The dataset thus provides an ideal basis to study the complex relationship between farm labor and farm (household) income.

The present dataset allows testing a couple of hypotheses. Firstly, we are interested to analyze whether Norwegian farmers cover their opportunity costs with regard to labor. Norway is a high-income country, so Norwegian farmers may face greater challenges than other farmers in the developed world in this respect. Secondly, we want to study which source of income is more important for farm household income. Norwegian agriculture is small-scale, and opportunities to grow are limited partly by natural conditions. Therefore, we hypothesize that off-farm income is of principal significance in explaining farm household income. Thirdly, we address the question whether farmers' age is related to household income. We hypothesize that younger farmers have higher opportunity costs than older farmers. This is because once a decision to enter farming is made, investments generate sunk costs. Finally, our dataset allows for the detailed study of regional and local characteristics, as it covers the entire farming population. We hypothesize that those characteristics matter in form of differences in the local labor and land markets (e.g. through urban sprawl).

Norwegian agriculture and agricultural policy

Norway is a small, open economy heavily relying on international trade in order to satisfy the needs of its population. The agricultural sector's (including forestry) contribution to the Gross Domestic Product (GDP) was about 0.5 per cent in 2013 with a falling trend. This small figure is partly due to the oil and gas sector that amounted to about 20 per cent of GDP. If the food, beverages and tobacco industry is included, then the share increases to 1.75 per cent. This agro-food sector is Norway's second largest industry sector in terms of GDP and largest industry sector in terms of employment.

About 3 per cent of Norway's surface is cultivated land. Natural and climatic conditions make Norwegian agriculture costly, as the vegetation period is short and fields are scattered. The structure of the agricultural holdings is small-scale compared to many other European countries. The size of a typical farm was 23 ha on average in 2014. An average livestock farm kept 24 cows or 61 sheep in the same year. Dairy is most important in terms of value of production, land use and employment. Its contribution to the sector's gross revenues (excluding subsidies) was almost 30 per cent in 2014. Beef, often produced in combination with dairy, adds another 13 per cent. Horticulture is important with respect to gross revenues (14 per cent), but less important with respect to land use. The cereal sector (9 per cent of gross revenue at sector level) is crucial for domestic food supply (measured in calories), which is an important determinant of the current agricultural policy.

Despite unfavorable natural conditions, Norwegian agriculture enjoys quite favorable political conditions that have led to the development of a comprehensive agricultural policy with a complex system of institutions for policy decision-making and market regulation. Norwegian farmers enjoy a high level of support compared to other farmers in the developed world. According to the Organization for Economic Co-operation and Development (OECD), total support including border protection amounts to around 60 per cent of the sector's gross income at farm gate (OECD 2015). Subsidies are provided in the form of output payments, input subsidies, animal and area payments as well as agro-environmental payments. All payments are coupled to current outputs, inputs, or other factors of production. The payment rates of most programs differ by region. Per unit rates are higher in regions with natural disadvantages and for smaller farms.

Data

The analysis is based on data from the Norwegian Direct Payment Register (NDPR) for the year 2009 (Norwegian Agriculture Agency 2015). The register contains information about agricultural area by crop and number of animals by type of animal (126 different crop and animal activities are distinguished) for every farm that applies for subsidies. A farm is defined by its property number. If a farmer owns several farms, he or she has to apply for direct payments for each farm. Eligibility for direct payments is subject to certain conditions, one of which is a minimum economic size of the farm (measured by turnover) in order to prevent small "hobby-farms" from receiving subsidies. As a consequence, the total acreage and numbers of animals may be somewhat underestimated when compared with other official sources, such as the decennial total farm census.

The data from the NDPR are matched with two data sources provided by Statistics Norway. The first source is the decennial total farm census for 2009 (Statistics Norway 2011a), from which we have information about the self-reported total farm labor input. This includes both family-owned and hired labor as well as paid and unpaid labor. The second source is the annual tax statistics of personal taxpayers for 2010 (Statistics Norway 2011b). It contains a complete overview of household income distinguished by sources and the taxes paid. The unit of analysis in our study is thus the farm household defined by its property number in the NDPR. In 2009, the number of farms was 40 583. With this as a starting point, we kept only those farms which could be identified in the total farm census for 2009 and the annual tax statistics. The merging process was carried out by Statistics Norway and left us with 38 072 farms. In addition, we applied outlier management by cutting off 1 per cent of the remaining farms at both ends of the tail with regard to agricultural area, labor input and total income. This left us with 37 366 farms that entered our analysis.

Farm household characteristics and income differences to average household

The average farm size was 22.3 ha, with some farms cultivating less than 1 ha and the largest farms growing almost 300 ha (Table 9.1). It can be inferred from the table that the largest farms measured in terms of area grow cereals. The largest dairy farms have more than 100 dairy cows. The median and mean for cereals area and number of dairy cows should be less emphasized, as it includes those farms that do not grow cereals or have dairy cows. The official Norwegian definition of one "man-year" in agriculture corresponds to 1 875 working hours. In terms of labor input, the average Norwegian farm is slightly larger than one man-year. The largest farm reports 4.3 man-years.

Taxable agricultural income for the average farm is lower than subsidies it received (Table 9.1). While the median agricultural income was 145 800 nkr, the average farm received subsidies worth 223 600 nkr. The data reveal a large variation in agricultural income ranging from a loss of 3.4 mill nkr to a positive income

Table 9.1 Descriptive statistics of the dataset for active farms in 2009 (37 366 observations)

Variable	Code	Unit	Median	Mean	Std. dev.	Min	Max
Agricultural area	agr_area	Ha	17.7	22.3	18.706	< 0.1	287
Cereals area	cere_area	Ha	0.0	6.9	15.447	0	287
Dairy cows	dairy_cow	Heads	0.0	5.2	10.352	0	125
Farm labor	labor	Hours	1 620.0	1 971.4	1 583.904	20	8 390
Farmer's age	age	Years	48.0	48.2	10.936	7	90
Agricultural subsidies	subs	1000 nkr	223.6	279.4	217.137	0	2 284
Agricultural income	agr_inc	1000 nkr	145.8	219.5	275.850	−3,400	2 042
Wage income	wage_inc	1000 nkr	314.3	351.3	321.394	0	2 000
Total household (hh) inc.	tot_inc	1000 nkr	663.7	694.6	332.901	0	2 047
Disposable hh income	disp_inc	1000 nkr	520.8	535.5	233.706	−948	1 859
Income difference	difference	1000 nkr	123.8	138.5	233.706	−1 345	1 462

of 2.0 mill nkr. The median wage income at the farm household level was about 1.5 times the median income from agriculture. Including income from other sources such as wage income, the total household income for the median farm was about 660 000 nkr. Hence, agricultural income made up a little more than 20 per cent of the total income for the median farm household. The absolute difference regarding wage income and total household income is about the same, ranging between zero and 2 mill nkr. However, the median total household income is more than twice the median wage income. There is also a large variation in disposable income at the farm household level, ranging from a negative 1 mill nkr to a positive 1.9 mill nkr.

The difference between a farm household's disposable income and the disposable income of an average household is denoted as the "income difference" (or "difference" for short). Table 9.1 reveals that the average farm household has a larger disposable income than the Norwegian average household. The income difference is 123.800 nkr in favor of the farm household. However, there is a large variation with a minimum of −1.34 mill nkr and a maximum of 1.5 mill nkr. The distribution of the income difference is shown in Figure 9.1 as a kernel density.

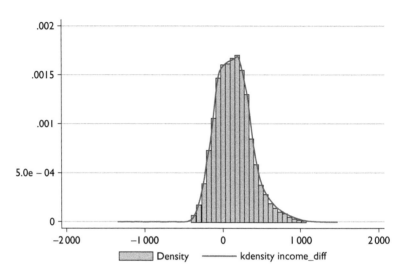

Figure 9.1 Distribution of the income difference among farm households compared to Norwegian average household (1 000 nkr)

About 30 per cent of the farm households have a negative income difference, with a median of −100 000 nkr. The positive income difference of the remaining households is 213 000 nkr (median). The farm households seem to be approximately normally distributed around the mean. About 70 per cent of the households are located within ± 1 std. dev. around the mean, while 15 (13) per cent lie at the remaining lower (upper) end of the tail. In order to gain a better understanding on the variation of farm and farm household characteristics for different income levels, the farm households are divided into four groups of equal size according their income difference (Table 9.2). The group with the lowest (i.e. negative) income difference ("low" in Table 9.2) comprises all households with an income difference of less than −29 958 nkr. The following group ("middle low") extends to a positive income difference of 123 803 nkr. The third group ("middle high") is made of all households with an income difference between 123 803 nkr and 278 298 nkr, while the last group ("high") covers all households above the latter limit.

The group with the lowest income difference is distinguished by lower averages regarding all agricultural characteristics like agricultural area, cereals area, dairy cows and farm labor. Consequently, those households also receive lower agricultural income and lower subsidies compare to the other groups. However, we can see that the differences in wage income contribute more to assigning the group members to the different groups. Apart from the "low" group, wage income is more than agricultural income and the wage income in the "high" group is five times higher than the wage income in the "low" group.

Performance at the farm level seems to be important. Table 9.2 reveals some interesting differences among the four groups. The households with the highest

Table 9.2 Characteristics of farm households by income difference quartiles, 2009

Variable	Code	Low	Medium low	Medium high	High
Agricultural area	agr_area	18	21	22	28
Cereals area	cere_area	4	6	7	11
Dairy cows	dairy_cow	4	5	5	7
Farm labor	labor	1810	1926	1958	2191
Farmer's age	age	49	49	48	47
Subsidies	subs	243.265	267.275	282.085	324.827
Agricultural income	agr_inc	142.038	199.817	227.296	308.775
Wage income	wage_inc	112.486	251.782	428.679	612.160
Tot. household (hh) income	tot_inc	317.907	560.607	772.166	1127.789
Disposable hh income	disp_inc	259.821	444.516	596.453	841.296
Income difference	difference	−137.179	47.516	199.453	444.296

Source: Authors' calculations

income difference use 25 per cent less farm labor per ha compared to the "low" group. More investigation would be needed to find out whether that observation is linked to differences in the farms' location and natural conditions, to the farms' production activities or are related to farm management. Households at the upper end of the scale make almost twice as large an income from agriculture per hour compared to households at the opposite end of the scale, which is likely a consequence of lower labor input per ha.

The 25 per cent farm households with the highest income difference are portrayed as larger farms in terms of farmed land, dairy cows and labor input, leading to higher agricultural income and subsidies. Farmers in the "high" income group also tend to be slightly younger compared to the "low" income group on average.

Another interesting aspect is the role of subsidies. The lowest group has marginally higher subsidy intensity. This group receives 13 512 nkr per ha in budget support, while the corresponding amount for the highest group is 11 401 nkr per ha. The numbers for the two groups in the middle are in between. The small differences illustrate the structural profile of the payment system where subsidy rates for the first hectares and animals are frequently higher than for the subsequent input factors. The income situation of farm households is compared to those of other households from two different perspectives: household size and type as well as regional differences in disposable income.

Table 9.3 shows how farm households perform with respect to the type and size of other households. We distinguish between three types of households: farm households, working households and all households. A working household is defined as household of the working population in which the age of the main household member is between 30 and 66 years. Through this definition, we exclude, for example, the households of students and those of senior citizens. All households include also farm households. As can be inferred from Table 9.3, the share of farm households of all households is less than 2 per cent. A comparison of the numbers in Table 9.3 indicates that both, household type and household size matters for the evaluation whether farm households achieve the income level of other households. The average farm household achieves a disposable household income of 536 000 nkr. When compared with all households, this is 77 000 nkr higher than the disposable income of the average household. However, if the comparison is made with respect to households representing the working population ("work"), the difference drops to only 9 000 nkr.

The question of what kind of households to compare with farm households becomes even more decisive when only non-single households are compared. Non-single households are defined as households with at least two adult household members. Non-single farm households have a disposable income of 634 000 nkr on average and perform slightly better than the average household (627 000 nkr). If only working households are considered, the positive income difference of 7 000 nkr turns into a negative difference of 35 000 nkr. The reason why farm households perform better on average than all households may be found by investigating single households. Here, farm households achieve a much higher disposable income when compared to both all households (88 000 nkr) and working households (49 000 nkr).

The data do not provide detailed information about the various sources of income for the different households. Non-agricultural income for farm households is substantially lower when compared with all households irrespective of size and type. Interestingly, single farm households achieve, in relative terms, more of their total income from agriculture compared to non-single households. Also, the agricultural income does not seem to differ considerably in absolute terms between single households and non-single households. Single farm households achieve about 80 per cent of the agricultural income of non-single farm households. This may be an indication that the farm size does not differ very much between those households. These observations together indicate that the primary difference between single and non-single households is not at the farm level, but that there is a second person in the household who contributes with non-agricultural income. Farm households seem to be less taxed than average households. The tax burden of all farm households is 23 per cent of total income compared to 27 per cent of working households and 26 per cent of all households.

Table 9.3 Income situations for households by size and type of household, 2009

	Single households			Non-single households			All households		
	Farm	Work[1]	All	Farm	Work[1]	All	Farm	Work[1]	All
Number of hh	13	607	1011	24	930	1141	37	1537	2152
Agr. income	191	n.a.	n.a.	235	n.a.	n.a.	219	n.a.	n.a.
Non-agr. income	266	391	337	575	897	834	465	697	601
Allowances[2]	4	18	13	14	23	19	10	21	17
Total income	461	409	351	824	920	853	695	718	617
Taxes paid	103	101	81	190	250	226	159	191	158
Disposable income	358	309	270	634	669	627	536	527	459

Source: Authors' calculations

Note: Number of households in 1 000; mean values in 1 000 nkr

[1]Working population: Age of main household member between 30 and 66

[2]Non-taxed allowances such as children allowance and housing allowance

The data allow a closer look not only with regard to the absolute income difference, but also with regard to regional variation. The data contain the geographical location for each farm while the annual tax statistics for personal taxpayers is available at the county level. Norway is divided into 19 counties. Figure 9.2 shows the median disposable household income of all households (light shaded bars), while the income difference of farm households is marked with dark shaded bars on top of the income for all households. The sum of the two thus displays the median disposable income of the farm households by county.

While the Norwegian average household achieved a median disposable income of about 400 000 nkr in 2009, farm households realized an additional 123 000 nkr. The figure reveals a few regional differences, which are smaller for all households compared to farm households. All households achieve the highest median disposable income in Akershus, which is the preferred residential area for much of the work force commuting to Oslo. The average income of all households is about equally high in the county of Rogaland that includes the "oil capital" Stavanger. There are minor differences for the other counties, with the exception of Oslo having a somewhat lower average disposable income. We assume the reason to be a larger share of single households compared to other counties.

The regional differences of disposable income for all households are to some extent mirrored in the regional difference for the farm households. The highest

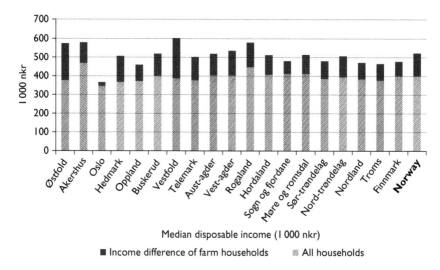

Median disposable income (1 000 nkr)

■ Income difference of farm households   ▨ All households

Figure 9.2 Median disposable incomes for agricultural households and all households by county

incomes are achieved in the Oslofjord-region (Østfold, Akershus and Vestfold) and in Rogaland. One reason may be that the labor market opportunities are particularly strong in these regions, such that the opportunity costs of farm labor may be higher than in other counties. An exception is Vestfold, where all household income does not differ from the Norwegian average, while the income difference of farm households is almost twice the national average. An explanation for this observation may be sought in regional variation in agricultural production. Compared to the national average, farm household income seems to be a bit lower in the counties in Western Norway, Central Norway and Northern Norway ranging from Hordaland to Finnmark. Finally, we analyze regional differences of the farm households with respect to income sources.

It appears that the average Norwegian farm household achieves precisely half of its total pre-tax income from wage income. About 30 per cent stem from agriculture, while other income covers most of the remaining income. Allowances play a minor role throughout the country.

The share of wage income ranges from 60 per cent in Oslo (only seven observations) and Hordaland down to 40 per cent in the northernmost counties of Nordland and Finnmark. The high share in Hordaland can be explained by offshore employment. In relative (to total income) and absolute terms, wage income seems to contribute most in southern Norway and least in Northern Norway as the counties are ordered from South to North in Table 9.4. A similar South-North decline emerges for other income.[1] But agricultural income generally decreases in absolute and relative terms when moving from Northern to Southern Norway with some

Table 9.4 Sources of income for farm households by county, 2009

	Number of hh	Agricultural Income		Wage Income		Other Income		Allowances		Taxes
Østfold	1975	206	(26.3)	414	(52.8)	155	(19.7)	10	(1.2)	183
Akershus	1940	171	(20.9)	424	(51.6)	217	(26.4)	9	(1.1)	204
Oslo	7	28	(3.7)	454	(60.1)	258	(34.1)	16	(2.1)	158
Hedmark	3034	210	(30.1)	342	(49.1)	136	(19.5)	9	(1.3)	151
Oppland	4245	192	(29.9)	312	(48.6)	129	(20.2)	9	(1.4)	141
Buskerud	1971	163	(21.9)	385	(51.7)	187	(25.1)	10	(1.3)	183
Vestfold	1108	236	(28.0)	427	(50.7)	168	(20.0)	10	(1.2)	206
Telemark	1255	130	(18.6)	402	(57.3)	161	(22.9)	9	(1.3)	167
Aust-Agder	536	187	(26.5)	352	(50.0)	153	(21.7)	13	(1.8)	159
Vest-Agder	914	170	(24.3)	361	(51.7)	155	(22.2)	13	(1.9)	152
Rogaland	3321	312	(39.5)	360	(45.5)	106	(13.5)	13	(1.6)	179
Hordaland	2804	150	(21.4)	422	(59.9)	121	(17.2)	11	(1.6)	166
Sogn og Fjordane	2890	197	(30.3)	343	(52.7)	100	(15.4)	10	(1.5)	147
Møre og Romsdal	2393	240	(34.7)	341	(49.1)	103	(14.8)	10	(1.5)	156
Sør-Trøndelag	2713	241	(36.6)	317	(48.0)	91	(13.8)	10	(1.5)	145
Nord-Trøndelag	2958	266	(38.6)	323	(46.9)	89	(12.9)	11	(1.6)	146
Nordland	2040	297	(47.0)	259	(40.9)	65	(10.4)	11	(1.7)	129
Troms	987	290	(45.7)	274	(43.1)	59	(9.4)	12	(1.8)	133
Finnmark	275	265	(41.8)	260	(40.9)	96	(15.1)	15	(2.3)	118
NORWAY	**37366**	**219**	**(31.1)**	**351**	**(49.8)**	**124**	**(17.6)**	**10**	**(1.5)**	**159**

Source: Authors' calculations

Note: Mean values in 1 000 nkr, percentage share in parentheses

notable exceptions. Rogaland has the highest absolute average agricultural income as the county is particularly known for its dense agriculture. About 20 per cent of all dairy cows and 30 per cent of all slaughter pigs are held in the county, although it covers only 12 per cent of the country's total agricultural area.

Regressing income differences on farm household characteristics

In order to gain further insights in the relationships between labor use and farm household income, we regressed the individual farm income difference on the variables in Table 9.1. In addition, we included the size of the farm household and a dummy to account for regional characteristics not captured by the other regressors. Instead of counties, the regional dummy is based on labor market regions, which are expected to provide a better proxy for the opportunity costs of labor compared to the rather arbitrary administrative barriers of a county. Norway is split into eight labor market regions (*lmr*). *Lmr1* consists of the municipalities around the Oslofjord, while *lmr2* is comprised of municipalities in the valleys of Eastern Norway. The municipalities along the coastline in Southern Norway make up *lmr3*, while the region around Stavanger in Southwestern Norway is denoted *lmr4*. *Lmr5* consists of the municipalities of Western Norway, while *lmr6* is comprised of the region around Trondheim in Central Norway. Northern Norway is split in two labor market regions, where *lmr7* takes the Southern part of Northern Norway, while *lmr8* collects the Northern part.

Table 9.5 shows the correlation coefficients of the explanatory variables in the regression. Agricultural variables are quite strongly correlated such as agricultural area (*agr_area*) and cereals area (*has_cere*). As subsidies are mainly paid on a per unit of area or animal basis, the correlation between subsidies, area and dairy cows is

Table 9.5 Correlation coefficients of the regression variables, 2009

	Agr_area	Cere_area	Farm labour	Dairy_cow	Subs	Farmer's age	HH_size
agr_area	1						
has_cere	0.6495	1					
Labour	0.4192	−0.0318	1				
has_dairy	0.3377	−0.1344	0.6127	1			
Subs	0.741	0.1422	0.708	0.6478	1		
Age	−0.0481	−0.0326	−0.0068	−0.0066	−0.0211	1	
HH_size	0.0221	0.0193	0.0729	0.0233	0.0215	−0.012	1

Source: Authors' calculations

also relatively high. Age and size of the household (*hh_size*: 0 if single household, and 1 if non-single household) are (linearly) uncorrelated with agricultural activities. In order to account for potential non-linearity, the variables in Table 9.6 enter the regression with both linear and squared terms. An exception is cereals area (*has_cere*), as the squared term was not significant. Table 9.6 provides the results of the regression analysis on the income difference. The regional dummy for labor market region 4 (*lmr4*) is omitted, as the income difference in this region has the highest average.

Due to the large number of observations, most coefficients of the regression analysis are significant at the 1 per cent level. The one exception is the linear coefficient for dairy cows, with a significance level of 5 per cent. The fit of the regression is quite high for a cross sectional analysis explaining 39.6 per cent of the variation in income differences. Figure 9.3 visualizes the estimated marginal income effects for selected explanatory variables. The income difference is calculated for the average farm household by keeping all regression variables apart from the variable investigated, at mean values. The chosen range for the variables corresponds to the 80 per cent interval. The lower 10 per cent and the upper 10 per cent are omitted to avoid a misinterpretation of the marginal effects. Regarding cereal area and dairy cows, the interval is calculated only for those farms that have cereals and dairy cows, respectively.

Cereal area and agricultural area, which are highly correlated (see Table 9.3), seem to have the largest effect on the income difference in absolute terms within the given range. The income difference varies between 160 000 nkr and almost 250 000 nkr in the case of cereal area. These cropping-oriented farms are expected to more easily combine on-farm activities with off-farm employment. This is in line with the finding depicted in Table 9.2 that farms in the high-income class have relatively more cereal area than dairy cows compared to the low-income class. It suggests that some of the variation in income differences across farms is explained by differences in farm specialization, with cereal farms having a higher income differences compared to other farms. This finding is further supported by the estimated effect of dairy cows on income differences. Here we find a slightly quadratic relationship. For small numbers of dairy cows the marginal effect is almost zero and increases slowly with increasing numbers. Overall the effect, however, is considerable smaller than an increase in cereal area.

For farm labor, subsidies and farmer's age we find a decreasing diminishing effect, with coefficients for the related linear and the quadratic variables showing negative and positive signs, respectively. For low values of these variables, the income differences decrease until the minimum from which the income difference increases again. Although the squared terms in the regression analysis are significant from an economic perspective the non-linear effects are small. The figure suggests some non-linearity for farm subsidies. One should expect that subsidies always increase farm household income. The regression analysis suggests, however, a weakly negative relationship between subsidies and household income for farms with low subsidies.

Table 9.6 Result of regression on income difference, 2009

Variable	Coefficient	Std.Error	t-value	P>|t|	[95% Conf. interval]	
Constant	230.40640	14.99228	−5.1	0.000	−79.92	−35.67
Agric_area	2.71706	0.17169	15.4	0.000	201.02	259.79
Agric_area ^2	−0.01694	0.00118	15.8	0.000	2.38	3.05
Has_cere	1.91639	0.11729	−14.4	0.000	−0.02	−0.01
Has_dairy	−0.46745	0.22686	16.3	0.000	1.69	2.15
Has_dairy ^2	0.04084	0.00448	−2.1	0.039	−0.91	−0.02
Labor	−0.02578	0.00228	9.1	0.000	0.03	0.05
Labor ^2	0.00000	0.00000	−11.3	0.000	−0.03	−0.02
Subs	−0.09967	0.02003	10.3	0.000	0.00	0.00
Subs ^2	0.00020	0.00002	−5.0	0.000	−0.14	−0.06
Age	−10.68244	0.61898	11.1	0.000	0.00	0.00
Age ^2	0.10095	0.00632	−17.3	0.000	−11.90	−9.47
HH_size	273.50260	1.99834	16.0	0.000	0.09	0.11
Imr1	−18.33174	3.55713	136.9	0.000	269.59	277.42
Imr2	−52.41485	3.26890	−5.2	0.000	−25.30	−11.36
Imr3	−33.54985	4.23815	−16.0	0.000	−58.82	−46.01
Imr5	−27.41388	3.43296	−7.9	0.000	−41.86	−25.24
Imr6	−40.83886	3.34441	−8.0	0.000	−34.14	−20.69
Imr7	−60.67606	4.84334	−12.2	0.000	−47.39	−34.28
Imr8	−57.79253	11.28821	−12.5	0.000	−70.17	−51.18

(R2 = 0.3962)

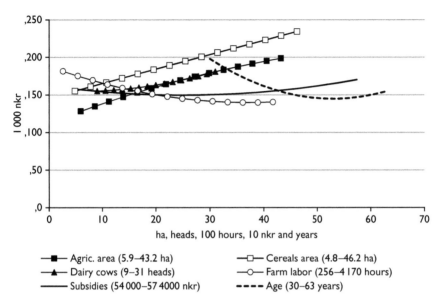

Figure 9.3 Marginal effects of agricultural variables on the income difference in labor market region 1

Labor has (*ceteris paribus*) a negative effect on the income difference with diminishing rate. The effect of labor levels out at around 3 000–3 500 hours, which is about two man-years. One explanation for this could be that for small farms an increase in farm labor comes at the expense of a reduction in off-farm labor and hence wage income, leading to an overall decline in household income. Once the "farm family" works full time, further increases in farm labor are realized primarily due to hired labor with no negative effect on off-farm labor and hence wage income. The income difference thus stays unaffected or might even increase due to additional farm income.

The household size corrects for the number of persons in the household. The coefficient is large, indicating the considerable difference it makes if the household is a single or non-single household.

The regional dummies are partly substantial, indicating that local characteristics matter. Given a mean income difference of 130 000 nkr, the difference between labor market region 4 and labor market region 8 is almost half that amount. As revealed in Figure 9.2, there are differences across counties both with regard to the non-agricultural household income and the income difference achieved by farm households. Age has a substantial negative effect. This implies that, *ceteris paribus*, younger farmers obtain a higher household income than older once. This might reflect differences in opportunity costs that might be higher for younger farmers and that only those farms remain active who manage to achieve a total household income that compares to the average income of other households. Hence, while young farmers may be willing to accept lower rates of return for labor in agriculture, they do not seem to be willing to accept lower rates of return for labor at the household level. During generational transfer, a farm might remain active only if it is either profitable or, considering the results in Table 9.2, can be combined with attractive off-farm incomes.

Conclusion

This study investigates the role of off-farm income to close the income gap between farm households and non-farm households. The analysis uses a comprehensive database covering detailed economic and tax-related information for the entire farm population in Norway.

First of all, Norwegian farmers cover their opportunity costs for labor at the household level. Unfortunately, the data do not allow investigating whether this observation is true at farm level as well, as the data do not distinguish between family and hired labor. At the same time, the analysis has revealed significant variation within the farm households, and even more pronounced for all households. Therefore, the above result is valid foremost for average levels. When farm households are compared with households that seem closer related with regard to type and size, the income difference observed at average level, considerably shrinks and the positive income difference may even turn into a negative one. The literature is clear that the household is the appropriate level for income comparison. However, our analysis highlights that one should be very careful how to define the non-agricultural households used for such comparison purposes.

Another important finding is that the wage income seems to be more decisive than income from agriculture when it comes to the income difference between farm households and other households. The farm households with the highest income difference are those that manage to derive a high wage income. In comparison, differences in income from agriculture are somewhat smaller between those households. In addition, differences in household incomes decrease with an increase in agricultural labor input, thus further supporting the hypothesis that differences in household incomes are primarily explained by wage income rather than by income from agriculture. This does not mean, however, that farm performance is unimportant. Farms with a larger income difference clearly outperform other farms with regard to income from agriculture per unit of land and per unit of labor. It remains to be analyzed whether these indicators are related to the farm's location and natural conditions, to the farms' portfolio of production activities, or are caused by differences in farm management issues. Our results provide some first indication that some of the variation in income differences can be attributed to differences in farms' portfolio. Primarily, cereal farms seem to be more capable of achieving a higher income difference compared to dairy farms. An explanation could be that cereal farms can more easily combine farming with off-farm work.

With respect to regional variation, our study suggests that the regions with the highest overall household income (Akershus, Rogaland) are also associated with the highest farm household income. This may reflect higher opportunity costs of farming close to urban areas with a high pressure on land prices. The economic impact of the regional dummies suggests that location matters. It remains to be analyzed whether such locality effects reflect variation in the labor market, in the land market, or is embedded in social or cultural differences across regions.

Differences in household incomes are larger for younger farmers, reflecting differences in opportunity costs. We hypothesize that farms are only maintained across generations when it is possible to combine the farm income with comparably high off-farm income. It follows that decisions to take over a farm are made on the household level, not on the farm level. A policy that aims at preventing active farms from closing down should therefore not only target intervention towards agriculture, but also focus on making it easier for potential farmers to combine agriculture with off-farm employment. There is a balance, however. The data reveal that larger farms on average perform better than smaller farms. This implies that continuing farms need to grow, which can happen only if existing farms quit. Our analysis thus reinforces a well-known conflict of objectives regarding the speed of structural change in agriculture. In this respect, our analysis covered only a particular year. Future research should focus on the question how a farm's income difference in a particular year relates to the decision whether the farm continues or exits in the course of future generational transfer. After all, our analysis does not reveal the causes of the large variation in the income difference across farm households. Some variation may be in fact explained by the inherent preferences of the farm operator.

Note

1 Other income makes up the difference between total income and the sum of agricultural income and wage income. It is not further defined in the database. It consists, in general, of other income from self-employment and capital income.

Acknowledgments

This research has received funding from the Research Council of Norway under grant no. 233810.

References

Ahearn, M.C., El-Osta, H. and Dewbre, J. 2006. The Impact of Coupled and Decoupled Government Subsidies on Off-Farm Labor Participation of U.S. Farm Operators. *American Journal of Agricultural Economics* 88(2): 393–408.

Benjamin, D. 1992. Household Composition, Labor Markets, and Labor Demand: Testing for Separation in Agricultural Household Models. *Econometrica* 60(2): 287–322.

Gardner, B.L. 1992. Changing Economic Perspective on the Farm Problem. *Journal of Economic Literature* (30): 62–101.

Mishra, A., El-Osta, H.S., Morehart, M.J., Johnson, J.D., and Hopkins, J.W. 2002. Income, Wealth, and the Economic Well-Being of Farm Households. Washington DC: U.S. Department of Agriculture, Economic Research Service, Agricultural Economic Report Number 812.

Norwegian Agriculture Agency. 2015. Direct payments. (https://www.slf.dep.no/en/agriculture-and-market/direct-payments, accessed 10.11.2015)

OECD. 2015. Producer and Consumer Support Estimates database. OECD: Paris.

Schmitt, G. 1989. Simon Kuznets' "Sectoral Shares in Labor Force": A Different Explanation of His (I+S)/A Ration. *American Economic Review* 79(5): 1262–1276.

Schultz, T.W. 1990. *Restoring Economic Equilibrium*. Cambridge MA: Basil Blackwell.

Statistics Norway. 2011a. Census of Agriculture 2010. (http://ssb.no/en/jord-skog-jakt-og-fiskeri/artikler-og-publikasjoner/landbruksteljing-2010, accessed 10.11.2015)

Statistics Norway. 2011b. Tax statistics for personal tax payers 2010. (http://www.ssb.no/en/inntekt-og-forbruk/statistikker/selvangivelse/aar-forelopige/2011-07-05, accessed 10.11.2015)

Chapter 10

Does the post-2013 CAP reduce the disparities in the distribution of decoupled payments across Europe?

A farm-level assessment

Maria Espinosa, Kamel Louhichi, and Sergio Gomez y Paloma

Introduction

The Common Agricultural Policy (CAP) has undergone a gradual change from market intervention instruments (e.g. price support) to decoupled measures attempting to enhance the environmental performance of the EU agricultural sector and to ensure a more equitable distribution of support between farmers. This became evident with the introduction of the single payment scheme (SPS) in 2005 in the Fischler reform.

Under the SPS, farms receive annual payments that do not depend on the current or future quantities of agricultural production, but are linked to farmland (Ciaian *et al.*, 2014). These payments are conditional on the farm compliance with the minimum environmental, food safety and animal welfare standards (GAEC, "Good Agricultural and Environmental Conditions"). Member states (MS) were given the option to implement the SPS based on regional, historic, static-hybrid or dynamic hybrid model. MS implementing a regional model opted for a redistribution of support among farms, while MS implementing a historical model opted to keep existing differences in direct payments among farms; while hybrid models implied that part of the payments are farm-specific and others are not.

In the new MS that joined the EU in 2004 and 2007, the direct payments were managed through the SAPS (single area payment scheme) (with the exception of Malta and Slovenia). The SAPS is a standard area subsidy paid per hectare of land without entitlements; all land is eligible and all farms receive a uniform payment. Conceptually, this payment corresponds to the regional SPS model with its surplus (infinite) stock of entitlements (Ciaian *et al.*, 2014).

In 2012, decoupled payment (SPS and SAPS) represented more than 90% of direct payments, highlighting their importance on the EU agricultural income support. Moreover, according to a recent study based on FADN (Farm Accountancy Data Network) data, the contribution of direct payments in the farm net value added[1] was about 31%, ranging from 72% in Finland to 12% in the Netherlands (European Commission, 2012). This implies that a drastic reduction of direct support may strongly impact the viability of certain farms in the EU. Nowicki *et al.* (2010) provided evidence that a sharp decrease in the direct payment budget would result in a large number of farms going bankrupt (Bureau and Mahé, 2015).

Despite its importance, the austerity measures in many MS due to the financial crisis as well as the persistence of disparities among farms, regions and MS have put public and political pressure on the budget allocated to SPS and SAPS and led to a new reform of the CAP in 2013.[2] Other factors such as the WTO (World Trade Organization), the sustainable management of natural resources, climate change and balanced territorial development have also played a key role in this reform.

The 2013 CAP reform (EU, 2013) goes further in the direction of more equitable, green, and market-oriented. It included a new system of direct payments called the "Basic Payment Scheme" (BPS) which replaced the SPS and the SAPS with an explicit goal to introduce a more selective form of support, with payments better targeted and more equitably distributed among farms, sectors and regions within each MS and across MS. In this respect, in addition to 'degressivity' (i.e. progressive reduction of support on larger beneficiaries) and 'external convergence' (a mechanism included in the Multiannual Financial Framework (MFF) 2014–2020), the reform introduces a more uniform distribution of the per-hectare basic farm payments ('internal convergence'), payments for young farmers, a 'redistributive payment' shifting support from larger farms to smaller ones and payments for farms located in areas with natural constraints.

Focusing on the convergence as one of the key criterion of the 2013 CAP reform, the main aims of this chapter are (i) to quantify the changes in the total budget allocation and in the average decoupled unit payments (including redistributive payment, capping and greening) under the post-2013 CAP, in comparison to the former CAP, and (ii) to assess to what extend the post-2013 CAP will reduce the intra- and inter-MS disparities in the distribution of funds. To reach these aims, we use the Farm Accountancy Data Network (FADN) data in year 2012 and we consider the changes derived from the final implementation of the CAP 2014–2020 by MS. MS decisions regarding the implementation of the entitlements, the BPS (as well as SAPS), the redistributive payment, the capping and the greening are also taken into account.

Results are presented in form of box-plot to show the distributive effects of the post-2013 CAP as well as via standard measurement approach, the Lorenz Curve, to compare the size of inequality at EU level under both pre- and post-2013 CAP. A summary table and graph, showing the potential winners and losers from the post-2013 CAP decoupled payments among EU-MS, farms and regions, are also presented.

The chapter is structured as follows: in the first section, an overview of the 2014–2020 CAP and its implementation by MS is provided. In the second section, the used data and methodology is described. In the third section the results are presented and discussed, and in the final section we highlight the main conclusions and directions of further research.

The 2014–2020 CAP and the MS implementation

Brief overview of the 2014–2020 CAP

One of the main objectives of the post-2013 CAP reform related to the direct payments[3] is to improve efficiency and equity of the CAP through more targeted and equitable direct payments. Within this reform, the SPS and SAPS have been substituted by the BPS, which operates on the same principle, but is slightly more restricted. The BPS is therefore similar to the regionalized SPS in which all farms in a region have entitlements with the same unit value. The other application of the SPS are the historical model in which the SPS is calculated at farm level, depending on the support received during the "reference" period, and the hybrid model, which is a combination of the historical and the regional model (in Table 10.2 the application is specified by MS).

Coupled support has been maintained for a number of products. Other measures such as the young farmer scheme, Areas of Natural Constraints (ANC), small farmer scheme and green payment and redistributive payment have been introduced under

Table 10.1 New design of direct payments (and share of direct payments envelopes)

Basic Payment Scheme (**)
- no fixed percentage
- 5% degressivity over €150.000

Green payment (**)
- mandatory 30%
- greening practices or equivalent

Redistributive Payment(**)
- up to 30%
- max. of 65% of average direct payments (first ha)

Young Farmer(*)
- up to 2%
- +25% payments (max 5 years)

Natural constraint support(*)
- Up to 5%

Coupled support(*)
- Up to 10% or 15%

Small farmer scheme(*)
- up to 10%
- max. 1250 EUR
- simplified

Source: DG-AGRI (2013).
*voluntary
**compulsory

the direct payments budget (see Table 10.1). MS are given more flexibility in the budgeting and implementation of direct payments (see Table 10.2). The MS applying the Single Area Payment Scheme (SAPS) may extend the use of this system until 2020.

Focusing on the BPS, the main aims of this income support measure are (i) the convergence of the value of the payment entitlement towards a more uniform unit value payment within a MS (internal convergence), (ii) the convergence of CAP financial resources among MS (external convergence), and (iii) the rebalancing of total payments (redistribution, degressivity and capping) between farmers.

The internal convergence mechanism is one of the core elements of the 2013 CAP reform. It seeks to reduce by 2019, or eliminate completely, the differences in the basic unit payment among farmers within each MS; therefore the direct payments will no longer be based on historic parameters but rather will move towards more homogenous payments. To achieve this, MS could choose from these different options:

- Full convergence in 2015 or 2019: all farms in one MS will have the same unit value per payment entitlement (flat rate from 2015 or from 2019).
- Partial convergence: MS will move towards a flat rate in 2019. Farms getting less of the (regional/national) average rate will have a gradual increase. No payment should be lower than 60% of the (national/regional) average. The payment entitlements with an initial value lower than 90% (100%) of the average will be increased, by 2019, by at least one-third of the difference between the initial value[4] and the 90% (or 100%) of the final convergence value. This increase in payments will be financed by the farmers who are getting the payments above the average. The specific criteria are determined by MS based on non-discriminatory criteria.

These models are applicable at national or at regional level if the MS chose the option of regionalizing the BPS (Article 23 of Regulation 1307/2013 (EU, 2013)).

The external convergence is related to a fairer distribution of CAP financial resources among MS that have been reflected on the 2014–2020 MFF (Multiannual Financial Framework). MS with average direct payments above the EU average have reduced their allocation progressively to finance those with an average direct payment below 90% of EU average. Due to the external convergence, all the new MS (with the exception of Cyprus, Malta and Slovenia) have observed an increase in their national ceilings; while the EU-15 MS, with the exception of Spain and Portugal, have registered a reduction of their national envelope (Anania and Pupo D'Andrea, 2015). In addition, the external convergence ensures that, first, the average direct payment per ha in MS where the envelope has been reduced cannot be lower than the EU average, and second, the average direct payment per ha in all MS cannot be lower than 196 Euros/ha (in nominal prices) by 2019.

In addition to internal and external convergences, MS have further opportunities to rebalance payments with the introduction of the redistributive payment, capping and the degressivity (reduction) of payments. The redistributive payments aims to increase support for small- and medium-sized farms by allocating higher levels of aid for the first 30 hectares (or up to the average farm size, if higher) of a holding. MS can devote up to 30% of their national ceiling for this purpose. This feature aims to improve the distributional equity of EU farm payments. In fact, on average 80% of the direct payments beneficiaries receive around 20% of the payments (DG AGRI, 2014). Moreover, the high level of aid received by some beneficiaries is seen as too high to be justified as an income support (i.e. large farmers are assumed to benefit from economies of scale) and, therefore, it should be decreased proportional to the farm size.

The second key element of the rebalance of payments is the compulsory degressivity and voluntary capping aiming to reduce the BPS for the largest economic farms. MS shall reduce basic payments, by at least 5%, for the part exceeding €150.000 with a sliding scale leading ultimately to a cap at €300.000.[5] MS could increase this percentage up to 100% (therefore leading to the capping). MS are also exempted to apply degressivity if it has decided to implement the voluntary redistributive payments, and these absorb more than 5% of the direct payments. Funds generated from degressivity and capping payments would be shifted to Rural Development projects in the same region/MS.

In addition to the BPS, the 2013 CAP reform has introduced a "greening" payment for respecting certain agricultural practices beneficial for the climate and the environment. In particular, 30% of the national envelope needs to be linked to the provision of three greening measures: crop diversification, maintaining permanent grassland and establishing Ecological Focus Areas (EFAs). MS are flexible in defining the EFA and the equivalence practices. This greening payment can be paid as a flat rate or as a percentage of the BPS of the individual farmer.

Finally, it is important to highlight that under the post-2013 CAP, MS have the possibility to transfer up to 15% of their national envelopes between pillars.

CAP 2014–2020 implementation by MS

The post-2013 CAP reform offers the MS certain flexibility regarding its implementation. Table 10.2 shows the options adopted by each MS regarding the application of the internal convergence mechanism, the redistributing of payments, the capping and the details of the Partial Convergence model. The ten new MS previously applying SAPS have decided to maintain this form of basic payment until the end of 2020. Among the 18 remaining MS, six decided to regionalize the BPS: France (two regions: Corcega and Hexagon), Germany (by administrative regions), Finland (two regions determined by natural constraints), Spain (50 regions determined by historical land uses (irrigated, non-irrigated, permanent crop and grassland) and county), Greece (regions determined by historical land uses: grazing areas, arable land and permanent crops), the United Kingdom (in England, three regions determined by natural characteristics,[6] and in Scotland, three regions determined by land uses and natural characteristics). The remaining 12 MS applying BPS have implemented it at the national level.

Eleven MS (and Northern Ireland) have decided to apply a Partial Convergence, while six MS (and England, Scotland and Wales) have opted for a flat rate (Germany, Malta and England already in 2015, while the rest of MS/regions by 2019). The percentage of the national ceiling dedicated to the basic payments and the SAPS is very heterogeneous among MS (ranging from 34% in France to 68% in Luxemburg). Regarding the allocation of the payment entitlements, the set of farmers eligible for direct payments has been expanded to include virtually all active farmers.[7] Therefore, new payment entitlements have been allocated to farmers who (i) were producing fruit and vegetables, ware potatoes, seed potatoes, ornamental plants and grapes; (ii) had entitlements from the national reserve and (iii) never held, owned or leased entitlements and can probe those who were farming in 2013. In addition, some MS limit the entitlements to the ones in 2013 (DK, FI, SE, UK-England), while others limit the number of entitlements to the eligible hectares in 2013 (BL-Flanders, ES, IR, PT) if that number is lower than the hectares the farmer declares in 2015. Furthermore, in FR vineyards are not eligible, while in NL and EL arable land under permanent greenhouses are not eligible. Austria and UK-Scotland have applied a reduction coefficient to permanent grassland (1 ha of permanent grassland gives right to 0.2 entitlements in Austria and 0.9 in UK-Scotland).

A total of eight MS will implement the redistributive payment: BE (Wallonia only), BG, DE, FR, HR, LT, PL and RO, ranging from 5% of the national ceiling in BG to 20% in FR. Among these MS, six have decided not to apply the reduction of payments mechanism; PL and BG will grant the redistributive payment while applying the reduction of payments mechanism. Nine MS[8] will cap the amounts of the basic payments, ranging from €150.000 to €600.000 (Table 10.2), while 15 MS have opted for applying only the minimum reduction of 5% on amounts of basic payments above €150.000. MS have also some freedom concerning the final application of the Partial Convergence and, therefore, the approximation towards flat rate. In particular, MS can choose the distance to the target value that should be reduced for the farmers receiving below the average.

Therefore, farmers can increase their unitary value of payment entitlements by an amount that reduces the distance to the target value by 33%, 70% or 83% (*increase target* in Table 10.2). This target value is settled either at the 90% or 100% of the average in 2019 (*ref. value* in Table 10.2). In addition, MS can decide on the minimum level (compared to the average) of the PE (Payment Entitlement) in 2019 (*min* column in Table 10.2) and the maximum decreased

Table 10.2 Implementation decisions of CAP 2014–2020 by member state

MS	Internal Convergence					Convergence criteria for MS in PC				Redistributive payment			Capping	
	Former Model	Model	% of total	NMI/RM	Increase target	Ref. value	Min.	Max	Model	ha	Euros/ha	%	Threshold (in 1000 €)	Reduction (%)
Belgium WL	HI	PC	29.9	NM	0.33	0.9	0.6	0.3	RP	30	115	17	150	100
(BL) FL	HI	PC	56.8	NM	0.33	0.9	0.6	0.3	RP	—	—	—	150	5
Bulgaria (BG)	SAPS	SAPS	47	—	—	—	—	—	—	30	77	7	150/300	5/100
Czech Republic (CZ)	SAPS	SAPS	54.8	—	—	—	—	—	—	—	—	—	150	5
Denmark (DK)	HYS	PC	65	NM	0.33	0.9			LR	—	—	—	150	5
Germany (DE)	HYD	FR2015	62.1	RM	—	—	—	—	—	1–30 30–46	50/30	6.9	—	—
Estonia (ES)	SAPS	SAPS	65.3	—	—	—	—	—	—	—	—	—	150	5
Ireland (IR)	HI	PC	67.8	NM	0.33	0.9	0.6		LR	—	—	—	150	100
Greece (EL)	HI	PC	60	RM	—	—	—	—		—	—	—	150	100
Spain (ES)	HI	PC	56	RM	0.33	0.9		0.3	LR	—	—	—	150	100
France (FR)	HI	PC	34	RM	0.7	1	0.6	0.3	RP	52	25	20		
Croatia (HR)	HI	PC	43	NM	0.33	1	0.6		LR	20	34	10		
Italy (IT)	HI	PC	58	NM	0.33	0.9	0.6	0.3	RP				150/500	50/100
Cyprus (CY)	SAPS	SAPS	61.1	—	—	—	—	—	—	—	—	—	150	5
Latvia (LV)	SAPS	SAPS	55.1	—	—	—	—	—	—	—	—	—	150	5
Lithuania (LT)	SAPS	SAPS	38.3	—	—	—	—	—	—	30	50	15	—	
Luxembourg (LU)	HYS	PC	68	NM	0.33	0.9	0.6	0.3	RP	—	—	—	150	5
Hungary (HU)	SAPS	SAPS	54.8	—	—	—	—	—	—	—	—	—	150/176	5/100
Malta (MT)	R	FR2015	34	NM	—	—	—	—	—	—	—	—	150	5
Netherlands (NL)	HI	FR2019	67.5	NM	—	—	—	—	—	—	—	—	150	5
Austria (AT)	HI	FR2019	65.9	NM	—	—	—	—	—	—	—	—	150	100

(continued)

Table 10.2 Implementation decisions of CAP 2014–2020 by member state (continued)

MS	Internal Convergence				Convergence criteria for MS in PC					Redistributive payment			Capping	
	Former Model	Model	% of total	NM/ RM	Increase target	Ref. value	Min.	Max	Model	ha	Euros/ ha	%	Threshold (in 1000 €)	Reduction (%)
Poland (PL)	SAPS	SAPS	46	—	—	—	—	—	—	0–3/3–30	0/41	8	150	100
Portugal (PT)	HI	PC	47	NM	0.33	0.9	0.6	0.3	LR	—	—	—	150	5
Romania (RO)	SAPS	SAPS	51	—	—	—	—	—	—	0–5/5–30	5/45	5	—	—
Slovenia (SI)	R	PC	54	NM	0.33	0.9	0.6	0.3	RP	—	—	—	150	5
Slovak Republic (SK)	SAPS	SAPS	56.4	NM	—	—	—	—	—	—	—	—	150	5
Finland (FI)	HYD	FR2019	49	RM	—	—	—	—	—	—	—	—	150	5
Sweden (SE)	HYS	PC	55.4	NM	0.83	0.9	—	—	LR	—	—	—	150	5
United Kingdom (UK) NI	HYS	PC	68	NM	0.7	1	—	LR	RP	—	—	—	150	100
EN	HYD	FR2015	68	RM	—	—	—	—	—	—	—	—	150	5
SC	HI	FR2019	61.8	RM	—	—	—	—	—	—	—	—	150/600	5/100
WA	HI	FR2019	68	NM	—	—	—	—	—	54	128	—	150/200/250/300	15/30/55/100

Source: European Commission (2015).

WL = Wallonia; FL = Flanders; NI = Northern Ireland; SC = Scotland; WA = Wales

HI = SPS Historical; HYS: SPS Hybrid Static; HYD: SPS Hybrid Dynamic; R: Regional

PC = Partial Convergence/FR2015 = Flat Rate by 2015/FR2019 = Flat rate by 2019/SAPS = Single Area Payment Scheme

% of Total = Percentage of the national financial allocation of the basic and the SAPS payments

NM = National Model/ RM = Regional Model. In DE the regional model will change to a national one in 2019.

RP = Reduction proportional to the distance to the average PE value/ LR = Linear reduction of the value of the PE for the farmers receiving above the average (*max* in Table 10.2). Finally, MS decide on whether the reduction of the PE above the average is conducted linearly or proportionally (*model* in Table 10.2). In the linear reduction the same percentage of reduction is applied for the share of the PE above the average, while in the proportional reduction the percentage of the reduction increases with the difference between the unit value of the PE and the 2019 average.

For a better understanding of the potential distributive effects of the post-2013 CAP decoupled payments, it is important to take into account the change of the national ceilings between the former and the post-2013 CAP. In the case of the former CAP we have considered 2012 data, as it is the year in which we have the FADN data; while for the CAP 2014–2020 it has been considered the budget in the year 2019, as it corresponds to the year in which the MS should achieve the final convergence. Table 10.3 provides the total direct payments (DP) and the ratio of total decoupled payments by MS under the previous and post-2013 CAP reform in million Euros (ME). In the post-2013 CAP there is flexibility between pillars. The net transfer is a total transfer from Pillar I to Pillar II of €3 billion over the 6 years. Eleven MS have decided to transfer from DP to RD (FR, LV, UK, BE, CZ, DK, DE, EE, EL, NL, RO), while HR, MT, PL, SK and HU transfer from RD to DP.

The decoupled payments in the former CAP correspond to SPS/SAPS and are calculated based on budget execution (EAGF (European Agricultural Guarantee Fund) data), while the ones for the CAP 2014–2020 correspond to the BPS and SAPS in the year 2019 with and without redistributive payment and greening (envelope reported by MS). Given the importance of the greening and of the

Table 10.3 Comparison of CAP budget between pre- and post-2013 CAP reform

	BPS-SAPS (2019)/ SPS-SAPS (2012)	BPS-SAPS + REDP (2019)/ SPS-SAPS (2012)	BPS-SAPS + REDP + GREEN (2019)/SPS-SAPS (2012)	TOTAL 2019-DP (ME)	TOTAL 2012-DP (ME)	TOTAL DP (2019)/ (2012)
AT	72.61%	—	105.67%	691.7	706.4	97.92%
BG	80.79%	92.76%	150.82%	792.5	494.4	160.30%
BL	44.27%	53.39%	81.41%	515.3	600.5	85.81%
CY	73.26%	—	109.30%	48.6	43.8	110.96%
CZ	62.99%	—	97.47%	856.7	824.1	103.96%
DE	56.56%	62.94%	90.31%	4792.6	5253.9	91.22%
DK	58.32%	—	85.37%	818.3	939.2	87.13%

(*continued*)

Table 10.3 Comparison of CAP budget between pre- and post-2013 CAP reform
(continued)

	BPS-SAPS (2019)/ SPS-SAPS (2012)	BPS-SAPS + REDP (2019)/ SPS-SAPS (2012)	BPS-SAPS + REDP + GREEN (2019)/SPS-SAPS (2012)	TOTAL 2019-DP (ME)	TOTAL 2012-DP (ME)	TOTAL DP (2019)/ (2012)
EE	105.32%	—	152.95%	143.9	91.9	156.55%
EL	54.81%	—	82.21%	2022.4	2282.3	88.61%
ES	61.18%	—	93.93%	4953.1	5237.2	94.57%
FI	54.87%	—	87.41%	524.6	531.8	98.64%
FR	35.36%	56.17%	87.37%	7189.5	7967.5	90.24%
HU	71.39%	—	110.47%	1273.9	1203.4	105.86%
IR	67.06%	—	96.76%	1211.0	1250.9	96.81%
IT	58.59%	—	88.89%	3702.4	3959.6	93.50%
LT	61.37%	85.44%	133.57%	517.0	345.6	149.60%
LV	124.21%	—	191.65%	279.8	132.9	210.52%
MT	13.44%	—	46.00%	5.2	4.8	107.55%
NL	58.93%	—	85.12%	700.8	823.0	85.16%
PL	63.35%	74.86%	116.44%	3430.2	2769.5	123.86%
PT	67.50%	—	109.35%	599.4	648.7	92.40%
RO	88.00%	97.76%	152.47%	1903.2	1086.8	175.12%
SE	56.08%	—	86.67%	699.7	689.3	101.50%
SI	59.23%	—	92.13%	134.3	130.2	103.16%
SK	78.94%	—	120.88%	448.7	354.3	126.64%
UK	65.56%	68.06%	97.56%	3200.8	3286.0	97.41%
EU	57.48%	63.84%	96.46%	41771.8	41658.3	100.27%

Source: European Commission (2014a, 2015) and EU (2013, 2014).

Note: Consider that while the 2012 data is based on actual expenditure, the 2019 data is based on expected expenditure based on envelopes.

The year 2012 has been taken as a reference for the period 2007–2013 to maintain consistency in the results section (based on FADN-2012).

Belgium and Luxembourg are merged as "BL".

Croatia is not included, as it is not implemented in the IFM-CAP model.

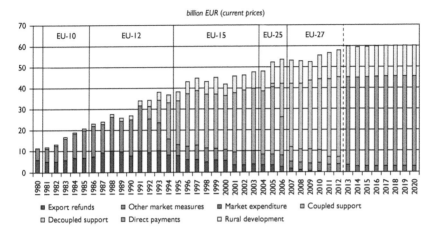

Figure 10.1 Distribution of Common Agricultural Policy payments, 2013

Source: DG-AGRI (2013).

redistributive payments, it is essential to isolate their effects while comparing the total decoupled supports under the former and the post-2013 CAP. It is also important to mention that neither the young farmer scheme (there is no data available in FADN to accurately assess this measure[9]) nor the small farmer scheme (it is voluntary measure and therefore it is difficult to be captured in our analysis) are considered in the calculation of this ratio. From Table 10.3, it can be highlighted that considering only the BPS/SAPS (first column), all MS will have fewer national payments compared to the 2012 level, except for EE and LV. However, when redistribution and greening are considered, all the MS applying SAPS – as well as some other MS such as AT, PT and SI – will have more decoupled budget assigned. The other MS will register a reduction of the decoupled payments budget below the 20%, except for Malta, where the budget decrease is about 46% due to the high share of coupled payments (57% of the national ceiling).

When considering all direct payments (therefore including coupled payments[10]), there is an increase in total funds allocated to direct payments in 2019, with respect to 2012, of less than 1% (Croatia not considered).[11] The CAP budget over time and the share of each measure are reflected in Figure 10.1.

Data and methods

As explained above, the main aims of this chapter are (i) to quantify the changes in the total budget allocation and in the average decoupled unit payments (including redistributive payment, capping and greening) under the 2013-CAP reform and

(ii) to assess to what extend the post-2013 CAP will reduce the disparities in the distribution of funds among EU MS, regions and farmers. Agricultural producers face very heterogeneous circumstances across the EU due to the very different economic and natural conditions and, therefore, an equal distribution of payments may not mean an equitable distribution; however, the definition of the equality criterion is out of the scope of this chapter.

To obtain the decoupled payments in 2020, we use the 2012 decoupled payments reported on EU-FADN database[12] and we apply the post-2013 CAP as it will be implemented by each MS in 2019 (target year for achieving the internal convergence), taking into account MS decisions regarding the calculation of entitlements, the BPS (as well as SAPS), the redistributive payment and the capping (see Figure 10.2). Distributional effects are presented in box-plots and via the Lorenz Curve in order to compare the size of inequality at the EU level under the pre- and post-2013 CAP. A summary table and graph, showing the set of potential winners and losers from the post-2013 CAP by MS, regions, farm types and individual farms, are also presented.

Data: The Farm Accountancy Data Network (2012)

The FADN (Farm Accountancy Data Network) is the only source of microeconomic data that is harmonized within the EU. It is a key dataset for both policy makers and researchers, as it serves as a basis for compiling statistics and policy analysis at farm level. In 2012, the FADN sample covered 83.292 commercial holdings (representing a population of around 5 million farms in the EU). Even if more than 7 million farms (corresponding to non-commercial farms[13]) are not represented by the FADN sample, the FADN sample covers around 90% of total UAA, 90% of total production (FADN) (FADN website). The FADN is a representative stratified sample with regard to regional disaggregation (FADN regions), production specialization and farm size. An individual weighting scheme is applied to each farm in the sample corresponding to the number of farms it represents in the total population. In FADN-2012 (data used for the analysis) all current EU MS[14] are represented except Croatia (which accessed the EU in 2013).

As stated before the FADN data is representative of the EU commercial agricultural holdings in term of number of holdings (in a certain region, farm specialization and economic size), but not in terms of production area (nor quantities), subsidies and entitlements. To illustrate this issue, we show in Figure 10.3 the representativeness of FADN data in terms of decoupled payments and entitlements (eligible area for SAPS) for the year 2012. The national data on total decoupled payments have been extracted from EAFG (European Agriculture Guarantee Fund, European Commission (2014a)), while the data on entitlements and the total area for SAPS are coming from the European Commission (2014b and 2014c).

As the FADN represents only commercial farms, it is expected that its representativeness in terms of total decoupled payments is below 100%; however, when

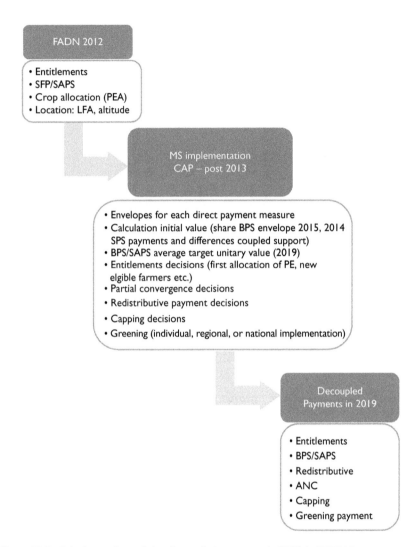

FADN 2012

• Entitlements
• SFP/SAPS
• Crop allocation (PEA)
• Location: LFA, altitude

MS implementation
CAP – post 2013

• Envelopes for each direct payment measure
• Calculation initial value (share BPS envelope 2015, 2014
  SPS payments and differences coupled support)
• BPS/SAPS average target unitary value (2019)
• Entitlements decisions (first allocation of PE, new
  elgible farmers etc.)
• Partial convergence decisions
• Redistributive payment decisions
• Capping decisions
• Greening (individual, regional, or national implementation)

Decoupled
Payments in 2019

• Entitlements
• BPS/SAPS
• Redistributive
• ANC
• Capping
• Greening payment

Figure 10.2 Calculation flow of the decoupled payments in 2019 in FADN farms

looking at the results it is not the case in several MS. As shown in Figure 10.3, in RO the share (FADN data divided by reported data) is approximately 1.2. This is due to the fact that the holdings receiving greater decoupled payments are over-represented in this MS (this ratio for the area receiving SAPS is 1.06)). On the other hand for CY, EL, MT and PT representation on decoupled payments is below 0.80. In the case of CY and PT the entitlements (or area receiving SAPS) ratio is as well below 0.8, however in the case of EL and MT the entitlements are over 0.8 (0.88

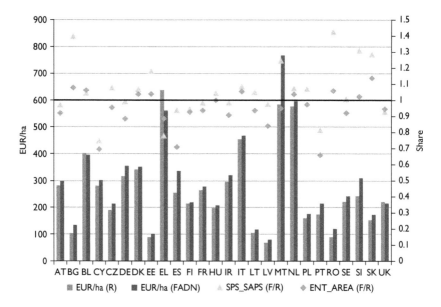

Figure 10.3 Representativeness of decoupled payments and entitlements in FADN compared to be population in the former CAP (2012)

R = reported

F = FADN data (2012)

Source: MS data on expenditure based on EAFG (European Commission, 2014a). MS information on entitlements (and area receiving decoupled payments) based on European Commission (2014b, 2014c).

Note: We are taking the EAFG report 2013 because MS pay farmers in year n; however, the EU reimbursed MS in year n + 1; therefore, for the calendar year 2012, the EAFG budged is taken to be for the financial year 2013.

Croatia is not represented in results as it is not in implemented in IFM-CAP.

and 0.94 respectively). This indicates that in EL and MT farmers with lower average unitary values are more represented in FADN.

Table 10.4 shows the representativeness of decoupled payments and potential eligible area (PEA) in FADN under the post-2013 CAP (2019), in comparison to the budget allocation envelope and the total population eligible area extracted from Eurostat (ESTAT), respectively. Results show that the representation of the Potential Eligible Area is between 0.8 and 1.2, except for CY, EL, MT and LV, where this area is underrepresented (a similar pattern as for entitlements in 2012). These MS are also underrepresented (below 0.8) in the FADN sample in the simulated year 2019. On the other hand, BPS and greening in AT and FR are overrepresented. This may be explained by the fact that farmers above the average payment per ha are overrepresented in the FADN sample.

Table 10.4 Representativeness of decoupled payments and potential eligible area (PEA) in FADN under the post-2013 CAP (2019)

	Budget and eligible area comparison between FADN and reported data (new CAP)			
	PEA (FADN/ESTAT)	*SPS(SAPS) (FADN/env)*	*REDP (FADN/env)*	*GREEN*
AT	1.03	1.25	—	1.25
BG	1.1	1.03	0.89	0.91
BL	1.05	1.11	0.81	1.2
CY	0.73	0.73	—	0.73
CZ	0.96	0.96	—	0.96
DE	0.98	0.95	0.92	0.95
DK	1.05	1.1	—	1.1
EE	1.05	0.98	—	0.98
EL	0.7	1.15	—	1.15
ES	0.98	0.86	—	0.86
FI	0.95	0.99	—	1.03
FR	0.89	1.4	0.83	1.4
HU	0.91	0.91	—	0.91
IR	0.84	0.98	—	0.98
IT	0.94	1.11	—	1.11
LT	0.89	0.89	0.71	0.89
LV	0.79	0.79	—	0.79
MT	0.67	0.66	—	0.66
NL	1	1.01	—	1.01
PL	0.95	0.95	1.12	0.95
PT	0.9	0.71	—	0.71
RO	1.05	1.04	1.17	1.04
SE	0.94	0.91	—	0.91
SI	0.98	1.04	—	1.04
SK	1.15	1.14	—	1.14
UK	0.87	0.95	0.78	0.99

Source: Authors' elaboration based on FADN data and MS implementation new CAP (European Commission, 2015).

ESTAT: Eurostat data

env: MS envelopes in year 2019

Average and distribution of decoupled payments under the former and the 2014–2020 CAP

In this section we compare, using FADN data, the average and the distribution of the basic decoupled unit payment under the former and the post-2013 CAP. The analysis has been conducted in successive steps for the CAP 2014–2010, starting with the BPS (or SAPS) and adding gradually the redistributive payment (RED), the capping/degressivity (CAP) and finally the greening (GREEN).[15] As shown in Table 10.5, all MS, except Latvia (LV), will register a reduction in the basic decoupled unit payment under the post-2013 CAP, reaching two-thirds in France (FR) and Greece (EL) due to the low share of decoupled payment scheme on the national ceiling. When considering the redistributive payment and the capping, the new decoupled unit payments get closer to the values of 2012. The average value becomes even higher for some MS such as Bulgaria (BG) and Latvia (LV). Finally, when adding the greening payment all new MS (except Malta (MT) due to the high share of coupled payments) will have a higher decoupled average payment, while in the old MS the range is between 0.49 in Greece (EL) and 0.99 in Ireland (IR). However, this is not surprising, since it aligns with one of the main goals of the post-2013 CAP reform, which is "fairer" distribution of CAP financial resources among MS (i.e. MS with average direct payments above EU average have reduced their allocation progressively to finance those with an average direct payment below 90% EU average).

Table 10.5 Comparison of unit value payment (EUR/PEA) in the former (2012) and post-2013 CAP reform (2019)

	Average (SPS/PEA) in 2012	SPS(BPS)/PEA (2019/2012)	(SPS(BPS) + RED + CAP)/PEA (2019/2012)	(SPS(BPS) + RED + CAP + GREEN))/PEA (2019/2012)
AT	247.37	0.60	0.60	0.88
BG	123.96	0.76	1.25	1.73
BL	355.09	0.42	0.49	0.75
CY	338.77	0.71	0.71	1.05
CZ	212.43	0.63	0.63	0.97
DE	329.76	0.52	0.63	0.88
DK	350.79	0.60	0.60	0.88
EE	100.4	0.99	0.99	1.43
EL	923.08	0.59	0.59	0.88

	Average (SPS/PEA) in 2012	SPS(BPS)/PEA (2019/2012)	(SPS(BPS) + RED + CAP)/PEA (2019/2012)	(SPS(BPS) + RED + CAP + GREEN))/PEA (2019/2012)
ES	351.75	0.51	0.51	0.79
FI	213.58	0.57	0.57	0.92
FR	275.01	0.34	0.59	0.89
HU	204.71	0.67	0.67	1.04
IR	313.18	0.67	0.67	0.97
IT	411.02	0.46	0.46	0.70
LT	117.6	0.58	0.92	1.37
LV	71.25	1.17	1.17	1.80
MT	421.79	0.13	0.13	0.43
NL	570.03	0.50	0.50	0.72
PL	174.97	0.62	0.77	1.18
PT	264.65	0.30	0.30	0.49
RO	116.88	0.77	0.86	1.34
SE	247.26	0.55	0.55	0.86
SI	259.74	0.62	0.62	0.96
SK	171.72	0.78	0.78	1.19
UK	262.89	0.64	0.67	0.96

Source: Authors' elaboration, based on FADN data and MS implementation new CAP (European Commission, 2015).

For simplicity, SPS and BPS both represent SAPS in the column headings.

The information on the SPS (EUR/PEA) in 2012 is the average over all the farms that may differ from the ones presented in Figure 10.1 that are calculated based on the ratio of the total values in numerator and denominator.

The box-plot Figures 10.4 to 10.6 show the distribution of the basic unit payment in EUR/PEA[16] (EUR/ha) under the former and the post-2013 CAP. The bottom of each box is the 25th percentile, the top is the 75th and the line in the middle is the 50th percentile. The whiskers represent the lowest datum within 1.5 IQR (Interquartile Range) of the lower quartile and the highest datum still within the 1.5 IQR of the upper quartile. The marks represent the mean.[17]

To facilitate comparison, MS are grouped into different graphs according to the applied internal convergence mechanism: SAPS, flat rate in 2019 (or 2015) and Partial Convergence. Two other box graphs (Figures 10.7 and 10.8) showing the distribution by farm production specialization and farm size aggregated over all MS are also plotted. UK has been presented in the set of countries applying flat rate (FR) because England, Wales and Scotland are applying flat rate and only Northern Ireland is applying partial convergence (PC). In each graph, four different box plots have been presented:

1   SPS (SAPS) (2012): representing the decoupled payments under former CAP.
2   BPS (SAPS) (2020)[18]: representing the BPS (or the SAPS) under the post-2013 CAP.
3   BPS (SAPS) + RED_CAPP (2020) where the redistributive payment and the capping have been added to BPS (or SAPS).
4   BPS (SAPS) + REDP_CAPP + GREEN (2020) where the greening payment has been added to BPS (or SAPS) and RED_CAPP.

It is important to highlight that the "greening payment" is linked to the farmers complying with the greening requirements. In the current analysis, we have assumed that all the concerned farms will fully comply with the requirement and, consequently, they will receive the greening payments. The unit value of the greening payment depends on the share of the BPS in the total budget as well as whether the greening is applied at national, regional or individual level.[19] When it is applied at individual level, the greening payment is related to the individual BPS and, therefore, will not have any distribution effect (just moving upwards the box-plot); however, when it is at regional level, there may be distributional effects on the basic payment as it is not linked to the calculated individual BPS.

The redistributive payment and the capping have also been included in this analysis because both of them affect the redistribution of direct payments between small and big farms, even if in opposite directions: redistribution increased the BPS/SAPS payments for the first hectares, while capping decreased the total basic payments for farmers exceeding a threshold (specified in Table 10.2). In MS applying both (PL, UK and BG), capping is applied before applying the redistributive payment. The effects of the redistributive payments (compared to the capping) are 26, 9 and 17 times higher for UK, BG and PL respectively. At EU level, the average amount devoted to redistributive payments is 17 times higher than the capping; therefore, the effects are more targeted in the direction of compensating small farmers rather than capping the payments for big farms.

Before providing the comparative distribution, it is interesting to highlight that, first, in CY, ES, IT, PT, EL, MT and NL there is a small proportion of farms with a very high unit value of basic payment that raise the mean significantly in the basic payment for the year 2012, but have little impact on the median. Second, the FADN values for 2012 should be homogenous within a MS; however, there are smooth variations as reflected in the box plot for CY (and in less prominent in BG). This is probably due to a reporting issue when farmers complete the FADN survey. From these graphs, we can notice that the implementation of the post-2013 CAP would lead, as expected, to an internal convergence towards uniform unit value of payments in all MS. In addition, the box-plot figures shows that, compared to former CAP, the application of Art.25 (4), in which it is stated that the PE value in 2019 should be higher than 60% of the average over the MS (or region depending on the BPS application), has a substantial effect in distribution of the payments in the lower whisker. The internal convergence is quite different among MS depending on the applied mechanism. For example, in MS applying SAPS (Figure 10.4) the convergence is almost total, except in BG, RO and LT, where the redistributive payment creates minor heterogeneity in the unitary decoupled payments among farms.

In the set of countries applying Partial Convergence (PC), it can be stated that there is heterogeneity in the final basic payments in 2019, but it is less pronounced than under the former CAP due to the internal convergence (Figure 10.5). From this graph, it is also interesting to notice the significant effect of the redistributive payment in France (FR), which almost doubles the average unit value.

In the MS applying a flat rate, it can be highlighted that there is a homogenous unit value payment at MS level, except in FI and UK, where the flat rate are differentiated by regions (Figure 10.6). In the case of FI, the average payments for the two regions are 112 and 125 EUR/ha and in the UK range between 7 EUR/ha

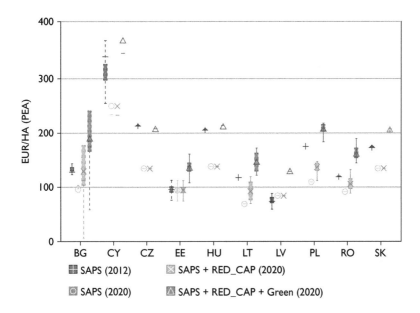

Figure 10.4 Distribution of unitary decoupled payments (EUR/HA(PEA)) under the pre- and post-2013 CAP reforms for MS applying SAPS

Source: Authors' elaboration.

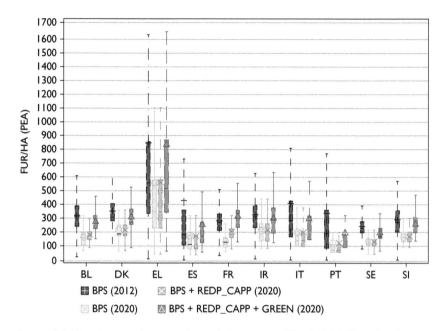

Figure 10.5 Distribution of unitary decoupled payments (EUR/HA(PEA)) under the pre- and post-2013 CAP reforms for MS applying Partial Convergence.

Source: Authors' elaboration.

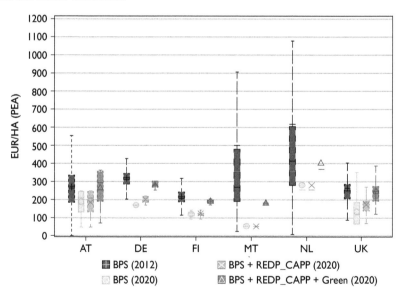

Figure 10.6 Distribution of unitary decoupled payments (EUR/HA(PEA)) under the pre- and post-2013 CAP reforms for MS applying Flat Rate

Source: Authors' elaboration.

in rough grazing in LFA in Scotland to 169 EUR/ha in England (particularly in regions not located in SDA (Severely Disadvantaged Areas) and in non-moorland areas located in SDA).[20] Among the MS applying a flat rate, only the UK and DE are applying the redistributive payment, as reflected in Figure 10.6.

As show in Figure 10.7, in all farm types there is a small proportion of farms with a very high unit value payment and a larger proportion of farms with low values (this is depicted by the higher values of the mean compared to the median). The most pronounced deviations are observed for the specialist olives and the specialist milk and cattle. In all the sectors, the average unit payments (considering only BPS) will decrease under the post-2013 CAP; this decrease ranges from 9 EUR/PEA (EUR/ha) in specialist horticulture to 281 EUR/PEA (EUR/ha) in specialist sheep and goats. This decrease is adjusted when greening, redistribution, and capping measures are considered. Moreover, as shown in Figure 10.7, in some specializations the average payment increases when all the decoupled payments are considered (this increase is over 50 EUR/PEA in specialist horticulture, specialist orchards and specialist wine). As expected, the spread of payments within each specialization is also shortened in the post-2013 CAP BPS.

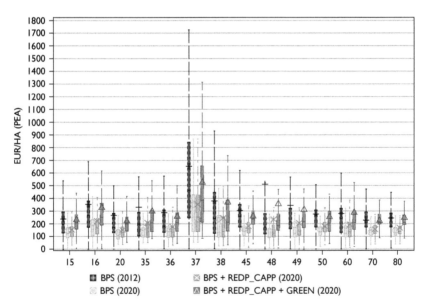

Figure 10.7 Distribution of unitary decoupled payments (EUR/HA(PEA)) under the pre- and post-2013 CAP reforms presented by farm type

15: Specialist COP, 16: Specialist other fieldcrops, 20: Specialist horticulture, 35: Specialist wine, 36: Specialist orchards – fruits, 37: Specialist olives, 38: Permanent crops combined, 45: Specialist milk, 48: Specialist sheep and goats, 49: Specialist cattle, 48: Specialist sheep and goats, 50: Specialist granivores, 60: Mixed crops, 70: Mixed livestock, 80: Mixed crops and livestock.

Source: Authors' elaboration.

The same trends are being observed while looking to the average and distribution of unit payments by Economic Size Class (ESC) (Figure 10.8): (i) a decrease in the average unit payments in all the size groups when only BPS/SAPS is considered, (ii) when redistributive and capping is considered this effect is attenuated and (iii) a reduction in farm heterogeneity within each group due to the internal convergence mechanism. The most homogenous payment is shown in the lowest ESC, explained by the fact that only farms in BG and RO are sampled in this class (i.e. all other MS have a threshold value in the FADN sample higher than 2×10^3 EUR, and therefore there are no farms of the other MS of this ESC represented in the FADN sample). It is also interesting to highlight that the effects of the internal convergence are depicted in the distribution of the ESC, as the median levels (considering BPS, redistributive and greening payments) show an increase in the smallest ESC (ESC 2 to ESC 7) and an decrease in the largest (ESC 8 to ESC 14).

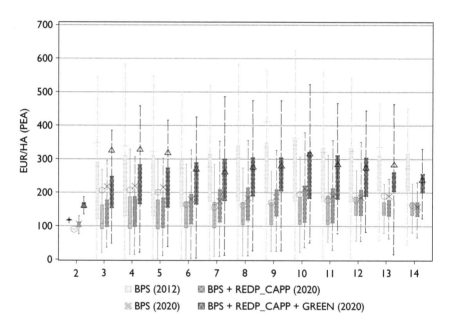

Figure 10.8 Distribution of unitary decoupled payments (EUR/HA(PEA)) under the pre- and post-2013 CAP reforms presented by economic size classes

Economic size of the farms represented by the Standard Output (SO): 2 = 2 – 4 × 10^3 EUR; 3 = 4 – 8 × 10^3 EUR; 4 = 8 – 15 × 10^3 EUR; 5 = 15 – 25 × 10^3 EUR; 6 = 25 – 50 × 10^3 EUR; 7 = 50 – 100 × 10^3 EUR; 8 = 100 – 250 × 10^3 EUR; 9 = 250 – 400 × 10^3 EUR; 10 = 500 – 750 × 10^3 EUR; 11 = 750 – 2000 × 10^3 EUR; 12 = 1 – 1.5 × 10^6 EUR; 13 = 1.5 – 3 × 10^6 EUR; 14 = 3 × 10^6 EUR.

Source: Authors' elaboration.

Figure 10.9 displays the distribution of decoupled payments across the whole commercial farms population in the EU (based on FADN samples) under the former and the post-2013 CAP (BPS/SAPS with and without the capping and the redistributive payment). These Lorenz Curves[21] show the cumulative proportion of decoupled payments (Y-axis) received by the cumulative proportion of beneficiaries (X-axis).

The graph shows that decoupled payments are not equally distributed among agricultural holdings under the pre- and post-2013 CAP reform. If that were the case, the cumulative decoupled payments would increase linearly from the bottom left to the upper right corner. The implementation of the post-2013 CAP has moved the redistribution of the decoupled payments closer to the diagonal, implying a more equal distribution of CAP decoupled payments among holdings. Under the former CAP, 50% of the farms were receiving 14% of the payments; while in the post-2013 CAP, 50% of the farms will receive 19% of the payments. The introduction of the redistributive/capping payments will improve slightly the equity distribution among farms. This is mainly shown in farms that represent over 50% of the cumulative difference of decoupled payments.

Figure 10.10 shows the cumulative differences between the decoupled payments under the former and the post-2013 CAP for the whole commercial farms population in the EU (based on FADN samples). In the X-axis is presented the

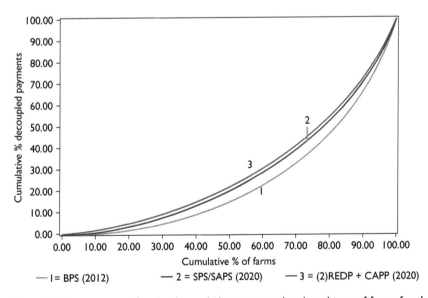

Figure 10.9 Lorenz curve for the decoupled payments related to the nr of farms for the pre- and post-2013 CAP

Source: Authors' elaboration.

cumulative frequency of farms, while in the Y-axis is presented the cumulative differences (sorted in ascending order) between the decoupled payments under both CAPs. The last farm (cumulative frequency = 100%) represents the value of the decoupled payments gained at EU-level due to the implementation of the post-2013 CAP. The cumulative differences of the payments are reported based on (i) the difference between the BPS (or SAPS) and the former CAP SPS (or SAPS) (represented in the graph by the blue line), (ii) the difference adding to BPS (or SAPS) the redistributing and capping payments (represented in the graph by the red line) and (iii) adding to (ii) the greening payment (represented in the graph by the green line).

As shown in Figure 10.10, the comparison of the post-2013 BPS (or SAPS) with the SPS (or SAPS) leads to a loss of −16333 million of Euro (ME); where the redistributive payment is added the loss is −14300 (ME), while when adding the greening the loss is −2711 (ME). Results show also that around 9% of the farms did not receive any decoupled payments in the base year and did not experience any change with the implementation of the post-2013 CAP. In addition, around 81% of the farms experienced a decline, while the remaining 10% gained payments. When the redistributive and the capping payments are considered, around 78% of farms experienced a decline, while the remaining 13% gained payments. As presented in

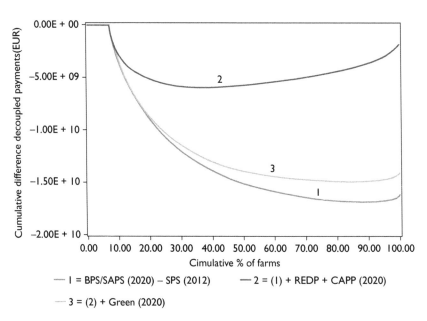

Figure 10.10 Cumulative difference in decoupled payments between the pre- and post-2013 CAP

Source: Authors' elaboration.

the aggregated results, the incorporation of the "greening payment" changes the picture of the redistribution of decoupled payments, as 48% of the farms are losing payments while 43% are gaining payments.

Table 10.6 summarizes the net redistribution of decoupled payments. It reports the amount of farms losing payments and farms gaining payments at four levels of aggregation (MS, regions, farm specialization, farm size and individual farms). The difference has been presented as in previous graphs, by considering first the post-2013 CAP BPS (or SAPS), and then adding successively the redistribution, capping and greening payments.

The main conclusions coming out from this table is that, as expected, the loss in the total amount of payments (the net difference, losing minus gaining payments) corresponds to the final value in Figure 10.10. As highlighted in previous results, only SAPS MS would benefit from the post-2013 CAP (when considering all the decoupled payments) with a net gain of 1252 ME, while the MS applying partial convergence and flat rate would register a loss rounding to −2829 ME and −1134 ME, respectively.

Table 10.6 Summary of redistribution effects of the CAP 2014–2020 relative to the former CAP by farms, regions, MS and farm type levels

Type of internal convergence	Disaggregation level	BPS (1)		(2) = (1) + REDP + CAP		(3) = (2) + GREEN	
		Losing payments	Gaining payments	Losing payments	Gaining payments	Loosing payments	Gaining payments
Overall	FARMS	−17070	737	−15134	834	−6228	3517
	REG	−16363	31	−14344	45	−4623	1911
	MS	−16351	19	−14320	19	−4108	1396
	FTYP	−16332	0	−14300	0	−3163	452
	ESC	−16332	0	−14300	0	−3130	418
SAPS	FARMS	−2111	41	−1703	80	−98	1350
	REG	−2089	19	−1653	31	−45	1297
	MS	−2089	19	−1642	19	−41	1293
	FTYP	−2069	0	−1623	0	0	1252
	ESC	−2069	0	−1623	0	−34	1286
PC	FARMS	−10435	455	−9268	504	−4330	1501
	REG	−9986	7	−8773	9	−3134	305
	MS	−9979	0	−8764	0	−2922	92
	FTYP	−9979	0	−8764	0	−2954	0
	ESC	−9979	0	−8764	0	−2829	0

(continued)

Table 10.6 Summary of redistribution effects of the CAP 2014–2020 relative to the former CAP by farms, regions, MS and farm type levels (*continued*)

Type of internal convergence	Disaggregation level	BPS (1)		(2) = (1) + REDP + CAP		(3) = (2) + GREEN	
		Losing payments	Gaining payments	Losing payments	Gaining payments	Loosing payments	Gaining payments
FR	FARMS	−4524	241	−4163	250	−1800	666
	REG	−4288	5	−3918	5	−1444	309
	MS	−4283	0	−3914	0	−1145	11
	FTYP	−4296	13	−3936	22	−1289	22
	ESC	−4283	0	−3914	0	−1145	10

Source: Authors' elaboration.

The sum for the FTYP and ESC in the different regions (by the model application of the BPS) is not the same as the "overall" because the FTYP/ESC are not region specific and therefore when aggregating at different levels may give different results.

Conclusions

The Common Agricultural Policy post-2013 has introduced a new design of direct payments. In particular, the new BPS is no longer based on uneven historical references, but rather on more converging per hectare payment. MS have the flexibility to implement the BPS at national or regional level. Based on the FADN, we have evaluated the distributive effects of the post-2013 CAP decoupled payments across Europe. By post-2013 CAP decoupled payments, we are referring here to the BPS (SAPS) payments, combined with the redistributive, the capping and the "greening" payments. Payments under Pillar 2 as well as coupled payments, young farmer scheme, small farmer scheme or the national top-ups paid in the new MS are not considered in this analysis.

Due to the external convergence of the CAP, most of the new MS gained from the post-2013 CAP (compared to the 2012 payments), while former MS experienced a decline in the amount of decoupled payments. The distributional effects of the post-2013 CAP decoupled payments vary strongly among MS, depending whether the MS is applying internal convergence flat rate (in 2015 or 2019), partial convergence or SAPS. However, in all cases, an internal convergence of payments is observed. This convergence is also confirmed when analyzing the results at the MS, regional and farm-type (by specialization and size class) levels. The Lorenz Curve shows that the decoupled payments under the post-2013 CAP are more equitably distributed among EU farms, in comparison to the former CAP. The introduction of the redistributive/capping payments (BL, RO, PL, BG, FR, UK and LT) will improve slightly the equity distribution among farms.

As explained above, only decoupled payments of the post-2013 CAP are considered in this analysis. Therefore, a natural move forward is the assessment of the whole CAP effects, including decoupled and voluntary coupled supports. However, since the coupled payments are (crop and livestock) production-activity-specific, their introduction may lead to the change in farm land allocation and herd size and, therefore, their effects cannot be easily captured through a static analysis. A farm-level model like IFM-CAP (Louhichi *et al.*, 2015) that enables simulation of farm behavior is more suitable in such a case. With this model the effects of the decoupled payments can also be refined. In fact, farmers may decide to activate fewer entitlements if the income effect of capping and the redistributive payments is significant; or they may renounce the greening measures if they are costly and, in such cases, the distributional effects of decoupled payments may be different. Consequently, the overall impacts of the post-2013 CAP can be captured only by models/tools working at the micro (farm) level, applicable at EU-wide scale and able to capture the full heterogeneity across EU farms in terms of policy representation and impacts.

Notes

1 Farm net value added (FNVA) is equal to gross farm income minus costs of depreciation. It is used to remunerate the fixed factors of production (work, land and capital), whether they are external or family factors. As a result, agricultural holdings can be compared regardless of the family/non-family nature of the factors of production employed. FNVA = output + Pillar I and Pillar II payments + VAT balance − intermediate consumption − farm taxes (income taxes are not included) − depreciation. (source: FADN).
2 The chapter will be using the terminology of the former CAP, referring to the CAP implementation in year 2012 (as we are using data for this year to analyze the distribution of payments), with post-2013 CAP (reform) referring to the 2019 implementation of the 2014–2020 CAP.
3 It can be quoted as other objectives: enhance competitiveness, improve environmental performance and a more strategic approach to Rural Development spending (DG-AGRI, 2013); however, they will not be covered in this chapter.
4 The initial value is set by dividing a fixed percentage of the total value of the aid within the SPS (adjusted by the share of the national ceiling and deducting the coupled support for livestock and Article 68) divided by the number of entitlements allocated to that farmer in the first year of implementation of the basic payment scheme.
5 MS were given the option to apply the reduction after deducting from the basic payment labor costs in previous years.
6 English non-SDA (Severely Disadvantaged Area); English-SDA non-moorland; English SDA-moorland.
7 In the new regulation the definition of 'active farmer' is more restricted, as non-farm activities such as recreational activities are now explicitly excluded.
8 Nine MS will make use of the possibility to subtract the salaries actually paid by farmers before applying the reduction.
9 In FADN there is no information regarding whether the farmer has become for the first time the head of the agricultural holding.
10 The coupled support share of direct payments are AT: 2.1%, BL-Flanders: 11.25%, BL-Wallonia: 21.3%, BG: 15%, HR: 15%, CY: 7.9%, CZ: 15%, DK: 2.8%, EE: 4.2%, FI: 20%, FR: 15%, EL: 8%, HU: 15%, IR: 0.2%, IT: 11%, LV: 14%, LT: 15%, LU: 0.5%, MT: 57%, NL: 0.5%, PL: 15%, PT: 21%, RO: 12%, SK: 13%, SI: 15%, ES: 12%, SE: 13%, UK-Scotland: 8%.
11 When considering the data for 2013 there is a reduction in 2019 of 4% in nominal terms in comparison to 2013 (Croatia not considered).
12 The 2013 FADN data was not available at the time of conducting this analysis.
13 The delimitation of commercial farms is determined by the economic size of the farm (determined by the ESU of the farm). Due to the differences in the farm structure, the threshold to define a commercial farm varies among MS.
14 In the analysis of the data, BL represents the combination of Belgium and Luxembourg.

15 This order is consistent, as the capping is calculated based on the BPS/SAPS payments while the "greening" is based on a share of total direct payments. The calculation of the total direct payments is based on the BPS and the share of BPS in the total DP envelope.

16 The Unit Basic Payment has been calculated as well based on the entitlements (see Figures 10.11 to 10.13 in the Annex); however, due to extreme values, the average values based on PEA are more in line with DG-AGRI figures (DG AGRI, 2013) (reported as well, based on PEA).

17 The average mean presented in the box-plot are based on the FADN sample without weighting, while the ones presented in Table 10.5 are based on the population (applying the FADN weights).

18 The national direct payment ceilings for 2019 and 2020 are the same; therefore, in the chapter 2019 or 2020 are used indistinctly.

19 MS applying the greening at individual level = BL, DK, IR, EL, ES, FR, HR, IT, NL, AT, PT, SI, WE, UK-Northern Ireland, UK-Wales. MS applying greening at regional level = FI, UK-England, UK-Scotland. MS applying greening at national level = MT, DE, LU.

20 The average payments in UK regions applying FR are UK-Wales = 67 EUR/ha, UK-Scotland (arable land = 146 EUR/ha, grazing in non LFA and in LFA with > 0.2 LU/ha = 23 EUR/ha, grazing in LFA with <0. 2 LU/ha = 7 EUR/ha), UK-England (non-SDA, SDA non-moorland = 169 EUR/ha; SDA moorland = 49 EUR/ha). UK-Northern Ireland is applying Partial Convergence with an average value of 221 EUR/ha.

21 In order to draw the Lorenz Curve, the decoupled payments have been grouped in ascending order, and the percentage cumulative frequency has been represented on the Y-axis. The same has been done for the nr of beneficiaries on the X-axis.

Annex

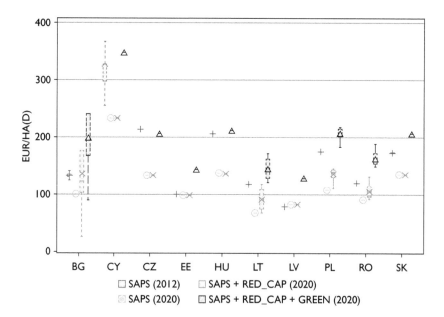

Figure 10.11 Distribution of unitary decoupled payments (EUR/HA (Declared)) under the pre- and post-2013 CAP reforms for MS applying SAPS

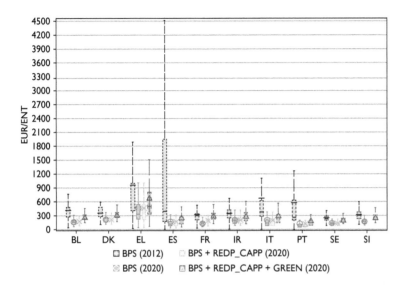

Figure 10.12 Distribution of unitary decoupled payments (EUR/ENT) under the pre- and post-2013 CAP reforms for MS applying Partial Convergence

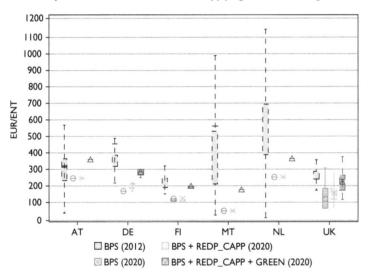

Figure 10.13 Distribution of unitary decoupled payments (EUR/ENT) under the pre- and post-2013 CAP reforms for MS applying Flat Rate

Acknowledgments

The views expressed are purely those of the authors and may not in any circumstances be regarded as stating an official position of the European Commission. We would like to thank Aurora Ierugan and Sophie Helaine from DG-AGRI

(DG-Agriculture and Rural Development, European Commission) for valuable comments and suggestions on an earlier version of this chapter.

References

Anania, G.; Pupo D'Andrea, M.R. (2015). The 2013 Reform of the Common Agricultural Policy, in J. Swinnen (ed.), *The Political Economy of the 2014–2020 Common Agricultural Policy: An Imperfect Storm*, CEPS Paperback, Centre for European Policy Studies, Brussels.

Bureau, J.C.; Mahé, L.P. (2015). Was the CAP Reform a Success? in J. Swinnen (ed.), *The Political Economy of the 2014–2020 Common Agricultural Policy: An Imperfect Storm*, CEPS Paperback, Centre for European Policy Studies, Brussels.

Ciaian, Pavel; D'Artis, K.; Swinnen., J. (2014). The Impact of the 2013 Reform of the Common Agricultural Policy on Land Capitalization in the European Union. *Applied Economic Perspectives and Policy* 36(4):643–673.

DG AGRI (Directorate General for Agriculture and Rural Development), Unit for Agricultural Policy Analysis and Perspectives. (2013). Overview of CAP reform 2014–2020. Agricultural Policy Perspectives Brief n 5/December 2013. http://ec.europa.eu/agriculture/policy-perspectives/policy-briefs/05_en.pdf

DG AGRI (Directorate General for Agriculture and Rural Development). (2014). Report on the distribution of direct aids to agricultural producers (financial year 2013). http://www.fega.es/sites/default/files/imported/PwfGcp/imagenes/es/ITEM_12-2_a_d-3550152-14-Report_FY2013_All_tcm5-48765.pdf

European Commission (2012). EU farm economics overview based on 2012 FADN data. DG Agriculture and Rural Development. http://ec.europa.eu/agriculture/rica/pdf/EU_FEO_FADN_2012.pdf.

European Commission. (2014a). 7th financial Report from the European Commission to the European Parliament and the Council on the European Guarantee Fund. Financial year 2013.COM(2014). 561 FINAL.

European Commission. (2014b). Direct Support-Horizontal. "SPS application accepted at MS level – Claim year 2012".

European Commission. (2014c). Direct Support-Horizontal. "Single Area Payment scheme (SAPS) at MS level – Claim year 2012".

European Commission (2015). Direct payments post 2014 Decisions taken by MS by 1 August 2014 – State of play on 07.05.2015-, European Commission, DG Agriculture and Rural Development. http://ec.europa.eu/agriculture/direct-support/direct payments/docs/implementation-decisions-ms_en.pdf

EU (European Union) (2013). Regulation (EU) No 1307/2013 establishing rules for direct payments to farmers under support schemes within the framework of the Common Agricultural Policy and repealing Council Regulation (EC) No 637/2008 and Council Regulation (EC) No 73/2009, *Official Journal of the European Union*, OJ L 347/608, Brussels.

EU (European Union) (2014). Commission delegated regulation (EU) No. 1378/2014 of 17 October 2014 amending annex I to Regulation (EU) No. 1305/2013 of the European Parliament and of the Council and Annexes II and III to Regulation (EU) No. 1307/2013 of the European Parliament and the Council.

Louhichi, K.; Ciaian, P.; Espinosa, M.; Colen, L.; Perni, A.; Gomez y Paloma, S. (2015). An EU-wide individual farm model for Common Agricultural Policy Analysis (IFM-CAP): first application to crop diversification policy. JRC Science and Policy Reports EUR 20910 EN, European Commission. http://publications.jrc.ec.europa.eu/repository/bitstream/JRC92574/jrcreport_jrc92574.pdf

Nowicki, P.; Goba, V.; Knierim, A.; van Meijl, H.; Banse, M.; Delbaere, B.; Helming, J.; Hunke, P.; Jansson, K.; Jansson, T.; Jones-Walters, L.; Mikos, V.; Sattler, C.; Schlaefke, N.; Terluin, I.; Verhoog, D. (2009). *Scenar 2020-II – Update of Analysis of Prospects in the Scenar 2020* Study. Contract No. 30–CE- 0200286/00-21, European Commission, Directorate-General Agriculture and Rural Development, Brussels.

Chapter 11

Cap post 2013: effects of a shift from Pillar I to Pillar II

Changes on land use and market effects among types of farms

Lilli Aline Schroeder, Sandra Marquardt, and Alexander Gocht

Introduction

The last Common Agricultural Policy (CAP) reform was finalised in 2013 (EU Reg No 1305-1308/2013) and includes the period 2014–2020. New aspects in this reform were the abolishment of production constraints (in the sugar, dairy and wine sectors), a new crisis reserve, the principle of supporting only active farmers, the additional Pillar I payment for young farmers, as well as voluntary coupled support payments. However, one of the major changes was the '*greening*' of Pillar I, which means that 30% of the national direct payments are linked to environmentally friendly management obligations (maintenance of permanent grassland, ecological focus areas, and crop diversification).

The budget for the period 2014–2020 has also changed: the total amount of CAP funding amounts EUR 362,787 billion, of which EUR 277,851 billion are allocated to Pillar I and 84,936 billion to Pillar II (EU COM, 2013). The distribution of payments across and within the Member States (MSs) was harmonised. However, in the CAP 2014–2020 MSs have more opportunity to adjust several elements of the new CAP to their specific priorities. For example, some MS are allowed to shift up to 15% or 25% of the budget between the two pillars. In Table 11.1, we show the final implementation decisions by the MSs concerning transfers between pillars and in Table 11.2 how the ceilings for Pillar I and II are defined. Furthermore, MSs can attribute higher payments to the first hectares of the farms to offer higher support for smaller farmers and can introduce a capping of direct payments for very large farms (EU COM, 2013).

Although the first discussions regarding a 2020 reform of the CAP have just begun, critical voices in the scientific and political community have expressed their views that a higher shift from Pillar I to Pillar II would be an important improvement of the CAP. In this regard, some scientists also discussed a complete shift of the greening budget from Pillar I to environmental measures in Pillar II. Hart et al. (2016) see this as one possible option beside others and point to issues that would need to be defined beforehand, such as payment rates, multi-annual programming, voluntariness, and co-financing. Buckwell (2015) lists a major shift in focus to rural development – by scaling back direct payments to a minimum – as one option for the CAP post-2020. He suggests that the greening should be absorbed into voluntary multiannual schemes using, e.g., a more-payment-by-results approach. In a discussion paper by the Dutch Presidency (2016) in the European Council from May 2016 on the CAP post 2020, the question is raised if the ecological focus of the introduced greening measures should be broadened. Therefore, to provide a first start to the design and evaluation of possible impacts of reform measures, in this study we examine the impacts of a 15% shift for all MSs from Pillar I to Pillar II, using the mathematical economic Common Agricultural Policy Regionalised Impact (CAPRI) model.

This chapter is structured as follows: First, we introduce the CAPRI model with its farm-type (FT) models, how land use and labour use are modelled and how the impact of Pillar II measures is simulated. Second, we describe the scenarios applied for this study: the 'Baseline' and the 'Shift-15%' scenario. Third, we present the results of this simulation by comparing the Shift-15% scenario to the Baseline, we report on effects on land use, yields and supply, prices, agricultural income, labour use and environmental indicators. In the last section of this chapter, we discuss our results, give conclusions, and offer an outlook on the situation.

The CAPRI model

To analyse land use, labour, price and production effects, we used the CAPRI model and its farm-level supply models that are differentiated by farm types. The model has been recently applied to assess direct payment harmonisation in the CAP (Gocht et al., 2013), effects of Rural Development Programmes (RDP) (Schroeder et al., 2015) and effects of CAP greening measures (Zawalińska et al., 2014). CAPRI is a comparative static partial equilibrium model, which iteratively links the farm-type supply modules with the global multi-commodity market module. The 2,450 farm-type supply models in CAPRI are representative for the EU27 (Gocht and Britz, 2011). The farm-type module mainly aims to capture the heterogeneity within a region in order to reduce aggregation bias when simulating the response of the agricultural sector to policy and market signals, with a specific focus on farm management, farm income and environmental impacts. The farm-type supply model was built from the Farm Accounting Data Network (FADN) and the Farm Structure Survey (FSS) data. It consists of independent non-linear programming models for each farm-type, representing the activities of all farms of a particular type and size class. The model captures the premiums paid under the CAP in detail, nutrient balances (nitrogen, phosphorus and potassium) and a feeding module covering animal nutrient requirements. In addition to the feed constraint, other model constraints relate to arable land and grassland. Grass, silage and manure are assumed to be non-tradable and receive internal prices based on their substitution values and opportunity costs. The farm-types are characterised along two dimensions: (i) 13 production specialisations (types of farming) and (ii) three economic farm size classes in terms of Economic Size Units (ESU, equivalent to EUR 1,200 gross margin). In total, this leads to 39 possible farm-types.

However, as not all farm-types can be modelled in each NUTS2 (Nomenclature des Unités Territoriales Statistiques) region, we apply a selection approach that ensures that the selection of farm-types maximises the representation of a region in terms of utilised agricultural area (UAA) and livestock units and that the total number of farm-types included in the model at the EU27 level is not over 2,450 (Gocht et al., 2014). The remaining farms (at the NUTS2 level) are contained in the residual farm-types aggregate, which are also represented by a mathematical supply model. Croatia is not yet included in the farm-type model. For a better readability of the results, we labelled the FT aggregates EU28 instead of EU27.

Land use and land market

The CAPRI model contains a supply and a demand curve for land, which together define the land rent clearing the balance. Furthermore, the model considers a land buffer, which means that in certain regions, additional land that was not used for agriculture before can be rented and vice versa.

Labour use

In the current version of the CAPRI model, labour use is modelled only for the agricultural sector and represented in terms of paid labour and family labour in agriculture, which are expressed in hours per ha, or head of livestock. These input coefficients are estimated from a Farm Accounting Data Network (FADN) sample and then combined with total labour requirements within a region (or aggregate national input demand reported in the Economic Accounts for Agriculture), using a Highest Posterior Density estimation framework (Britz and Witzke, 2014).

Modelling the impact of Pillar II

The Rural Development (RD) measures for Less Favoured Areas (LFA), Natura2000 (N2K) and Agri-environment Schemes (AES) are modelled in the Mathematical Programming (MP) farm-type models along with direct payments and other measures from Pillar I, while all other Pillar II measures can be captured in regional Computational General Equilibrium models (CGEs). However, CGEs were not used in this study for several reasons: First, as it was still unclear how the RD measures were designed by the MSs for the 2014–2020 period, it was not yet possible to include the changes into the model; second, the RD measures which are not assigned to AES, LFA or N2K have no effect on land use and are therefore not relevant for the research questions of this study; third, the agricultural sector receives the largest amount of Pillar II payments, and therefore modelling the RD measures which are relevant for agriculture (AES, LFA and N2K) will capture the majority of effects of the Pillar II.

The measures for AES, LFA and N2K are linked to the production activities and technologies in the MP farm-type models. AES are some of the most heterogeneous of all RD measures. They can be similar to LFA schemes, i.e., with minimal conditions for farmers, or very specific, requiring the establishment of buffer strips, hedges and low-intensity farming. However, these differences had to be ignored because of the lack of data on the appropriate classifications. Instead, they are treated as differentiated subsidies to particular activities and intensities. The actual payments, available from the budget model (Dwyer and Clark, 2010), were distributed using the FADN distribution of AES payments per ha, differentiated per farm type lying in or outside of LFA, to relate the payments to the activities contained in the CAPRI FT models. Thus, if, e.g., dairy farmers received a higher amount of payments than did pig and poultry farmers, this situation was interpreted as support to dairy farming relative to pork or poultry meat production. In addition, the information on the shares of each farm type located in or outside of LFAs was used. However, the extensive technology variant of each activity received a higher premium (50% above average) compared to the intensive variant (50% below average). This logic is currently applied to differentiate dairy cows, bulls and heifers for fattening, whereas low-yielding cows are typically found in more extensive production systems that rely more on fodder and less on concentrates. LFA payments were implemented as payments per ha, separately for arable land and grassland, and were specified using the known LFA shares of arable land/grassland in the NUTS2 regions from the dynamic model to simulate Conversion of Land Use and its Effects (CLUE). Because they are distributed to all crop activities of a certain type, their allocative impact was assumed to be minimal. N2K payments were implemented as per ha payments to the extensive technology variants of all agricultural crop activities. The per ha payments were calculated separately for arable land and grassland by using the known N2K shares for these land-use types from the CLUE model. The direct allocative impact (intervention logic) was assumed to be a support for extensification.

The scenarios

We considered two forward-looking simulations: The first is a scenario serving as a basis for the comparisons ('Baseline') and contains the CAP policy for the period 2014–2020, implying an implementation of the reform from 2013, and the second scenario ('Shift-15%') simulates a higher budget shift from Pillar I to Pillar II. Both simulations were modelled for 2025 using 2008 as the base year. To model price developments, we used the European Commission price outlook (EU COM, 2014). The effects of a higher shift from Pillar I to Pillar II are quantified by comparing the scenario containing a higher budget shift to the Baseline scenario. We evaluated differences in land use, income and supply, as well selected environmental indicators.

Our Shift-15% scenario is based on the Baseline scenario but involves shifting a more substantial and unified share of total CAP receipts away from direct payments in Pillar I and into RD aids under Pillar II. The shift amounts to 15% of direct payments (coming to the same extend from each Pillar I direct payment except for voluntary coupled support) because this is the maximum ceiling for transfers from Pillar I to II in the

CAP 2014–2020. The shifted budget is allocated to AES, LFA and/or N2K measures. It does not allow a shift from Pillar II back to Pillar I, which is currently used by certain MSs of the EU28, particularly new MSs. The scenario also makes the assumption that the reallocation in funds from Pillar I to II does not require national co-financing. All other elements of the CAP policy for the period 2014–2020 (Baseline) are unchanged.

Budget shift by Member State

For the Baseline, the currently known ceiling values for the year 2020 are presumed to be maintained up to our simulation year, 2025. The ceiling values depicted in Table 11.1 are final values, i.e., after the notified transfers between pillars have taken place. For the Shift-15% scenario, we simulated a 15% reduction in the original Pillar I ceilings with an associated increase in Pillar 2 payments.

Therefore, the final relative difference in Pillar I ceiling values between our Shift-15% scenario and the Baseline scenario is not 15% for all MSs. For the MSs France, Latvia, United Kingdom, Belgium, Czech Republic, Denmark, Germany, Estonia, Greece and the Netherlands, a lower final relative difference in Pillar I budget will occur, whereas for the MSs Croatia, Malta, Poland, Slovakia, and Hungary a higher final relative difference in Pillar I will occur. The highest relative decrease in Pillar I budget occurs for the Slovak Republic (21%), followed by Poland (20%) and the lowest relative decrease for the UK (5%), and followed by Latvia (8%) and Denmark (9%). The relative change in Pillar II budget depends on the amount, which is

Table 11.1 Re-allocation of ceiling funds between Pillars I and II

From Pillar I to Pillar II		From Pillar II to Pillar I	
Estonia	15.0%	Poland	25.0%
United Kingdom	10.8%	Slovakia	21.3%
Latvia	7.5%	Croatia	15.0%
Denmark	7.0%	Hungary	15.0%
Greece	5.0%	Malta	3.8%
Belgium	4.6%		
Germany	4.5%		
Netherlands	4.3%		
France	3.3%		
Czech Republic	1.3%		

Note: Percentages of the annual financial envelope for Pillar I and II that MS decided to transfer to the other pillar, respectively. MSs not named in this table did not shift any budget between the pillars in the CAP 2014–2020.

Source: EU COM (2015).

shifted from Pillar I, but it also depends on the amount of the initial budget in Pillar II in the CAP 2014–2020. Therefore, the highest relative increase in Pillar II budget occurs for Hungary (909%), followed by Bulgaria (118%), Poland (114%) and Portugal (113%). The lowest relative increase in Pillar II occurs for Finland and the UK (6%), followed by Austria (9%). No change in Pillar I and II budgets occur for Estonia. It can be expected that we will see higher effects of the budget shift in the MSs with high relative decreases in the Pillar I and high relative increases in the Pillar II budget. However, it needs to be considered that the entire budget of the ceiling values is not actually spent by the MSs. Therefore, the CAPRI model calculates an actual value paid, which considers entitlements and budget distribution patterns of each MS from the past CAP periods.

Table 11.2 Pillar I and II payments under the Shift-15% scenario and absolute change to Baseline values

	Sum of Pillar I payments	Sum of Pillar II payments		Sum of Pillar I payments	Sum of Pillar II payments
European Union 28	35,906	19,095	Sweden	595	793
	−5,425	5,425		−105	105
European Union 15	27,600	15,510	United Kingdom	3,053	2,526
	−3,796	3,796		−151	151
European Union 13	8,307	3,585	Czech Republic	742	530
	−1,629	1,629		−120	120
Belgium	458	188	Estonia	144	75
	−56	56		0	0
Denmark	748	278	Hungary	1,079	215
	−70	70		−194	194
Germany	4,266	1,977	Lithuania	439	257
	−527	527		−78	78
Austria	588	1,207	Latvia	257	138
	−104	104		−23	23
Netherlands	623	174	Poland	2,602	1,218
	−78	78		−649	649
France	6,322	1,782	Slovenia	114	103
	−870	870		−20	20

	Sum of Pillar I payments	Sum of Pillar II payments		Sum of Pillar I payments	Sum of Pillar II payments
Portugal	509	169	Slovak Republic	335	197
	−90	90		−88	88
Spain	4,159	1,681	Croatia	254	0
	−734	734		−45	−45
Greece	1,655	510	Cyprus	41	41
	−195	195		−7	7
Italy	3,149	2,179	Malta	4	5
	−556	556		−1	1
Ireland	1,029	903	Bulgaria	677	221
	−182	182		−119	119
Finland	446	1,353	Romania	1,618	584
	−79	79		−285	285

Budget shift by RD-measure

Looking at the distribution of the budget shift at the level of individual Pillar II measure groups shows us that in the EU28, 'AES for field crops' receive the highest absolute additional payments (EUR 989 Mio.), followed by 'AES for grassland farms' (EUR 956 Mio.) and the LFA measure (EUR 903 Mio.). In the EU15, the highest absolute additional payments are allocated to 'AES for grassland' (EUR 773 Mio.), followed by 'AES for field crops' (EUR 678 Mio.) and LFA payments (EUR 598 Mio.). In the EU13, 'AES for field crops' receive the highest absolute additional payments (EUR 311 Mio.), followed by LFA payments (EUR 305 Mio.) and 'AES for mixed farms' (EUR 253 Mio.).

Simulation results

To show the effects of a budget shift from Pillar I to Pillar II, we compare our Shift-15% scenario with the Baseline simulation as reference scenario. Both scenarios are simulated for the year 2025. The final net effects in this comparison are a result of reducing the Pillar I budget, on the one hand, while at the same time increasing the Pillar II budget, on the other hand. It needs to be considered that these two mechanisms and also other economic mechanisms in the model produce partially countervailing effects resulting in the final net effect. Furthermore, it should be noted that the effects of our simulation, shifting 15% of the Pillar I budget to Pillar II, lead to only modest impacts on the agricultural economy.

Land use

Utilised agricultural area

The UAA decreases in the EU28 by 0.02% (28,920 ha), in the EU15 by 0.06% and increases in the EU13 by 0.09%. Figure 11.1 shows the relative changes in land use at NUTS2 level. The highest relative decrease in UAA at MS level occurs in Sweden (0.5%, 14,390 ha), followed by Portugal (0.22%, 7,500 ha) and Finland (0.21%, 4,800 ha). The highest relative increase in UAA occurs in Lithuania (0.39%, 11,400 ha) followed by Latvia (0.31%, 6,120 ha). The largest absolute decrease in UAA occurs in France (27,540 ha), followed by Romania (20,400 ha) and Sweden (14,390 ha). The largest absolute increase in UAA occurs in Poland (43,960 ha), followed by Lithuania (11,400 ha) and Hungary (10,850 ha). Looking at the farm-type aggregates for the EU28 shows us that the 'FT14_60 general field cropping and mixed' shows the highest decreases in UAA (32,550 ha), followed by 'FT13 Specialist cereals, oilseeds and protein crops' (31,770 ha). The highest increase in UAA in the EU28 occurs for the 'FT41 Specialist dairying' (15,300 ha), followed by 'FT42_43 Specialist cattle-rearing and fattening' (14,440 ha) and 'FT_44 Sheep goats and other grazing livestock' (13,130 ha). In the EU15, it shows that the 'FT13 Specialist cereals, oilseed and protein crops' shows the highest decreases in UAA (49,780 ha), followed by 'FT14_60 General field cropping and mixed' (decrease in UAA by 28,020 ha). The highest increase in UAA occurs in the EU15 for the 'FT44 Sheep, goats and other grazing livestock' by 12,230 ha, followed by 'FT42_43 Specialist cattle-rearing and fattening' with an increase of 10,480 ha in UAA. In the EU13, for all farm-types the UAA increases; the most for the 'FT13 Specialist cereals, oilseeds and protein crops' (28,310 ha), followed by 'FT41 Specialist dairying' (15,090 ha).

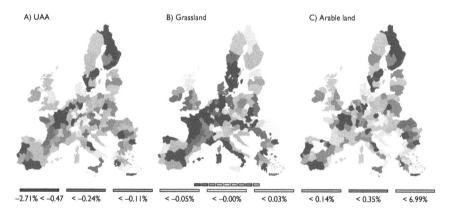

Figure 11.1 Relative change in land use to Baseline at NUTS2 level in EU28

Grassland

Grassland area decreases in the EU28 by 0.13% (80,830 ha), in EU15 by 0.17% and in EU13 by 0.02%. The highest decrease occurs in Sweden (1.16%, 4,680 ha), followed by Hungary (0.41%, 3,830 ha) and Belgium (0.32%, 1,780 ha). An increase in grassland area occurs in Lithuania (0.84%, 7,500 ha), the Czech Republic (0.05%, 580 ha) and Poland (0.03%, 1,090 ha). The highest absolute decrease in grassland area occurs in France (20,670 ha), Spain (15,310 ha) and Italy (10,060 ha). Looking at the farm-type aggregates for the EU28 shows us that grassland decreases for all farm-types. The highest decrease occurs for the 'FT44 Sheep, goats and other grazing livestock' (19,060 ha), followed by 'FT42_43 Specialist cattle-rearing and fattening' (13,640 ha). Also in the EU15, grassland decreases for all FTs. The highest decrease occurs for the 'FT44 Sheep, goats and other grazing livestock' by 17,470 ha, followed by 'FT41 Specialist dairying' (14,810 ha) and 'FT42_43 Specialist cattle-rearing and fattening' (14,740 ha). In the EU13, an increase in grassland dominates. The 'FT41 Specialist dairying' shows the highest increase (2,450 ha), followed by 'FT42_43 Specialist cattle-rearing and fattening' (1,210 ha). The highest grassland decrease in the EU13 occurs for the 'FT44 Sheep, goats and other grazing livestock' (decrease of 730 ha).

Arable land

Arable land increases in the EU28 by 0.04% (51,910 ha), mainly in the new MSs (51,800 ha, 0.12% in EU13). In the EU15 the sum in area of arable land remains nearly unchanged. The highest relative increase occurs in Slovenia (1.09%, 2,080 ha) followed by Latvia (0.5%, 6,680 ha). Only in very few MSs or regions arable land decreases. The highest relative decrease in arable land occurs in Sweden (0.39%, 9,700 ha), Portugal (0.31%, 7,280 ha) and Finland (0.22%, 4,800 ha). At EU28 farm-type level, it shows that the FTs change their amount of arable land very differently: The 'FT44 Sheep, goats and other grazing livestock' increases arable land the most, by 32,190 ha, followed by 'FT42_43 Specialist cattle-rearing and fattening' (28,080 ha) and 'FT41 Specialist dairying (27,770 ha); The highest decrease in arable land occurs for the 'FT14_60 General field cropping and mixed', by 28,450 ha, followed by the 'FT13 Specialist cereals, oilseeds and protein crops' (28,410 ha). In the EU15, the 'FT44 Sheep, goats and other grazing livestock' increase their absolute amount of arable land the most, by 29,700 ha, followed by 'FT42_43 Specialist cattle-rearing and fattening' (increase by 25,220 ha); 'FT13 Specialist cereals, oilseeds and protein crops' decrease their arable land the most (47,500 ha), followed by 'FT 14_60 General field cropping and mixed' (24,660 ha decrease). In the EU13, arable land increases for all FTs; the most for 'FT13 Specialist cereals, oilseeds and protein crops' (28,670 ha), followed by 'FT41 Specialist dairying' (12,640 ha).

Looking at the different types of arable crops, it shows that in the EU28, fallow land decreases by 1.09% and also area for fodder crops decreases, except for fodder maize, which increases by 1.58%; cereals are the arable crops which increase the most in the EU28 in relative terms (by 0.45%), followed by oilseeds (increase of 0.34%)

and vegetables and permanent crops (slight increase by 0.12%). The area of other arable crops decreases in the EU28 by 0.30%. In the EU15, the direction of the effect is nearly the same as in EU28 but to a lesser extent in relative terms. Also in the EU13, the direction of changes in the area of arable crops is nearly the same as in EU28 but with a higher decrease for fallow land (2.31%), a higher increase in fodder maize (2.63%) and oilseeds (0.52%), and a lower increase in vegetables and permanent crops (0.08%).

Yield and supply

As shown in Table 11.3, the yields on agricultural land decrease on average in the EU28 by 0.29%, in the EU15 by 0.23%, and in the EU13 by 0.45%. The decreases in yields in arable crops outweigh the increasing yields in grassland in all three MS aggregates. However, the decrease in yield in arable land is remarkably higher in the EU13 (0.48%) than in the EU15 (0.23%). In combination with the changes in land use, this leads to a decrease in supply for all arable crops in the EU28 and the EU15, except for fodder maize, for which the reduced yield is outweighed by the increased cultivated area. In the EU13, intensive grassland has increased slightly in area (0.06%) and yield (0.06%), which results in an increase in supply. The same holds true for vegetables and permanent crops (supply increase of 0.12%). Also the supply of fodder maize is increased in the EU13 (0.84%) for the same reasons as in the EU28.

The decreasing productivity in livestock production in the EU28, EU15 and EU13 cannot outweigh the increasing herd sizes, which results in an increase in stocking densities.

Table 11.3 Farm size, yield, and income, by farm type

	Hectares or herd size [1000 ha or hds]	Yield [kg, Const EU or 1/1000 head/ ha]	Supply [1000 t, 1000 ha or Mio Const EU]	Crop share/ Animal density [% or 0.01 animals/ha]	Income [Euro/ ha or head]
Utilised agricultural area	182,285	7,703	1,404,049	100	981
	−0.02%	−0.29%	−0.31%	0.00%	−0.53%
Pasture	59,946	23,319	1,397,888	33	33
	−0.13%	0.05%	−0.09%	−0.12%	−0.12%
Arable land	122,339	7,385	903,451	67	67
	0.04%	−0.30%	−0.26%	0.06%	0.06%
Fallow land	9,558			5	180
	−1.09%			−1.08%	−8.12%

	Hectares or herd size [1000 ha or hds]	Yield [kg, Const EU or 1/1000 head/ ha]	Supply [1000 t, 1000 ha or Mio Const EU]	Crop share/ Animal density [% or 0.01 animals/ha]	Income [Euro/ ha or head]
Vegetables and permanent crops	14,072	8,466	119,130	8	7,104
	0.12%	−0.12%	0.00%	0.14%	0.05%
Cereals	56,572	5,699	322,407	31	286
	0.45%	−0.67%	−0.23%	0.46%	−2.59%
Oilseeds	13,445	2,768	37,217	7	337
	0.34%	−0.54%	−0.20%	0.35%	−2.58%
Other arable crops	6,126	8,822	54,039	3	1,778
	−0.30%	−0.12%	−0.42%	−0.28%	−0.64%
Fodder maize	6,036	53,855	325,065	3	208
	1.58%	−0.97%	0.59%	1.59%	−5.64%
Fodder other on arable land	16,397	27,038	443,334	9	301
	−1.39%	0.84%	−0.56%	−1.37%	−5.97%
Gras and grazings extensive	29,653	13,725	406,988	16	77
	−0.28%	−0.05%	−0.33%	−0.26%	−11.81%
Gras and grazings intensive	30,292	32,711	990,900	17	−26
	0.01%	0.00%	0.01%	0.02%	−62.20%
Beef meat activities	17,358		5,853	10	−126
	0.18%		0.10%	0.19%	4.22%
All dairy	40,277		66,608	22	873
	0.15%		0.06%	0.17%	0.29%
Milk ewes and goat	74,166		4,577	41	23
	1.15%		1.10%	1.16%	16.58%
Sheep and goat fattening	56,147		912	31	44
	0.98%		0.88%	0.99%	2.73%

Price effects

Producer prices for arable crops increase slightly in the EU28: for cereals by 0.44%, for oilseeds by 0.53%, for vegetables and permanent crops by 0.03% and for other arable crops by 0.50%. Producer prices for nearly all animal products show a slight decrease: for beef meat by 0.21%, for pork meat by 0.14%, for sheep and goat meat by 0.89%, for dairy products by 0.08%, other animal products by 0.20%. Only the producer price for poultry meat slightly increases in the EU15 by 0.09%. The direction of price effects in the EU15 is the same and also the extent of change is nearly the same; only for dairy products the decrease in producer prices is slightly lower. The same holds true for the EU13 except for vegetables and permanent crops, for which the producer price decreases slightly by 0.05%; and for dairy products, for which the producer prices have a higher decrease in EU13 than in the EU28. The direction of producer price effects is in all MSs for nearly all products the same, only for vegetables and permanent crops the direction changes into slightly negative for some MSs: Malta, Czech Republic, Poland and Greece. The producer prices for dairy products increase only in Malta, Lithuania, Bulgaria and Poland; and for other animal products, producer prices increase only in Lithuania, Romania, Croatia, Bulgaria and the Netherlands.

Income effects

As shown in Table 11.3, through the budget shift, agricultural income per ha decreases in the EU28 by 0.53%. At the farm-type level aggregated to EU28, the income effect is different for the different FTs: An increase in agricultural income occurs for the 'FT44 Sheep, goats and other grazing livestock' by 0.74%, for the 'FT31 Specialist vineyards' by 0.34% and for the 'FT32 Specialist fruit and citrus fruit' by 0.03%; for all other FT-aggregates the agricultural income decreases, the most for the 'FT13 specialist cereals, oilseed and protein crops' by 1.86%, followed by 'FT7 Mixed livestock holdings' (decrease of 1.75%) and 'FT42_43 Specialist cattle-rearing and fattening' (decrease of 1.46%). For the EU28-FT-aggregates with increasing income, the sum of CAP premiums are increasing in our simulation, for the FTs with decreasing income CAP premiums are decreasing, except for the 'FT41 Specialist dairying' (income decrease of 0.35%), for which premiums are increasing but the agricultural outputs are decreasing and inputs are increasing (in monetary terms).

Overall, the positive income change for livestock activities and arable land is outweighed by the decrease in income for grassland and fodder production. In the EU15, the same direction of income effects occurs but results in a slightly lower total income decrease (0.19%). The decrease in income from grassland production is much higher in the EU15 than in the EU28, the income increase from beef meat activities is higher in the EU15 than in the EU28. Also in the EU13 the directions of income effects are nearly the same as in the EU28 but resulting in a considerably higher total income decrease (2.40%). Even though the income loss from grassland is lower, the decrease in income from fallow land is much higher in the EU13 than in the EU28 and EU15. Furthermore, in contrast to the aforementioned MS groups, in the EU13 income decreases for dairy production (by 4.66%) and sheep and goat fattening (by 2.81%). The income for the other livestock production increases in the EU13.

Effects on labour use in agriculture

In our study, we simulate labour use as paid labour, family labour and total labour in hours per hectare or per head of livestock for each agricultural production activity. Furthermore, we calculate the labour use for the gross production for each farm-type, NUTS2 region and MS, which is the labour use per hectare or head multiplied by the activity level (crop area or herd size).

In our Shift-15% scenario, total labour use for gross agricultural production in the EU28 increases by 0.17%, whereof family labour increases by 0.20% and paid labour by 0.10%. In the EU15, total labour use for gross agricultural production increases by 0.07%, family labour also by 0.07% and paid labour by 0.05%. In the EU13, total labour use for gross agricultural production increases by 0.30%, family labour by 0.31% and paid labour by 0.21%. At MS level, Slovenia increases total labour for gross agricultural production the most (by 0.57%), followed by Hungary (0.56%), Bulgaria (0.46%), Latvia (0.44%) and Poland (0.43%). A decrease in total labour use for gross agricultural production occurs in Sweden (by 0.35%) and Portugal (0.12%) and to lesser extent also in eight other MSs. At NUTS2 level, the change in agricultural labour use is different within the MSs. For example, in France and in the UK: Wales and Scotland decrease total labour use for gross agricultural production (by 0.12% and 0.11%, respectively), whereas in the other NUTS2 regions it increases or stays nearly constant. At farm-type level, nearly all EU28-farm-types increase total labour use for gross agricultural production with only three EU28-farm-types, reducing labour use only marginally (0.004–0.02%).

If we look at the total labour use for gross agricultural production for certain production activities at EU28 level, it shows that the total labour use for the gross production of cereals increases the most in relative terms (by 0.66), followed by oilseeds (increase of 0.53%) and 'all ruminants' (increase of 0.22%). For set-aside and fallow land the total labour use for the gross production decreases by 1.67% in the EU28; also for fodder activities labour use declines by 0.44% and for 'other arable crops' by 0.27%. If we look at total labour use per ha or livestock head in the EU28, it shows that labour use for cereals increases the most in absolute terms (by 5.4 min/ha), followed by oilseeds (increase of 4.2 min/ha) and 'beef meat activities' (increase of 2.4 min/head). For set-aside and fallow land the total labour use per ha decreases by 5.4 min/ha in the EU28, as well as for 'other arable crops' by 3.6 min/ha and for fodder activities by 1.8 min/ha.

Environmental effects

Nitrogen

In the EU28, through the budget shift total, nitrogen (N) surpluses decrease slightly by 0.46%. This is the net effect of two contrary components: the gaseous N-losses

A) CH4   B) N2O   C) GWP

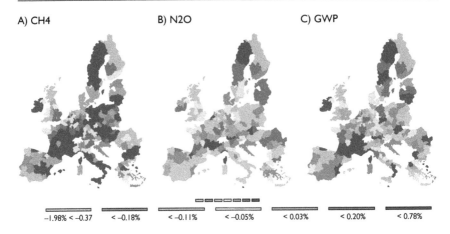

−1.98% < −0.37   < −0.18%   < −0.11%   < −0.05%   < 0.03%   < 0.20%   < 0.78%

Figure 11.2 Impact of Shift-15% scenario on A) methane, B) nitrous oxide, and C) global warming potential

from manure and the run-off of N from manure management increase but can be outweighed by the decreasing gaseous N-losses from mineral fertilisers, run-off N from mineral fertilisers and the N surplus at soil level. In the EU15, the decrease in total N-surplus is slightly lower (decrease of 0.36%) and in the EU13 the decrease is slightly higher (0.76%).

Greenhouse gas (GHG) emissions

The global warming potential (GWP) in the EU28 decreases slightly in total (0.06%) and also per ha (0.04%). This comes from the reduced N2O emissions, which decrease by 0.22% and cannot be outweighed by the increased CH4 emissions (increase by 0.14%). The direction of the effects on GHG emissions is the same for the EU15 and EU13, however, to different extents: in the EU15 the total decrease in GWP is slightly lower than in the EU28 and in the EU13, it is higher than in the EU28. At the MS level and NUTS2 level the effect on GHG emissions differs, as shown in Figure 11.2.

For the MSs Malta, Lithuania, Slovak Republic, Slovenia, Ireland, France and Cyprus, the total GWP slightly increases. For Hungary the highest decrease in total GWP occurs (0.5%), followed by Poland (0.4%), the Czech Republic, Spain and Bulgaria (all 0.3% decrease).

Discussion, outlook and conclusions

The simulation developed and applied for this study combines the effects of reducing Pillar I with a simultaneous increase in Pillar II and considering the impact of complex and individual Pillar II measures. To be able to fully grasp the complexity of these elements, we applied the mathematical economic model CAPRI. Due to the construction of the simulation in this study, we received final equilibrium effects, which did not allow for analysing interim results of the different influencing components of a simulation. A study showing the isolated impact of Pillar II by using the example of Germany was carried out by Schroeder et al. (2015).

Land use

The premiums in Pillar I of the CAP are reduced to the same extend for grassland and arable land, hence the revenue to land decreases. As a reaction, fallow land is taken out of agricultural production and as result the UAA decreases. In marginal regions, agricultural production without Pillar II support would no longer be profitable, especially for grassland. If these regions already received high AES payments in the Baseline simulation, these payments are further increased through the shift in our Shift-15% scenario. However, the increased Pillar II payments are not sufficient to compensate the decreased Pillar I payments, and grassland is taken out of agricultural production because it is less profitable than arable land; i.e., the UAA decreases further.

Income

The change in income for the agricultural sector as whole in our simulation is only very modest and far from being significant. It results mainly from the changes in CAP premiums but also from production and price changes. At the farm-type level, the change in agricultural income is very different. CAP premiums are transferred from intensive regions (reduction in Pillar I) to more extensive regions or farm-types (enhancement of Pillar II). Certain agricultural production systems are particularly suitable for receiving this shift in premiums, e.g., livestock holdings. Hence, the winners of the premium shift are particularly sheep and cattle farms and smallholdings. However, the other farm-types lose only very little of their income.

Labour use

The effect of our Shift-15% scenario on labour use in agriculture is only marginal, especially if we look at the per ha or per livestock head basis. However, the overall direction of the effect in the EU – an increase in total labour use – shows that our scenario is implemented correctly, because an increase in Pillar II budget means more labour-intensive production in agriculture. At the MS level, it shows that the decrease in UAA in Portugal, Finland and Sweden leads to a reduction of total labour use. This also holds true for most of the NUTS2 regions. At the farm-type level, it shows that if labour use increases, this is mainly due to the increase in labour for ruminant production systems but often also for cereals and oilseeds. The labour for ruminant production systems increases for all EU28-farm-types except for 'FT33 specialist olives', 'FT50 specialist granivores' and 'FT2 specialist horticulture', for which also the total labour use for gross production slightly decreases.

Environment

Through the enhancement of the Pillar II one would expect a positive impact on environmental indicators, because most Pillar II measures support an extensification of agricultural production. Even though our results support the extensification effect through reduced yields, they show, on the other hand, that the reallocation of CAP payments from Pillar I to Pillar II does not per se result in an improvement for the environment. Overall, in our simulation, the positive effect of reduced N2O emissions through reduced fertiliser use is weakened through the increased ruminant livestock production and the resulting increased CH4 emissions from manure management. Positive environmental impacts would be expected especially for marginal regions, were Pillar II payments are mostly allocated. This is, however, not the case because, due to the reduction in Pillar I, agricultural land use is reduced also in these regions. As we could show, for climate change the CAPRI model already has good instruments to measure the impacts. Also carbon sequestration in soil can already be modelled with CAPRI using a link to a biophysical model (as in Gocht et al., 2016), but was not realised in this study. At present a biodiversity indicator is still missing, but first attempts in this direction have been made. However, it should be kept in mind that for all indicators modelling makes sense only if larger effects are to be expected (e.g., through larger changes in the policy) at high regional or farm-type resolution.

Modelling issues and critical appraisal

Due to the different handling of the flexibility between pillars in the CAP 2014–2020 by the MSs, our 15% shift from Pillar I to Pillar II did not result in a 15% shift for all MSs. Hence, many of the big MSs had smaller relative shifts and many new MSs had larger relative shifts. Furthermore, it needs to be considered that the Pillar II in the Baseline had very different budgets for the MSs, which means relatively a much higher increase in Pillar II payments for new MSs than for old MSs.

It should be kept in mind that we modelled only the Pillar II measures LFA, AES and N2K. If CGEs would be linked to the CAPRI model, more detailed information on labour use could be provided because some Pillar II measures, e.g., village renewal or the promotion of agricultural investments in stables and new techniques mainly target the construction sector. This was shown in Schroeder et al. (2015). Other sectors benefiting in labour use from Pillar II measures are the education and the administration sector; this, however, could not be included in this study and will not cause significant effects, because the vast majority of Pillar II budget is allocated to the agricultural sector anyway. Another interesting point would be the monetary evaluation of labour and related market mechanisms which impact the price, supply and demand of labour for different regions and activities. Lastly, it should be noted that modelling labour use in agriculture is not simple, because the supply of labour is hard to define, as in many cases family labour can be very flexibly activated and can compensate upcoming higher demands.

Modelling the impact of Pillar II measures remains a challenging task, given the complexity of the grouping of measures, their implementation logic etc. The effects of Pillar II measures are partially contrary and the plurality of programmes between MSs and CAP programming periods can hardly be managed and or modelled with their names, grouping and design changing continuously so that they are hardly comparable over time. However, when MSs finally publish how the RD programmes and their budget are designed in detail for the current programming period, an update of the CAPRI data bases could be done and would help to obtain more realistic results. Regarding the uptake of AES, we assume in our model – based on historic FADN data – that those FTs, which had AES in the past, would continue to have them in the future. An update of the model which is data- and time-consuming could provide an improvement here in the future.

In our simulation the budget shift from Pillar I to Pillar II requires no co-financing by MSs. This assumption was made for three reasons. First, in times of fiscal austerity most MSs have limited public funds. The usual assumption that RD expenditure has to be co-financed is one of the reasons why expanding Pillar II has not been attractive to many MSs, in the current period. Second, a precedent was set by an agreement with the UK that its voluntary modulation (as applied 2007–2013) did not require national co-financing. Third, the European Council agreement of 8/2/13 specified that funds shifted to Pillar II voluntarily, using the proposed (Article 14) flexibility clause, do not have to be co-financed. For these reasons, this assumption appears plausible for a Pillar I to Pillar II fund-shifting scenario.

To isolate the impacts of reducing Pillar I and enhancing Pillar II, an intermediate scenario would be needed, which, however, is beyond the scope of this chapter. Nevertheless, the final net effect would remain the same.

Policy outlook

In our simulation, the Pillar I and therefore also the greening component of the Pillar I was reduced. If this is a sensible procedure remains questionable. On the one hand, many studies have shown that the greening does not yet produce positive environmental effects. On the other hand, the greening certainly needs some more time to prove its worth, and more Pillar II budget instead of greening is questionable because intensive regions would not be targeted anymore. If environmental protection in intensive regions should be clearly forced, more targeted regulations and standards would probably be the most effective way. However, with the current instruments, an effective greening with a targeted Pillar II would be the best. If the Pillar II should result in more significant effects, a more significant shift than shown in this chapter would be needed. But through such a shift, also the share between intensive and extensive regions and farming systems will get larger.

Conclusions

In our study we were able to simulate a highly complex policy scenario of the CAP for the manifold agricultural production sector, which is characterised by great regional differences in the EU. We found that the effects of a 15% shift from Pillar I to Pillar II of the CAP are only marginal, which is due to the small proportion of the budget but also due to the occurrence of cross effects within the sector and between regions, e.g., for environmental indicators, income and labour use. With the direction of the effects, we showed that our model implementation is correct and that the Pillar II measures affect the sector in the intended way. However, a relevant effect on the major policy goals for rural development, such as grassland maintenance, biodiversity protection or GHG mitigation, would be achieved only if a higher budget is assigned to these measures and they are regionally better targeted. We showed that the largest proportion of the additional Pillar II premiums in our Shift-15% scenario is allocated to regions and farming systems in which the uptake of Pillar II programmes was already much higher than in others. To also reach the regions with intensive production, politicians should consider more mandatory measures or should make the current Pillar II measures more attractive for intensive arable farming systems because here, no or much less additional GHG emissions from ruminants would occur and positive environmental effects would be much higher.

References

Britz, W. and Witzke, H.-P. (2014): CAPRI model documentation 2014. URL: http://www.capri-model.org/docs/capri_documentation.pdf

Buckwell, A. (2015): Where should the CAP go post-2020? pp. 509–529 in: Swinnen (ed.) et al. (2015): *The Political Economy of the 2014–2020 Common Agricultural Policy – An Imperfect Storm.* Published by Rowman & Littlefield International, Ltd. ISBN: 978-1-78348-484-3, 696 pp.

Dwyer, J. and Clark, M. (2010): CAPRI-RD Expenditure database report, CAPRI-RD Deliverable 2.1.1 (Draft).

EU COM (2013): Overview of the CAP Reform 2014–2020. European Commission Agricultural Policy Perspective Brief Number 5 / December 2013. URL: http://ec.europa.eu/agriculture/policy-perspectives/policy-briefs/05_en.pdf. 10 pp.

EU COM (2015): Direct payments post 2014. Decisions taken by Member States by 1 August 2014 – State of play on 07.05.2015 – information note. 31 pp.

Gocht, A., Britz, W. (2011): EU-wide farm-type supply models in CAPRI – How to consistently disaggregate sector models into farm-type models. *Journal of Policy Modeling* 33, 146–167.

Gocht, A., Britz, W., Ciaian, P., Gomez y Paloma, S. (2013): Farm-type effects of an EU-wide direct payment harmonisation. *Journal of Agricultural Economics* 64, 1–32.

Gocht, A., Leip, A., Espinosa, M., Van-Doorslaer, B., Schroeder, L.A., Gomez y Paloma, S., Lugato, E. (2016, accepted for publication): A Grassland strategy for farming systems in Europe to mitigate GHG emissions – An integrated spatially differentiated modelling approach. *Land Use Policy.*

Gocht, A., Witzke, H.-P., Espinosa, M., Gomez y Paloma, S. (2014): CAPRI-FARM methodological improvements: selection routine, input allocation and GHG reporting. Internal report IPTS, JRC-European Commission.

Hart, K., Buckwell, A., Baldock, D. (2016): Learning the lessons of the Greening of the CAP. A report for the UK Land Use Policy Group in collaboration with the European Nature Conservation Agencies Network, Institute for European Environmental Policy, London. 64 pp.

Netherlands Presidency (2016): Food of the Future – The Future of Food. Discussion paper of the Netherlands Presidency of the Council of the European Union. URL: http://english.eu2016.nl/documents/publications/2016/05/31/food-of-the-future

Schroeder, L.A., Gocht, A., Britz, W. (2015): The Impact of Pillar II Funding: Validation from a Modelling and Evaluation Perspective. *Journal of Agricultural Economics* 66, 415–441. doi: 10.1111/1477-9552.12091

Zawalińska, K., Was, A., Britz, W. (2014): Impact of "Greening" the Common Agricultural Policy on Sustainability of European Agriculture: From Perspective of the Baltic Sea Countries. *Journal of Agribusiness and Rural Development* 4, 191–212.

Chapter 12

Contribution of public policies to farm real estate values

Saleem Shaik

Introduction

Farm real estate comprises approximately 80 percent of farm assets. It is hypothesized that a large share of public policies like farm programs, public-private crop insurance program and politics is capitalized into farm real estate values. The Federal farm programs introduced as part of New Deal legislation address declines in farm prices and net farm income. Since 1933, 14 major farm bills introduced in 1948, 1954, 1956, 1965, 1970, 1973, 1977, 1981, 1985, 1990, 1996, 2002, 2008 and 2014, respectively, have provided protection to producers. The Federal Crop Insurance Corporation created in 1938 provided protection not only against price and income variation but also from the Great Depression. The United States Department of Agriculture Risk Management Agency for Federal Crop Insurance Corporation administers public-private crop insurance program in the United States. To increase the participation and demand changes in the crop insurance, policies and subsidies were proposed in 1940, 1977, 1980, 1996, 2000, 2002 and 2008. Finally, these farm policies are initiated in the U.S. Senate and/or House of Representatives and in rare cases the President, as in 1933.

These public policies on farm real estate values and agriculture economy in general play an important role in managing evolving risks in agricultural production. The magnitude of agriculture subsidies from farm program payments and crop insurance program payments relative to the general subsidies is relatively small, but on the rise. Concerns are being raised that current congressional emphasis on substantially reducing agriculture subsidies from traditional farm program and crop insurance program payments might adversely affect farm real estate values.

Literature in the last eight decades suggests the supply and demand factors including inflation, debt financing, financial speculation, and increasing urban and environmental influences were the primary drivers of farm real estate values (Gardner, 2002; Gertel, 1985; Harris, 1977; Lintner, 1965; and Wallace, 1926). However, this view is slowly but steadily changing. This is due to the continuous nature and predictability of farm program payments and crop insurance program payments, and also digressing from the expected correlation between risk and returns of agricultural production (Shaik, Atwood and Helmers, 2005 and 2012).

Even though the unique public-private crop insurance program has evolved into one of the major risk management tools for producers, the intended and unintended consequences of crop insurance along with farm program payments are yet to be evaluated. To evaluate the importance of premium subsidies and indemnities from the crop insurance program, the subsidies need to be defined as the difference between potential indemnities and premiums (returns on crop insurance for the producers) paid plus the government subsidies received by the producers. Hence reducing expected future transfer of farm program payments and crop insurance program payments is likely to reduce the upward pressure on farm real estate values and the burden on taxpayers' monies due to payments from farm programs and crop insurance programs (see U.S. GAO, 2008 and 2014).

In the past, variability in farm returns, farm program payments and crop insurance program payments have been observed due to changes in the market supply and demand as well as changes in the farm bill provisions. However, does this variability in farm returns, farm program payments and crop insurance program payments have differential effects on farm real estate values? Ideally, variability in farm returns could lead to lower farm real estate values due to lower investment back on the farm. This is due to uncertain farm income from production. In contrast, a similar view might or might not be true with respect to variability in farm program payments and crop insurance program payments. This could be due to the acreage controls and price support emphasis of farm program payments, and crop insurance is likely going to kick in if and only if there is a loss event or increased uncertainty in yield or revenue. To account for potential unknown state-level differences, temperature, precipitation and time trend are included in the extended income capitalization model.

The income capitalization framework also evaluates the contribution of the levels and variability associated with farm returns, farm program payments and crop insurance program payments to farm real estate. In addition, the perceived relationship between farm returns and farm program payments, farm returns and crop insurance program payments, and the bi-directional relationship between farm program payments and crop insurance program payments are also examined. The empirical application involves historical data from 48 states from 1949 to 2010. Due to the use of cross-section time-series data that involves spatial variation across states and temporal variation through time, three-way hierarchical linear model analyses are conducted.

Income capitalization model

The structural factors explaining farm real estate values have centered on the income capitalization model. The basic representation of the income capitalization model is derived from discounting expected future returns over an infinite life. The incorporation of individual components of the expected future returns will provide a mechanism for policy analyses. The individual components include farm receipts *(fcr)*, farm program payments *(fpp)*, crop insurance program payments *(cip)* along with an urbanization variable *(urban)*. This extended model is represented as:

$$V = f\left(\frac{fcr, fpp, cip}{r}, urban\right) \qquad (1)$$

where V is farm real estate, and r is a discount rate or real interest rate.

In reality, the politics or political party will contribute indirectly to the value of farm real estate, via farm program payments and crop insurance program payments. Even though there is no theoretical basis, there is an interest to evaluate if politics or political parties have any leftover or residual indirect or direct effects on farm real estate values. The political party controlling the State Governorship *(stparty)*, National Presidency *(usparty)*, Senate *(senate)* and House of Representatives *(house)* is included to evaluate the importance of politics on farm real estate values. The variable representing the political party controlling the National Senate, House and Presidency, and State Governorship is defined as an exogenous dummy variable with one (1) representing Democrats and zero (0) representing Republicans. The extended model with politics is defined as:

$$V = f\left(\begin{array}{c} \dfrac{fcr, fpp, cip}{r}, urban, \\[2mm] stparty, usparty, senate, house \end{array}\right) \qquad (2)$$

To evaluate the importance of risk or variability[1] in farm returns risk(*fcrR*), farm program payments risk (*fppR*) and crop insurance program payments risk (*cipR*) are included. Now, Equation (2) is represented as:

$$V = f\left(\begin{array}{c} \dfrac{fcr, fpp, cip}{r}, urban, fcrR, fppR, cipR, \\[2mm] stparty, usparty, senate, house \end{array}\right) \qquad (3)$$

To address potential endogenous issues, Equation (3) is extended to include two additional equations defining the endogenous farm program payment and crop insurance payment variables. Included in both these equations are the risk or variability of farm returns risk (*fcrR*), farm program payments risk (*fppR*) and crop insurance program payments risk (*cipR*).

In addition, the farm program payment equation includes the Herfindahl index of crop and livestock revenue measuring the degree of specialization or diversification of revenue *(hirev)*, the Herfindahl index of planted acreage measuring the degree of specialization or diversification of harvested acres *(hiacre)* and the farm size (*fsize*) (Shaik et al., 2012).The Herfindahl index of crop and livestock revenue and the Herfindahl index of crop program acreage are included to account for differences in the type of agriculture, supported commodities, farm program features, and farm size over time.The crop insurance payment equation includes the number of crops insured (*ncrops*), share of crop insurance acreage relative to the total acreage (*ciacres*), share of policies receiving indemnities relative to the total policies (*cipolys*) and the farm size (*fsize*). The number of crops insured in each state is included to account for state differences with respect to differences in the type of agriculture and supported commodities with crop insurance. The share of crop insurance acres relative to the total harvested acres is included to reflect the percentage of participation in the crop insurance program. To reflect the percentage of producers receiving indemnities, the share of crop insurance policies receiving indemnity relative to the total policies is included as well. Similarly, changes in farm size are included in the crop insurance program payments equation to account for the temporal changes.

To account for potential climate and technology changes, the coefficient of variation in precipitation (*precp*) and temperature (*temp*) across 12 months of a year and time trend (*trend*) is also included in each of the three equations.This is purely included to account for unknown potential spatial and temporal variation and does not truly represent precipitation and temperature. Now, the entire system is represented as:

$$
V = f\left(
\begin{array}{l}
\left(\dfrac{\widehat{fcr,\ fpp,\ cip}}{r}, urban \right), fcrR,\ fppR,\ cipR, \\[2mm]
stparty, usparty, senate, house, temp, precp, trend
\end{array}
\right)
$$

$$
fpp = f\left(
\begin{array}{l}
fcr, cip,\ fcrR, cipR, hirev, hiacre,\ fsize, \\[2mm]
stparty, usparty, senate, house, temp, precp, trend
\end{array}
\right)
$$

$$
cip = f\left(
\begin{array}{l}
fcr,\ fpp,\ fcrR,\ fppR, ncrops, ciacres, cipolys,\ fsize, \\[2mm]
stparty, usparty, senate, house, temp, precp, trend
\end{array}
\right) \tag{4}
$$

United States state data and construction of the variables

To be consistent with the agricultural land value per acre, all the variables are standardized to a per acre basis using acres in farms.[2] Additionally, the variables expressed in nominal dollars were converted into real 2000 dollars using the implicit gross domestic product price deflator. Farm real estate, farm returns, farm program payments and crop insurance program payments are reflected by real land values, expected farm crop receipts per acre, expected farm program payments per acres and expected crop insurance program payments per acre, respectively. The expected real interest rate definition is used where the expected rate of inflation (GDP Implicit Price Deflator) is subtracted from the Federal land bank nominal interest rate.The unit of expected real interest rate is percent.

The expectations of farm returns, farm program payments, crop insurance program payments and real interest rates were estimated by an autoregressive process in each state rather than using an ad hoc lag length. The order of the autoregressive model is selected by a stepwise autoregression. The stepwise autoregression method initially fits a high-order model with many autoregressive lags and then sequentially removes autoregressive parameters until all remaining autoregressive parameters have statistically significant t-tests. Once the lag length is estimated for farm returns, farm program payments, crop insurance program payments and inflation component of real interest rates for each in each state, the expected farm returns, expected farm program payments, crop insurance program payments and expected inflation are computed as moving averages. The moving average is computed based on past information of the variables using the lag length estimated from the stepwise autoregressive model.[3] These expected values of farm returns, farm program payments, crop insurance program payments and real interest rates are used in the analysis.

To reflect the importance of nonfarm demand for agricultural land and nonfarm economic influence on the value of land, urbanization is defined as urban population per acre. Diversity in agriculture production due to differences in farm structure, crop mixes, changes in the program crop acreages, livestock enterprises, etc., the Herfindahl indexes of crop acreage and crop-livestock revenue are included in the econometric estimation. Even though existing theory does not provide testable hypothesis, Herfindahl indexes[4] are used in the model to allow for temporal and spatial heterogeneity across states in the panel estimation. The Herfindahl index of crop and livestock revenue reflects variations in the crop and livestock mixes across a resource region over time. The Herfindahl index of crop program acreage accounts for the spatial variation of program crop acreage across a resource region over time. Farm size is computed as the land in farms divided by the number of farms.

The number of crops for which insurance is offered in each state is included to account for the heterogeneity among states with respect to differences in the type of agriculture and supported commodities with crop insurance. The share of crop insurance acres relative to the total harvest acres is included to reflect the percentage of participation in the crop insurance program. To reflect the percentage of producers receiving indemnities, the share of crop insurance policies receiving indemnity relative to the total policies is included as well. Similarly, changes in farm size are included in the crop insurance program payments equation to account for the temporal changes.

The political party controlling the National Presidency, Senate and House, and State Governorship is defined as set of dummy variables. However, the creation of each dummy variable is based on the detailed state-level information. This information included name of the President and Governor, their political affiliation and associated period in office. Similarly, the names of the individual members of Senate and House of Representatives, their political affiliation and associated period in office were collected. This information is used to generate a dummy variable.

It is relatively easy to create a State Governorship and National Presidency dummy variable of one (1) for Democrats and zero (0) for Republicans. The political affiliation of State Governor and National President is used to generate the dummy variable. If the Governor and President are affiliated with the Republican party, it is coded as zero (0) and one (1) if they are affiliated with the Democrat party. With the Senate and House, the dummy variable is created based on the number of members affiliated with the Republican or Democratic parties. If there are more Republicans compared to Democrats in the Senate or House of Representatives, the dummy was coded as zero (0), and one (1) otherwise. The summary statistics of the variables are presented in Table 12.1.

Table 12.1 Summary of the variables used in the analysis, 1949–2010

Variables	Mean	Minimum	Maximum
Real land value (V)	1,127.92	45.19	13,135.28
Real interest rates (r)	1.81	−17.24	10.96
Expected crop returns (frc)	157.42	3.54	1,384.72
Expected crop returns risk (frc)			
Farm program payments (fpp)	10.25	0.11	108.49
Farm program payments risk (fpp)			
Net crop insurance (nci)	0.02	0	0.73
Net crop insurance risk (nciR)			
Urbanization (Urban)	764.82	3.17	15,892.09
Revenue Herfindahl index (hirev)	26.74	10.74	69.89
Acreage Herfindahl index (hiacre)	37.97	16.45	100
Farm size (fsize)	585.87	39.83	6,645.16
Number of crops insured (ncrops)	9.55	1	51
Share of crop insurance acres (ciacres)	0.08	0	0.7
Share of policies receiving indemnities (cipolys)	0.15	0	1
State Party (1 = Dem)	0.587	0	1
National Party (1 = Dem)	0.507	0	1
National Senate Party (1 = Dem)	0.671	0	1
National House Party (1 = Dem)	0.781	0	1
CV of Precipitation (precp)	54.88	14.65	152.25
CV of Temperature (temp)	32.56	10.36	73.38

The mean United States farm real land value of $1,128 per acre with a minimum value of $45 and maximum value of $13,135 suggests stark differences across states and over time. Even though the average real interest rate was around 1.81 percent, the values oscillated from −17.24 percent to 10.96 percent. In contrast, the average expected crop returns, expected farm program payments, expected crop insurance program payments and urbanization were $157 per acre, $10.25 per acre, $0.02 per acre and 765 urban-population per acre, respectively. The maximum expected crop returns, expected farm program payments, expected crop insurance program payments and urbanization are 9 times, 11 times, 33 times and 21 times, respectively, higher than the average value. The average risk or variability of expected crop return, expected farm program payments and expected crop insurance program payments are $16 per acre, $3.88 per acre and $0.013 per acre, respectively.

The average crop-livestock revenue Herfindahl index and harvested program crop acreage Herfindahl index are 27 percent and 38 percent, respectively. The values closer to the lower end suggests diversification rather than specialization in revenue and harvested program crop acreage. The minimum farm size is six times lower (maximum farm size is 11 times higher) than the average farm size of 586 acres.

The average number of crops with insurance policies is around 10 crops with 51 crops and one crop on the two extremes. The average share of crop insurance acres and the policies receiving indemnities are 8 percent and 15 percent, respectively.

With the exception of national political party, the average of the State (*stparty*), Senate (*Senate*) and House (*House*) was great than 50 percent, suggesting for the time period used in the analysis, Democrats had control and could be potentially driving the farm policies.

Finally, the average coefficient of variation of precipitation is 55 millimeters with a minimum of 15 millimeters and maximum of 152 millimeters. In comparison the average coefficient of variation of temperature is 32 degrees centigrade with a minimum of 10 and maximum of 73 degrees.

Empirical model and results

To examine the factors including politics or political party affecting farm real estate along with counter-cyclical relationships between farm program payments (crop insurance program payments) and the relationship between farm program payments and crop insurance program payments, an application of the extended income capitalization is modeled for the United States using data from 48 states for the period 1949 to 2010. The contribution of expected crop returns, expected farm program payments, expected crop insurance program payments, urbanization and a set of four political parties to agricultural farm real estate for the United States were estimated. In addition, the importance of a set of four political party variables along with other variables to expected farm program payments and expected crop insurance program payments is examined. To accomplish this, Equation (4) is estimated, accounting for the panel structure of the data.

The recursive/triangular structure simultaneous equation model (Equation 4) accounting for time-series and cross-section data is represented as:

$$
\begin{aligned}
V_{it} &= \gamma_i + \gamma_t + \gamma_r r_{it} + \gamma_{fcr}\, fcr_{it} + \gamma_{fpp}\, \widehat{fpp}_{it} + \gamma_{cip}\, \widehat{cip}_{it} \\
&\quad + \gamma_{urban}\, urban_{it} + \gamma_{temp}\, temp_{it} \\
&\quad + \gamma_{precp}\, precp_{it} + \gamma_{trend}\, trend_{it} + \varepsilon_{it} \\
fpp_{it} &= \alpha_i + \alpha_t + \alpha_{fcr}\, fcr_{it} + \alpha_{cip}\, cip_{it} + \alpha_{fsize}\, fsize_{it} \\
&\quad + \alpha_{hirev}\, hirev_{it} + \alpha_{hiacre}\, hiacre_{it} + \alpha_{temp}\, temp_{it} \\
&\quad + \alpha_{precp}\, precp_{it} + \alpha_{trend}\, trend_{it} + \varepsilon_{it} \\
cip_{it} &= \beta_i + \beta_t + \beta_{fcr}\, fcr_{it} + \beta_{fpp}\, fpp_{it} + \beta_{ncrops}\, ncrops_{it} \\
&\quad + \beta_{ciacres}\, ciacres_{it} + \beta_{cipolys}\, cipolys_{it} + \beta_{fsize}\, fsize_{it} \\
&\quad + \beta_{temp}\, temp_{it} + \beta_{precp}\, precp_{it} + \beta_{trend}\, trend_{it} + \varepsilon_{it}
\end{aligned}
\tag{5}
$$

where γ_i, α_i and β_i are the fixed-effect state dummies and γ_t, α_t and β_t are the fixed-effect farm bill dummies in the land value equation, farm program payment equation and crop insurance program payments equation, respectively; ε_{it} is the remainder random error term; $i = 1, ..., N$ is the number of cross-sections (in our case 48 states); and $t = 1, ..., T$ is the number of years (in our case 62 years, from 1949 to 2010).

The simultaneous equation model is estimated in two stages. The first stage involves estimating the predicted expected farm program payments and predicted expected crop insurance program payments using the second and third equation, respectively, in Equation (5). In the second stage, the predicted expected farm program payments $\widehat{fpp}$ and the predicted expected crop insurance program payments $\widehat{cip}$ are used as exogenous variables in the first equation of Equation (5). Both stages are estimated using a two-way fixed effects model, accounting for temporal and spatial variation across states and farm bill periods.

Estimated coefficients for Equation (5) are presented in Tables 12.1 to 12.4. The mean and standard deviation of elasticity are estimated from individual elasticities estimated from each individual observation. The discussion of the results uses elasticity measures for ease of interpretation.

Farm real estate equation results

Results presented in Table 12.2 indicate the expected negative sign on real interest rates. This negative sign is consistent with the theory of income capitalization model and is around 3 percent across all 48 states from 1949 to 2010. The expected farm crop receipts, expected farm program payment, expected crop insurance program payments and urbanization variables are positive and statistically significantly related to farm real estate value. Based on the mean of individual observation computed elasticities presented in Table 12.2, the average elasticity of expected farm crop receipts, expected farm program payments, expected crop insurance program payments and urbanization is 33.70, 15.41, 8.88 and 26.14 percent, respectively. So, a 10 percent reduction in expected farm crop receipts, expected farm program payments, expected crop insurance program payments and urbanization leads to a decline in farm real estate values by $38, $17.40, $10 and $29.50,[5] respectively. Overall, a 100 percent joint reduction in expected farm crop receipts, expected farm program payments, expected crop insurance program payments and urbanization will reduce the value of farm real estate by $94.80 [$1,128 {*} (3.37 percent + 1.541 percent + 0.888 percent + 2.614 percent)].

Do risk or variability in expected farm crop returns, expected farm program payments and expected crop insurance program payments affect farm real estate values? The negative and statistically significant sign on expected crop returns risk shows an increase in the variability associated with farm crop returns will reduce the value of farm real estate. In contrast, increased variability in expected farm program payments and expected crop insurance program payments leads to increased value of farm real estate. This could be due to the increase in the magnitude of farm

Table 12.2 Farm real estate value equation results

Variables	Estimate	tValue	Probt	Mean Elasticity	Stdev Elasticity
Intercept	−681.590	−5	<0.0001		
Real interest rates	−18.326	−10.05	<.0001	−0.0288	0.4525
Expected crop returns	2.157	10.62	<.0001	0.3370	0.2234
Expected crop returns risk	−5.004	−9.29	<.0001	−0.0967	0.1321
Expected farm program payments	11.936	3.93	<.0001	0.1541	0.1353
Expected farm program payments risk	7.589	3.62	0.0003	0.0358	0.0396
Expected net crop insurance	2,179.140	1.76	0.0794	0.0888	0.1205
Expected net crop insurance risk	619.250	1.84	0.0658	0.0107	0.0233
Urbanization	0.588	22.22	<.0001	0.2614	0.4755
Precipitation	1.340	2.97	0.003	0.1736	0.2318
Temperature	3.512	1.85	0.0638	0.2608	0.3186
State Party (1 = Dem)	3.917	0.27	0.7905	0.0050	0.0086
National Party (1 = Dem)	5.661	0.37	0.7091	0.0077	0.0136
National Senate Party (1 = Dem)	−249.900	−8.76	<.0001	−0.4239	0.6069
National House Party (1 = Dem)	343.120	12.87	<.0001	0.6174	0.8190
Trend	17.148	10.41	<.0001	0.9496	0.8424

program payments and crop insurance program payments over time. So, it is not only the levels but also the variability in expected farm crop return, farm program payments and crop insurance program payments that explains farm real estate values. Finally, the trend and coefficient of variation in precipitation and temperature also are positive and significantly related to farm real estate values.

Finally, there could be indirect effects of politics or political party system via farm program payments and crop insurance program payments on farm real estate. In addition, the direct effects of the political party system on farm real estate are examined. The State Governorship and National Presidency are statistically insignificant and do not affect farm real estate values. However, a Democrat-controlled Senate and House would lead to a decrease and an increase, respectively, in the value of farm real estate.

Farm program payment equation results

An inverse relationship between expected farm program payments and expected farm crop returns is observed. Based on the elasticities presented in Table 12.3, the average elasticity of expected farm crop returns elasticity is 101.71 percent, with a standard deviation of 164.89 percent. A 10 percent increase in expected farm crop receipts implies a 10.17 percent decrease in expected farm program payments. The negative relationship indicates producers receive farm program payments only if there is a shortfall in farm crop receipts. In contrast, the variability in expected farm crop returns with positive and statistically significant sign shows an increase in the variability associated with farm crop returns will increase farm program payments.

Even though there is no a prior expectation, a positive and significant relationship between expected farm program payments and expected crop insurance program payments is observed. A 10 percent increase in expected crop insurance program payments will increase expected farm program payments by 0.76 percent. Identifying the reasons or rationale for the positive sign is difficult given that in the data, farm program payments and crop insurance program payments are not differentiated by different types of crops, different type of farm program payments and different types of crop insurance policies. This suggests a uni-directional relationship between expected crop insurance program payments and expected farm program payments.

An increase in the risk or variability associated with expected crop insurance program payments will reduce expected farm program payments due to the negative and statistically significant sign. Increased farm size is negatively related to expected farm program payments. This negative relation suggests producers tend to receive lower farm program payments on a per acre basis. As indicated in the model section, the state-level program crop acreage Herfindahl index and crop-livestock revenue Herfindahl index were included to account for state variation in non-observable differences in crop mixes, livestock enterprises, and other farm structure variables. The negative and significant sign of the program crop acreage Herfindahl indexes suggests for a 10 percent increase in specialization of program crop acreage, the expected farm program payments are expected to decline by 11.3 percent. This

Table 12.3 Farm program payment equation results

Variables	Estimate	tValue	Probt	Mean Elasticity	Stdev Elasticity
Intercept	1.269	0.52	0.6149		
Expected crop returns	−0.030	−10.26	<.0001	−1.0171	1.6489
Expected crop returns risk	0.038	3.63	0.0003	0.1427	0.2934
Expected net crop insurance	11.891	2.93	0.0034	0.0764	0.2251
Expected net crop insurance risk	−14.691	−1.92	0.0553	−0.0575	0.1855
Acreage Herfindahl index	0.148	4.17	<.0001	1.4919	3.2073
Revenue Herfindahl index	−0.085	−3.54	0.0004	−1.1303	2.1490
Farm size	−0.002	−3.63	0.0003	−1.1553	4.7401
Precipitation	0.003	0.29	0.7743	0.0558	0.1249
Temperature	−0.036	−0.92	0.3591	−0.3924	0.6251
State Party (1 = Dem)	−0.076	−0.26	0.7959	−0.0152	0.0355
National Party (1 = Dem)	−1.696	−5.53	<.0001	−0.2959	0.7169
National Senate Party (1 = Dem)	4.319	8.67	<.0001	1.0411	2.1588
National House Party (1 = Dem)	−3.537	−6.51	<.0001	−0.9674	1.8091
Trend	0.399	23.82	<.0001	3.8740	6.3256

suggests producers with diversified crop production system are expected to receive higher farm program payments. In contrast, the positive and significant sign of the crop-livestock revenue Herfindahl indexes suggests for a 10 percent increase in specialization of crop-livestock revenue, the expected farm program payments are expected to increase by 14.9 percent. This suggests producers generating revenue from specialized crop or livestock production system are expected to receive more farm program payments.

With respect to expected farm program payments, it does not matter which political party controls the State Governorship, as the variable is statistically insignificant. However, the negative sign on Presidency implies that a Democrat-controlled political party would lead to reduction in expected farm program payments on a per acre basis. A 10 percent shift in the Presidency from the Republican to the Democrat party will lead to a 2.959 percent decrease in expected farm program payments per acre. The positive and statistically significant sign with higher magnitude would lead to increased farm program payments if Democrats control the

Senate. The elasticity suggests, if there is 10 percent shift from a Democrat- to a Republican-controlled Senate, the expected farm program payments per acre will decrease by 10.4 percent. In contrast, with a negative sign, the Democrat-controlled House would lead to a reduction in farm program payments. So a 10 percent switch from a Democrat- to a Republican-controlled House would lead to an increase in expected farm program payments by 9.674 percent. Results for the expected crop insurance program payments shows positive sign of National Presidency, Senate and House, and State Governorship; however, only the Senate is statistically significant, suggesting the Senate plays a major role in expected crop insurance program payments. A 10 percent switch from a Democrat- to a Republican-controlled Senate would lead to decrease in expected crop insurance payments by 5.602 percent.

Finally, the trend and coefficient of variation in precipitation are positively related to farm program payments, while the coefficient of variation in temperature is negatively related.

Crop insurance payment equation results

A positive relationship between expected crop insurance program payments and expected farm crop returns is observed. A 10 percent increase in expected farm crop receipts implies a 5.07 percent increase in expected crop insurance program payments. The positive relationship indicates producers receive crop insurance program payments if there is a shortfall in yield/production or price. The risk or variability in expected farm crop returns is positive and significantly related to expected crop insurance program payments. This suggests that an increase in the variability associated with expected farm crop returns will increase expected crop insurance program payments.

Table 12.4 Crop insurance payment equation results

Variables	Estimate	tValue	Probt	Mean Elasticity	Stdev Elasticity
Intercept	0.00569	0.57	0.582		
Expected crop returns	0.00003	2.62	0.0088	0.5067	2.5871
Expected crop returns risk	0.00010	1.78	0.0753	0.1674	1.0351
Expected farm program payments	0.00032	3.33	0.0009	0.4033	0.8048
Expected farm program payments risk	−0.00043	−1.79	0.0733	−0.2160	0.4866
Crop insurance policies	−0.00061	−2.54	0.0111	−0.6716	1.5537
Share of crop insurance acres	0.01462	1.35	0.1786	0.1529	0.3729
Share of policies receiving indemnities	0.01912	3.93	<.0001	0.3566	1.4716

Variables	Estimate	tValue	Probt	Mean Elasticity	Stdev Elasticity
Farm size	0.00001	2.79	0.0053	0.5547	1.4713
Precipitation	0.00002	0.34	0.7321	0.1136	0.2820
Temperature	0.00021	1.06	0.2895	0.8073	2.1380
State Party (1 = Dem)	0.00041	0.29	0.7738	0.0210	0.0445
National Party (1 = Dem)	0.00085	0.56	0.5731	0.0330	0.0631
National Senate Party (1 = Dem)	0.01027	4.49	<.0001	0.5602	0.9687
National House Party (1 = Dem)	0.00098	0.39	0.6997	0.0806	0.2775
Trend	−0.00013	−1.18	0.2375	−0.6475	1.6735

A positive and statistically significant relationship is observed between expected farm program payments and expected crop insurance program payments. This suggests a 10 percent increase in expected farm program payments is expected to increase expected crop insurance program payments by 4.03 percent. Even though there is a positive relation between the two in the farm program payment equation and the crop insurance program payments equation, the magnitude of the causality is different. This also suggests the implications are expected to be different depending upon the changes to the policies in the future. This, in conjunction with the positive and statistically significant relationship in observed expected crop insurance program payments and expected farm program payments in the farm program payment equation, suggests bi-direction causality between expected farm program payments and expected crop insurance program payments.

A negative and statistically significant sign on the risk or variability associated with expected farm program payments will reduce expected crop insurance program payments. As the availability of insurance expands to greater numbers of crops, the expected crop insurance program payments is lower, given the negative sign. A 10 percent increase in the number of crops insured reduces the expected crop insurance program payments per acre by 8.6 percent. This suggests producers with specialized crops like corn, soybean, wheat, cotton or rice are expected to receive higher crop insurance program payments on a per acre basis. Similarly, as the share of crop insurance acreage relative to the total acreage increases, the expected crop insurance program payment per acre is lower. However, the magnitude is much lower, i.e., a 10 percent increase in the crop insurance acreage will reduce crop insurance program payments by only 0.36 percent.

In contrast, as the share of the policies receiving indemnities increases so does the crop insurance program payment. A 10 percent increase in the share of policies receiving indemnities is expected to increase crop insurance program payments by

2.7 percent. Unlike the farm program payment equation, the farm size is positively related to crop insurance program payments. This suggests, on average, large-size farms tend to receive high crop insurance program payments on a per acre basis.

Finally, the coefficient of variation in precipitation and temperature are positively related to farm real estate values with trend variable declining over time.

Summary and policy implications

The primary contribution of this research is to evaluate the importance of politics or political party controlling the National Presidency, Senate majority and House majority, and State Governorship in directly affecting expected farm program payments and expected crop insurance program payments programs as well the farm real estate values. The secondary contribution is to extend earlier research to include not only the levels but also the risk or variability associated with expected farm crop returns, expected farm program payments and expected crop insurance program payments in explaining farm real estate values. Finally, the research uses historical United States state-level data from 1949 to 2010 to examine the effect of expected farm program payments, expected crop insurance program payments and expected farm returns and urbanization on value of land. The majority in the Senate and House plays a statistically significant role in explaining expected farm program payments, expected crop insurance program payments and farm real estate values in United States for the period 1949 to 2010. The State Governorship did not play a statistically significant role in explaining expected farm program payments, expected crop insurance program payments and farm real estate values. The National Presidency played a significant role in explaining expected farm program payments and farm real estate.

The result of the study suggests a positive contribution of expected farm crop returns, expected farm program payments and expected crop insurance program payments to farm real estate values. Based on data from 48 states in the United States for the period 1949 to 2010, the average contribution of farm program payments and crop insurance program payments is 15 percent and 8.88 percent, respectively. Indeed, given the results of this study, it is likely that substantial cost reductions in the farm program and crop insurance program payments will lead to disproportionate effects on farm real estate values. Second, there is a negative and positive sign on the expected farm crop returns variable in the farm program payments equation and crop insurance program payments equation, respectively. This suggests the perceived counter-cyclic nature of expected crop insurance program payments (expected farm program payments) and farm returns is not consistent (consistent) with the intent of the federal programs. Further, this could be due to the intent of the different types of farm programs and crop insurance program apart from overlapping of the two programs to cover similar risks. Finally, the results do not quantify changes in the share of contribution of farm program payments and crop insurance program payments to the value of land over time and across regions. This would be a potentially valuable and fruitful research topic.

Notes

1 Risk or variability is defined as the standard deviation of last 5 years, excluding the current year. Even though 5 years seem to be a short time period, it is used to reflect potential changes reflected in the introduction of major farm bill every 5 years.
2 The sources and construction of historical data are available upon request from the author.
3 Alternatively, predictions from the autoregressive can also be used.
4 The Herfindahl index, also referred to as the Herfindahl-Hirschman index, is a commonly accepted measure of concentration. The value of the index is the sum of the squares of the shares of all firms (or in our case, crop and livestock variables) in an industry (or in our case, farm). The index takes a value of 100 percent when it is totally concentrated and zero percent when it is fully diversified.
5 The reduction in the value of farm real estate is obtained by multiplying the average farm real estate value by the average elasticity estimated from the regression analysis. For example, the average expected farm crop receipts elasticity of 3.37 percent is multiplied by \$1,128 to get \$38. Similarly, a reduction in farm real estate value of \$174 due to expected farm program payments is obtained by multiplying \$1,128 with average expected farm program payments elasticity of 1.541 percent. With respect to expected crop insurance program payments, a reduction of \$10 in farm real estate values is obtained as (\$1,128 {*} 0.888 percent). Finally, a reduction in urbanization leads to decline in farm real estate values by \$29.50 and obtained as (\$1,128 {*} 2.614 percent).

References

Gardner, B.L. 2002. U.S. Commodity Policies and Land Prices. WP 02-02, Department of Agricultural and Resource Economics, The University of Maryland, College Park.

Gertel, K. 1985. Differing Effects of Farm Commodity Programs on Land Returns and Land Values. USDA, *ERS Agricultural Economics Report* No. 544.

Harris, D.G. 1977. Inflation-Indexes, Price Supports, and Land Values. *American Journal of Agricultural Economics*, 59:489–495.

Lintner, J. 1965. The Valuation of Risk Assets and the Selection of Risky Investments in Stock Portfolios and Capital Budgets. *Review of Economics and Statistics*, 47:13–37.

Shaik, S., J. A. Atwood, and G. A. Helmers. 2005. The Evolution of Farm Programs and Their Contribution to Agricultural Land Values, *American Journal of Agricultural Economics*, 87:1190–1197.

Shaik, S., J. A. Atwood, and G. A. Helmers. 2012. Did 1933 New Deal Legislation Contribute to Farm Real Estate Values: A Regional Analysis, *Journal of Policy Modeling*, 34(6): 801–816.

U.S. General Accounting Office. 2014. *Farmers Have Been Eligible for Multiple Programs and Further Efforts Could Help Prevent Duplicative Payments*. GAO-14-428. Washington, D.C.: July 8, 2014.

U.S. General Accounting Office. 2008. *Federal Farm Programs: USDA Needs to Strengthen Controls to Prevent Payments to Individuals Who Exceed Income Eligibility Limits*. GAO-09-67. Washington D.C.: October 24, 2008.

Wallace, H.A. 1926. Comparative Farm-land Values in Iowa, *Journal of Land and Public Utility Economics*, 2:385–392.

Chapter 13

Land markets in Europe
Institutions and market outcomes[1]

Pavel Ciaian, d'Artis Kancs, and Dusan Drabik

Introduction

Agricultural land markets in the European Union are subject to significant policy interventions. Land market exchanges and land allocation as input in production are currently not taking place in a free market environment. Three types of land market interventions are present in the European Union: *tenure-/ownership regulations, environmental regulations*, and *area-based subsidies*. Tenure-/ownership regulations regulate land sales and rental transactions in terms of the right to use, control, and transfer land. Environmental regulations regulate land use by granting financial incentives or by imposing restrictions to farming activities with the aim of protecting and conserving land and the environment. The main part of the Common Agricultural Policy (CAP) support is allocated as land-based subsidies with the aim of supporting farmers' income and promoting sustainable development of rural areas.

Land market interventions vary considerably across the EU Member States, reflecting the variation in the quality and abundance of land as well as the differences in historical, societal and political developments. The implementation of *tenure-/ownership* regulations is not necessarily driven by efficiency gains for society but by political economy factors, largely determined by wealth redistributive effects among market participants (Swinnen 2002; Ciaian et al. 2010; Swinnen et al. 2014b). The primary motivation of the introduction of *environmental regulations* is to address market failures linked to the production of public goods and externalities by agricultural sector. *Area-based subsidies* are implemented to address income disparity between agriculture and other sectors of the economy, prevent depopulation of rural areas, and incentivize farmers to protect the environment (Swinnen 2015). The critics of the CAP argue that the political economy factors play a significant role in the design, implementation, and evolution of the CAP (Swinnen 2015). One reason is that farmers are, in general, a well-organized lobby group excreting pressure on politicians for support, whereas politicians gain their political support by providing subsidies.

Policy interventions can have severe implications for land market outcomes. First, land market interventions alter the costs and benefits of land market participants.

For example, land price interventions affect the income that landowners receive when selling or renting land. The CAP subsidies increase land returns to farmers. Second, land market interventions regulate which activities can be carried out on land. For example, environmental restrictions regulate the intensity of land use in agricultural production. Third, they determine which market participants have access to land and under what conditions. For example, pre-emption right provisions give preferential access to land to certain groups while other groups (e.g., foreigners) may get restricted access. Forth, they impact the outcome of land sales and rental market transactions. For example, long-term tenure contracts reduce the number of rental market transactions.

Agricultural land markets in the European Union

The farmland sales markets are relatively thin in the European Union. The share of the area of annually transacted agricultural land in the total utilized agriculture area (UAA) ranges between 0.1 percent in Slovakia to 8 percent in Lithuania (Table 13.1). The transacted area tends to be stable over time in Old Member States (OMS).[2] In New Member States (NMS),[3] the available evidence suggests an increase in the transacted area over time, probably induced by structural changes in agriculture due to the transition process and the EU enlargement (Ciaian et al. 2012c).

Table 13.1 Agricultural land sales as a percentage of the total utilized agricultural area

	Old member states	
	1998	*2006*
Belgium	1.63	1.28*
Finland	1.79	2.72
France	1.03	0.99*
Germany	0.58	0.58
Greece	0.41	0.35*
Ireland	3.04	2.90
Italy	1.60	1.42*
Netherlands	3.72	3.08
Spain	0.52	0.62
Sweden	0.63	0.62
UK	3.60	1.64*

(continued)

Table 13.1 Agricultural land sales as a percentage of the total utilized agricultural area
        (*continued*)

	New member states	
	*1998–2001***	*2005–2006***
Bulgaria	0.34	1.61
Czech Republic	2.8	3.30*
Estonia	n.a.	n.a.
Hungary	n.a.	3.6
Latvia	n.a.	n.a.
Lithuania	1.9	8.4
Poland	1.71	1.77
Romania	0.2	0.43
Slovakia	0.1	0.14

* Data from 2004.
** Bulgaria: data for 1999 and 2006; Czech Republic: data for 1998 and 2005; Estonia: data for 2005,
   transacted arable land as a percentage of UAA; Hungary: data for 2006; Lithuania: number of sales
   and gifts, data for 2000 and 2006; Poland: data for 1998 and 2005; Romania: data for 1999 and 2005;
   Slovakia: data for 2001 and 2005.

Sources: Ciaian et al. (2010); Swinnen and Vranken (2009; 2010).

Land sales price developments show greater dynamics. Overall, an upward trend
in price development tends to prevail in land sales across EU Member States in
the period 1995–2009 (Figure 13.1). The observed price increase can be explained
by the food price increase, a shift to a land-based subsidy system in the European
Union, and productivity growth (Ciaian and Kancs 2012; Michalek et al. 2014).

The levels of agricultural land sales prices vary strongly within the European
Union. Figure 13.1 compares the level of sales prices among EU Member States
in 1995, 2002, and 2009. The strongest difference in the price level is between
OMS and NMS. On average, land prices in OMS are several times higher than in
NMS and these price differences tend to persist over time. The lowest land price
is recorded in Lithuania, preceded by Latvia, Bulgaria, and Slovakia. In contrast,
the Netherlands reports the highest land prices in the EU. Land prices are also
high in Denmark and Luxemburg, in particular in 2009. From the reported NMS,
the Czech Republic has the highest land prices. Nevertheless, if compared to the
Netherlands for 2009, the Czech prices are lower by a factor of 20. Sweden and
France have more comparable price levels to NMS, though the gap is still substantial, more than 50 percent higher if compared to the Czech prices.

In most EU Member States, the land rental market seems to be more important than the sales market as a large share of the agricultural area, though a strong

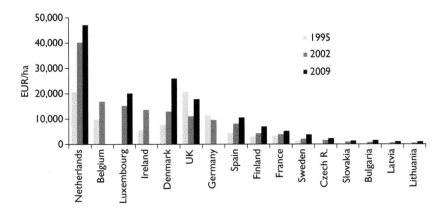

Figure 13.1 Development in land prices in the European Union (EUR/ha)

Source: Eurostat.
Notes: All prices are for agricultural land except for Bulgaria and France, for which arable price is reported. For the Netherlands and the UK the price for 1995 is the 1996 value; for Luxembourg the price for 2002 is the 2003 value; for the UK the price for 2009 is the 2008 value.

variation among Member States exists (Figure 13.2). In the OMS, the share of rented land in 2012 ranged between 19 percent in Ireland and 87 percent in France, while in the NMS it ranged between 26 percent in Poland and 95 percent in Slovakia (Table 13.2, Figure 13.2).

During the period 2004–2012, land renting decreased in roughly one-half of Member States, but increased in the other half. However, the increases in land renting tend to be larger (mostly varying between 3 and 18 percent) than the decreases (varying between -1 and -5 percent). Particularly strong expansion of land renting (more than 10 percent) occurred in Greece, Slovenia, Italy, Latvia, and Sweden. Countries with the most significant decrease in land renting (more than -5 percent) include Portugal and the Czech Republic (Table 13.2).

Rental price heterogeneity among Member States is less accentuated than land sales prices. Nevertheless, the cross-country variance has grown over time and has been driven mainly by NMS (from 1,000 percent between the lowest and highest countries in 2000 to over 4,200 percent in 2012). Although rental prices are in general higher in OMS, several OMS (e.g., Portugal, Spain, the UK) report comparable levels to NMS. Rental prices varied in 2012 from €20 per hectare in Latvia to €869 per hectare in the Netherlands. However, in most Member States the land rental prices were in the range between €150 per hectare and €300 per hectare in 2012 (Table 13.3). With the exception of Greece and the UK, rental prices increased in the period 2004–2012. The rental price increase is significantly higher in NMS than in OMS, which was likely induced by productivity growth and the introduction of the CAP subsidies after the EU accession of NMS (Ciaian and Kancs 2012; Swinnen et al. 2013).

Table 13.2 Land renting in the European Union

	2000	2004	2012	Change 2012/2000	Change 2010/2004
		% of UAA			% change
Old Member States					
Belgium	75	75	73	−2.6	−2.7
Denmark	25	29	29	15.5	0.0
Germany	70	70	67	−3.6	−4.4
Greece	36	42	52	42.6	22.9
Spain	32	31	37	16.1	17.1
France	81	84	88	8.6	3.9
Ireland	18	19	19	5.8	3.7
Italy	36	36	43	19.8	18.8
Luxembourg	48	49	54	12.3	8.9
Netherlands	39	41	41	5.9	0.7
Austria	26	30	28	6.8	−4.9
Portugal	28	36	27	−4.3	−25.9
Finland	32	34	34	5.8	−0.4
Sweden	40	48	54	36.2	11.8
UK	39	40	44	10.4	7.7
New Member States					
Bulgaria	n.a.	n.a.	89	n.a.	n.a.
Cyprus	n.a.	66	67	n.a.	2.0
Czech R.	n.a.	91	83	n.a.	−8.9
Estonia	n.a.	61	62	n.a.	2.2
Hungary	n.a.	66	62	n.a.	−4.8
Latvia	n.a.	41	48	n.a.	17.8
Lithuania	n.a.	52	54	n.a.	3.6
Malta	n.a.	84	82	n.a.	−2.1

	2000	2004	2012	Change 2012/2000	Change 2010/2004
			% of UAA		% change
Poland	n.a.	27	27	n.a.	0.0
Romania	n.a.	n.a.	57	n.a.	n.a
Slovakia	n.a.	97	95	n.a.	−1.6
Slovenia	n.a.	29	35	n.a.	20.1

Source: FADN, 2016.

Figure 13.2 Share of rented land as a percentage of the total utilized agricultural area (UAA), 2012

Source: FADN, 2016.

Table 13.3 Rental prices in the European Union (EUR/ha)

	2000	2004	2012	Change 2012/2000	Change 2012/2004
		EUR/ha		% change	
Old Member States					
Belgium	142	174	204	44.0	17.2
Denmark	88	130	191	117.9	47.4
Germany	144	152	168	16.7	10.5
Greece	105	123	111	5.3	−10.0
Spain	29	34	44	52.0	28.5
France	124	131	150	21.3	14.9
Ireland	52	48	50	−3.6	4.9
Italy	60	72	86	42.8	19.3
Luxembourg	91	97	117	28.3	20.3
Netherlands	276	319	359	30.4	12.8
Austria	50	57	64	28.9	12.7
Portugal	17	19	25	43.4	30.1
Finland	48	57	75	57.6	31.1
Sweden	66	68	119	80.9	74.7
UK	70	66	63	−11.0	−4.9
New Member States					
Bulgaria	n.a.	n.a.	146	n.a.	n.a.
Cyprus	n.a.	105	113	n.a.	6.9
Czech R.	n.a.	25	59	n.a.	136.3
Estonia	n.a.	3	15	n.a	338.0
Hungary	n.a.	35	77	n.a.	119.1
Lithuania	n.a.	8	21	n.a.	175.0
Latvia	n.a.	4	10	n.a.	126.7

	2000	2004	2012	Change 2012/2000	Change 2012/2004
	EUR/ha			% change	
Malta	n.a.	89	88	n.a.	−1.1
Poland	n.a.	10	18	n.a.	91.3
Romania	n.a.	n.a.	55	n.a.	n.a.
Slovakia	n.a.	23	39	n.a.	69.1
Slovenia	n.a.	11	34	n.a.	211.8

Source: FADN, 2016.

Tenure-/ownership regulations

There is great diversity of tenure-/ownership regulations in the European Union. They span from strictly regulated to largely liberal markets. According to land regulation indicators reported by Swinnen et al. (2014a), France and Hungary have the most stringent land market interventions in the EU. These two countries strictly regulate both sales and rental markets. Sweden, Germany, Finland, the UK, Greece, and Ireland have the least regulated land markets. Several countries – such as Belgium, Italy, the Netherlands, Portugal, Poland, and Slovenia – implement a moderate level of land market regulations. Typically, these countries regulate one side of the land market: either the sales or the rental market. For example, in Belgium, where about 70 percent of land is rented, most regulations concern the land rental market. Another example is Poland, where farmers own most of the land. Therefore, there is relatively little protection of tenants but there are important sales market regulations protecting family farms that operate on owned land (Table 13.4) (Swinnen et al. 2014a, 2014b; Ciaian et al. 2010).

There are various explanations why a particular land tenure-/ownership regulation or institution emerged in different countries. According to Swinnen (2002) and Swinnen et al. (2014b), changes in tenure-/ownership regulations in Europe were not necessarily efficiency-driven, meaning they did not emerge because they were more efficient than the existing alternatives. Swinnen (2002) and Swinnen et al. (2014b) argue that mainly political economy factors determine land institutional choices in the European Union. Changes in land tenure-/ownership imply redistribution of wealth among different market participants, in particular between landowners and tenants (or between domestic and foreign owners). These wealth distributional aspects have likely affected the emergence of a particular path, depending on the power balance between different land market groups present at a given point of time (de Janvry, 1981; Baland and Platteau 1998; 2002; Swinnen et al. 2014b).

According to Swinnen (2002) and Swinnen et al. (2014b), tenure-/ownership market regulations in OMS can largely be explained by the economic and political changes that took place in the late nineteenth and early twentieth centuries. Historically, large and wealthy landlords renting land to small and poor tenants dominated European countries. Large landlords controlled both the economic and the political power in the eighteenth and nineteenth centuries. The industrialization and democratization in the subsequent period increased the participation of workers, small farmers, and tenants in the political process through voting, thus reducing the political power of landlords. This political process resulted in adoption of regulations giving tenants (and landless workers and small farmers) more access to land either through enhancement of tenancy regulations or supporting land purchases. The improved access to land through tenancy was implemented in countries such as Belgium, France, and the Netherlands. These countries gradually introduced regulations throughout the twentieth century aiming at improving the rental conditions for tenants; for example, better conditions in case of contract termination, and automatic rights for rental contract renewal, and pre-emptive right options. Other countries, like Ireland and Denmark, followed the second approach by introducing measures to help the tenant to become the owner of land through government subsidies to buy the land (stimulating the demand for land) or through increased land and inheritance taxes (stimulating the supply of land as it induced landlords to sell (part of) their estate). These two separate patterns of institutional change largely explain the present tenure-/ownership regulations existing in the land markets in OMS (Swinnen 2002; Swinnen et al. 2014b).

In NMS, the current land tenure-/ownership regulations are heavily affected by the communist regime before the fall of the iron curtain and the subsequent land reforms and privatization processes as well as the EU accession. In these countries, the power strangles between landlords and tenants was less pronounced. The primary political battle was on the type of land privatization to be implemented after the collapse of the communist regime. The choice was between allocating the land to former (pre-collectivization) owners or to farm labor. The choice of the privatization strategy determined the structure of the land ownership and the importance of tenancy (Kancs and Ciaian 2010). However, overall, sales and rental markets (with some exceptions) remained relatively liberal. The key land regulation introduced in the land market in NMS was aiming at restricting foreigners' access to land acquisitions. This was introduced as a result of the accession of NMS to the European Union. The accession was expected to drive competition for land from OMS where land is considerably more expensive.

Table 13.4 Tenure-/ownership regulations in the European Union

Type of Regulation	Countries
Measures to protect the tenant	
Maximum rental prices	Austria, Belgium, France, the Netherlands
Minimum rental contract duration	Austria, Belgium, France, Italy, the Netherlands, Portugal, Slovakia, Slovenia, the UK (Scotland)

Type of Regulation	Countries
Measures to protect the tenant	
Automatic rental contract renewal	Belgium, the Czech Republic, France, Germany, Italy, the Netherlands, Portugal, Spain, Sweden, Slovakia, Slovenia
Conditions for rental contract termination	Belgium, France, the Netherlands
Pre-emptive buying right of the tenant	Belgium, France, Italy, Portugal, Sweden, Hungary, Latvia, Lithuania, the Netherlands, Romania, Slovakia, Slovenia, the UK (Scotland)
Measures to protect the owner-cultivator	
Requirements for the (new) landowner (e.g., residence, qualification, conduct of agricultural activity)	Austria, Denmark, Spain, Hungary, Lithuania, Poland, Slovakia
(Maximum) sales price regulations	Austria, France, Poland
Pre-emptive right for neighboring farmers	France, Italy, Portugal, Hungary, Latvia, Lithuania, Romania, Slovakia, Slovenia
Maximum transacted / Owned area	Denmark, France, Hungary, Lithuania, Poland
Measures to protect the (non-farm) land owner	
Maximum duration of rental contract	Denmark, Finland, Sweden, Hungary, Poland, Slovakia, the UK (Scotland)
Minimum rental prices	Austria, the Czech Republic, France, the Netherlands
Measures to prevent land fragmentation	
Regulations on pre-emptive buying rights of the co-owner	Italy, Portugal, the Czech Republic, Hungary, Lithuania, Poland, Romania, Slovakia, Slovenia
Minimum plot size	Germany, Bulgaria, Estonia, Lithuania, and Slovakia

Sources: Swinnen, Van Herck and Vranken (2014a); Drabik and Rajčániová (2014); FestForest (2014); Thomson, Moxey, and Butler (2014).

Table 13.4 summarizes the diversity of land tenure-/ownership regulations in different EU Member States. Following Swinnen et al. (2014a), we distinguish four categories of specific tenure-/ownership regulations: (i) measures to protect the tenant, (ii) measures to protect the owner (cultivator), (iii) measures to protect the (non-farm) land owner, and (iv) measures to prevent land fragmentation..

Rental market regulations

Rental market measures regulate both rental prices and contractual arrangements. The regulations are stronger in OMS than in NMS. In several EU Member States, governments impose price restrictions on rental markets for agricultural land. These restrictions take the form of a maximum or a minimum rental price. The maximum price aims to reduce pressure on farmers' rental costs, whereas the minimum rental price protects the rental income of landowners. For example, in Belgium and the Netherlands, there is a maximum rent. In France, there is a combination of a minimum and a maximum rent. However, in most Member States, there are no rental price restrictions. The maximum price restriction may induce illegal (grey) markets, as farmers may be willing to pay more than the maximum regulated amount by offering additional unofficial payments in the presence of competitive pressures. Indications of this practice can be found, for example, in Belgium, France and the Netherlands (Ciaian et al. 2012b; Thomson et al. 2014).

Regulation of rental contract duration is relatively common across Member States. For example, in Belgium and France, it is at least 9 years; in the Netherlands, at least 6 years; and in Spain at least 5 years. Moreover, in several countries (e.g., Belgium, France) even the renewal/inheritance of rental contracts is regulated. For example, in Belgium, there are several types of (long-term) tenancy contracts. First, there is a "traditional" tenancy contract with a duration of at least 9 years. Second, it is possible to have a contract for 18 years or more. Third, there is also a "career contract," whose duration is equal to the duration of the expected career of the farmer. Contracts of 9 and 18 years are automatically prolonged by successive periods of 9 years, whereas a career contract ends automatically when the tenant turns 65. In contrast, Ireland does not regulate the contract duration, while Denmark, Hungary, and Poland specify maximum lease durations without an automatic right of renewal (Swinnen et al. 2014a; Ciaian et al. 2012b; Thomson et al. 2014).

The duration of rental contracts for agricultural land gives an indication of rental market flexibility for farmers to adjust their production to changes in the external environment. Therefore, long-term rental contracts allow less adjustment to external changes than do short-term contracts. On the other hand, short-term contracts offer tenants less security, which reduces investment incentives for farmers.

In most countries, rental markets are free and unrestricted in relation to regulations on the quantity of land rented. In general, there are no constraints on the amount of land that is transacted (except in Hungary) and transactions do not need to be approved by a government agency (except in France, Germany, and the Netherlands) (Ciaian et al. 2012b).

Sales market regulations

In general, sales markets for agricultural land are less vulnerable to regulations than rental markets. Only in France, some regions in Germany, and some NMS (e.g., Hungary, Slovakia) there are strict sales market regulations. In France and Germany, there are special agencies that deal with agricultural land sales. In France, regional organizations (SAFERs) effectively control the local land markets through their power to buy, sell, and rent out agricultural land.[4] Effectively, they ensure that active farmers only own land. The SAFERs also control the level of farm restructuring and growth by requiring farmers to get authorization for farm expansion (Latruffe et al. 2013). The most widespread sales market regulation is the pre-emptive right provision to certain land market participants. Regulations in Member States vary with respect to who has the pre-emptive right to land acquisition such as tenants, neighbors, or co-owners. The most common priority groups of buyers are tenants followed by co-owners and neighboring farms. The motives behind granting the preferential treatment vary across Member States and include facilitating the access to land to certain groups of buyers or an attempt to prevent excessive land fragmentation.

Different countries have a form of land taxation: either ownership (property), transaction (e.g., capital gains tax for sales, registration tax for purchases), or inheritance tax. The tax system varies strongly across countries and usually agricultural land is favored in comparison to other property types by providing some form of favorable treatment. For example, such a special treatments are provided in Finland, Lithuania, and Poland (Ciaian et al. 2012a; UN-HABITAT 2013). To reduce competitive pressures from non-agricultural sector, some countries require a new buyer to provide a proof of competence in the agricultural sector through experience or education (e.g., Austria, Denmark, Lithuania, Poland, Slovakia), or impose a legal obligation to ensure that the land is cultivated after the purchase (e.g., Hungary, Lithuania). Other types of sales restrictions protect local or domestic buyers by requiring either local or country residence of the buyer. In Austria, new owners of agricultural land are required to reside close to the land plot. In Denmark, for an area smaller than 30 hectares, buyers need to have permanent residence rights in the country. Also Slovakia and Lithuania have residence requirements.

According to the EU accession treaties, NMS could impose up to a 10-year (12 years in Poland) transitional ban on agricultural land acquisitions by foreign individuals and legal persons (companies) from the EU Member States (European Commission 2014a). These restrictions were introduced as transitional measures to allow land markets to gradually adjust to competitive pressures rising from the single EU market. The primary reason for the transitional restrictions was the existence of substantial differences in agricultural land prices between OMS and NMS. As shown in Figure 13.1, prior to the EU accession, land prices in OMS where several times higher than in NMS. Note that, these price differences were not eliminated over the transitional period and still persist. As a result, the fear among the farming community of potentially strong competition coming from OMS remained in NMS after the expiration of the transitional period in 2014 (2016 in Poland).

As a response to pressures from farmers, NMS introduced new regulations attempting to indirectly restrict land purchases by foreigners. Although the new regulations do not directly target foreigners (as this would be illegal under the EU treaties), the motivation behind their introduction was the expiration of transitional retractions. The new measures target predominantly sales markets by restricting the purchase of agricultural land to different groups of individuals and by making land sales transactions administratively more cumbersome. That is, the most frequently adopted new measure in NMS is the pre-emptive buying right to farmers, neighbors, or domestic residents. However, if we compare the new adopted measure in NMS, such measures are present also in OMS. These measures add to the existing measures in NMS prior to the expiration of the transitional bans. The strongest prior restrictions existed in Poland and Hungary – two countries with strong political representation of small farmers and bordering with countries that have significantly higher land prices (Germany and Austria).

The most restrictive new lands sales measures were introduced in Slovakia, Lithuania, and in combination with exiting restrictions also in Poland. The new regulation in Slovakia gives the pre-emptive right to buy agricultural land to family relatives, co-owners, and farmers conducting their activity for at least 3 years in the cadastral zone where the offered land is located.[5] The second priority group includes farmers (individual farms, farm employees, or companies) with permanent residence (or headquarters) in Slovakia of at least 10 years and conducting agricultural activity for at least 3 years.[6,7] Selling land to the second group of potential buyers requires an announcement of the offer (free of charge) for at least 15 days in the online registry of agricultural land offers administered by the Ministry of Agriculture and on a public board in the village where the land is located. If none of the pre-emption right holders express their interest in acquiring the land plot within a 6-month period, it can then be sold to any buyer (not necessarily working in agriculture) from the European Union. The complex conditions under which agricultural land can be sold imply that individuals without permanent residence in Slovakia practically cannot buy land in the country (Drabik and Rajčániová 2014). These new measures make Slovakia, in addition to France and Hungary, one of the most protected land sales markets in the European Union.

In Lithuania, according to a new measure, any new buyer must have at least 3 years of experience (in the last 10 years) in agricultural production, qualification in agriculture, and obtain a government permission to buy agricultural land. The new owner also needs to conduct agricultural activity on the purchased land for at least 5 years after the purchase agreement and maintain a pre-defined minimum income level per hectare (defined by the Ministry of Agriculture). Further, an owner cannot own more than 500 ha of agricultural land in total (FestForest 2014). In anticipation of the expiration of transitional restrictions in 2016, Poland adopted new measures in 2015 with the aim of restricting land purchases by foreigners. The existing regulations in Poland require the land to be used for agriculture, buyers have qualification in agriculture, and an owner does not own more than 300 hectares of agricultural land.

Note that not all NMS introduced as restrictive sales regulations as Lithuania, Poland, or Slovakia. For example, new measures in Romania give the pre-emptive buying rights to farmers, neighbors, and co-owners. However, there is no residence requirement implying that foreigners are not excluded from the sales market.

The regulation treats foreign and domestic buyers fairly equally in Romania. Compared to other EU Member States, Romania remains one of the countries with the most liberal sales market. In Romania, where farmers own a significant share of land, renting is less important, which may partially explain the adoption of a rather liberal sales market regulation.

Environmental regulations

Various public goods and (positive or negative) externalities (e.g., landscape features, biodiversity and the environment) are linked to agricultural production. Markets are often inefficient in delivering their optimal production level (Cooper et al. 2009). The market failure has motivated the European Union to introduce policies targeting the provision of agricultural public goods and externalities. Currently, several EU-level measures target these objectives and are linked to the agricultural land cultivation. The most important EU-wide environmental instruments include agro-environmental payments, Less Favored Area (LFA) payments, the Natura 2000 network, and the Nitrates Directive.

First, under the CAP there are various support instruments targeted at motivating farmers to adopt sustainable management practices on land to prevent land abandonment. The two most important instruments include agro-environmental payments and LFA payments granted under the Rural Development Program. Agri-environmental payments are offered on a voluntary basis for the provision of environmental management services. They are granted for a range of farm activities aimed at improving the environment on the farm. They cover additional costs and foregone farm income resulting from the adoption of environmental management practices. Agri-environmental payments affect particularly farm input use, because they are conditional on the adoption of environmentally friendly production practices, such as fertilizer reduction, organic farming, intensification of livestock, conversion of arable land to grassland, rotation measures, and support of biodiversity (EC 2005). LFA payments support farmers located in less productive regions by granting a per-hectare payment. The aim of this support is to prevent land abandonment in places where natural conditions (e.g., difficult climatic conditions, mountainous regions, low soil quality) make land cultivation less attractive.

Other EU-wide environmental regulations targeted at land use include the Natura 2000 network and Nitrates Directive. The Natura 2000 is an EU-wide network of nature protection measures (implemented as part of the Birds and Habitats Directives) and aims to preserve the survival of European Union's most valuable and threatened species and habitats. It includes two types of areas: Special Areas of Conservation (SACs) and Special Protection Areas (SPAs). SACs cover areas that provide rare and vulnerable animals, plants and habitats increased protection, while SPAs includes areas that are important for rare and vulnerable birds that use them for breeding, feeding, wintering, or migration. Around 10 percent of the EU agricultural area is under Natura 2000. However, Natura 2000 also covers other areas (e.g., costal area) designated as vulnerable from a natural and ecological point of view. Conservation measures are required to be applied on these areas in order to maintain or restore the natural habitats and/or the populations of the species for which the sites are designated. Conservation measures are financially supported both by national and EU-level funding (e.g., LIFE-Nature instrument). It should be mentioned that agricultural production is not excluded from the Natura 2000 areas. However, agricultural production taking place in these areas are subject to strict regulations in line with conservation requirements. In cases when the land owner-ship structure and use rights are contrary to the conservation objectives of Natura 2000, land is purchased in public domain or by recognized non-governmental organizations (European Commission 2014b; Kettunen et al. 2014).

The Nitrates Directive regulates the fertilizer and manure use in agriculture in order to reduce nitrates pollution in ground and surface waters. Countries designate nitrate-vulnerable zones that could pollute waters from high applications of manure and fertilizers on land. However, a number of countries (e.g., Austria, Denmark, Finland, Germany, Ireland, Lithuania, Luxembourg, Malta, the Netherlands, and Slovenia) include their whole territory in these zones (European Commission 2015).

The Nitrates Directive legally regulates annual farm application of manure and fertilizers on land by imposing upper limits per hectare. Further, countries define codes of good practice for farmers, to be implemented on a voluntary basis in all territory, and specific practices compulsory for farmers located in nitrate-vulnerable zones. For example, these practices regulate the periods of prohibition of the appli-cation of certain types of fertilizer, manure storage methods, spreading methods and crop rotation in certain zones (e.g., on steep slopes; frozen or snow-covered ground, near water courses) and other land management measures (European Commission 2015). A number of Member States have decided to impose stricter regulations than required by the Nitrates Directive, particularly in countries with intensive livestock production. For example, in Belgium, Denmark, and the Netherlands livestock manure nitrogen limits are stricter than those defined in the Nitrates Directive; fer-tilizer application standards vary depending on crop and soil types as well (Le Goffe 2013). Overall, the Nitrates Directive affects the use rights of land, as it requires adoption of specific good farming practices (application of manure and fertilizers).

Given that environmental regulations affect land management and its use, they alter the functioning of land markets in the European Union. In particular, they affect land allocation and the benefits and costs of landowners and users. Environmental regulations are also expected to generate welfare benefits to the society in general, as they are designed to increase the provision of public goods or to reduce negative externalities on land. However, public welfare benefits are not necessarily internal-ized by land owners/users. Environmental regulations are associated with additional costs, forgone income, or produced public benefits. To partially or fully compensate for the costs, the regulations are typically implemented in combination with subsi-dies (e.g., agri-environmental payments).

Nilsson and Johansson (2013) find for Sweden, and Kilian et al. (2012) for Germany, that agro-environmental payments are negatively correlated with land prices. This suggests that environmental constraints linked to these measures impose additional costs for farmers. It is also possible that the land receiving agri-environmental support has less favorable natural conditions for agricultural production, which is ultimately reflected in lower land prices. This hypothesis is indirectly supported by Ciaian et al. (2015), whose estimates show that agri-environmental and LFA payments are fully translated in higher farm income, suggesting that these payments may exercise minimal impact on other factors such as land prices. The estimates of Mary (2013) show that LFA payments have negative and significant impact on farm productivity of French crop farms, whereas agri-environmental payments are found to have no impact on productivity. Mary's (2013) findings suggest that an increase in LFA payments by €100 would decrease farm productivity by 0.016 percent.

The environmental regulations may not always reduce land values or land productivity. For example, the limitations imposed by the Nitrates Directive on manure application on land may actually boost land competition, as farmers need to spread manure on a larger surface in zones with a nitrogen surplus in order to comply with requirements. The resulting higher demand for agricultural land would result in higher land prices. This positive price effect of the Nitrates Directive is confirmed by Latruffe et al. (2013) for Brittany in France and Vukina and Wossink (2000) for the Netherlands. Also LFA payments are found to increase land prices as they increase land returns for less productive land and thus stimulate competition on land markets (Patton et al. 2008; Kilian et al. 2012). For Natura 2000, although valuation estimates vary widely across studies, the evidence tends to show that these areas generate public welfare benefits to society and that societal benefits often significantly exceed private benefits (Hoyos et al. 2012).

Area-based subsidies

The emphasis of the CAP before 1992 was on encouraging agricultural productivity, maintaining a stable supply of affordable food for consumers and ensuring a viable agricultural sector. The support to farmers was implemented predominantly through a price support system that guaranteed high prices to farmers. The early CAP had a major impact on agricultural product markets, leading to large distortions and high budgetary costs. To address these issues, important changes were made to the CAP starting from 1992. To reduce the market imbalances, domestic prices were reduced and the income loss to farmers was redressed through coupled compensatory direct payments. The subsequent reforms implemented in 2003, 2005, and 2013 shifted the main part of the CAP support towards area-based payments, which are decoupled from agricultural production but linked to land. In order to receive decoupled payments, farmers were required to implement minimal environmental practices (cross-compliance and "greening" measures).

Two types of area payments are implemented in the European Union: the Single Area Payment Scheme (SAPS) and the Single Payment Scheme (SPS) (Table 13.5). A key difference between the SAPS and the SPS is the area eligible for the payment.

Table 13.5 The SAPS and SPS implementation by Member States under the 2003 CAP reform

Model SPS / SAPS	Member State (start date)
SPS historical	Austria (2005), Belgium (2005), France (2006), Greece (2006), Ireland (2005), Italy (2005), Netherlands (2006), Portugal (2005), Spain (2006), the UK (Wales and Scotland)
SPS regional	Malta (2007), Slovenia (2007)
SPS hybrid	Denmark (2005), Finland (2006), Germany (2005), Luxemburg (2005), Sweden (2005), the UK (N. Ireland, 2005), the UK (England, 2005)
SAPS	Bulgaria (2007), Czech R. (2004), Estonia (2004), Cyprus (2004), Latvia (2004), Lithuania (2004), Hungary (2004), Poland (2004), Romania (2007), Slovakia (2004)

Notes: Starting year of implementation in parentheses.

Source: European Commission.

Under the SAPS, the entire area that framers use can receive a payment per hectare. Under the SPS, the farmer is entitled to a yearly payment depending on the number of payment entitlements the farmer possesses. The number of entitlements is based on the reference (historical) area of the farm. To receive the SPS, farmers need to match each entitlement with one hectare of land. Thus, the SPS is linked to land because, in the absence of eligible land, farms cannot activate (cash in) their entitlements. Farms can expand or decrease their stock of entitlements by buying or selling entitlements on the market from other farms.

Another key difference between the SAPS and the SPS is the value of the per hectare payment. Under the SAPS, all farms in a given Member State (or region within a Member State) receive an equal per hectare payment. Under the SPS, the payment value can differ between farms in a given region. This depends on the type of the SPS model a Member State implemented under the 2003 CAP reform, that is, historical, regional, or hybrid model. Under the historical model, the SPS is farm-specific (and thus heterogeneous) and equals the support the farm received in the reference period. Under the regional model, an equal per-hectare payment is granted to all farms in a given Member State (or region within a Member State). The hybrid model is a combination of the historical and regional models.[8]

An important implication of the SAPS and the SPS for land markets is that they increase returns to land. The two types of payments do not oblige farms to produce on land. Land only needs to be maintained in good agricultural conditions and minimal environmental requirements need to be respected. As a result, the SAPS and SPS subsidies tend to increase competition for land as market participants seek to acquire more land (either through rental or purchase) to benefit from subsidies. In well-functioning markets, the enhanced competition will be reflected (capitalized) in higher land values (rental and sales prices) and thereby benefit mainly landowners instead of farmers who are actual subsidy addressees. Depending on competition on land markets, type of the implemented SPS model and other factors, the size of capitalization differs between the SAPS and the SPS as well as between different SPS models.

To illustrate the differences in the area-based payment, we show the effects graphically using a stylized land rental model of Ciaian et al. (2014), which is shown in Figure 13.3. For the sake of graphical tractability, we assume that (i) the entire land is owned by "landowners," who rent the land to "farms," (ii) there are two identical regions except for the land supply, and (iii) entitlements are allocated to farms (in accordance with EU rules).

The horizontal axis shows the quantity of land, A, the vertical axis measures the rental price, r, and the SAPS/SPS subsidy, t. The aggregate land demand without subsidies is given by the downward sloping curve DD. Land supply in region 1 is given by curve S_1, and land supply in region 2 is given by curve S_2. The land market

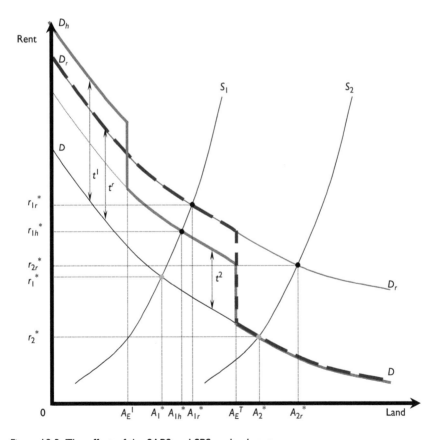

Figure 13.3 The effect of the SAPS and SPS on land rents

equilibriums in the zero support regime, are (A_1^*, r_1^*) and (A_2^*, r_2^*) in region 1 and region 2, respectively. Although, the productivity is the same for all farms (i.e., land demand is the same in region 1 and region 2), there is less land used in equilibrium in region 1 than in region 2 due to lower land supply.

As a starting point, we consider the SAPS. Under the SAPS, the entire land is eligible for support and payment value is uniform across all farms. We denote the hectare value of the SAPS by t'. The SAPS shifts land demand upward from DD to D_rD_r. Farms' willingness to pay for land increases by the SAPS value, t'. The land market equilibrium shifts from (A_1, r_1) to (A_{1r}, r_{1r}) in region 1 and from (A_2, r_2) to (A_{2r}, r_{2r}) in region 2. Land use and land rent increase by $A_{1r}^* - A_1^*$ $(A_{2r}^* - A_2^*)$ and by $r_{1r}^* - r_1^*$ $(r_{2r}^* - r_2^*)$, respectively, in region 1 (region 2). Competition for land drives up land rental prices and thus the SAPS gets capitalized into land rents. The capitalization level is equivalent in both regions. The capitalization is higher when the supply of land is less elastic. In the extreme case, with fixed land supply (not shown in Figure 13.3), the SAPS may become fully capitalized into land prices, that is, all subsidies will go to landowners because land rents increase proportionally to the SAPS (Ciaian and Kancs 2012). The capitalization effect of the SPS is more complex as the amount of subsidies that farms receive depends on the number of entitlements they possess. The two key determinants of the SPS capitalization are (i) the size of entitlements relative to the total land area and (ii) the heterogeneity of the SPS payment (i.e., the type of the SPS model) (Courleux et al. 2008; Ciaian et al. 2008, 2010, 2014; Kilian and Salhofer 2008).

The capitalization of the SPS depends strongly on the ratio of the eligible area to the total number of entitlements. If there are more entitlements than the eligible area ("surplus"), then the SPS leads to a land price increase. However, if there are fewer entitlements than the eligible area ("deficit"), then the SPS does not increase land prices. This is shown in Figure 13.3 for the regional SPS model. For comparison, we assume a SPS rate of t', that is, the same value as in the case of the SAPS. However, under the SPS, the stock of entitlements determines the maximum amount of land that can receive payments. We assume a total amount of entitlements A_E^T. The land demand with the regional SPS model is given by the bold (kinked) line D_rD. Given that farms need land to activate their entitlements and cash-in the SPS, farms' willingness to pay for land increases by the value of the entitlement, t'. This holds until all entitlements are exhausted, that is, up to A_E^T. After this point, land demand is the same with and without the SPS, as there are no unused entitlements available.

The effects of the SPS on the land market are very different in the two regions. In region 1, where entitlements are in surplus compared to the total land area $(A_1^* < A_E^T)$, the SPS gets capitalized into land rents. That is, the equilibrium changes from (A_1, r_1) without support to (A_{1r}, r_{1r}) with the regional SPS model. The effect is the same as in the case of the SAPS. However, the effect is different in region 2 where entitlements are in deficit relative to land $(A_2^* > A_E^T)$. The equilibrium (A_2, r_2) is not altered by the SPS. The SPS has a zero-distortive marginal effect on farm rental decisions. This implies zero capitalization of the SPS in region 2.

The main intuition behind these results is that, in the presence of surplus entitlements, farms will not be able to activate all their entitlements with the current area of land. Profit-maximizing farms will compete for additional land, seeking to activate their unused entitlements. Competing farms will overbid the market price for land until it equals the marginal profitability and the entitlement value. As a result, the SPS will be capitalized into land rents. The effect of competitive pressure in the case of deficit entitlement is the reverse. If land is in surplus relative to entitlements, farmers will compete for entitlements to benefit from the SPS. The SPS will benefit the entitlement owners, but will not be reflected in higher land rental prices. The same intuition holds for all SPS models. However, in reality the SPS capitalization is expected to be smaller in countries implementing the historical model than in countries implementing regional or hybrid models because fewer entitlements relative to total area were allocated under the former than under the latter (Ciaian et al. 2008, 2010, 2014).

When the SPS is capitalized into land values, the share of payments that is capitalized into land rents decreases in the payment heterogeneity. That is, the subsidy capitalization is higher under the regional SPS model than under the historical or hybrid models. We illustrate this effect in Figure 13.3 by comparing regional and historical models. We assume the same regional model as above. For the historical model, we consider two types of entitlements. The stock of type 1 entitlements, A_E^1, has unit face value t^1, and the stock of type 2 entitlements, A_E^2, has face value t^2. The aggregate stock of entitlements, A_E^T, is the sum of the two types, that is, $A_E^1 + A_E^2 = A_E^T$ where $t^1 > t^2$. This implies a land demand function such as represented by the (double kinked) curve $D_h D$. Relative to a no-support regime, the historical SPS model shifts land demand by t^1 up to A_E^1, where all high value entitlements are activated. In the interval from A_E^1 to A_E^T (where $A_E^T - A_E^1 = A_E^2$) it is higher by t^2, and it is the same after all entitlements are activated at A_E^T (= $A_E^1 + A_E^2$).

To compare the effects of the different models (regional SPS, historical SPS and SAPS), we keep the total amount (value) of the SPS entitlements constant. Above we have shown that under the regional model, the equilibrium was (A_{1r}^*, r_{1r}^*) in region 1 – where the entitlements were in surplus relative land. Under the historical SPS model, the equilibrium in region 1 is (A_{1h}^*, r_{1h}^*). Hence, land use increases and land rents go up in both models though less under the historical than under the regional SPS model (and the SAPS). This implies lower capitalization under the historical than under the regional SPS model (and the SAPS).

The intuition behind these results is that as farms with high value entitlements compete with farms with low value entitlements, farms owning high value entitlements can afford to pay higher rents, but will only bid up the rent to the maximum that the low value entitlements can (no longer) afford. Therefore, the low value entitlements will determine the SPS capitalization at the margin. This implies that the SPS capitalization decreases in the heterogeneity of the SPS levels. Thus, the capitalization of the SPS in land prices will be stronger under the regional SPS model than under the historical SPS model. The capitalization rate under the hybrid model is between the regional and historical SPS models (Ciaian et al. 2008, 2010, 2014).

In region 2, there is no effect of the SPS with both regional and historical SPS models because of the deficit entitlements relative to the total area. The SPS had no impact on the land market—the equilibrium remains unchanged at (A_2^*, r_2^*). Hence the SPS does not lead to capitalization of subsidies in region 2, irrespective of the SPS model.

Overall, the capitalization of the SAPS is expected to dominate the capitalization of the SPS as there are no entitlements (all agricultural area is eligible) and the per-hectare payments are uniform across farms under the SAPS. The impact of the SPS on land capitalization is expected to be the largest for the regional model, followed by the hybrid model, while the historical model is associated with the smallest capitalization rate. This is because under the regional model entitlements are more abundant relative to the total land area and the SPS is homogenous across farms. The opposite is true for the historical model: fewer entitlements were allocated relative to total land and the payment value varies across farms. The hybrid model is an intermediary case as it is similar to the regional model with respect to the entitlement stock, while payments are heterogeneous across farms but less than under the historical model.

Empirical evidence

There are a growing number of studies empirically estimating the capitalization of EU land-based subsidies. The results of these studies are summarized in Table 13.6. The studies can be grouped into two broad categories: land sales price studies and land rent studies.[9] Most studies focus on land rental prices since data on land rents are more widely available. Land sales price studies usually estimate the capitalization elasticity representing the percentage change in land price per 1 percent increase in subsidies, whereas rental studies typically estimate capitalization rate measuring the share of subsidy capitalized into land rents.

Table 13.6 Empirical evidence of area-based payment capitalization into land values

Study	Type of area CAP subsidy (Country)	Percentage change in land sales price per 1 percent increase in subsidies	Share of subsidy capitalized into land rents) (%)
Michalek, Ciaian and Kancs (2014)	SPS (EU, OMS)	—	6–10
Kilian et al. (2012)	SPS, hybrid (Germany, Bavaria)	—	44–94
Feichtinger and Salhofer (2015a)	SPS, hybrid (Germany, Bavaria)	—	35

Study	Type of area CAP subsidy (Country)	Percentage change in land sales price per 1 percent increase in subsidies	Share of subsidy capitalized into land rents) (%)
Guastella et al. (2014)	SPS, historical (Italy)	—	0
O'Neill and Hanrahan (2013)	SPS, historical (Ireland)	—	Short-run: 7–25 Long-run: 21–53
		—	
Ciaian and Kancs (2012)	SAPS (EU, NMS)	—	19
Van Herck and Vranken (2013)	SAPS (EU, NMS)	—	15–32
Nilsson and Johansson (2013)	SPS, hybrid (Sweden)	0.54	—
Karlsson and Nilsson (2014)	SPS, hybrid (Sweden)	0.00	—
Feichtinger and Salhofer (2015b)	SPS, hybrid (Germany, Bavaria)	0.20–0.28	—

Two studies, using very different datasets, have estimated the impact of the SAPS on land rents in the NMS. Ciaian and Kancs (2012) use a firm-level panel dataset of more than 10,000 farms in 7 NMS in 2004 and 2005. Van Herck et al. (2013) use country level-data on average land rents and the SAPS for 6 NMS over the period 1994–2009. Both studies find remarkably similar results: they find that between €0.15 and €0.32 per additional euro of the SAPS is capitalized in higher land rental prices. These estimates appear somewhat low given that theory suggests a considerably higher capitalization rate. One explanation for this small capitalization level could be the presence of land market rigidities (including regulations) that hamper the full adjustment of land sales and rental prices.

The estimates of the capitalization rates for the SPS vary more across studies. This is mainly because of different regional coverage by the studies, which captures different SPS implementation models (Table 13.5). Michalek et al. (2014) estimate the capitalization of the SPS into land rents using farm-level data across OMS for the early period of the SPS implementation (2004 to 2007). They find a relatively low capitalization rate of only 6 to 10 percent. However, Michalek et al. (2014) also show that there is a significant variation in the SPS capitalization rate across OMS, among regions and among farms. Moreover, their estimates confirm the theoretical predictions on lower SPS capitalization in the historical compared to the hybrid model. O'Neill and Hanrahan (2013) estimate the short-run capitalization rate in the same magnitude for Ireland (historical model) as Michalek et al. (2014): between 7 and 25 percent. In the long run the capitalization rate is larger: between 21 percent and 53 percent. Guastella et al. (2014) find a statistically insignificant impact of the SPS on land rents in Italy, where the historical SPS model is implemented.

Nilsson and Johansson (2013) analyze the SPS impacts in Sweden, whereas Kilian et al. (2012) and Feichtinger and Salhofer (2015b) analyze the SPS impacts in Bavaria (Germany) and find a comparably high capitalization rate. The former study finds that the elasticity of agricultural land sales price with respect to the SPS is 0.54 (i.e., a 1 percent increase in the SPS increases land sales price by 0.54 percent), whereas the latter two studies find that 35 to 94 percent of the SPS are capitalized into land rental prices. Both Sweden and Germany implement the hybrid model where the entitlements are more abundant relative to total land, which, according to the analysis depicted in Figure 13.3, is expected to cause a higher capitalization of the SPS.

In contrast, Karlsson and Nilsson's (2014) estimates suggest no impact of the SPS on land sales prices in Sweden (hybrid model). This contradicts the findings of Nilsson and Johansson (2013). Both studies use the same data from the Swedish Mapping, Cadastral, and Land Registration Authority for the period January 2007 to December 2008. The two studies differ in the methodology they employ. Karlsson and Nilsson (2014) use a spatial multilevel model that accounts for spatial spillover effects and interdependencies, while Nilsson and Johansson (2013) apply asset-pricing model where land price is determined by the expected returns from its current and potential future uses. These differences in methodology imply that when controlling for interdependencies between local and regional factors and spatial spillover effects between neighboring farms, the SPS becomes unimportant in determining land sales prices. Similarly, Feichtinger and Salhofer (2015b) control for spatial spillover effects and interdependencies and find lower capitalization elasticity for sales prices in Bavaria in Germany (0.20–0.28) than do Nilsson and Johansson (2013).

In general, with some exceptions, the estimated capitalization of the SPS appears to be more in line with the theoretical predictions than in the case of the SAPS. However, the estimated capitalization rates for both types of payments could be underestimated due to the presence of various tenancy regulations. In particular, long duration rental contacts and maximum rental price interventions applied in several countries can prevent full price adjustments or cause sluggish adjustment of land rents to subsidies, implying that the effect may not be full and immediate. Studies that focus specifically on short-term or new contracts find considerably higher capitalization rates. For example, Patton et al. (2008) in their analysis of Northern Ireland only include farms with rental contracts of 1 year or less, and exclude all longer-term rental contracts. They find that the capitalization of land-based subsidies is more than 100 percent. Also Kilian et al. (2012) find that the SPS capitalization effect is significantly higher for newly signed rental contracts in Bavaria (Germany). Further, Latruffe et al. (2013) find that land regulation linked to intervention of public authority (i.e., SAFER) in land markets reduces land sales prices in Brittany (France). This is because of the pre-emptive rights of SAFER, which allows maintaining lower market prices by purchasing land if the price is too high and selling it back at a lower price.

Conclusions

This chapter analyzes the government interventions in land markets in the European Union with a focus on three main areas: tenure-/ownership regulations, environmental regulations, and area-based payments. The analysis shows that agricultural land markets in the European Union are far from operating in a free market environment. It is generally acknowledged that the well-functioning land markets plays an important role in promoting economic development of rural areas, because it allows a more efficient use of land by facilitating transfer of land from less to more productive farmers and structural adjustment of farming sector. As a result, the presence of land market interventions may have important implications by constraining these developments in general and land market structural adjustments in particular. However, not all interventions may be detrimental to society. For example, the regulations attempting to address market failures linked to provision of agricultural public goods and externalities may actually generate net welfare gains.

Unlike land subsidies or environmental regulations, tenure-/ownership regulations are generally not subject to joint EU policies, but remain essentially a national matter. This is one of the reasons why they tend to vary strongly across countries, as they reflect national political economy preferences. They include a wide range of measures targeting either sales or rental markets. Almost all EU Member States have in place some type of land market intervention. Rental markets tend to be under stronger regulation in OMS than NMS. However, there are some OMS (e.g., France) that have implemented complex regulatory systems, which intervene in land markets. Generally, NMS have relatively liberal rental markets. However, sales transactions are subject to stricter rules in particular toward foreigners or non-residents aimed to protect domestic land markets against competitive pressures from OMS.

The European Union has put in place several regulations with the aim of addressing land market failures linked to provision of public goods and externalities. The most important EU-wide environmental instruments targeting land markets include agri-environmental payments, LFA payments, the Natura 2000 network, and the Nitrates Directive. While these instruments may reduce private benefits of owning or using land (e.g., by reducing land market price or productivity) due to imposed land use restrictions, they may generate substantial welfare gains to society by improving the environmental services on land such as landscape or biodiversity.

The EU land markets are also significantly affected by area-based subsidies – the SAPS and the SPS – granted under the CAP. The theoretical models suggest that land market outcomes would differ between the SAPS and the SPS. In a well-functioning land market, the SAPS should get incorporated into land values, thereby benefitting mainly landowners instead of famers. For the SPS, the theoretical analysis suggests that the subsidy capitalization may vary from a full to a zero rate, and that it decreases with the variation in the payments value among farms. The empirical findings tend to suggest a lower capitalization rate than predicted by theoretical models. This is especially the case for the SAPS for which empirical studies report a relatively low capitalization rate. One explanation for the smaller capitalization rate could be the presence of land market rigidities induced by land tenure-/ownership regulations that hamper the full adjustment of land sales and rental prices to external shocks.

Notes

1 The authors are solely responsible for the content of the chapter. The views expressed are purely those of the authors and may not in any circumstances be regarded as stating an official position of the European Commission.
2 OMS refers to Austria, Belgium, Denmark, Germany, Greece, Finland, France, Ireland, Italy, Luxembourg, the Netherlands, Portugal, Spain and Sweden, and the United Kingdom.
3 NMS refers to eight Member states from Central and Eastern Europe which joined the EU in 2004: the Czech Republic, Estonia, Hungary, Latvia, Lithuania, Poland, Slovakia and Slovenia.
4 In addition to having a pre-emptive right, SAFER also participates in the negotiation process between the buyer and the seller of agricultural land. If the parties cannot reach a mutual agreement on a certain price, SAFER can propose another buyer or another price that is more in line with the observed market price. In some cases, SAFER can even decide to exercise its pre-emptive right and acquire agricultural land to sell to another buyer or to rent out when this better fits SAFER's mission objectives. Even if an agreement has been established between a buyer and a seller, SAFER can intervene and exercise its pre-emptive right, for example when agricultural land is sold at a price that is considered too low and SAFER suspects that it is being purchased for speculative reasons (Ciaian et al. 2012a).
5 It should be noted that farmers in Slovakia rent as much as 90 percent of land which makes them more vulnerable to foreign land acquisitions.
6 Young farmers (for both groups) are exempted from the requirement of conducting agricultural activity for at least three years before the transaction.
7 Further, the second group is distinguished by whether farmers conduct their agricultural activity in the neighboring village with respect to the sold land or in other location. The former farmers have the priority over the latter type of farmers in acquiring the land.
8 Conceptually, the SAPS corresponds to the regional SPS model with an infinite stock of entitlements.
9 The capitalization effect on land sale price is equivalent to the capitalization effect on rental prices if the sale prices follow the asset pricing formula where land price equals the sum of discounted future rental prices.

References

Baland, J.M. and Platteau, J.P. (1998). "Wealth Inequality and Efficiency in the Commons, Part II: The Regulated Case." *Oxford Economic Papers* 50: 1–22.
Baland, J.M. and Platteau, J.P. (2002). "Collective Action and the Commons: The Role of Inequality." In J.M. Baland, P. Bardhan and S. Bowles (eds.) *Inequality, Cooperation and Environmental Sustainability*. Centre for Research and Economic Development, University of Namur, Belgium.

Ciaian, P. and Kancs, D. (2012). "The Capitalization of Area Payments into Farmland Rents: Micro Evidence from the New EU Member States." *Canadian Journal of Agricultural Economics* 60(4): 517–540.

Ciaian, P., Kancs, D., and Gomez y Paloma, S. (2015). "Income distributional effects of CAP subsidies, Micro evidence from the EU." *Outlook on Agriculture* 44(1): 19–28.

Ciaian, P., Kancs, D. and Swinnen, J.F.M. (2008). "Static and Dynamic Distributional Effects of Decoupled Payments: Single Farm Payments in the European Union." LICOS Discussion Paper 207/2008, Centre for Institutions and Economic Performance (LICOS), Leuven.

Ciaian, P., Kancs, D. and Swinnen, J.F.M. (2010). *EU Land Markets and the Common Agricultural Policy.* Brussels : Centre for European Policy Studies (CEPS).

Ciaian, P., Kancs, D. and Swinnen, J.F.M. (2014). "The Impact of the 2013 Reform of the Common Agricultural Policy on Land Capitalization in the European Union." *Applied Economic Perspectives and Policy* 37(3): 1–31.

Ciaian, P., Kancs, D., Swinnen, J., Van Herck K. and Vranken L. (2012a). "Sales Market Regulations for Agricultural Land in EU Member States and Candidate Countries." *Factor Markets WP 14, Centre for European Policy Studies (CEPS)*, Brussels.

Ciaian, P., Kancs, D., Swinnen, J., Van Herck K. and Vranken L. (2012b). "Rental Market Regulations for Agricultural Land in EU Member States and Candidate Countries." *Factor Markets WP 15, Centre for European Policy Studies (CEPS)*, Brussels.

Ciaian, P., Kancs, D., Swinnen, J., Van Herck K. and Vranken L. (2012c). "Institutional Factors Affecting Agricultural Land Markets." *Factor Markets WP 16, Centre for European Policy Studies (CEPS)*, Brussels.

Cooper, T., Hart, K. and Baldock, D. (2009). *The Provision of Public Goods Through Agriculture in the European Union.* Report Prepared for DG Agriculture and Rural Development, Contract No 30-CE-0233091/00-28, Institute for European Environmental Policy: London.

Courleux, F., Guyomard, H., Levert, F. and Piet, L. (2008). How the EU Single Farm Payment Should Be Modelled: Lump–sum Transfers, Area Payments or … What Else? Working Paper No. 08–01, Agricultural Structures and Markets, Resources and Territories (SMART), Economic Studies and Research Unit (LERECO), National Institute of Agronomic Research (INRA).

de Janvry, A. (1981). "The Role of Land Reform in Economic Development: Policies and Politics." *American Journal of Agricultural Economics* 63(2): 385–392.

Drabik, D. and Rajčániová, M. (2014). "Agricultural Land Market in Slovakia under the New Land Acquisition Law." *Review of Agricultural and Applied Economics* 17(2): 84–87.

European Commission (2005). "Agri-environment Measures Overview on General Principles, Types of Measures, and Application." Directorate General for Agriculture and Rural Development, European Commission, Brussels.

European Commission (2014a). "Extension of transitional periods for the acquisition of agricultural land." *MEMO/11/244*, European Commission, Brussels, 14 April 2011, http://europa.eu/rapid/press-release_MEMO-11-224_en.htm?locale=en.

European Commission (2014b). "Farming for Natura 2000." Report prepared for the European Commission by Concha Olmeda (Atecma/N2K GROUP), Clunie Keenleyside, Graham Tucker and Evelyn Underwood (IEEP) under contract No. 070307/2010/580710/SER/B3 European Commission, Brussels.

European Commission (2015). "The Nitrates Directive." Directorate General for the Environment, European Commission, Brussels, 17/09/2015. http://ec.europa.eu/environment/water/water-nitrates/index_en.html.

FADN (2016). "FADN Public Database." Farm Accountancy Data Network, European Commission, Brussels, http://ec.europa.eu/agriculture/rica/database/database_en.cfm.

Feichtinger, P. and Salhofer, K. (2015b). "The Fischler Reform of the Common Agricultural Policy and Agricultural Land Prices." Discussion Paper No. DP-58-2015, Institut für nachhaltige Wirtschaftsentwicklung, Universität für Bodenkultur Wien.

FestForest (2014). "Important changes to the law regarding ownership of farmland in Lithuania." HD FestForest, 1st May 2014, http://www.hdfestforest.com.

Guastella, G., Moro, D. Sckokai, P. and Veneziani, M. (2014). "The Capitalization of Area Payment into Land Rental Prices: A Panel Sample Selection Approach." Paper presented at the EAAE Congress: 'Agri-food and Rural Innovations for Healthier Societies', 26–29 August 2014, Ljubljana, Slovenia.

Hoyos, D., Mariel, P. Pascual, U. and Etxano, I. (2012). "Valuing a Natura 2000 network site to inform land use options using a discrete choice experiment: An illustration from the Basque Country." *Journal of Forest Economics* 18: 329–344.

Kancs, D. and Ciaian, P. (2010). "Factor content of bilateral trade: the role of firm heterogeneity and transaction costs." *Agricultural Economics* 41(3–4): 305–317.

Karlsson, J. and Nilsson, P. (2014). "Capitalisation of Single Farm Payment on farm price: an analysis of Swedish farm prices using farm-level data." *European Review of Agricultural Economics* 41(2): 279–300.

Kettunen, M., Torkler, P. and Rayment, M. (2014). "Financing Natura 2000 in 2014–2020: Guidance Handbook." *Publication commissioned by the European Commission DG Environment, Institute for European Environmental Policy (IEEP), WWF and ICF GHK.*

Kilian, S., Anton, J., Salhofer, K. and Roder, N. (2012). "Impacts of 2003 CAP Reform on Land Rental Prices and Capitalization." *Land Use Policy* 29(4): 789–797.

Kilian, S. and Salhofer, K. (2008). "Single Payments of the CAP: Where Do the Rents Go?" *Agricultural Economics Review* 9(2): 96–106.

Latruffe, L., Minviel, J.J. and Salanié, J. (2013). "The Role of Environmental and Land Transaction Regulations on Agricultural Land Price: The Example of Brittany." Factor Markets WP 14, Centre for European Policy Studies (CEPS), Brussels .

Le Goffe, P. (2013). "The Nitrates Directive, Incompatible with Livestock Farming? The Case of France and Northern European Countries." Policy Paper No. 93, Notre Europe, Jacques Delors Institute.

Mary, S. (2013). "Assessing the Impacts of Pillar 1 and 2 Subsidies on TFP in French Crop Farms." *Journal of Agricultural Economics* 64: 133–144.

Michalek, J., Ciaian, P. and Kancs, D. (2014). "Capitalization of the Single Payment Scheme into Land Value: Generalized Propensity Score Evidence from the European Union." *Land Economics* 90(2): 260–289.

Nilsson, P. and Johansson, S. (2013). "Location Determinants of Agricultural Land Prices." *Review of Regional Research* 33: 1–21.

O'Neill, S. and Hanrahan, K. (2013). "An Analysis of the Capitalisation of CAP Payments into Land Rental Rates in Ireland." Factor Markets WP 68, Centre for European Policy Studies *(CEPS),* Brussels.

Patton, M., P. Kostov, S.A. McErlean, and Moss, J. (2008). "Assessing the Influence of Direct Payments on the Rental Value of Agricultural Land." *Food Policy* 33(5): 397–405.

Swinnen, J.F.M. (2002). "Political Reforms, Rural Crises, and Land Tenure in Western Europe." *Food Policy* 27(4): 371–394.

Swinnen, J.F.M. (ed.) (2015). *The Political Economy of the 2014–2020 Common Agricultural Policy: An Imperfect Storm.* Brussels : Centre for European Policy Studies (CEPS).

Swinnen, J.F.M., Ciaian, P., Kancs, D., Van Herck, K. and Vranken, L. (2013). "Possible Effect on EU Land Markets of New CAP Direct Payments." Report No. PE 495.866, Policy Department B: Structural and Cohesion Policies, European Parliament.

Swinnen, J. Van Herck, K. and Vranken, L. (2014a). "Land Market Regulations in Europe." LICOS Discussion Paper No. 354, LICOS Centre for Institutions and Economic Performance.

Swinnen, J. Van Herck, K. and Vranken, L. (2014b). "The Diversity of Land Institutions in Europe." LICOS Discussion Paper No. 355, LICOS Centre for Institutions and Economic Performance.

Swinnen, J.F.M. and Vranken, L. (2009). "Review of the Transitional Restrictions by New Member States on the Acquisition of Agricultural Real Estate." CEPS Working Paper, Centre for European Policy Studies, Brussels.

Swinnen, J.F.M. and Vranken, L. (2010). "Review of the Transitional Restrictions Maintained by Bulgaria and Romania with Regard to the Acquisition of Agricultural Real Estate." CEPS Working Paper, Centre for European Policy Studies, Brussels.

Thomson, S., Moxey, A. and Butler, A. (2014). "Scottish Agricultural Tenure Evidence Review." Agriculture, Fisheries and Rural Affairs, The Scottish Government.

Van Herck, K., Swinnen, J. and Vranken, L. (2013). "Capitalization of Direct Payments in Land Rents: Evidence from New EU Member States." *Eurasian Geography and Economics* 54(4): 423–443.

Vukina, T. and Wossink, A. (2000). "Environmental Policies and Agricultural Land Values: Evidence from the Dutch Nutrient Quota System." *Land Economics* 76(3): 413–429.

UN-HABITAT (2013). "Property Tax Regimes in Europe." *The Global Urban Economic Dialogue Series, UN-HABITAT the United Nations.*

Chapter 14

Impact of public subsidy on farmland values

The case of South Korea

Hyunjeong Joo, Ashok K. Mishra, and Jinsoon Lim

Introduction

Agriculture was the main industry in the 1960s, but the share of agriculture growth in the GDP has shrunk ever since industrial growth took over. Data show that, in 2013, 6.3% of total households were engaged in farming work and vocational farmers comprised 5.7% of the total population. During the same time period, 5.9% employed persons worked in the agricultural sector. As of 2013, the agricultural sector consisted of 2% of the nominal GDP, 2.3% if forest and fishery sectors were included.[1] The majority of Korean farmers own small-scale family farms. In 2013, the total agricultural land area was 1.7 million hectares, which was comprised of 963,876 ha of rice and 747,560 ha of dry fields. In the same time period, 9,984 farm households lived on uncultivated land, while 1.1 million farm households lived on cultivated land; 65.7% among the cultivated land residents lived on an area under 1 hectare, and about 1% of the cultivated land residents had 10 hectares and over.

The staple food of South Korea is rice; therefore, early Korean farmers focused on the production of rice. However, because of an increased rice supply from high-yielding production technology, reduction in rice consumption, and mandatory rice imported by the World Trade Organization, Korean farmers have diversified farm production (42% paddy rice; 24% vegetables and wild greens; 15% fruits; 9% food crops; and 5% livestock farm households in 2013).[2] According to the Farm Household Economic Survey (FHES), total farm household income, which includes farm income, off-farm income, transfer income, and other income, increased from ₩26.9 million in 2003 to ₩34.5 million in 2013. Until 2006, farm income (₩12 million) was greater than off-farm income (₩10 million), but since 2007, off-farm income has exceeded farm income; indeed, off-farm income accounts for 45% of the total farm household income while farm income contributes only 29%. In the same data resource, assets were ₩400 million and the debt of farm households was ₩27 million. Twelve percent of farm households had no profits, 51% of farm households earned between ₩1 and ₩10 million, and only 3% of farm households received more than ₩100 million in total sales.

Table 14.1 shows trends in farm household income and government subsidies (or public subsidies) in Korea. Total farm household income increased slightly from ₩3.14 million to ₩3.2 million during the 2008–2012 period; off-farm income (off-farm employed income) was greater than the income from farming. Also, note that the share of off-farm income increased, while the share of farming income decreased over the time period. The share of public subsidy to farm household[3] is smaller than off-farm income; however, they are higher than off-farm self-employed business income. In South Korea, as is the case in the United States, public subsidies/government subsidies and off-farm income are important sources of income for farm households. As in other developed countries, the agricultural sector in South Korea has long been heavily dependent on government support to compete with cheaper imports from abroad and transition to modern farming practices. Korea was also identified as having some of the highest subsidy levels, with government support accounting for 54% of farmers' income. Only Norway, Switzerland and Japan had higher subsidy levels among OECD members.

In addition to looking at income of farm households, it is also important to consider wealth to accurately assess the economic wellbeing of farm households in South Korea. To this end, like any farmers in developed countries, farmland is an important asset for Korean farmers as well. In 2013, farmland comprised about 53% of total farm assets in South Korea. Farmland provides agricultural products

Table 14.1 Trends and composition of farm household income in South Korea

Year	Total household income	Farming income	Non-farm income	Transfer income	Irregular income	% non-farming income
2003	31,436	12,365	10,991	2,375	5,705	35
2004	32,956	13,693	10,845	3,416	5,001	32.9
2005	34,312	13,290	11,118	4,587	5,315	32.4
2006	36,377	13,617	11,303	5,502	5,956	31.1
2007	35,167	11,448	12,208	5,455	6,057	34.7
2008	32,610	10,314	12,129	5,651	4,516	37.2
2009	31,800	10,008	12,516	5,656	3,619	39.4
2010	32,121	10,098	12,946	5,610	3,467	40.3
2011	29,673	8,615	12,745	5,367	2,946	43
2012	30,245	8,896	13,241	5,472	2,636	43.8
2013	33,389	9,705	15,189	5,652	2,843	45.5

(2010 = 100), (in ₩1,000)
Source: Korea Statistics, Bank of Korea.

for present farmers and provides rental revenue for retired farmers in the form of pensions (Offutt, 2003). In addition, farmland is one of the essential inputs, including labor and capital, that has a production cost, and affects farm production decisions. In Korea, the trend of total land area is increasing; however, farmland area is simultaneously diminishing. From 2009 to 2013, total land area in South Korea increased from 9.9 million hectares to 10 million hectares, however, total farmland area has decreased slightly or remained same, about 1.7 million hectares. However, it should be pointed out that farmland values have increased significantly. For instance, the value of farmland per acre has increased from ₩29,862 per acre in 2008 to ₩34,783 per acre in 2012.[4]

Government subsidies or farm subsidy programs typically transfer income from consumers and taxpayers to farm operators, especially to owners of farmland and other resources used in farm production. Recall that agricultural subsidies in South Korea, similar to other developed countries with agricultural subsidies, can be capitalized into the value of farmland. A plethora of literature points (see Moss and Schmitz, 2003) to assessing the impact of government subsidies on farmland values. However, literature falls short on the impact of such subsidies on farmland value in highly subsidized country like South Korea. Therefore, the objective of this chapter is to assess the impact of government subsidies farmland values among South Korean farm households. To examine this, the unconditional quantile regression method is used.

Agricultural sector of South Korea

South Korea is located in Northeast Asia. It lies between China in the West and Japan in the East and is considered to be an important geographical area. After the Korean War in 1953, the peninsula was divided into North Korea and South Korea based on the Korean Demilitarized Zone (DMZ), which crosses the 38th parallel North. The total population of South Korea was about 50 million in 2011; it is projected to be 51 million in 2015. Approximately 20% of the total population lives in the capital city, Seoul.[5] About 70% of land in South Korea is mountainous. The total land area is approximately 100,033 square kilometers, similar in size to the State of Kentucky in the US (104,659 square kilometers).[6] Based on 2011 data, the population density in South Korea is about 497 persons per square kilometer. The South Korea administrative district is split into 16 regions. These are similar to counties in the United States and consist of one special city, six metropolitan cities, eight provinces, and one special self-governing province (77 cities, 88 districts, and 69 boroughs).

In the early 1960s, South Korea was referred to as one of Asia's "four dragons" alongside Taiwan, Hong Kong, and Singapore. These so-called Newly Industrializing Countries (NICs) showed rapid economic growth after World War II. During the 1970s through the 1990s, South Korea's gross domestic product (GDP) grew at an average rate of 5% per year. However, the financial crisis in 1997 put a damper on this growth rate. Surprisingly, the real GDP growth rate fell to 2.3% in 2012. And it should be noted that South Korean economy dropped back even further to about 0.5%, at the end of second quarter of 2014. Similar to other developed countries, the agricultural economy in South Korea has been sluggish. In order to accelerate economic growth, the agricultural sector has been neglected, while preference has been given to sophisticated industries. Although agriculture has been ignored, it still played a crucial role in the economic well-being of rural farm households in South Korea. The agricultural sector has implications on food security, maintaining rural communities, and environmental and local conservation.

Agricultural policy and government subsidies in South Korea

Before the start of industrialization in the 1960s, historical events shaped the agricultural sector of South Korea. For example, during the Japanese colonial era from 1910 to 1945, South Korea was used primarily for rice production and food supplies for the Japanese; agricultural policy was focused on increasing rice productivity and regulating prices in order to stabilize supply and prices. In 1949, after independence, South Korea introduced farmland reform in order to deal with Japanese-owned farms and to distribute farms to tenant farmers who would eventually become farm owners. The tenant farmers did not receive fair contracts with the farm owners. However, during the process of purchasing farms, farmland reform increased farm productivity (Lee et al., 2011).

There were some specific goals for agricultural policies for the period following the Korean War. Kim and Lee (2003) studied South Korean agricultural policy by decades and found that in the 1950s, agricultural policies were focused on solving the food shortage and price stabilization. After the Korean War (1950–1953), infrastructure in South Korea was demolished and its economy lagged behind that of North Korea. The South Korean government created economic policies to provide a stable source of food and fiber to combat hyperinflation. The government also invested in reconstruction and national defense in order to restore confidence in the government. To improve the food shortage problem, the government controlled the sales price. During this period, the government implemented polices that stabilized price of rice. In the second half of the 1960s, in an effort to reestablish the agricultural sector, agricultural policy concentrated on increasing production of agricultural goods and creating a farm-price-support system. In 1961, the South Korean government enacted the *Price Maintenance of Agricultural Products Act*. Under this Act the government could now purchase agricultural products, make collateral loans, and export subsidies to maintain a price level that benefited farmers. However, despite the efforts to improve food production, agricultural production fell short of self-sufficiency along with two bad harvests in the late 1960s.

From the late 1960s until the late 1970s, the South Korean economy grew rapidly. During the 1970s, farm policy focused on the double grain price system, progress and productivity, and the improvement of agricultural technology.

In the double grain price system, the government bought staple grains from farmers and sold them to consumers at a lower cost. The goal of agricultural policy focused on protecting agriculture, creating a two-tier price scheme via the government purchase program, supporting productivity enhancement programs, and encouraging farmers to adopt new technologies. The government initiated "Saemaeul-Undong" or "The New Village Movement" for comprehensive development of agricultural areas. This movement focused on constructing programs, eradication of poverty, improving income of farm households, and rural development.

In the 1980s, under pressure to open the agricultural market to foreign counties, the government's role in the market decreased, and the foreign market became dominant. To comply with the opening market, agricultural policy focused on improving farm structure, fostering large-scale professional farmers, and creating non-farm income to enhance farm productivity and efficiency. In this period, non-agricultural work was actively introduced, and farmers pursued new income resources such as producing high-income crops or livestock in conjunction with their original farming work. In 1989, "Agricultural development comprehensive plans" started to emerge. These aimed to enhance productivity, competitiveness, and stability of income as the scale of farming grew and technology accelerated, which enabled agricultural land mobility and an improvement of rural life.

In the 1990s, South Korean agricultural policy focused on preparing and opening the agricultural market. The settlement of Uruguay Round in 1993 and the establishment of the WTO (World Trade Organization) in 1995 intimidated domestic farmers. Therefore, the South Korean government endeavored to stabilize farmers' incomes and lessen the effect of imported agricultural products through the enhancement of non-agricultural income and the improvement of the agricultural structure. In 1991, the "Farming and fishing villages structural improvement plan" was enacted to enhance competitiveness. Government subsidies, mainly in the form of payments or loans, accompanied government policies. To examine government subsidies in South Korea, Lee et al. (2011) separated the South Korean agricultural policy into two time periods: the time prior to the agricultural market opening and the time after the agricultural market opening. The first period was further subdivided into three parts: pre-1960, 1961–1976, and 1977–1992. In order to explain the after-market opening period, the authors categorized the period into three sectors denoted by presidential terms: 1993–1997, 1998–2002, and 2003–2007.

Between 1993 and 1997, under the "New Agricultural Administration" program ₩42 trillion was allocated for "Farming and fishing villages." These funds were to support structural improvement work over a 10-year period, from 1992 to 2001. This investment and loan program was meant to consolidate agriculture and fishery's power and improve rural areas. The plan lasted from 1992 to 1998 and cost ₩35 trillion. In addition, from 1994 to 2004, ₩15 trillion was allocated for the "Farming and fishing villages' special tax." This tax was used to enhance agricultural competitiveness and improve rural amenities, lifestyle, and welfare. From 1998 to 2002, the fifteenth president, Dae-Jung Kim, signaled the start of a challenging time for the South Korean economy. The year before he came into office, in 1997, South Korea had a currency crisis and received relief money from the International Monetary Fund (IMF). In accordance with the economic crisis, many farmers went bankrupt and relinquished their farming work. Agricultural policymakers reacted with six main objectives to recover the agricultural economy and to design a new paradigm: to nourish sustainable agriculture, increase competitiveness, foster the exportation of agricultural products, strengthen agricultural trade power, improve rural welfare and to stabilize farm management (Lee et al., 2011).

In 1999, the "Agriculture and farm village development plan" and the "Agriculture and farm village fundamental law" were enacted. In 2001, direct payment for paddy rice farming was instituted. Under this law if a farmer had a rice paddy, then he/she would earn payment by hectare to compensate for the multifunctionality and public good of agriculture. In 2002, direct payments were made for the preservation of rice income. This policy supported and maintained the income of rice farmers; it also had fixed and flexible payment options. Flexible payment meant that the government compensated 85% of the difference between the targeted price and the average rice market price each year. In 2003, farmland law was enacted and rice product control was conducted. To support agricultural policy (1999–2004) about ₩45 trillion was allocated to the agricultural sector.

The sixteenth president, Mu-Hyun Roh (2003–2007), focused his agricultural policies on market oriented farms, welfare, rural development, non-farm income creation, and food industrialization. In 2003, the "Special law of farmer and fisherman debt relief" program was enacted. In the plan, about 66% of the funds were planned for public subsidies (government payments) and 34% for financing projects. Half was given directly to farmers, while the other 50% was invested in SOC and research development. These subsidies were meant to support enhancement of agricultural competitiveness (65%), stability of management and income (16%), food safety and distribution (9%), and local development and welfare (10%) (see Park et al., 2005).[7] The main usage of the fund was to stabilize farm management, farm household income, and grain market management. In 2014, a special law passed for the improvement of quality of life for those involved in agriculture, forestry and fishing. Previous agricultural policies were focused on the support of SOC, production base, and the enforcement of competition.

Current agricultural policies are diverse. For example, the government has implemented programs to ensure food safety, target farm programs, promote environmentally friendly agricultural production, support large-scale farms, and improve rural residential life. The 2008 Organization for Economic Cooperation and Development (OECD) report points out that the South Korean government implemented agricultural policy reforms that, in many aspects, were broadly consistent with the principles of transparency, targeting, flexibility, and equity outlined in the OECD Ministerial Council Statement. Agriculture in South Korea needs to be allowed to evolve into an efficient, modern enterprise that provides a positive economic contribution to society in line with other sectors of the economy. Although the WTO and other agricultural exports countries are pressing South Korea to reduce public subsidies, it is not a simple change to make. To compensate, South Korean farmers relied on public subsidies or farm subsidies. The amount of producer support in South Korea is approximately three times the OECD average.[8] South Korea's policy support towards its agricultural sector ranks among the world's highest.[9]

In 2015, planned public subsidies/government subsidies for agriculture was about ₩14 trillion, an increase of 3.4% compared to the 2014 budget. The main goals of the 2015 budget are to secure agricultural and food products for future industrialization, enhance competitiveness, disaster prevention for food safety, maintain farm income and management safety, enhance farm household welfare, promote high value-added food industry, impose agricultural marketing and price stabilization, and discover new agribusiness items. Among the working expenses, over 60% of the total public subsidies are accounted for by grain management and agricultural marketing, reinforcement constitution of agriculture, and stabilization of farm income and management sections. Item-wise, rice production receives about 37% of the public subsidies. In sum, the two mainstream policies still strive to strengthen self-sufficiency and to reduce the income gap between farmers and people working in other industrial sectors. It's also important to recognize that South Korea places significant importance on self-sufficiency in food staples and achieving income parity between rural and urban households.

Model and estimation procedure

A plethora of literature on the factors affecting farmland values has been published and the empirical relationship is well recognized in the agricultural economics literature. These include the income capitalization model (see Alston, 1986; Burt, 1986; Pope et al., 1978) and hedonic models (Palmquist and Danielson, 1989; Shonkweiler and Reynolds, 1986). Recent literature on farmland values has focused on the effect of government payments. In the last two decades, studies of government payment impacts have also included those of specific crops and specific programs (Goodwin and Ortalo-Magne, 1992). Payments linked to program bases and resulting impacts on agricultural land values were examined by Gardner (2002). Weersink et al. (1999) and Gardner (2002) found that government payments increased agricultural land values. Goodwin, Mishra, and Ortalo-Magne (2003) and Lence and Mishra (2003) concluded that government payments positively affected cash rents.

Most empirical evaluations of the determinants of farmland values adopt a present value model, where the value of a productive asset (farmland) is given by the capitalized values of current and expected future streams of net income generated by the asset. Under standard assumptions, farmland values are determined by the present value of future rents

$$V_t = \sum_{i=1}^{\infty} \frac{\mathrm{E}\left[CF_{t+i} \mid \Omega_t\right]}{\prod_{j=1}^{i}\left(1 + r_{t+j}\right)}$$ (14.1)

where V_t is the value of farmland, $\mathrm{E}\left[CF_{t+i} \mid \Omega_t\right]$ is the expected cash flow from farmland (typically the Ricardian rent defined as the excess of returns over the variable factors of production), and r_t is the discount rate parameterized as the weighted average cost of capital. Expanding this formulation to consider government payments

$$V_t = \sum_{i=1}^{\infty} \frac{\mathrm{E}\left[CF_{t+i}^M \mid \Omega_t\right] + \mathrm{E}\left[GP_{t+i} \mid \Omega_t\right]}{\prod_{j=1}^{i}\left(1 + r_{t+j}\right)}$$ (14.2)

where $\mathrm{E}\left[CF_{t+i}^M \mid \Omega_t\right]$ is the expected cash flow from the market, and $\mathrm{E}\left[GP_{t+i} \mid \Omega_t\right]$ are the cash inflows from government payments. The following empirical model is used to estimate the impact of government payments and debt-to-asset, including returns to asset on farmland values in South Korea:

$$\ln\left(v_t\right) = \beta_0 + \beta_1 \ln\left(R_{At}\right) + \beta_2 \ln\left(r_t\right) + \beta_3 \ln\left(T_t\right) + \beta_4 \ln(GP).$$ (14.3)

where R_A is returns to farmland (*net farm income*), r is regional location of farms, T is a debt-to-asset ratio and GP represents government payments.

Equation 14.3 can be estimated using classical least squares (OLS) regression method; OLS shows us how the conditional mean function of y changes with the vectors of covariates x. However, the OLS regression is also very sensitive to outliers and does not provide an accurate result if the assumptions of linearity, homoscedasticity, normality, and independence of the residuals are not satisfied (Rao and Toutenburg, 1999). Surprisingly only a few published studies have used a more flexible semi-parametric regression model to explore potentially complex and heterogeneous relationship between public subsidies in agriculture and farmland valuation. However, Koenker and Bassett (2001) argue that covariates may influence the conditional distribution of the response in a number of other ways, for example, stretching one tail of the distribution, compressing the other tails, or inducing multimodality. Koenker and Bassett (2001) point out that quantile regression can provide a more nuanced view of the stochastic relationship between variables, and therefore a more informative empirical analysis. However, the conditional quantile regression (CQR) offers a narrower interpretation as the effect of the public subsidies program would explicitly depend on the level of other conditioning variables in the quantile. Therefore, this study uses the unconditional quantile (UQR) method developed by Firpo, Fortin, and Lemieux (2009) using longitudinal data. The UQR approach has been rarely used in current empirical work and addresses a question that the CQR method of estimation cannot answer. Moreover, from a policy standpoint, policymakers are generally interested in learning about the influence of a specific program or policy on the unconditional distribution of an outcome.

Specifically, we use the Re-centered Influence Function (RIF). UQR measures the minuscule change of a real-valued function; it is based on the concept of the influence function developed from the field of robust statistics and summarized in Hampel et al. (2005). Frölich and Melly (2013) also summarized additional advantages of the UQR approach, showing that the estimator is √n consistent, asymptotically normal, and efficient. They noted that the unconditional effects are averages of the conditional effects and are more precisely estimated than conditional effects. Consequently, quantile effects are also robust to outliers that may be prevalent in reported income and sales measures. Finally, Fipro, Fortin, and Lemieux (2009) prove the unconditional property of the RIF regression, and this implies that the RIF regression results have a similar interpretation as coefficients from an OLS regression.

Korea Farm Household Economic Survey (FHES) data

The data used in this study were obtained from the 2008 to 2012 Farm Household Economy Survey (FHES) of South Korea. The FHES is administered annually and collects information about farming practices, demographics, and financial status from approximately 2,800 farm households. The survey changes the sample of farmers every 5 years. In other words, over each 5-year period, the sample consists of the same farm households. These farm households operate farms of about 10 acres (1,000) or more, or generate annual sales (of farm products) of at least 500,000 won. We are using the most recent data available: the 2008 to 2012 FHES. It's important to note that not included in the survey are single households, foreign households, non-family households, business farms having over five regular employees, and semi-farm households such as churches, schools, agricultural and test sites.

The survey is conducted using an interview method. There are two types of logs: a questionnaire and an original register. The questionnaire is conducted monthly and has items about the current state of the farm households, assets (for example, land, buildings, machinery, and intangible assets), debts, and financial assets. The original register is surveyed twice per year (early year and late year) and has questions regarding cultivated crops, livestock, receipts, expenses, agricultural labor hours, agricultural production cost, and the amount of grain consumption and stock. In the farm household survey data, the farm household income is segregated into sources of income as shown in Figure 14.1. In Figure 14.1, the total farm household income is disaggregated into regular income and irregular income. Regular income is further disaggregated into net farm household income, which includes income from the farm and non-farm sector, and transfer income. Transfer income includes public subsidies or government subsidies to agricultural household and private subsidies (not related to production agriculture). In this study, *net farming income* is defined as income from farming, shown in Figure 14.2 as "*Farm Income.*" In addition to the FHES data, population and unemployment rate data were obtained from the South Korean Statics department, and the information regarding distance from Seoul data was collected from *DistanceFromTo.net*; is used as a proxy variable to indicating access the off-farm income. Variable definition and summary statistics are provided in Table 14.2.

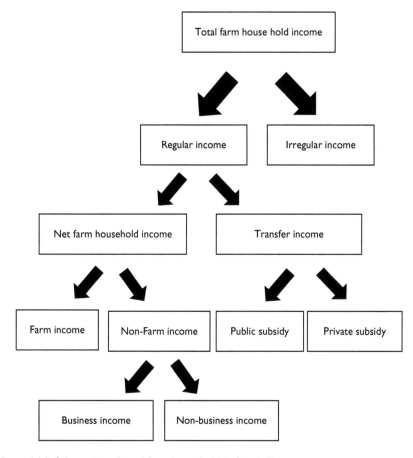

Figure 14.1 Schematics of total farm household in South Korea

Source: Korea Farm Household Economic Survey (FHES) data.

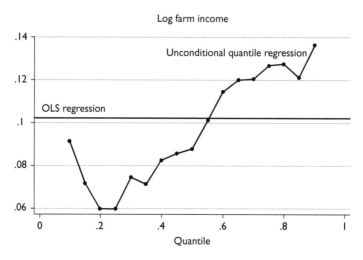

Figure 14.2 Quantile relationship between farm income and farmland values, South Korea (2008–2012)

Table 14.2 Variable description and summary statistics, South Korea (2008–2012)

Variable	Definition	Pooled	2008	2009	2010	2011	2012
Land_value	Farmland value per hectare	323,604	319,138	321,738	315,981	321,882	339,084
Farm_Inc	Net farm income per hectare	26,914	23,398	29,835	30,046	26,150	25,140
Public_sub	Public subsidies in agriculture per hectare	15,365	10,566	13,203	15,964	17,982	19,058
DebtAsset	debt/asset	0.08	0.09	0.09	0.08	0.07	0.07
F_Crop	=1 if crop (paddy rice, upland crop)	0.25	0.30	0.25	0.22	0.24	0.23
F_FruitVeg	=1 if fruit and vegetable farm	0.33	0.28	0.30	0.34	0.36	0.36
F_Special	=1 if specialty crops and flower farm	0.04	0.06	0.06	0.05	0.03	0.03

Variable	Definition	Pooled	2008	2009	2010	2011	2012
F_Livestk	=1 if livestock farm	0.07	0.06	0.09	0.09	0.05	0.06
F_Other	=1 if other harvested crops farm	0.31	0.31	0.30	0.30	0.32	0.32
Pop_density	Person/km^2	418.58	395.89	413.80	420.03	426.88	436.05
Un_emp	Unemployment rate %	2.44	2.28	2.54	2.70	2.43	2.26
Distance	Distance from Seoul, (km)	191.63	192.18	191.41	191.77	191.15	191.64
Observations		12,642	2,515	2,528	5,517	2,555	2,522

Results and discussion

We apply the RIF regression model to provide estimates of the unconditional quantile marginal effects. As a result, Table 14.3 presents the unconditional quantile regression estimators of the logarithm of farmland values (hence presence of off-farm income) for the 0.10, 0.25, 0.50, 0.75, and 0.90 quantiles with controls for farm income, public subsidies (= government subsidies), farm type, geographic location of the household, and market conditions (such as unemployment rate and pollution density) where the farm is located. For comparison purposes we also present the results for OLS regression. The R^2 for the OLS regression in model 1 is 0.40. Table 14.3 shows that the impacts of farm income on farmland values in South Korea are uniformly positive across the unconditional quantile regressions, indicating that farm income increases farmland values across all quantiles; the estimates are lower at the low quantiles. The findings suggest usage of UQR is more efficient than OLS. Results indicate that a 10% increase in public subsidies in South Korea increases farmland values between 1.0% at the 10th quantile to about 1.3% at the 90th quantile (see Figure 14.2). Findings are consistent with those in the literature—albeit they are from US farmland valuation studies (Moss and Schmitz, 2002; Goodwin, Mishra and Ortalo-Magne, 2003; Lence and Mishra, 2003). These findings directly support Melichar's (1979) hypothesis that growth in real returns (or farm income) to land pushes up farmland values.

The coefficient on public subsidies (also known as government payments) is positive and statistically significant at the 1% level of significance. The elasticities suggest that a 1% increase in public subsidies increases farmland values in South Korea by 0.10% at the 25th quantile to about 0.15% at the 90th quantile (Figure 14.3).

Table 14.3 Unconditional quantile regression estimates for farmland values, South Korea

Variables	OLS	10th	25th	50th	75th	90th
Ln Farm_Inc[1]	0.102***	0.0882***	0.0620***	0.0913***	0.130***	0.135***
	(0.005)	(0.007)	(0.005)	(0.006)	(0.009)	(0.014)
Ln Public_Sub[2]	0.121***	0.0938***	0.0738***	0.0945***	0.146***	0.154***
	(0.006)	(0.007)	(0.005)	(0.007)	(0.010)	(0.015)
Ln debtasset	−0.226***	−0.0757	−0.0594	−0.278***	−0.395***	−0.202*
	(0.044)	(0.080)	(0.062)	(0.060)	(0.073)	(0.090)
Farm type dummies (crop farm s = base)						
F_FruitVeg	−0.0252	−0.157***	−0.0912***	0.0507	−0.0174	0.0917*
	(0.020)	(0.032)	(0.026)	(0.028)	(0.034)	(0.042)
F_Special	0.0220	−0.260***	−0.145**	0.0295	0.115	0.496***
	(0.041)	(0.063)	(0.048)	(0.054)	(0.062)	(0.092)
F_Livestk	−0.0873**	−0.111*	−0.0358	0.0126	−0.0962	−0.241***
	(0.029)	(0.051)	(0.040)	(0.044)	(0.053)	(0.059)
F_Other	0.383***	0.0887**	0.222***	0.407***	0.540***	0.648***
	(0.020)	(0.029)	(0.024)	(0.028)	(0.037)	(0.048)
Pop_density	0.0004***	0.0001***	0.0002***	0.0003***	0.0004***	0.0006***
	(0.000)	(0.000)	(0.000)	(0.000)	(0.000)	(0.000)
Distance	0.0003	−0.0011**	−0.0012***	0.0004	0.0004	0.001*
	(0.0001)	(0.0004)	(0.0003)	(0.0003)	(0.0004)	(0.0005)
Regional dummies (Capital region = base)						
Gangwon-do	−0.945***	−0.224***	−0.222***	−1.028***	−1.897***	−1.543***
	(0.0451)	(0.0490)	(0.0442)	(0.0588)	(0.0837)	(0.126)
Chungcheong-do	−0.867***	−0.0528	−0.0639	−0.877***	−1.862***	−1.636***
	(0.039)	(0.038)	(0.036)	(0.048)	(0.075)	(0.119)
Kyeongsang-do	−1.111***	−0.340***	−0.407***	−1.159***	−1.814***	−1.606***
	(0.057)	(0.081)	(0.068)	(0.071)	(0.099)	(0.152)

Variables	OLS	10th	25th	50th	75th	90th
Jeolla-do	−1.554***	−0.345***	−0.847***	−1.826***	−2.434***	−2.016***
	(0.064)	(0.086)	(0.079)	(0.082)	(0.112)	(0.170)
Jeju-do	−0.600***	0.592***	0.578***	−0.663***	−1.236***	−1.677***
	(0.111)	(0.167)	(0.142)	(0.146)	(0.192)	(0.273)
Year dummies (2008 = base)						
Year=2009	−0.057*	−0.044	−0.043	−0.052	−0.049	−0.087
	(0.024)	(0.035)	(0.029)	(0.033)	(0.042)	(0.054)
Year=2010	−0.079***	−0.044	−0.052	−0.094**	−0.088*	−0.085
	(0.024)	(0.035)	(0.028)	(0.033)	(0.042)	(0.054)
Year=2011	−0.099***	−0.094**	−0.078*	−0.115***	−0.098*	−0.106
	(0.0245)	(0.0358)	(0.0291)	(0.0332)	(0.0425)	(0.055)
Year=2012	−0.036	0.013	−0.019	−0.051	−0.033	−0.071
	(0.024)	(0.033)	(0.028)	(0.033)	(0.042)	(0.055)
Intercept	5.467***	3.966***	4.546***	5.473***	6.769***	6.962***
	(0.041)	(0.042)	(0.039)	(0.051)	(0.080)	(0.126)
N	12,642	12,642	12,642	12,642	12,642	12,642

(*Dependent variable*: log total farmland value per hectare)
Robust standard errors in parentheses: * $p < 0.05$, ** $p < 0.01$, *** $p < 0.001$
[1]Unit of farm income is ₩1 million per hectare.
[2]Unit of government subsidies is ₩1 million per hectare.

Note that elasticity increases with higher quantiles and the OLS coefficient is well below the median—but closer to the 50th quantile. Findings here are consistent with those found in the US and Canadian farmland valuation studies (Featherstone and Baker, 1988; Clark, Klien, and Thompson, 1993; Moss, 1997; Just and Miranowski, 1993). The coefficient on the debt-to-asset ratio (or leverage) is negative and statistically significant for the South Korean farmland values, but at the higher quantiles (50th and higher quantiles). Results suggest that an increase in leverage decreases real farmland values. A plausible explanation is that farms with higher land values are more likely to be large and productive farms; hence large farms usually make better use of borrowed capital.[10] Findings here are consistent with the debt model

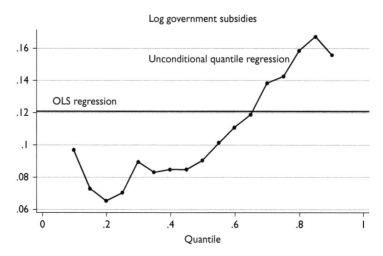

Figure 14.3 Quantile relationship between public subsidies and farmland values, South Korea (2008–2012)

presented by Merton (1974), Mishra, Moss, and Erickson (2008) as well as the farm credit results in Shalit and Schmitz (1982).

Turing our attention to the type of farms (commodity specialization), our analysis reveals that, compared to crop farms, fruits and vegetable farms and specialty crop farms have higher land values, but at the 90th quantile. The population density has a positive and significant effect on farmland values, in both the OLS and the quantile models. A 1% increase in population density increases farmland value by 0.03% and 0.06% in the OLS and 90th quantile, respectively. Finally, our analysis reveals that farms located in regions other than the capital region (base group) have significantly lower farmland values. Results in Table 14.3 show that the coefficient on the regional location dummies is negative and statistically significant for all quantiles.

Conclusions

This chapter examined the impact of public subsidies in agriculture on farmland valuation in South Korea. To study this we used data from the Household Economic Survey (FHES) of South Korean farm households, unconditional quantile regression (UQR) method. Our analysis indicates that a 10% increase in public subsidies in agriculture increases farmland value by 1.0% to 1.5%, depending on the quantile. Note that higher impact is noted at the higher quantiles. Additionally, farm income had a positive effect on farmland value and significant a across all quantiles. Consistent with the theory, we found that high debt-to-asset ratio has a significantly negative impact on farmland valuation. Farms with higher farm financial risk have lower farmland valuation. Finally, our study found that farms located in urban areas and farm types had significant impact on farmland valuation.

Results of our study show that there is a significant positive impact of public subsidies on farmland value in South Korea. While there is a concern that higher farmland values increase costs of production and decrease (through higher rental costs) the overall performance of agricultural production, they tend to have a positive effect on the wealth and economic well-being of farm households, who own farmland as an asset, in the longer term. On the contrary, higher farmland values act as a barrier to entry for new and beginning famers. Therefore, understanding the impact of the public subsidies on the agricultural sector is critical to decision making by policymakers.

Notes

1 Source: STATISTICS KOREA (http://www.kosis.kr).
2 Source: STATISTICS KOREA (http://www.kosis.kr).
3 Public subsidies, government payments, government subsidies and agricultural policy payments are used interchangeably in this chapter.
4 Won (₩) is the Korean monetary unit, where $1 = ₩1,109 (12.09.2014) Korea Exchange Bank.
5 Sources: Korean Statistical Information Service (KOSIS), Korean Census in 2010, and the Bank of Korea.
6 Sources: http://english.visitkorea.or.kr/enu/AK/AK_EN_1_1_1.jsp (Korea Tourism Organization), http://en.wikipedia.org/wiki/Geography_of_South_Korea (Geography of South Korea), & http://kentucky.gov/ (State of Kentucky website).
7 This plan would run for a 10-year period from 2004 to 2013. Unlike previous government subsidies, which used funds from the national treasury, local government, and self-payment, this subsidy came from only the national treasury.
8 http://www.oecd.org/tad/agricultural-policies/producerandconsumersupportestimates database.htm
9 Rice, soybean and barley are the most heavily supported commodities, but beef, pork and dairy also receive some support.
10 Indeed, Mishra, Moss, and Erickson (2008) argue that the interest rate charged by banks is an increasing function of the debt-to-asset ratio. Large farms are more likely to have debts, and they are the ones who make greater and more efficient use of the debt.

References

Alston, J.M. 1986. An Analysis of Growth of U.S. Farmland Prices, 1963–1982. *Am. J. Agr. Econ. 68*, 1–9.
Burt, O.R. 1986. Econometric Modeling of the Capitalization Formula for Farmland Prices. *Am. J. Agr. Econ. 68*, 10–26.
Clark, J.S.; Klein, K.K.; Thompson, S.J. 1993. Are Subsidies Capitalized into Land Values? Some Time Series Evidence from Saskatchewan. *Can. J. Agr. Econ. 41*, 55–163.
Featherstone, A.M.; Baker, T.G. 1988. Effects of Reduced Price and Income Supports on Farmland Rents and Values. *NC J. Agr. Econ. 10*, 177–190.
Firpo, S.; Fortin, N.; Lemieux, T. 2009. Unconditional Quantile Regressions. *Econometrica 77* (3), 953–973.

Frölich, M.; Melly, B. 2013. Unconditional Quantile Treatment Effects Under Endogeneity. *Journal of Business & Economic Statistics 31*(3), 346–357.

Gardner, B. 2002. *American Agriculture in the Twentieth Century*. Cambridge, MA, and London: Harvard University Press.

Goodwin, B.K.; Mishra, A.K.; Ortalo-Magne, F.N. 2003. What's Wrong with Our Models of Agricultural Land Values? *Am. J. Agr. Econ. 85*, 744–752.

Goodwin, B.K.; Ortalo-Magne, F.N. 1992. The Capitalization of Wheat Subsidies into Agricultural Land Values. *Can. J. Agr. Econ. 40*, 37–54.

Hampel, F.R.; Ronchetti, E.M.; Rousseeuw, P.J.; Stahel, W.A. 2005. *Robust Statistics: The Approach Based on Influence Functions*. Wiley-Interscience: Wiley Series in Probability and Statistics, New York.

Just, R.E.; Miranowski, J.A. 1993. Understanding Farmland Price Changes. *Am. J. Agr. Econ. 75*, 156–168.

Kim, H.; Lee, Y. (2003). Agricultural Policy Reform and Structural Adjustment: Historical Evidence from Korean Experience. Policy Reform and Adjustment Workshop, Imperial College London, Wye Campus from International Agricultural Policy Reform and Adjustment Project (IAPRAP).

Koenker, R.; Hallock, K. 2001. Quantile Regression. *Journal of Economic Perspectives 15*, 143–156.

Lee, T.; Lim, J.; Ahn, D.; et. al. (2011). *The Research on Interim Evaluation of the Agricultural Policies of Current Korea Administration and Reform Project*. Agricultural Economics Association (Written in Korean).

Lence, S.H.; Mishra, A.K. 2003. The Impacts of Different Farm Programs on Cash Rents. *Am. J. Agr. Econ. 85*, 753–761.

Melichar, E. 1979. Capital Gains versus Current Income in the Farming Sector. *Am. J. Agr. Econ. 61*, 1086–1106.

Merton, R.C. 1974. On the Pricing of Corporate Debt: The Risk Structure of Interest Rates. *Journal of Finance 29*, 449–470.

Mishra, A.K.; Moss, C.B.; Erickson, K.W. 2008. The Role of Credit Constraints and Government Subsidies in Farmland Valuation in the U.S.: An Options Pricing Model Approach. *Empirical Economics 34*(2), 285–297.

Moss, C.B. 1997. Returns, Interest Rates, and Inflation: How They Explain Changes in Farmland Values. *Am. J. Agr. Econ. 79*, 1311–1318.

Moss, C.B.; Schmitz, A. 2003. *Government Policy and Farmland Markets: The Maintenance of Farmer Wealth*. Ames, Iowa: Iowa State University Press.

Offutt, S. (2003). The Significance of the Value of Farmland. In C. B. Moss; A. Schmitz, eds. *Government Policy and Farmland Markets: The Maintenance of Farmer Wealth*. Ames, IA: Iowa State Press.

Palmquist, R.B.; Danielson, L.E. 1989. A Hedonic Study of the Effects of Erosion Control and Drainage on Farmland Values. *Am. J. Agr. Econ. 71*, 55–62.

Pope, R.D.; Kramer, R.A.; Green, R.D.; Gardner, B.D. 1978. An Evaluation of Economic Models of U.S. Farmland Prices. *West. J. Agr. Econ. 4*, 107–119.

Shalit, H.; Schmitz, A. 1982. Farmland Accumulation and Prices. *American Journal of Agricultural Economics 81*, 710–719.

Shonkwiler, J.S.; Reynolds, J.E. 1986. A Note of the Use of Hedonic Price Models in the Analysis of Land Prices at the Urban Fringe. *Am. J. Agr. Econ. 69*, 58–63.

Weersink, A.; Clark, S.; Turvey, C.G.; Sarker, R. 1999. The Effect of Agricultural Policy on Farmland Values. *Land Econ. 75*, 425–439.

Chapter 15

The succession decision

The case of small- and medium-sized midwestern farms

Renee D. Wiatt and Maria I. Marshall

Introduction

Farm family business sustainability is a topic that merits increased attention. Research has shown that family business sustainability can be a hard fought process (Bowman-Upton, 1991; De Massis et al., 2008; and Gersick et al., 1997). Family business sustainability is often greatly influenced by the succession planning process and the way decisions within a family business are made. Studies in the past have mainly focused on analyzing the success of the succession process (Calus and Van Huylenbroeck, 2008; Mishra and El-Osta, 2007; Morris et al., 1996; Venter et al., 2005; and Weigel and Weigel, 1990) and the characteristics of successors taking over the family business (Morris et al., 1996; Potter and Lobley, 1992). Sureshwaran (2008) estimated that 70% of U.S. farmland will change hands in the next 20 years and more than 50% of current farmers are likely to retire in the next 5 years. However, only 34% of current farmers retiring in the next 5 years have a succession plan for the farm business (Mishra and El-Osta, 2007).

Succession planning is important for the continuity of a business. When a farm family does not adequately plan for succession, the family business is more likely to go out of business, be absorbed by other businesses, or have its farmland converted to non-farm uses (Sureshwaran, 2008). Recent U.S. studies show that the majority of farmers do not have updated estate plans or adequate succession plans (Hachfeld et al., 2009). One anecdotal reason may be that farmers do not really exit but transfer labor, management, and/or power to a successor slowly and informally. They begin by mostly transferring labor and, more slowly, management and power, causing increased conflict in the family and family business. It is important to understand how this intergenerational transfer actually takes place in farm family businesses.

Literature review

The transfer of a business's ownership from one individual to the next is a decision affecting as much as 40% of American businesses at any one point in time (Bowman-Upton, 1991; De Massis et al., 2008). Gersick et al. (1997) cited that as many as 65–80% of the business enterprises in the world are family-owned or family-managed. Yet, a very small percentage of family businesses survive when transferred from one generation to the next (Bowman-Upton, 1991; De Massis et al., 2008).

Bowman-Upton (1991) noted that possibly the most difficult decision that a family business has to make is to whom the family business will be transferred. Some businesses may choose to focus on skill level, others on demographic characteristics, interpersonal characteristics, or motivation levels of a potential successor (Morris et al., 1996). Whether or not a successor has been named could greatly influence how a family business is managed and strategically placed for the future (Potter and Lobley, 1992).

An extensive amount of research was conducted on succession planning for intergenerational transfer, and many factors such as successor's education level, owner age, total assets, experience of owner, business income or size, age of the business, growth intensions, owner's gender and presence of children (ages 13–18) were identified to affect that transition (Bowman-Upton, 1991; Calus and Van Huylenbroeck, 2008; De Massis et al., 2008; Laband and Lentz, 1983; Mishra and El-Osta, 2007; Morris et al., 1996; Weigel and Weigel, 1990; Wilson et al., 1991). However, there is relatively little research on farm family businesses. Intergenerational transfer is especially important for farms because of the profession's high occupational inheritance rate (Laband and Lentz, 1983). Farm asset transfer and intergenerational management succession are critical to the sustainability of farm family businesses.

Research regarding succession has to be approached differently when examining family businesses than when examining non-family business entities (Mishra et al., 2004). When the "family" is integrated with the business, there are familial bonds and interactions that affect succession decisions. When the family unit becomes intertwined in the decision-making process of the family business, objectives and goals of the business may become skewed or altered in order to maintain family bonds. The maintenance of family relationships can sometimes come as an expense to the family business. The succession process of a family business can be extremely complicated because personal feelings can easily play a role in decision-making and the process of succession is not strictly adherent to numbers and contracts.

Most research focused on either business characteristics, owner characteristics, or family characteristics (or at best two out of three facets) (Tagiuri and Davis, 1996). Few have been able to focus on all three aspects of the family business. We contribute to the literature by investigating how all three – family, business, and owner characteristics – affect the selection of a successor.

Family business characteristics

The "Succession Effect," as proposed by Calus and Van Huylenbroeck (2008), noted that when a successor was present, then the family business had an incentive to expand. Their research found that a farmer was more likely to invest in his or her own business when there was a likely successor. Calus and Van Huylenbroeck also found that in the presence of a known successor, business owners were more likely to have expanded the business by investing in capital or by increasing output. Generational transfer in farm family businesses usually meant that more human and physical capital were acquired by each generation (Mishra et al., 2010).

There has been a limited amount of research focused on the goal orientation and family business succession or for that matter success. Danes and Lee (2004) hypothesized that spouses would differ in their perceived success of their business goals; their hypothesis was not supported. Danes and Lee's research did not link the discussion of goals to the success of succession. Lee and Marshall (2013) directly linked goal orientation to family business performance. We posit that increased family business communication about goals will lead a family business to take part in succession planning and name a successor.

Meeting with an estate planning professional is an important part of succession planning. Many family businesses had not met with an estate planning professional, often due to the stress caused from estate planning (Fetsch, 1999, p. 2). An estate plan could be a very important piece of information for both the business unit and the family unit, especially when voiced from a neutral party, e.g., a tax attorney (Sander and Bordone, 2006).

It is important for the senior generation to be willing to hand the business down to the next generation. Salamon et al. (1986) found that, in general, the business owner was hesitant to retire and hand over the business, which ultimately delayed management succession. One of the most cited reasons for the hesitancy to retire was the fear for loss of salary and benefits. Moreover, the owner usually did not want to relinquish control, for fear that the business would not be run the way that he or she had envisioned (Bowman-Upton, 1991).

The number of generations involved in the day-to-day management of the business could have an effect on naming a successor (Olson et al., 2003). Bennedsen et al. (2007) found that having more than one possible successor could delay the succession process, as again it reduced the sense of urgency for the senior generations. Wolf (2003) found that in dairy farms where senior and junior generations worked together the likelihood of succession was high.

As demonstrated by the Sustainable Family Business Model (Stafford et al., 1999), the family and the business were continuously competing for both time and resources from both systems. Danes and Lee (2004) found that in farm businesses, the highest level of tension between couples was generated from the struggle to balance work and family. There were constraints and resources shared between and among the two systems – the family and the business – which in turn affected the sustainability of the family business as a whole. Basco and Pérez Rodríguez (2009) found that when the family business decided to focus on both the family and the business instead of just on the business, then family success increased and business success remained constant. If the business owner put the business first, then it was likely that the family would then have fewer resources and be less successful because the resources that were once shared had gone to the business (Stafford et al., 1999). Overall, businesses were more successful when the family and business share time instead of emphasizing one over the other (Basco and Pérez Rodríguez, 2009; Stafford et al., 1999). One would expect that family businesses that had a balance between the family system and the business system were more likely to have chosen a successor.

Business characteristics

Family business literature has used income to calculate business size. Past research found that farm income and farm size affected farm transition (Calus et al., 2008; Gibson and Cassar, 2002; Mishra and El-Osta, 2007). Calus et al. (2008) found higher levels of farm assets when a named successor was present in a farm business, just as Stavrou (1999) found that as business size increased, the offspring's intentions to join the family business also increased. Studies thus far showed that total sales volume, total farm assets, number of employees, and business size all had a positive influence on the incidence of business succession planning (Calus et al., 2008; Gibson and Cassar, 2002; Mishra and El-Osta, 2007). We focus on annual family business income as a measure of business size.

Each family business could have different goals, ranging from maximizing profit to integrating family members into the business. The act of setting business goals helped members of the family who were involved in the business have a sharper vision of where the family business was headed in the future (Bowman-Upton, 1991). The differences in business goals could define where a business was going and what it would accomplish, whether their goal was profit or passing the business to a family member. Bizri (2016) found that founders first look to their nuclear family when determining who would take control of the business. Due to the very high occupational inheritance rate found among farmers (Laband and Lentz, 1983), we could assume that the most important goal for farmers would be to pass their business down to their son or daughter.

Business owner

Demographic characteristics such as gender, age, and education could have an effect on succession (Weigel and Weigel, 1990). The generation of the owner could affect whether or not he or she had thought about naming a successor. In the case that owners were either second generation or higher, they had experienced a succession process in one way or another – either passing the business down to their next heir(s) or having the business passed down to them.

Both age and education could have an effect on the succession process. Kimhi and Nachlieli (2001) found that as an owner's amount of education increased, the probability of having a family member built into the succession plan increased. The likelihood that the older generation of the business had given up the power and ownership of the business increased as the owner (older generation) aged (Remble et al., 2010). Mishra et al. (2003) stated that age had an effect on the timing of business succession, or business transfer. Of the farmers interviewed, Mishra et al. found

34% of them had a succession plan if they planned on retiring in the next 5 years, and 80% of those had a family member named as the successor.

Data

The data used are from the 2012 Intergenerational Farm and Non-Farm Family Business Survey. The 2012 Intergenerational Farm and Non-Farm Family Business Survey was a 30-minute telephone survey of rural small and medium family businesses. The population for this survey was obtained from a list of 2,163 small and medium farm and agribusinesses in Illinois, Indiana, Michigan, and Ohio who are registered in Food Industry MarketMaker. Registered members of the interviews were conducted from April 2011 to February 2012. The final sample contains 736 family businesses for an overall response rate of 34%. To qualify for the study as a family business, one of the following metrics had to be met: At least one other member of the family besides the respondent had to have ownership interest in the business (86% of the sample). At least one other member of the family besides the respondent had to work at least part-time in the business (92% of the sample). The respondent inherited the business (18% of the sample). The respondent planned to transfer the business to a family member (55% of the sample).

The Family Business Succession Survey (FBSS) consisted of eight sections of questions for the business owner or operator to answer. The sections include the following: business demographics, succession, family business organization, management strategies, business success, family tensions, business and household finances, and life-cycle questions. A mixture of continuous, Likert-type, and binary variables measured the responses of the surveyed business owners.

Our data was fairly consistent with past research that has been conducted in regard to a business having an identified successor. We omitted non-farm family businesses from our dataset so that the analysis was strictly related to farm family businesses. Out of the 409 usable observations, 30% had a designated successor. Calus et al. (2008) and Calus and Van Huylenbroeck (2008) found that in their study only 19% of their businesses had a designated successor, in contrast to those who did not have a designated successor (37%) and those who were not certain who their successor would be (45%). In a nationwide study, Mishra et al. (2003) found that only 27% of farm operators had named a successor.

Setting the stage for succession planning: what we can learn from the data

It should not come as a shock that many family businesses are not prepared for succession. It is also not shocking that many family businesses make ungrounded decisions when it comes to planning and continuity of the business. Family businesses can be a twisted maze of managing finances, operations, human resources, relatives, and emotions. Nothing demonstrates this more than delving into the data to see misalignments in responses.

Being prepared for and preparing for a transfer, whether it be an ownership or management transfer, can be very important elements for a family business to consider. Only 43% of family business owners responded that their family was prepared for a management succession if it were to happen today, but 63% of business owners responded that there is enough capital or money to implement the transfer of the business. So, what could be existing in that gap that makes businesses feel unprepared? The gap comes down to lack of planning and/or unwillingness of owners to relinquish at least some control of the business to their heirs. Whether they sense their son, daughter, or family member is not yet responsible enough to take over the business or they feel as if a longer training period is needed, these insecurities often result in a lack of planning.

Even though businesses may not be prepared for a transfer or have sufficient business stability for a transfer, their drive for the family business to continue can overshadow transfer decisions. For example, 38% of business owners worry about their heirs being able to afford to purchase the family business. Even though they worry about putting heirs at risk, business owners are often willing to put their own livelihood at risk for the sake of business continuity. When asked if they plan to transfer the family business to a family successor even if it puts their own personal wealth and livelihood at an increased risk, 47% at least somewhat agreed that they would. These statistics show how distorted business decisions can become when the emotions of the family enter into the equation.

Expectations and viewpoints between generations can vary, and this can cause a roadblock in the succession process. Our data showed that 25% of the senior generation had not at all attempted to explore or discover the preferences of the heirs as part of the planning process and only 31% had made a large effort to explore these preferences. This result is echoed in that only 28% of the senior generation are prepared to give up control of the family business by delegating management to heirs or successors. The result of this lack of communication can be expectations that are severely fragmented. Only 53% reported they actively engaged heirs or successors in a discussion of possible transfer plan alternatives. Lack of common goals among family members was found to influence the successful transfer of 59% of family businesses. More communication between the two generations could greatly improve succession planning effectiveness and create a family business environment that is more inviting to the new generation.

When it comes to transferring the family business, there are multiple approaches that can be taken. The decision as to who receives which piece(s) of the family business can be very complicated. Sweat equity, equal division, or heir's individual abilities can help guide these transfer decisions. Pontet et al. (2007) cite that confidence in a successor's abilities does not necessarily tie to ownership. Only 21% of family businesses report any amount of tension generated from unequal ownership of the business by family members. Owners of businesses are fairly equally distributed in response when the question arose of "Should each hair share equally in business ownership even if this distribution of ownership is not the most profitable for the business?" Roughly half of respondents (53%) disagreed, 14% neither agreed nor disagreed, and 33% of respondents agreed. It is interesting to note that 63% of business owners agree that the heir with the most ability should have the largest management role, even if all heirs have chosen the family business as a career. Delving into the data reconfirms that many inconsistencies exist amid family businesses, and transfer decisions in family businesses are not strictly adherent to numbers.

Methodology: probit model estimation

A probit model was used to model the factors that affect the likelihood of a business having a named or designated successor. Glauben et al. (2004) used a probit model to estimate effects on the likelihood of farm succession; Lange et al. (2011) also used a probit model to estimate transfer decisions on family farm businesses. The response variable, whether or not a business has named a successor, is binary: 1 signifies that a successor has been named or identified and 0 signifies that no successor has been named or identified. The coefficients on each of the independent variables can be interpreted as individual influences on the probability of the model, ceteris paribus. An example of the model form is as follows:

$$P\ (y = 1 \mid \mathbf{x}) = G(\beta_0 + \beta_1 x_1 + \ldots + \beta_k x_k) = G(\beta_0 + x\beta) \tag{15.1}$$

where G is a function taking values strictly between 0 and 1: $0 < G\ (z) < 1$, for all real numbers z (Wooldridge, 2009). This rule of G (z) lying between 0 and 1 ensures that the estimated probability generated from a given linear probability model will not project a negative probability or a probability over the value of 1. For this model, we are assuming a standard normal distribution for the error term, ε. In order to account for the heteroskedasticity that is often inherent to survey data, we used robust standard errors instead of normal standard errors.

$$P\Big(id\_a\_successor = 1\Big) = \alpha + \beta_1 \star Business + \beta_2 \star Family + \beta_3 \star Owner + \varepsilon \tag{15.2}$$

The variables of interest are (1) the presence of sufficient amounts of capital to implement a transfer and (2) the regular family discussions of business goals. The family business owner indicated whether there was enough capital present to implement the transfer of the family business. The options for discussing business goals were "never" discuss goals, "yearly" discuss goals, "quarterly" discuss goals, "monthly" discuss goals, or discuss goals "all the time." In the case that the business answered "quarterly," "monthly," or "all the time" to the question, it was grouped into the "regularly discuss goals" binary dummy variable.

We modify Smilkstein et al.'s (1982) family and work APGAR assessments by combining the two to encompass both family and work (in our case, family business) into one assessment. This assessment contains four questions, focused on how the family and business share time, turn to others when they are troubled, accept and support ideas and thoughts, and how much conflict is generated by making business versus family decisions. We adapt the experience of the owner from Mincer's (1991) formulation, which includes both age and education levels. Each variable's name, definition, dummy structure, and unit of measurement are shown below in Table 15.1. Also included are frequencies of the binary variables as well as the descriptive statistics of continuous variables.

Table 15.1 Variable definition and summary statistics

Variable	Definition	No Identified Successor Means (n = 288)	Identified Successor Means (n = 121)
Business Characteristics			
Income between $50,000 and $99,000	= 1 if the business had gross income of between $50,000 and $99,000; = 0 otherwise	0.1806	0.1818
Income over $100,000	= 1 if the business had gross income over $100,000; = 0 otherwise	0.3403	0.5289
Successful Business	= 1 if business owner says that the business is somewhat successful or successful; = 0 otherwise	0.8993	0.9587
Sell or Give Business to Family	= 1 if distribution of the business to the next generation includes selling or giving the business to family successors; = 0 if business will be sold to someone outside of the family or liquidated	0.5451	0.8678
Capital	= 1 if there is enough capital or money to implement a transfer of the business; = 0 otherwise	0.6146	0.7934
Goal of Family as a Priority	= 1 if the primary business goal is business survival, keeping the business in the family, or the opportunity to work with family members; = 0 otherwise	0.3611	0.5041
LLC, Corporation, or Trust	= 1 if the business is organized as an LLC, Corporation, or Trust; = 0 if business is solely owned or a partnership	0.3194	0.3802
Family Characteristics			
Regularly Discuss Goals	= 1 if the family discusses business goals on a quarterly basis or more frequently; = 0 otherwise	0.5069	0.7190

Variable	Definition	No Identified Successor Means (n = 288)	Identified Successor Means (n = 121)
Estate Plan Discussion	= 1 if the family has ever met with an accountant, financial planner, lawyer, or business consultant to discuss estate planning; = 0 otherwise	0.5313	0.7521
Senior Generation Ready	= 1 if the senior generation is very much or extremely prepared to give up control of the family business by delegating management to heirs or successors; = 0 otherwise	0.2153	0.4298
Generations in Management	= number of generations of family members involved in the day-to-day management of the business	1.4549	1.8595
Modified APGAR	16-point Likert scale of how functional a family and business interact and work with one another (0 = most dysfunctional and 16 = most functional)	10.3472	10.5537
Owner Characteristics			
Experience	= business owner's age in 2010 less years of education obtained	44.4306	47.0413
Female	= 1 if business owner is female; = 0 otherwise	0.3889	0.4050
Married	= 1 if the business owner is married; = 0 otherwise	0.8854	0.8926
Constant	= intercept		

Results: business, family and individual (owner) factors

Results of the probit model as well as the marginal effects are shown below in Table 15.2. The probability of naming a successor increases by 11% when there is sufficient capital present in the family business to implement a business transfer. The frequency of the discussion of goals is also significant to a family business having an identified successor, at the 1% level. The discussion of goals increases the probability that a business has a named successor by 14%.

Table 15.2 Parameter estimates of factors affecting farm succession

Variable	Probit Coefficients (n = 409)	Robust Standard Errors	Marginal Effects
Income $50,000 to $99,000	0.1678	0.2104	0.0541
Income over $100,000	0.2251	0.1782	0.0711
Successful Business	0.2394	0.3152	0.0691
Sell or Give Business to Family	0.8555***	0.1779	0.2405***
Capital	0.3661**	0.1605	0.1087**
Goal of Family as a Priority	0.2172	0.1485	0.0685
LLC, Corporation, or Trust	−0.1175	0.1562	−0.0361
Regularly Discuss Goals	0.4658***	0.1572	0.1411***
Estate Plan Discussion	0.3713**	0.1581	0.1123**
Senior Generation Ready	0.2750*	0.1634	0.0890
Generations in Management	0.2521**	0.1104	0.0785**
Modified APGAR	0.0039	0.0380	0.0012
Experience	0.0155**	0.0063	0.0048**
Female	0.0675	0.1554	0.0211
Married	0.0266	0.2417	0.0082
Constant	−3.6370***	0.6677	—

Note: Single, double, and triple asterisks (*, **, ***) denote statistical significance at the 10%, 5%, and 1% levels, respectively.

Business characteristics

The intention of the owner to sell or give the business to a relative after he or she exits the business increases the probability of naming a successor by 24% when compared to an owner having the intention to liquidate the business or sell to a non-relative. Other business controls were not found to be significant.

Family characteristics

The discussion of an estate plan can encompass effects from both the family and the business as separate but intersecting entities as they relate to succession planning. Roughly 60% of the total owners in our survey have met with an accountant, financial planner, lawyer, or business consultant to discuss their estate planning strategies, which leaves almost half of them who have not. Discussing an estate plan with a professional has a significant positive association with the probability of a business having a named successor. The model shows that the effect of discussing an estate plan increases the probability of having identified a successor by roughly 11%.

Often discussed in the literature is the senior generation's willingness to hand over the business (Venter et al., 2005). The model shows that when the senior generation is ready to hand over the business, there is a statistically significant positive effect on the probability that a family business has a named successor. Winter et al. (2004) found that the most frequently cited reason that managers were no longer involved in the business differed between those ages 45 and older versus those younger than 45. When managers were over 45, the most frequent reason cited was retirement, but for those younger than 45 years of age, the reason most cited was resource issues. When the senior generation is ready to hand over the business (versus when the senior generation is not ready to hand over the business), the probability of naming a successor increases by 9%.

The number of generations involved in the day-to-day management of the business were found to be positive and statistically significant. For each generation that is involved in the daily management of the business, the likelihood that a business has identified a successor increases by 8%.

Individual characteristics

In our model, the owner's years of experience has a positive influence on the business's probability of having a named successor. For each year of experience that the owner of the business has, the likelihood of naming a successor increases by 0.12%.

Conclusions

This study analyzed the characteristics that influence the probability of a family business having a named successor. This study focused on the business, family and individual characteristics that affect the probability that a farm family business has a named successor. In particular the study focused on the presence of sufficient capital in order to implement a transfer, and the frequency of discussion of future business goals. The findings of this research prove that both of these variables have an effect on naming a successor. The findings also highlight the importance of good family business management.

The results of the models show a true disconnect between the business owner's perceptions and what is actually happening in his or her business. The business owners are likely to gauge success in a different way than would non-family business owners. For example, respondents perceived their business as successful (92% of sample), yet their income was below $50,000 per year (44% of sample). With family businesses, the owners are more likely to have a feeling of success stemming from the incorporation of their family and their work into their life and may also feel more prepared for a business disruption, because people in their business know the business and could step in temporarily if need be.

The model shows that business and family characteristics have more significance to a business having a named successor than do individual characteristics of the owner. The only individual characteristic that was influential to a business having identified a successor was the owner's years of experience. The business characteristics that had an effect on a family business having a named successor are the intent of the owner(s) to sell or give the business to a family member and if there is enough capital or money to implement a transfer. Family characteristics that had an impact on the business having a named successor are regular discussion of business goals as a family, if the family has met with a professional to discuss an estate plan, if the senior generation is ready to give up control of the family business, and the number of generations involved in the daily management of the business.

For family farm businesses, the traditionalist view of passing the farm down through the family and treating the farm as a "family affair" is evident in the results. For example, the intention of the business owner to sell or give the business to a relative is a prevalent force driving the naming of a successor. The frequency of discussion of future business goals, whether it be yearly, quarterly, or monthly, is a management strategy that can easily be implemented into a family agribusiness, but has a large impact on leading a family business to successful succession.

Identifying the barriers that family businesses face when naming a successor will help Extension Services and other small and family business consulting agencies and organizations to formulate a guide to assist families when working through this process. Some of these include devising a set of guidelines for families to follow to assist them in their succession process or making a list of those "difficult subjects" that families must talk about to make their process as successful as possible. Helping family businesses name a successor will increase their sustainability and help to make the occupational inheritance rate more successful.

For farm family businesses, the focus should be put on planning in a formal way. For instance, farm business owners who want to name a successor (ultimately leading to having a successful succession process) should make sure that it is their intention to sell or give the business to a relative when they retire or otherwise exit the business. Farm businesses should meet with an estate planning professional, integrating the family and the business into one legal plan. This not only helps prepare the business for a shock of some kind but it also makes the plans accessible to all the family members. Family farm businesses can also formally plan without a professional in the sense that they can have an official family business meeting where the family members can openly discuss issues relevant to business planning.

During these meetings, the members of the family business should plan on discussing future business goals, at least on a quarterly basis.

Policy implications: capital and financial planning and options

Transferring a farm family business can be a very expensive transaction and can weigh heavily on the minds of business owners. As we saw from the previous analysis, family businesses must conduct strategic family business management in order to succeed their business to the next generation. There are different options that family businesses can take when transferring a business, including to gift the business or shares of the business to relatives or other heirs, allow family members to purchase shares of the business or the whole business, or allow non-relatives to purchase shares of the business or the whole business. According to the Family Business Succession Survey, 38% of family business owners worry whether their heirs or successors can afford to purchase the family business. Yet, 14% of business owners plan on selling the business to someone outside of the family, 56% of business owners plan on giving or selling the business to relatives, 26% of business owners plan on liquidating business assets, and 5% of business owners do not know what will happen when they exit the business.

The encouraging news is that 63% of business owners from the FBSS survey responded that there is enough capital to implement the transfer of the business. Successors finding financing for the purchase of that family business is another story. Acquiring such financing can be the first of many stumbling blocks in the transfer of a family business. Even when financing is an option (when there is not enough cash to buy the business or business shares outright), the principal payments can sometimes be so high that they are crippling. A standard farm family business, for example, contains high-value assets such as land, structures (barns, outbuildings, and grain bins), equipment, and livestock. In a world where a new combine with attachments can cost half a million dollars or more, the value of a family business's capital can quickly add up.

Small- and medium-sized farm family businesses have to be mindful of the delicate balance between having enough capital to employ more than one generation in the business (to have someone to transfer that business to) while also being heedful to not create a business so heavy in assets that potential new owners cannot afford to "buy in" to the business. To get around such stumbling blocks, careful planning needs to occur. The United States Department of Agriculture Farm Service Agency offers Beginning Farmers and Ranchers Loans as well as Minority and Women Farmers and Ranchers Loans. In order to qualify as a "beginning farmer or rancher," the individual had to start "farming or ranching less than 10 years ago" (USDA, 2012, p. 17). In order to qualify as socially disadvantaged and qualify for a Minority and Women Farmers and Ranchers Loan, the individual must be one of the following: American Indian or Alaskan Native, Asian, Black or African American, Native Hawaiian or other Pacific Islander, Hispanic, or a woman (p. 17).

Different types of loans are available for each group, including direct loans for farm ownership, operating, and emergency situations. Rates and terms vary across loams, but all interest rates are fixed and are almost always lower than market rates. There are upper bounds on possible loan amounts. Direct farm ownership loans and direct operating loans can be no more than $300,000 and direct emergency loans can be no more than 100% of actual or physical losses or $500,000 (whichever is lower). Direct farm ownership loans can have terms up to 40 years, while direct operating loans can be a maximum of only 7 years. Direct emergency loans are typically no more than 7 years as well.

This chapter leads us to recognize that competent business management is likely to indicate a successful succession. When family businesses are correctly managed, there is a higher rate of planning present and better integration between the family and the business. Characteristics such as having more than one generation involved in the day-to-day management of the business, the business owner having the desire to sell or give the business to family successors, the family business having enough capital to implement the transfer of the business, the family regularly discussing business goals, if the business has discussed an estate plan with a professional, if the senior generation is ready to give up control of the business, and the experience level of the owner – all are distinct indicators of naming a successor.

Acknowledgment

This chapter reports results from the Intergenerational Transfer for Strong and Sustainable Small and Medium-Sized Farm Family Businesses Project which was supported by Agricultural and Food Research Initiative Competitive Grant no. 2009-55618-05056 from the USDA National Institute of Food and Agriculture.

References

Basco, R., and M.J. Pérez Rodríguez. March 2009. "Studying the family enterprise holistically: evidence for integrated family and business systems." *Family Business Review*, 22(1), 82–95.
Bennedsen, M., K.M. Nelson, F. Perez-Gonzalez, and D. Wolfenzon. 2007. "Inside the family firm: The role of families in succession decisions and performance." *Quarterly Journal of Economics*, 122: 647–691.
Bizri, R. 2016. "Succession in the family business: Drivers and pathways." *International Journal of Entrepreneurial Behavior & Research*, 22(1), 133–154.
Bowman-Upton, N. 1991. "Transferring Management in the Family-Owned Business, U.S. Small Business Administration." <http://www.sba.gov/idc/groups/public/documents/ sba_homepage/serv_sbp_exit.pdf>.
Calus, M., and G. Van Huylenbroeck. 2008. "The succession effect within management decisions of family farms." *Proceedings of the 12th Congress of the European Association of Agricultural Economists* (pp. 1–5).
Calus, M., G. Van Huylenbroeck, and D. Van Lierde. 2008. "The relationship between farm succession and farm assets on Belgian farms." *Sociologia Ruralis*, 48(1), 38–56.

Danes, S. M., and Y.G. Lee. 2004. "Tensions generated by business issues in farm business-owning couples." *Family Relations*, 53(4), 357–366.

De Massis, A., J.H. Chua, and J.J. Crisman. 2008. "Factors preventing intra-family succession." *Family Business Review*, 21(21), 183–199.

Fetsch, R.J. 1999. "Some do's and don'ts for successful farm and ranch family estate transfers." *Journal of Extension*, 37(3), Retrieved from <http://www.joe.org/joe/1999june/iw2.php>.

Gersick, K.E., J.A. Davis, M.M. Hampton, and I. Lansberg. 1997. *Generation to Generation: Life Cycles of the Family Business*. Boston, MA: Harvard Business School Press.

Gibson, B., and G. Cassar. 2002. "Planning behavior variables in small firms." *Journal of Small Business Management*, 40(3), 171–186.

Glauben, T., H. Tietje, and C. Weiss. 2004. "Succession in agriculture: a probit and a competing risk analysis." Selected paper for the annual Meeting of the American Agricultural Economist Association (AAEA) in Denver.

Hachfeld, G.A., D.B. Bau, C.R. Holcomb, J.N. Kurtz, J.W. Craig, and K.D. Olson. 2009. "Farm transition and estate planning: Farmers' evaluations and behavioral changes due to attending workshops." *Journal of Extension*, 47(2): 2FEA8. http://www.joe.org/joe/2009april/a8.php

Kimhi, A., and N. Nachlieli. 2001. "Intergenerational succession on Israeli family farms." *Journal of Agricultural Economics*, 52(2), 42–58.

Laband, D.N., and B.F. Lentz. 1983. "Occupational inheritance in agriculture." *American Journal of Agricultural Economics*, 65(2), 311–314.

Lange, K., J. Johnson, P. Johnson, D. Hudson, and E.J. Belasco. 2011. "Parental motivation in family farm intergenerational transfers." Poster prepared for presentation at the Agricultural & Applied Economics Association's 2011 AAEA & NAREA Joint Annual Meeting, Pittsburgh, Pennsylvania, July 24–26, 2011.

Lee, Y.G., and M.I. Marshall. 2013. "Goal orientation and performance of family businesses." *Journal of Family and Economic Issues*, 34, 265–274.

Mincer, J. 1991. *Education and unemployment* (NBER Working Paper No. 3838). Cambridge, MA: National Bureau of Economic Research.

Mishra, A K., and H.S. El-Osta. 2007. "Factors affecting succession decisions in family farm businesses: evidence from a national survey." *Journal of the American Society of Farm Managers and Rural Appraisers*, 70(1), A1–A10.

Mishra, A.K., H.S. El-Osta, and J.D. Johnson. 2004. "Succession in family farm business: empirical evidence from the U.S. farm sector." Proceedings of the Agricultural and Applied Economics Association Meeting in Denver, CO.

Mishra, A.K., H.S. El-Osta, and S. Shaik. 2010. "Succession decisions in U.S. family farm businesses." *Journal of Agricultural and Resource Economics*, 35(1), 133–152.

Mishra, A.K., J.D. Johnson, and M.J. Morehart. 2003. "Retirement and succession planning of farm households: results from a national survey." Paper for presentation at the National Public Policy Education Committee, Salt Lake City, UT.

Morris, M.H., R.W. Williams, and D. Nel. 1996. "Factors influencing family business succession." *International Journal of Entrepreneurial Behavior & Research*, 2(3), 68–81.

Olson, P.D., V.S. Zuiker, S.M. Danes, K. Stafford, R.K.Z. Heck, and K.A. Duncan. 2003. "The impact of the family and the business on family business sustainability." *Journal of Business Venturing*, 18(5), 639–666.

Pontet, S.B., C. Wrosch, and M. Gagne. 2007. "An exploration of the generational differences in levels of control held among family businesses approaching succession." *Family Business Review*, 20(4), 337–354.

Potter, C., and M. Lobley. 1992. "Ageing and succession on family farms: the impact on decision-making and land use." *Sociologia Ruralis*, 32(2–3), 317–334.

Remble, A.A., R. Keeney, and M.I. Marshall. 2010. "Multiple generation farm households: what determines primacy in management?" Selected paper prepared for presentation at the Southern Agricultural Economics Association Annual Meeting, Orlando, FL, February 6–9, 2010.

Salamon, S., K.M. Gengenbacher, and D.J. Penas. 1986. "Family factors affecting the intergenerational succession to farming." *Human Organization*, 45(1), 24–33.

Sander, F.E.A., and R.C. Bordone. March 2006. "All in the family: Managing business disputes with relatives." *Negotiation*, (March), 3–5.

Smilkstein, G., C. Ashworth and D. Montano. 1982. "Validity and reliability of the family APGAR as a test of family function." *The Journal of Family Practice*, 15, 303–311.

Stafford, K., K.A. Duncan, S. Danes, and M. Winter. September 1999. "A research model of sustainable family businesses." *Family Business Review*, 7(3), 197–208.

Stavrou, E.T. 1999. "Succession in family businesses: exploring the effects of demographic factors on offspring intentions to join and take over the business." *Journal of Small Business management*, 37(3), 43–61.

Sureshawran, S. 2008. "Farm transition – exit, entry and planning." in *Family Farm Forum*, CSREES, USDA, May 2008.

Tagiuri, R., and J. Davis. 1996. "Bivalent attributes of the family firm." *Family Business Review*, 9(2), 199–208.

USDA (United States Department of Agriculture. 2012. *Your Guide to FSA Farm Loans [PDF]*. June 2012. United States Department of Agriculture, Farm Service Agency. <http://www.fsa.usda.gov/Internet/FSA_File/fsa_br_01_web_booklet.pdf>.

Venter, E., C. Boshoff, and G. Maas. 2005. "The influence of successor-related factors on the succession process in small and medium-sized family businesses." *Family Business Review*, 18(4), 283–303.

Weigel, D.J., and R.R. Weigel. 1990. "Family satisfaction in two-generation farm families: the role of stress and resources." *Family Relations*, 39(4), 449–455.

Wilson, S., R. Marotz-Baden, and D.P. Holloway. 1991. "Stress in two-generation farm and ranch families." *Lifestyles: Family and Economic Issues*, 12(3), 199–216.

Winter, M., S.M. Danes, S. Koh, K. Fredericks, and J.J. Paul. 2004. "Tracking family businesses and their owners over time: Panel attrition, manager departure and business demise." *Journal of Business Venturing*, 19(4), 535–559.

Wolf, C. 2003. "The influence of financial, production, and operator characteristics on dairy farm transfer plans." *Journal of the American Society of Farm Managers and Rural Appraisers*, 66, 129–133.

Wooldridge, J.M. 2009. *Introductory econometrics, a modern approach*. South-Western Pub.

Chapter 16

The impacts of common agricultural policy on farm succession in Slovenia

Boštjan Kerbler

Farms are most often under family ownership (as family farms) and are therefore the only part of society that must ensure its own social and professional reproduction. On family farms, supervision over farm management and ownership is transferred within the family between generations (Gasson and Errington 1993). Succession on a farm is therefore the basis for a farm's existence and development. According to Laband and Lantz (1983), succession on family farms is five times more frequent than in other professions and represents the best example of intergenerational transfer of physical and human capital. During the socialization process, a potential successor on a farm receives detailed insight into the work of the farm owner and the farming lifestyle, direct experience, and intergenerational transfer of knowledge, and at the same time develops respect for all of this, especially for the land as a primary resource for making a living on the farm. Therefore, according to Laband and Lentz (1983), the transfer of human capital between generations in the same family also represents its enrichment, and at the same time this increases the value of physical capital—both its actual value as well as awareness of its value. In order for this to happen, basic conditions must be fulfilled; specifically, that the takeover of the farm and continuation of farming actually take place, and that the transfer of the farm to the successor takes place in a timely manner.

One of the major problems in agriculture in developed countries, including Slovenia, is a reduction in the number of farm takeovers or the transfer of farms to successors. The European Union is trying to stop these negative trends through certain measures under its common agricultural policy. Slovenia, as an EU member state since 2004, is entitled to funds under these measures. This chapter presents the impacts of common agricultural policy on farm succession in Slovenia to date. In order to better understand the issue at hand, the sociodemographic conditions on Slovenian farms before Slovenia's accession to the EU are described in greater detail. In addition, some other characteristics of Slovenian agriculture are also presented that are believed to (directly or indirectly) influence young people's decisions regarding farm takeover and are reflected in the effectiveness and efficiency of the common agricultural policy measures addressing this issue.

Two years before Slovenia acceded to the European Union, in his book *Aktualna vprašanja kmetijske politike* (Current Agricultural Policy Issues) Bojnec (2002, 358) wrote the following:

> Slovenian agriculture faces natural, economic, and social problems that make it impossible to increase agricultural efficiency and improve farmers' social equality. The biggest problems are the unfavorable natural conditions, the fragmented land holding structure, and the age and educational structure of the farming population.

His findings are based on data obtained during the last agricultural census before Slovenia's accession to the EU. It was carried out in 2000 and it first and foremost revealed distinctly unfavorable sociodemographic characteristics of Slovenian farms. In terms of the age structure of family farm households, a large share of elderly family members stood out. People over age 55 accounted for nearly a third of all household members. A comparison of the data with those recorded in previous censuses (in 1981 and 1991; cf. Kovačič, 1996) even shows that by 2000 the age structure of family farm households had distinctly deteriorated. For example, the aging index stood at 78 in 1981 and at 85 10 years later, but during the 2000 census it had already increased to 135. Especially striking were the data on the age structure of farm owners: 56.3% were older than 55, of whom more than half were over 54. There were 20.5% of farm owners younger than 45 and only 5.2% younger than 35. Kovačič (1996), who had already drawn attention to the trend of aging farm owners and the high average age of farm owners even before the census, also argued that this reduced the development orientation of Slovenian farms. However, despite farm owners' alarming age structure, the census revealed an even more alarming fact: only 23% of family farms had selected a successor. In addition to the unfavorable age structure and succession situation, the 2000 census also showed an unfavorable education structure of Slovenian farms, even though even before the census Hribernik (1993, 1996) had already drawn attention to the great importance of the education process and (ongoing) learning for the development of agriculture and farms, as well as farm succession. As he states, "investing in farmers' education is an investment without which the development of agriculture is condemned to stagnation and farmers as a social class are condemned to social marginality" (1993, 458) and "the educational path of young people on farms plays an important role in fulfilling their parents' aspirations for ensuring intergenerational continuity, which their basic profession stems from" (1996, 24). Hribernik argues that farm owners and their successors should be part of the full-time education system as long as possible, after which they should participate in continuous professional training in order to improve on what they have learned so far. However, the 2000 census showed a different picture: only 38% of farm owners had completed vocational or secondary school, and as many as 58.4% had only completed primary school or not even that; the majority of the latter were over age 65 (Dernulc et al. 2002). Judging from the criteria for formal agricultural education obtained, the situation regarding farm owners' professional qualifications was even less favorable: only 16.1% of farm owners had completed at least one agricultural education program, among whom only 2% were age 65 or older. Even though the general education level of farm successors was higher on average than that of farm owners (65% of farm successors had completed vocational or secondary school), there were no major differences between farm owners and successors in terms of professional agricultural qualifications.

In addition to the unfavorable sociodemographic conditions, Slovenia had to deal with an exceptionally unfavorable size structure and above-average ownership and land fragmentation prior to its accession to the EU. After the Second World War, Slovenian agriculture developed in a specific communist political and economic environment, which did not favor private farming. Whereas in western European countries, farm size increased relatively quickly in parallel with improvements in farming technology, during this period and partly also in the 1990s the opposite process took place in Slovenia, characterized by continuous deterioration in the size and ownership structure as well as a low level of professionalization reflected in the age and educational structure described above (Ministry of Agriculture, Forestry, and Food 2007). Based on the data from the 2000 agricultural census, Slovenia had 86,467 agricultural holdings. According to Vrišer (2005), family farms predominated, accounting for 86,336 or 99.85% of all agricultural holdings. They occupied 93.9% of utilized farmland.[1] The remaining 0.15% of agricultural holdings with 6.1% of utilized farmland included agricultural companies and cooperatives— that is, the socialist sector from the communist period, which ended in 1991 with Slovenia breaking away from Yugoslavia and gaining its independence. Because of denationalization or poor management in the newly democratic state many agricultural companies and cooperatives went bankrupt or converted to other activities. As a result, their number decreased significantly, with only eleven remaining in 2000. The main feature of the Slovenian ownership structure before Slovenia joined the EU was therefore the distinct predominance of small farms (0–5 ha of land), which accounted for 61.6% or just under two-thirds of all agricultural holdings or 26.1% of utilized farmland. Another feature was the large share (26.5%) of extremely small farms (0–2 ha), which covered 5.4% of utilized farmland. The majority of extremely small and small farms were made up of family farms. Vrišer (2005) further reports that the comparison of past statistical agricultural censuses shows that the average size of family farms continued to decrease, finally stopping at only 5.3 ha of utilized farmland in 2000. Even if all agricultural holdings are taken into account, including agricultural companies and cooperatives, in 2000 an average agricultural holding owned only 5.6 ha of utilized farmland, which is 3.5 times less than the EU average at that time. In addition to the unfavorable size structure, the census also proved that land and ownership fragmentation were among the biggest developmental problems of Slovenian agriculture. This was especially true for family farms, for which it turned out that they worked a total of over 600,000 pieces of farmland, or 7.2 pieces of land per farm on average. The average size of an individual piece of farmland was less than 1.4 ha. Only one-eighth of farms owned their entire land in one piece and they worked just under a tenth of all utilized farmland. However, the majority of land was worked by family farms that owned two to ten pieces of farmland (Dernulc et al. 2002). The situation in Slovenian agriculture regarding the size and ownership structure is alarming and also affects young people's decisions regarding farm takeover; a number of experts had already drawn attention to this before the census, including Hribernik (1996, 16), who wrote:

> Farmers with a few hectares of farmland cannot generate an income compara-
> ble to the working and dependent members of a farm household and thereby
> also cannot provide the level of social security that would encourage young
> people to maintain farms as production and ownership units.

Rural sociologist Ana Barbič (1993, 265) substantiated this further, claiming "young people that remain involved in agriculture do this increasingly less for emotional reasons and increasingly more for economic reasons."

In addition to the size and ownership structure, achieving economic viability, which has thus proved to be a key factor in young people's decisions to take over farms, is further hindered by unfavorable natural conditions. Even before Slovenia's entry into the EU, Naglič (1998) and other experts (e.g., Gams 1983; Volk et al. 1992; Cunder 1997; Plut 1998) had drawn attention to the fact that Slovenia is among the countries with the most difficult natural conditions for agriculture (alongside Scandinavia, Switzerland, and Austria). Slovenia is characterized by extremely dynamic terrain, which means much of its farmland is highly sloped. Due to dynamic terrain, high elevations, and Slovenia's location itself (at the inter-section of the Alps, the Dinarides, the Pannonian Plain, and the Mediterranean), the climate is also unfavorable. Exceptional weather conditions, such as frost, glaze, storms, droughts, and so on are very common. In addition, 44% of Slovenian ter-ritory is covered in karst areas characterized by poor soil composition and specific hydrological conditions. The natural conditions described generally do not hinder farming in Slovenia, but the agricultural production capacity is smaller, production is more expensive, and the competitive capacity and market flexibility are lower compared to farms with better natural conditions for farming. This was already highlighted in the early 1990s by Volk et al. (1992). Based on the natural factors that have a negative impact on farming and the unfavorable economic and social factors resulting from poor natural (and hence also production) conditions, approximately in that same period Robič (1988) divided all of Slovenian territory into two types of farming areas: lowland areas and areas with limited factors for farming. It turned out that as much as 80.6% of farmland is located in areas with limited natural con-ditions for farming.[2]

In 2004, when Slovenian agriculture was dealing with the conditions described above, Slovenia became a full member of the EU and hence also part of the

EU common agricultural policy. Opportunities for securing EU budget funds to improve its agricultural conditions, including the transfer of family farms to the following generation, opened up to Slovenia. The incentives connected with this were included in the 2004–2006 Rural Development Program of the Republic of Slovenia, a development document drawn up in accordance with the Accession Treaty and the relevant Council and Commission Regulations. One of the program measures included under its second priority (i.e., Economic and Social Restructuring of Agriculture) was also the "early retirement" measure. Its goal was to improve the unfavorable age (and educational) structure of farm owners and provide an income (annuity) to elderly farmers that decided to stop farming and hand down their farms to younger transferees. Annuity beneficiaries included older transferors of farms across all of Slovenia that had to meet the following conditions:

- They had to be older than 45 and younger than 61 (women) or 63 (men).
- They had to own at least 3 ha of comparable farmland.[3]
- They had to have worked the farm they wanted to transfer for at least the past 10 years.
- They had to have had retirement and disability insurance coverage as farmers or members of a farmer's family for at least the past 5 years.
- They were not allowed to retire under the national retirement scheme.

The farm transferees had to meet the following conditions:

- They had to be at least 18 and no more than 50 years old as of the day of the transfer.
- They had to agree to work the farm transferred to them for at least 10 years, using good farming practices.
- They had to have adequate farming qualifications (at least 5 years of farming experience or they had to have completed at least 3 years of secondary education in farming or another relevant field, or have at least 3 years of farming experience and have completed additional training in farming).

This measure also stipulated that farm transferors receive an annuity for 10 years, paid out to them in equal monthly installments. The annuity included a fixed part (€4,121) at the annual level and a variable part. The variable part depended on the size of the land transferred and amounted to €358 per hectare of comparable farmland a year, but only up to a maximum of 24 ha.

As laid down in the program, "such support should facilitate structural and organizational changes on farms" (Ministry of Agriculture, Forestry, and Food 2003, 164), and in addition to having a social impact, this was also intended to improve the farms' economic status. Specifically, the annuity paid to the transferors would provide an adequate standard of living and by changing the ownership structure, the farms would be taken over by younger farmers that Harmel et al. (2008, 142) believed were "considerably more flexible in introducing new and additional forms of farming, securing funds, and introducing supplementary activities." The authors further argued that

> in the long run only those promising agricultural holdings will be retained that will be able to survive on the common EU market with the help of the common agricultural policy. It is therefore even more important to ensure the takeover of farms that prove promising.

Initially, €12.7 million were envisaged for this measure out of the €312.6 million of total funds envisaged to cover all the measures within this program, but later on this figure was reduced to €7.2 million despite an increase in the total funds. In addition to this measure, from 2004 to 2006 other measures were also made available to improve economic efficiency, increase the competitiveness of family farms, and consequently promote farm transfer and takeover, such as measures aimed at investment in agricultural holdings, improving the processing and marketing of agricultural products, diversifying agricultural activities and activities related to agriculture, marketing high-quality agricultural and food products, and so on. These measures were part of the 2004–2006 Single Programing Document—that is, an agreement on securing funding from EU structural funds that Slovenia concluded with the European Commission (cf. Government of the Republic of Slovenia 2003). However, it should be noted that the measures within this document were intended for the entire farming population, whereas the early retirement measure was targeted specifically at elderly farm owners and their successors.

In addition to the EU common agricultural policy measures, from 2004 to 2006 Slovenia also carried out its own national rural development policy measures. These are not the topic of this study, but nonetheless, one should be presented here in greater detail: the one-off financial support for young farmers that was part of the support programs for restructuring and reforming agricultural production, and very similar to the concurrent common EU agricultural policy measure regarding the allocation of setting-up aid to facilitate the establishment of young farmers detailed in the EU Official Journal (1999). The purpose of the national measure was to improve the age structure and social status of farms. The financial aid beneficiaries were young farm owners under the age of 40 who were taking over a farm for the first time, and possessed adequate farming qualifications and experience. They had to use at least 5 ha of comparable farmland, of which they had to own at least 3 ha, and had to agree to pursue their farming activity at the farm for at least 5 years after receiving the financial aid. The farm had to be entered in the register of agriculture holdings and had to demonstrate economic viability at the time the application for the financial aid was submitted, which means it had to generate an annual income equivalent to at least the minimum Slovenian gross annual salary from the agricultural and forestry activity performed at the farm. Beneficiaries were able to obtain grants for partially covering the costs of the farm takeover. Justifiable costs included notary fees, legal expenses, the costs of preparing documentation, the payout of hereditary shares, and certified appraiser fees. For example, in 2006 the Slovenian Official Gazette stipulated that the highest amount of financial support for young farmers setting up farms was €16,274 per beneficiary (Uradni list Republike Slovenije 2006). It was allocated based on the collected points and criteria specified in the call for applications, taking into account the developmental, regional, and social aspects of agricultural holdings, and the marketing or economic elements and the environmental aspect of agricultural production (Volk et al. 2005, 2006, 2007).

At the end of the 2004–2006 period, the Slovenian Ministry for Agriculture, Forestry, and Food commissioned the study "Naknadno ex-post vrednotenje programa razvoja podeželja za Republiko Slovenijo" (Ex-Post Evaluation of the 2004–2006 Rural Development Program of the Republic of Slovenia; cf. Harmel et al. 2008) to evaluate the efficiency and effectiveness of the 2004–2006 Rural Development Program of the Republic of Slovenia and examine its long-term impacts on agriculture and society as a whole. The study's findings regarding the effectiveness of meeting the goals of the early retirement measure, and regarding its efficiency and impacts, are summarized on pages 299–302. In this study, effectiveness was determined based on the monitoring and control indicators defined in the program, and the data for determining the efficiency and impacts were obtained from various reports and by surveying the funds' recipients. These study findings are also tied in with some other insights that follow.

As part of the early retirement measure, the program envisaged 780 applications from beneficiaries during the 2004–2006 period. It was expected that 9,200 ha of comparable farmland would be transferred from elderly farm owners to younger transferees. The program evaluation study showed that the realization of the contracts concluded for transferring the ownership from elderly to younger farmers was 48.1% on average, with only 375 contracts concluded in total. Realization was the highest during the first year the measure was implemented (i.e., 92.5%), with 185 of the envisaged 200 contracts being concluded. During the second year, it decreased by nearly half to 45.5% (107 of the envisaged 235 contracts concluded); and in 2006 it decreased by a further half, down to 24.1% (with only 83 contracts concluded out of the 345 envisaged). The average share of comparable farmland transferred stood at 40.6% for all 3 years, with similar annual fluctuation as in the realization of the contracts concluded. In all 3 years, a total of 3,739.5 ha of comparable farmland were transferred to younger farmers. It can be concluded that the effectiveness of carrying out the measure was lower than expected. Despite the low realization of the transfer of farm ownership from elderly owners to younger farmers, the payment of funds as part of this measure reached 90.2%, with €6.5 million out of the envisaged €7.2 million being paid out.

One of the priorities of the early retirement measure was to improve the unfavorable age structure of Slovenian farm owners. In this regard, the survey conducted as part of the program evaluation study showed that the average age of transferees when submitting their applications was 34 and the average age of transferors was 59. The average age difference between the transferor and the transferee was thus 25 years. The majority (56%) of the transferees surveyed were between 30 and 39 years old, and there was also a significant share of transferees less than 30 (28%). The remaining 16% were between 40 and 50 years old. Nonetheless, this measure had no broader impact on improving the age structure of farm owners in Slovenia. According to the Statistical Office of the Republic of Slovenia (2007), at the end of the program period the share of farm owners over age 55 was even 2.1 percentage points higher than during the 2000 census and amounted to 58.4%. In contrast, the share of owners less than 45 years old decreased by 3.5 percentage points to 16.9%. Hence, the share of elderly farm owners was a full 8.7 percentage points higher than the EU average (not taking into account Romania and Bulgaria, which only joined the EU in 2007). There were only 4% of farm owners younger than 35 years old, which meant Slovenia was among countries with the lowest share of young farm owners (European Commission 2007).

The program evaluation study also provided the answer to the question of whether the annuity offered was sufficient to encourage farm owners to stop farming, hand their farms over to their successors, and use the annuity to secure a suitable living standard for themselves. Based on various data it was established that in 2006 the average monthly annuity installment paid out under the measure discussed amounted to €727.31, whereas the average farmers' old-age pension amounted to €428.5. This shows that the measure should have had a stimulating effect. However, because the amount of annuity was determined primarily based on the quantity of farmland transferred, the information on the farm owner's average annuity and average old-age pension per hectare of the average farmland transferred (in the case of the annuity) and per hectare of the average farm size (in the case of the pension) is more valid. The study shows that the annuity amounted to €72.7 a month and the old-age pension amounted to €66.9. From this perspective, the difference between the annuity and pension are no longer significant enough for this measure to be perceived as stimulating. The survey results also show that 32% of the annuity recipients surveyed believed that the annuity under the early retirement measure was insufficient to cover the costs of those who decided to transfer their farms to their successors. Moreover, even those reporting that the annuity covered the farm transferor's costs added that it covered only the costs of the farm transfer and nothing else.

The implementation of the early retirement measure was also supposed to improve the economic viability of agricultural holdings and increase their competitiveness. According to the study described above, as many as 72% of farms with more than 10 ha of utilized farmland were involved in the early retirement measure, which means that these farms were larger than the average size of Slovenian farms determined at the end of the program period, which equaled 6.5 ha of utilized farmland or 6.1 ha in the case of family farms. Hence, the average size was also somewhat larger than the one established in the 2000 census, which was primarily the result of a 12.9% decrease in the number of (mostly small) farms. On the other hand, during this period the share of farms with over 10 ha of utilized farmland increased from 12.7% to 15.6% or nearly by 3 percentage points; exactly the same increase was determined with regard to the share of farms owning up to 5 ha of utilized farmland (Statistical Office of the Republic of Slovenia 2007). All of this confirms that farm takeovers under the early retirement measure indeed took place on promising farms, which was also this measure's primary goal. A positive impact of this measure is also reflected in the fact that 44% of the transferred farms included in the survey reported a higher income after the transfer; specifically, the majority of them increased their income by approximately 10%. On some farms the impact of farm transfer was even greater, with an up to 50% increase in income. The majority of respondents from farms with a reported increase in income also reported that they improved the established farming practices after the transfer, especially by renting additional land, and modernizing the farm machinery and equipment. However, it should be noted that the same share of respondents (44%) reported no change in the farm's income after its transfer to a younger farmer and 12% even reported a decrease in income.

The goal of improving the economic viability and competitiveness of farms is indirectly connected with the farm owners' age structure. Younger farm owners are largely better educated and usually

> better qualified to work in agriculture, are more entrepreneurial, and can therefore adapt more effectively to the technological changes and conditions on the market, which is a precondition for increasing work productivity and consequently the competitiveness of agriculture and preserving it. (Ministry of Agriculture, Forestry, and Food 2007, 23)

The 2007 statistical data on the farm owners' general education show that the farm owners' educational structure improved compared to 2000, which had a stimulating effect on achieving the goal discussed. The share of farm owners who had or had not completed primary education or even had no education decreased by 8 percentage points during this period. This means that even if the farms were taken over by farmers who were not young, their general educational level was still higher than that of their predecessors: the share of those who had completed vocational or secondary school was 6.2 percentage points higher, and the share of those with a college, university or any other form of a higher education degree was 1.4 percentage points higher. Nonetheless, it should be noted that in 2007 the general educational level of more than half (50.4%) of farm owners was still low (cf. Statistical Office of the Republic of Slovenia 2007). The data on agricultural education are somewhat more encouraging. During the 2000 census, as many as 83.9% farm owners had only practical farming experience, but by 2007 this percentage decreased to 65.3%, mainly due to various agricultural training courses taken during this period. Thus for example, during the 2000 census only 8.2% of farm owners reported having taken an agricultural course, whereas by 2007 this share had already increased to 27.1%. Such an increase is not connected with the early retirement measure, but with the implementation of other measures under the common (and national) agricultural policy, as part of which farm owners had to acquire adequate agricultural expertise and skills at training courses in order to be able to apply for funds in public tenders or (continue) to perform certain activities.

Due to the participation of farms in various measures, one needs to be extra cautious in analyzing the effectiveness and efficiency of the early retirement measure. The related evaluation study shows that half the farms involved in the early retirement measure also acquired funds from other financial support schemes envisaged by the rural development program for the period studied. For example, because nearly all farms (98.7%) that obtained funds for their transfer to younger owners were located in areas with limited farming factors, more than three-quarters (77.6%) were also involved in the measure providing assistance to farms in areas with limited farming factors, and a large portion also secured funds from the national agricultural policy for rural development, especially the one-off financial support for young farmers. However, the evaluation study did not analyze the synergistic effects between these measures, nor did it separately analyze the effectiveness and efficiency of the measure providing the one-off financial support to young farmers, as part of which €6.1 million was paid out between 2004 and 2006 (Volk et al. 2005, 2006, 2007); namely, this measure was not included in the common agricultural policy rural development program evaluated by this study.

In early 2007, when the 2004–2006 Rural Development Program of the Republic of Slovenia had concluded and Slovenian agriculture was in the state described above, Slovenia and other EU member states entered a new program period. A new program document concluded between Slovenia and the European Commission titled the 2007–2013 Rural Development Program of the Republic of Slovenia entered into force and provided the program basis for securing funding from the European Agricultural Fund for Rural Development. Nearly €1.2 billion were envisaged for its implementation. It contained four priority axes that included various agricultural structural policy and rural development policy measures. In terms of promoting the transfer of farm ownership from elderly to younger owners and encouraging young people to take over farms, the first priority axis is relevant because it was intended to improve the competitiveness of agriculture and forestry. Two measures were implemented as part of this priority axis: measures 112 and 113. Measure 112 offered assistance to young farmers in farm takeovers, which had been carried out as a national measure during the 2004–2006 period, and measure 113 was the early retirement measure for farmers, which was also supported through the common agricultural policy funds in the previous period. The funds allocated for the implementation of measures 112 and 113 totaled €35.2 million and nearly €38.1 million, respectively (Ministry of Agriculture, Forestry, and Food 2007).

The goal of providing assistance to young farmers taking over farms (measure 112) was to promote the transfer of farms to younger generations and thus improve the age structure of farm owners, facilitate farm takeover and structural adaptations after the takeover, increase the developmental capacity of the transferred farms, and thus contribute to increased work productivity in agriculture. The assistance to young farmers in taking over farms was carried out in the form of a one-off financial support to facilitate the takeover and the farm's structural adaptations after it. As specified in the program,

> young people often decide against taking over a farm, even though they have the opportunity to do so, because takeover is connected with the problem of paying off other heirs and securing start-up capital for the farm's structural adaptations after the takeover. (Ministry of Agriculture, Forestry, and Food 2007, 100)

The amount of the financial support was determined based on the number of points collected in the assessment of the applications submitted and amounted to a maximum of €70,000 per beneficiary (at the end of the program period). In scoring the market and economic elements of production, the developmental, regional, social, and environmental aspects of the farms and the costs of farm transfer were taken into account. The measure further required that young transferees enclose a business plan with their applications, outlining the development of agricultural activity at the agricultural holding being transferred. This way they could also apply for support under the measure for modernizing agricultural holdings for planned investment on farms (and at the beginning of the program period also under the measure for providing training for jobs in agriculture, forestry, and food industry). In addition to the business plan, other requirements had to be fulfilled in order to acquire funds under measure 112:

- The farm had to be economically viable and manage at least 3 ha of comparable farmland.
- The young transferee had to be older than 18 and younger than 40 years old, and was allowed to take over the ownership of a farm for the first time, whereby he had to take over the entire holding.
- The young transferee had to possess adequate professional expertise and skills (at least completed primary school with a minimum of 5 years of farming experience and a national vocational qualification in farming or a farming-related activity, or at least completed vocational secondary school in a farming or farming-related program and at least 3 years of farming experience). If the young farmer failed to meet the relevant professional expertise and skill requirements when submitting his application, he had to agree to fulfill these requirements within 36 months of the issue of the decision on the allocation of funds at the latest.
- The young transferee had to remain the head and owner of the agricultural holding for at least 5 years after receiving the funds under this measure, and maintain the farmland in the size reported in the application.
- The young transferee had to start monitoring the farm's operating results 1 year after receiving the funds at the latest and had to report them for at least 5 years after the funds had been paid out.

- The measure envisaged that an audit be carried out at the farm no later than 5 years since the issue of the decision on the allocation of funds; should the transferee have failed to meet the goals set up in the business plan, he was required to return all of the funds received under this measure.

The goal of providing assistance to farmers to retire early (measure 113) was the same as that of measure 112: to improve the age structure of farm owners, facilitate structural changes at agricultural holdings, and increase the developmental capacity of the transferred farms, thereby contributing to increased work productivity in agriculture. In substantiating this goal, the program provided that

> delaying the transfer of the holding to a younger generation indirectly reduces the farm's developmental orientation and impedes the process of concentration and consolidation of agriculture. The promotion of early retirement of elderly farmers and the transfer of farms to younger owners indirectly creates new jobs on farms. (Ministry of Agriculture, Forestry, and Food 2007, 103)

Early retirement support was provided (the same way as during the previous program period) in the form of annuities paid out to elderly farm owners that decided to stop performing gainful agricultural activity on their farms and transfer these to a younger and more active generation or the head of another farm that planned to increase his or her holding through the takeover. The program specified that the annuity be paid in monthly installments for a maximum of 10 years and until the transferor reached the maximum age of 70 years; after the transferor's retirement, the annuity was to be reduced to the amount of pension received. The annuity included a fixed part of €5,000 per farm a year and a variable part that depended on the size of the transferred farm. The variable part was calculated based on the data on the size and utilization of farmland. For every hectare of comparable farmland transferred €300 a year were envisaged to be paid out, but only for a maximum of 20 ha of comparable farmland. If the transferred farm was larger than that, all of the farmland had to be transferred, but the annuity did not increase in this case. The total amount of annuity paid out throughout its payment period was not allowed to exceed €110,000 per transferor. The requirements for obtaining funds under measure 113 were similar to those in the previous program period, with certain adjustments:

- The agricultural holding had to manage at least 5 ha of comparable farmland (in contrast to the 3 ha required in the previous program period).
- The transferor had to be older than 57 years (55 in the previous program period).
- The transferor had to have had farming retirement and disability insurance coverage for at least the past 7 years (5 years in the previous program period).

- The farm transferee had to be over age 18, with no maximum allowed age defined (as opposed to the previous program period).
- In the case of 3 years of farming experience, the transferee was required to have completed at least a vocational secondary school in a farming or farming-related program (in the previous program period, additional agricultural training sufficed in this case).

In addition to measures 112 and 113, other measures were also available during the 2007–2013 period for improving the economic viability and increasing the competitiveness of family farms, and thereby promoting farm transfer and takeover: for example, measure 121 (modernizing agricultural holdings), already mentioned above; measure 123 (adding value to agricultural and forestry products), for which the majority of funds were allocated as part of the first priority axis; measure 311 (diversification into non-agricultural activities); and measure 111 (providing training for jobs in agriculture, forestry, and food industry), also already mentioned above, whose goal was to support training and the provision of information (acquiring new expertise, skills, and information through seminars, workshops, talks, practical field demonstrations, modules or obtaining a national vocational qualification certificate), and consequently increase the work productivity and innovation in agriculture. If farms participated in several measures that complemented one another, the program even provided certain benefits. Thus, for example, a farm that obtained funds under measure 112 was also entitled to receive a higher co-funding share under measure 121 if it decided to also participate in this measure, as well as to a larger number of points in the case of participating in measure 311. On the other hand, those applying for funds under measure 123 received a larger number of points if they were younger than 40 years old (which was the maximum age for a transferee allowed under measure 112). More points in applying for funds under measure 112 were also given to farms located in areas with limited farming factors, whereby farms receiving funds under measure 112 that were located in areas with limited farming factors could also apply for funds under other relevant measures (e.g., as part of measures 211 and 212 with funds earmarked for compensatory allowances for farms with limited farming conditions).

Even though the program period concluded in 2013, at the time of writing this chapter (in August 2016) a study on the ex-post evaluation of the 2007–2013 Rural Development Program of the Republic of Slovenia has not been prepared yet. Therefore, data from the annual program implementation reports, the ongoing program evaluation reports, and available statistical data were used to determine the effectiveness of achieving the goals of measures 112 and 113, and their efficiency and impacts. One of the more important features of program implementation noted during the evaluation was that, due to the changed needs for funds under individual measures during the program period, multiple changes occurred in the distribution of funds by individual axes and measures, including measures 112 and 113. By the end of the program period, funds for measure 112 increased by approximately €20.4 million (from €35.2 to €55.6 million), whereas funds for measure 113 decreased by nearly the same amount (from envisaged €38.2 million to €17.9 million; Ministry of Agriculture, Forestry, and Food 2007, 2015b). The preliminary program evaluation (cf. Ministry of Agriculture, Forestry, and Food 2006) already drew attention to certain deficiencies of measure 113 and advantages of measure 112. Regarding measure 113 (which was only at the stage of proposal at that time) the evaluators explained that it was justified, considering the structural problems Slovenian agriculture was dealing with, but that it had been fairly poorly formulated. They expressed concern over its potentially insufficient effectiveness and efficiency. "To make this measure more effective, it should be extended to a significantly larger number of beneficiaries. The measure's efficiency is further reduced by the additional tax imposed on the funds received and this should be decreased or abolished" (Ministry of Agriculture, Forestry, and Food 2006, A12). One of the options proposed to improve the measure's efficiency was to increase the funds allocated and another, more radical option was to cancel the measure and transfer the funds envisaged for it to measure 112. Upon its entry into force, the program partly took into account this recommendation. As explained in the program, this measure was not cancelled because it was considered appropriate for implementation, considering the experience and response from the previous program period. However, the measure was thoroughly reshaped based on the pre-liminary evaluation recommendations and as such incorporated into the officially approved program. On the other hand, the preliminary evaluators suggested that the option of increasing the funds allocated to measure 112 be examined in order to increase its efficiency. Predictions that this measure would be well received by potential fund beneficiaries proved to be correct already during the first year of program implementation. According to Volk et al. (2008), the first call for allocating funds under this measure met with such a wide response that it was closed even before the end of 2007 because the envisaged number of applications had already been reached. This bit of information is even more surprising (and positive) con-sidering that the envisaged amount of support for farm takeovers as part of this first call—that is, at the beginning of the program period and before the changes or the introduction of increased funds for this measure—was significantly lower than later on, amounting to a maximum of €40,000.

However, the implementation of measure 112 was not effective and efficient only at the beginning of the program period, but throughout its duration. This was also confirmed by Bedrač et al. (2015) during the most recent regular program evalu-ation. They established that measures for which the funding from the European Agricultural Fund for Rural Development was used up to the best possible extent and that were extremely well evaluated during the regular program evaluations had the greatest impact on strategic goals. These measures also included measure 112 and the related measures 121 and 123 mentioned above. According to the authors, all three had significant synergistic effects and contributed extremely positively to the increased competitive capacity of the agriculture and food industry. With its young transferees, measure 112 in particular contributed to an improved agrarian structure (i.e., overall living and production conditions in agriculture). Measure 113 had a smaller impact on meeting the strategic goals; according to Bedrač et al. (2015), it even partly duplicated measure 112. Even though there were some differences between the two measures regarding the requirements for obtaining the funds (such as the maximum allowed age of the transferee under measure 112 and the minimum allowed age of the transferor under measure 113), according to the authors, 92% of farms involved in the early retirement measure simultaneously carried out the transfer to young transferees under measure 112. On the other hand, only 7% of farms that obtained funds for implementing measure 113 also secured funds from measure 112 (Ministry of Agriculture, Forestry, and Food 2015a). This is additionally confirmed by the finding that Slovenian farmers did not receive measure 113 as well as measure 112.

The effectiveness and efficiency of implementing measure 112 are reflected not only in the increased funds for this measure during the program period, but also in the number of young transferees receiving the funds, the number of farm takeovers carried out, and the total area of farmland transferred to young farmers. The program envisaged that 1,700 young transferees would receive the one-off financial support under measure 112 over the entire program period, but the data show (cf. Ministry of Agriculture, Forestry, and Food 2015a) that this figure was exceeded by a full 133.2%, with 2,656 applicants being granted support in seven calls for applications. Taking into account that at the beginning of the program period (i.e., before the changes), the program envisaged that support would be provided to 1,200 young farmers, the realization rate was even higher than that: the planned figure was exceeded by 221.3%. The percentage of accepted applications was also high (88%). A total of 3,015 individuals applied for financial support to young transferees as part of all seven calls and only 359 were rejected. This means that the applicants were well prepared for the calls and wanted to take over the farms. Every young transferee whose application for funds under measure 112 was accepted received an average of €20,971 of one-off financial support. A total of 64,642 ha of all land (agricultural and forest areas) were transferred, corresponding to an average of 24.4 ha per farm, and 36,671 ha of utilized farmland, corresponding to an average of 13.8 ha per farm. This means that the farms that young individuals decided to take over were larger and even more promising than the farms that elderly farm owners had transferred to young successors under the early retirement measure during the previous program period. In this regard, the age structure of young transferees was also more favorable, with their average age being 33. The measure also justified its purpose in terms of improving the age structure of the heads of agricultural holdings. Specifically, the data show that the share of young transferees that had completed only primary education was significantly lower compared to the owners of the farms they had taken over, and the share of those with higher education (a college or university degree) was considerably higher. The majority of transferees (34%) had completed secondary school and more than two-thirds had at least a vocational or secondary education. Bedrač et al. (2015) further determined that their applications in the calls for securing funds under measure 112 were generally more successful, which is also indicated by the share of accepted applications among those submitted.

Based on the features of implementing measure 112 described above, Bedrač et al. (2015) also provided a general assessment of its effectiveness and efficiency. Because the values of the measure's effectiveness indicators were strongly surpassed in nearly all the cases, they assessed it as highly effective. They ascribed this to the fact that it had been carried out continually throughout the program period, the calls for applying for funds under this measure were clear and comprehensible and included precisely specified requirements and scoring criteria, and that the measure was compatible with other measures or program goals. For example, the latter is confirmed by the fact that at the end of the program period, as many as 33% of recipients of funds under measure 121 were young farm transferees, whereby they were entitled to a 10% higher share of financial support. The effectiveness of measure 112 (thanks to its compatibility with other measures) is also proven by the fact that as many as 77% of farms participating in measure 112 also received financial support for farms in areas with limited farming conditions (Ministry of Agriculture, Forestry, and Food 2015a). Considering that under measure 112 on average fewer funds were used up per transferee than planned, Bedrač et al. (2015) reported that the measure was not only effective, but also demonstrated above-average efficiency. The average amount of the one-off financial support paid out to young transferees in Slovenia was even 25% lower than in other EU member states. The authors therefore argued that the measure might have not been set up ambitiously enough. According to them, it would make sense to continue to implement it during the 2014–2020 program period.

Bedrač et al. (2015) did not share the same opinion regarding the effectiveness and efficiency of measure 113. They believed this measure was less efficient and therefore they did not recommend its implementation during the 2014–2020 period. There were no problems with its implementation in the 2007–2013 period, but it presented a great "financial burden because long-term liabilities had to be adopted due to the nature of its implementation" (Ministry of Agriculture, Forestry, and Food 2015a, 33). Based on the financial liabilities adopted in the previous program period, funds for 375 farm owners that had entered the early retirement scheme in the 2004–2006 period thus continued to be paid out throughout the 2007–2014 period. Hence, the funds earmarked for the implementation of measure 113 during the 2007–2013 program period also included these payments. During the 2007–2013 program period, four public calls for applications were issued for the early retirement measure and they were responded to by 216 elderly farm owners who wanted to retire; transfer their farms to a new, younger owner; and join the annuity payment system. Among the applications submitted, 201 were accepted, which represented a 95.7% realization of the program plan (with 210 early retirements envisaged). The average 10-year annuity approved amounted to €87,283 (cf. Ministry of Agriculture, Forestry, and Food 2015a), which represented nearly €18 million new financial liabilities over the period of 10 years. The majority of transferors were between 55 and 64 years old (59 on average) and a total of 2,511 ha of comparable farmland or an average of 12.5 ha per accepted application were transferred. Even though the average size of the transferred farmland was larger than in the previous program period and the anticipated transfer rate was 143.4% (the program envisaged the transfer of 1,751 ha of comparable farmland), according to Bedrač et al. (2015), the level of efficiency (viewed from the perspective of the funds approved per application and the farmland transferred) nonetheless shows that Slovenia lagged behind the EU average. The average 10-year annuity approved in the EU amounted to €70,000 (approximately 20% lower than in Slovenia) and the average size of the farmland transferred was larger (i.e., 16 ha). The authors also concluded that due to a small number of transfers the impact of this measure on other measures within the first priority axis was very limited, as was its influence on individual goals of the overall program. Its poorer effectiveness was also the result of considerable limitations included in the measure, which had a negative impact on its implementation and achieving the goals set:

> The fairly high threshold of the size of agricultural holdings under the measure (5 ha) often meant that not as many potential transferors decided to participate in the measure as could have. In addition, paying retirement and disability insurance contributions was another factor that made farm owners decide against early retirement. Returning funds in some cases and the loss of other social transfers were further factors that had a negative impact on the implementation and achievement of the goals set." (Bedrač et al. 2015, 31)

Despite everything, the authors added that "to a certain extent this measure nonetheless facilitated intergenerational farm takeovers and was thus effective in pursuing the goals of improving the age and educational structure of the heads of Slovenian agricultural holdings."

The effectiveness and efficiency of implementing measures 112 and 113 (and other related measures) during the 2007–2013 program period, and their impact on improving the age and educational structure of Slovenian farm owners, are also confirmed by statistical data. According to Eurostat (cf. European Commission 2013), the share of elderly farm owners began to decrease and the share of younger owners began to increase. The share of elderly farm owners in Slovenia was still high at the end of the program period, but the important point is that it started to decrease, which had a stimulating effect. This trend already began to show after the first 3 years of the program period and continued until its end. In 2010, the share of farm owners over 55 years old decreased by 1.8 percentage points compared to 2007 and amounted to 56.6%, and by 2013 it fell by further 2.2 percentage points to 54.4%, which was 0.5 percentage point lower than the EU average and 1.9 percentage points lower than in 2000 (i.e., before Slovenia's entry into the EU). On the other hand, the share of farm owners below age 45 was 18.3% in 2010 or 1.4 percentage points lower than in 2007; the share in 2013 was 19.1%. The increase in the share of farm owners younger than 35 was also encouraging, increasing by 0.8 percentage points over the entire program period. Nonetheless, at the end of the program period the share of young Slovenian farm owners was still under the EU average, but the difference to this average decreased compared to 2007: it fell from 5.0 to 1.9 percentage points among farm owners below age 45, and from 2.3 to 1.1 percentage points among farm owners below age 35. Encouraging data regarding the decreasing age of Slovenia farm owners were also revealed by the 2010 Slovenian agricultural census: the share of farms with a designated successor was 44.4%, which represented an exceptional increase over the 23% established during the 2000 census. In addition to the age structure, farm transfers to younger owners also improved the educational structure of farm owners, continuing the trend from the previous program period. During the 2007–2013 program period, the share of farm owners who had or had not completed primary education or had no education fell from 50.4% to 31.7%, and the share of those who had completed vocational or secondary education increased from 44.5% to 58.9%. The share of farm owners with a college or university degree also increased considerably, from 4.2 % to 9.4 % (Statistical Office of the Republic of Slovenia 2007, 2013). A positive trend continuing from the previous program period was also evident in improved agricultural qualifications of farm owners. In 2013, the share of farm owners that had only practical farming experience decreased further, by 15.2 percentage points, to 50.1%, whereas the share of those that had at least completed a training course in farming increased by 11.3 percentage points over 2007, reaching 38.3%. In 2013, 11.6% of farm owners had completed one of the forms of formal agricultural education; the share increased by 4.1 percentage points compared to the beginning of the program period. A positive trend could thus be established in terms of the age and education structure of farm owners; however, the same cannot be reported for the size structure of the farms. At the end of the program period, this was almost the same as at its beginning: the average size of farmland used by family farms was 6.2 ha or 6.6 ha if agricultural companies are also included; in both cases this means an increase of 0.1 ha. In this period, too, the number of farms decreased. In fact, it was only the number of family farms that decreased: it fell by 4%, which was considerably less than during the 2000–2007 period, when a 12.9% decrease was recorded. What is the most surprising is that the share of farms with 3–20 ha of utilized farmland decreased by 1.6%, whereas the share of small farms (with fewer than 3 ha of utilized farmland) increased by 1.3%. The share of large farms (with more than 20 ha of utilized farmland) increased by 0.6%, but some of this increase has to be ascribed to the increased number of agricultural companies: there were 201 of them or 70 more than in 2007; this was their first increase after the 2000 census and Slovenia's entry into the EU. Despite the larger number of large farms, their share continued to be modest at the end of the program period: only 4.8%.

Despite the effective and efficient implementation of measures 112 and 113 during the 2007–2013 program period and their positive impact on the age and educational structure of farm owners, the size structure of Slovenian farms certainly did not offer good prospects for Slovenia when it entered the new program period. This was also highlighted in the 2014–2020 Rural Development Program of the Republic of Slovenia, a joint program document concluded between Slovenia and the European Commission on securing funding from the European Agricultural Fund for Rural Development:

> Agriculture is dealing with a very small average size of agricultural property and great fragmentation of farmland. These two factors hinder production intensity, increase production costs, and reduce the competitiveness of agriculture compared to production in other EU member states. Slovenia is ranked among countries with the smallest average size of utilized farmland per agricultural holding in the EU. (Ministry of Agriculture, Forestry, and Food 2015c, 73)

Because the size structure of farms is closely connected with their productivity and competitiveness, and thus the young people's decision to take over farms and continue farming on them, one of the priorities that Slovenia defined in the program based on the analysis of conditions and the current state of affairs in agriculture was also "facilitating the structural adaptation process in agriculture and thus creating conditions for increasing productivity of Slovenian agriculture." Its goal was to enhance the farms' survival capacity and the competitiveness of all types of agriculture. One of the measures supporting this task was measure M06 (development of farms and companies), which had a double goal: to encourage young people to take over farms (sub-measure M06.1) and to promote the development of non-agricultural activities (sub-measure M06.4), which was "especially important for small farms ... with a low level of market orientation, ... which can generate additional sources of income through the development of non-agricultural activities and thus ensure their economic and social stability" (Ministry of Agriculture, Forestry, and Food 2015c, 266). This way the measure tried to continue the effective and efficient implementation of measure 112 from the previous program period, while also focusing on solving the issue of competitiveness connected with the small size of Slovenian farms, which was the goal of measure 311 (diversification into non-agricultural activities) during the 2007–2013 program period. At the beginning of the program period, €125.3 million (11.4% of all the program funds) were earmarked for the implementation of measure M06, of which €60.6 million were earmarked for sub-measure M06.1 (setting up support to kick-start the activities for young farmers). An additional €5.3 million of financial liabilities adopted under the early retirement measure were transferred to the 2014–2020 program period from both previous program periods (Ministry of Agriculture, Forestry, and Food 2015d). Because measure 113 was cancelled in the 2014–2020 program period, funds for further improvement of the age structure of Slovenian farm owners were allocated only under sub-measure M06.1. These funds were planned to support the farm takeovers by young farmers on 3.5% of Slovenian farms throughout the program period. Funds for continuing the trend of improving the educational structure of farm owners were earmarked under measure M01 (transfer of knowledge and information activities); more specifically, €12.5 million were planned to help young transferees acquire new expertise and skills through targeted professional training in order to be able to perform activities on farms. Similar to the previous program, the 2014–2020 rural development program also substantiated allocating funds to improve the age and educational structure of farm owners with findings that this was

> [a]n important developmental need of Slovenian agriculture … younger heads of agricultural holdings are better educated on average, they introduce innovations more quickly, are more entrepreneurial, adapt more quickly to conditions on the market, and are usually also more motivated to acquire additional expertise, introduce improvements and innovations … The structural adaptation processes in Slovenian agriculture will thus be faster if they coincide with the processes of generational rejuvenation on farms and improved qualifications of young owners. The decision to kick-start this activity [taking over the ownership of a farm] is not simple because it is connected with economic risk. Young people also find it more difficult to access the funds required for purchasing farmland, machinery, and equipment, and establishing or expanding the production capacities. The support for kick-starting and developing young farmers' farms under measure M06 can make the first years of setting up a farm easier, thereby encouraging young people to decide to continue farming and find employment in agriculture. Measure M01 can help young farmers improve their qualifications for performing their activity. (Ministry of Agriculture, Forestry, and Food 2015c, 74, 108)

The requirements for obtaining funds from sub-measure M06.1 were similar to those in the previous program period, but with some adjustments, such as the following:

- The required educational level was raised: the planned young transferees had to have at least a lower vocational qualification (completion of primary school thus no longer sufficed); if they had a vocational qualification in a non-agricultural program, they were required (the same as in the previous period) to also have a national vocational qualification certificate in farming (although this time at least SQF level 4).
- The farm had to operate at least 6 ha of comparable farmland (compared to 3 ha in the previous program period) and its maximum size was set at 80 ha of comparable farmland.

The amount of financial support also changed: it decreased to a maximum of €45,000 per young transferee entitled to this support, whereby he or she had to be a full-time employee at the farm or had agreed upon submitting the application to get employed within 9 months after the date of issue of the decision granting him or her the right to receive the relevant funds. For all other beneficiaries the amount of the financial support was lower: they could receive a maximum of €18,600. In contrast to the previous program period, the financial support was paid out in two installments; the first installment (70% of the funds allocated) was paid out upon the issue of the decision granting the right to receive the funds or after the beneficiary got employed on the farm, and the second installment (up to 30% of the funds allocated) was paid out after the proper implementation of activities specified in the business plan that the young beneficiary had to submit together with the application for obtaining funds under this sub-measure.

Similar to the previous program period, beneficiaries of the funds under sub-measure M06.1 were also able to obtain financial support from other measures (for example, allowances for farming in areas with natural or other special limitations available under measure M13, or financial support for investments in fixed assets included in measure M04). Because at the time of writing this chapter (August 2016) this program period has not concluded yet, the results of the first regular program evaluation have not been published yet, and no more recent official statistical data than those presented have been made available, an evaluation of the effectiveness and efficiency of sub-measure M06 cannot be provided. Hopefully, the positive impacts of implementing common agricultural policy measures on promoting farm takeovers and thus on improving the age and educational structure of Slovenian farm owners will also be evident at the end of the 2014–2020 program period. It is also to be hoped that these measures for improving the size structure of Slovenian farms will be more effective than in the past because this could have an even stronger stimulating effect on potential successors, encouraging them to decide to take over farms in (even) larger numbers.

The EU common agricultural policy measures for promoting the takeover of farms and their timely transfer to young successors have thus proven effective and efficient in Slovenia. However, as highlighted by Kerbler (2012), financial support for young transferees is only the "last stage" in the available incentives aimed at increasing the number of takeovers and transfers of (Slovenian) farms. It is only important when a successor has already been provided for and already appointed at a farm, and when this successor decides with certainty to take over the farm and continue to farm after the takeover, or when the farm owner decides to hand over the farm to a successor in a timely fashion. However, these decisions must have first taken place on a farm at all. In order to meet this condition, important steps must already be taken far in advance; specifically, farm succession must be part of a long-term planning process. In the future, promoting farm succession planning could constitute a new common agricultural policy measure, which would definitely facilitate the number of takeovers of (Slovenian) farms and their timely transfer to successors.

Notes

1 Utilized farmland is farmland that agricultural holdings use for farm production. It is divided into:
  • Tilled fields and gardens;
  • Orchards;
  • Vineyards;
  • Meadows and pastures.

2 Later calculations showed that this share was even a few percent higher.
3 1 ha of comparable farmland corresponds to:
- 1 ha of tilled fields or gardens; or
- 2 ha of meadows or extensively managed orchards; or
- 4 ha of pastures, or
- 0.25 ha of intensively managed (plantation) orchards, vineyards, or hop yards; or
- 8 ha of forest; or
- 5 ha of forest plantations; or
- 6 ha of swampy meadows or other areas.

References

Barbič, Ana. 1993. "(Samo)obnavljanje kmečkega sloja v Sloveniji." *Sodobno kmetijstvo* 26(6): 258–266.

Bedrač, Matej, Tomaž Cunder, Klemen Koman, Damjan Kavaš, and Renata Slabe Erker. 2015. *Izdelava sprotnega vrednotenja programa razvoja podeželja 2007–2013 v letu 2014.* Ljubljana: Agricultural Institute of Slovenia.

Bojnec, Štefan. 2002. "Aktualna vprašanja kmetijske politike." *Sodobno kmetijstvo* 25(9), 357–361.

Cunder, Tomaž. 1997. "Naravne danosti in socio-ekonomska struktura." In *Slovensko kmetijstvo in Evropska unija*, edited by Erjavec, Emil, Mirolav Rednak, and Tina Volk, 143–155. Ljubljana: ČZD Kmečki glas.

Dernulc, Simona, Uršula Iljaš Petrovič, Barbara Kutin Slatnar, Irena Orešnik, Tomaž Cunder, Mojca Golež, and Luka Juvančič. 2002. *Agricultural Census, Slovenia, 2000.* Ljubljana: Statistical Office of the Republic of Slovenia.

European Commission. 2007. *Eurostat: Agriculture – Key Farm Variables.* Luxembourg: European Commission.

———. 2013. *Eurostat: Agriculture – Key Farm Variables.* Luxembourg: European Commission.

Gams, Ivan. 1983. "Hribovske kmetije Slovenjegraškega Pohorja." *Geografski zbornik* 23: 141–199.

Gasson, Ruth, and Andrew Errington. 1993. *The Farm Family Business.* Wallingford: CAB International.

Government of the Republic of Slovenia. 2003. *Enotni programski dokument.* Ljubljana: Government Office for Structural Policy and Regional Development.

Harmel, Matjaž, Jurij Kobal, Mojca Hrabar, Pia Primec, Simona Knežević Vernon, Andrej Stres, and Jerneja Kovačič. 2008. *Naknadno ex-post vrednotenje programa razvoja podeželja za Republiko Slovenijo 2004–2006.* Ljubljana: Ministry of Agriculture, Forestry and Food.

Hribernik, Franc. 1993. "Vloga izobraževanja v razvoju kmetijstva." *Sodobno kmetijstvo* 26(11): 458–462.

———. 1996. "Ali lahko kmetije v Sloveniji zagotavljajo primerno socialno varnost kmečkemu prebivalstvu?" *Socialno delo* 35(1): 15–30.

Kerbler, Boštjan. 2012. "Factors affecting farm succession: The case of Slovenia." *Agricultural Economics (Zemědělská ekonomika)* 58(6): 285–298.

Kovačič, Matija. 1996. *Socio ekonomska in velikostna struktura kmetij v Sloveniji v obdobju 1981–1991.* Ljubljana: Biotechnical Faculty, Department of Agronomy.

Laband, David N., and Bernard F. Lentz. 1983. "Occupational Inheritance in Agriculture." *American Journal of Agricultural Economics* 65(2): 311–314.

Ministry of Agriculture, Forestry, and Food. 2003. *Program razvoja podeželja za Republiko Slovenijo 2004–2006.* Ljubljana: Ministry of Agriculture, Forestry, and Food.

———. 2006. *Predhodno vrednotenje Programa razvoja podeželja Republike Slovenije za obdobje 2007–2013.* Ljubljana: Ministry of Agriculture, Forestry, and Food.

————. 2007. *Program razvoja podeželja Republike Slovenije za obdobje 2007–2013.* Ljubljana: Ministry of Agriculture, Forestry, and Food.

————. 2015a. *Poročilo o napredku v okviru Programa razvoja podeželja Republike Slovenije 2007–2013 za leto 2014.* Ljubljana: Ministry of Agriculture, Forestry, and Food.

————. 2015b. *Program razvoja podeželja Republike Slovenije za obdobje 2007–2013: 9. sprememba.* Ljubljana: Ministry of Agriculture, Forestry, and Food.

————. 2015c. *Program razvoja podeželja Republike Slovenije za obdobje 2014–2020.* Ljubljana: Ministry of Agriculture, Forestry, and Food.

————. 2015d. *Program razvoja podeželja Republike Slovenije za obdobje 2014–2020: Osnovne informacije o ukrepih.* Ljubljana: Ministry of Agriculture, Forestry, and Food.

Naglič, Miran. 1998. "Pomen kmetijstva v območjih s težjimi razmerami za pridelavo." In *Kmetijstvo in okolje,* edited by Rečnik, Metka, and Jože Verbič, 85–90. Ljubljana: Agricultural Institute of Slovenia.

Official Journal of the European Communities. 1999. *Council Regulation (EC) No. 1257/1999 of 17 May 1999 on support for rural development from the European Agricultural Guidance and Guarantee Fund (EAGGF) and amending and repealing certain Regulations.* Brussels.

Plut, Dušan. 1998. "Slovensko kmetijstvo in sonaravni regionalni razvoj." In *Kmetijstvo in okolje,* edited by Rečnik, Metka, and Jože Verbič, 29–35. Ljubljana: Agricultural Institute of Slovenia.

Robič, Tone. 1988. "Razvojni cilji kmetijsko nerazvitih območij." In *Kmetijski priročnik 1989,* edited by Savina Dreu, 28–53. Ljubljana: ČZP Kmečki glas.

Statistical Office of the Republic of Slovenia. 2007. *Okolje in naravni viri: Kmetijstvo in ribištvo.* Ljubljana: Statistical Office of the Republic of Slovenia.

————. 2013. *Okolje in naravni viri: Kmetijstvo in ribištvo.* Ljubljana: Statistical Office of the Republic of Slovenia.

Uradni list Republike Slovenije (Official Gazette of the Republic of Slovenia). 2006. *Javni razpis za dodeljevanje sredstev iz naslova pomoči mladim kmetom za prevzem kmetij v letu 2006,* no. 88. Ljubljana.

Volk, Tina, Miroslav Rednak, Tomaž Cunder, Matej Bedrač, Tine Štebe, Marjeta Pintar, Barbara Zagorc, Ben Moljk, Andrej Zemljič, and Mojca Škof. 2005. *Poročilo o stanju kmetijstva, živilstva in gozdarstva v letu 2004.* Ljubljana: Agricultural Institute of Slovenia.

————. 2006. *Poročilo o stanju kmetijstva, živilstva in gozdarstva v letu 2005.* Ljubljana: Agricultural Institute of Slovenia.

————. 2007. *Poročilo o stanju kmetijstva, živilstva in gozdarstva v letu 2006.* Ljubljana: Agricultural Institute of Slovenia.

Volk, Tina, Miroslav Rednak, Tomaž Cunder, Matej Bedrač, Marjeta Pintar, Ben Moljk, Andrej Zemljič, and Mojca Škof. 2008. *Poročilo o stanju kmetijstva, živilstva in gozdarstva v letu 2007.* Ljubljana: Agricultural Institute of Slovenia.

Volk, Tina, Miroslav Rednak, and Lojze Senegačnik. 1992. *Strategija razvoja slovenskega kmetijstva.* Ljubljana: Ministry of Agriculture, Forestry, and Food.

Vrišer, Igor. 2005. "The Size of Agricultural Holdings in Slovenia." *Geografski vestnik* 77(1): 9–25.

Chapter 17

Does the elderly farmer pension program affect the off-farm labor decisions of younger adults in family farms in Taiwan?

I-Chun Chen, Hung-Hao Chang, and Lih-Chyun Sun

Introduction

In 2005, the average age of farmers in Taiwan was 62 (Chang, 2013). Older farmers forming the structure of the agricultural sector is a phenomenon that has been observed in many of the developed East Asian countries (Biddlecom et al., 2001; Chang, 2013; Chuang, 2011; Fan, 2010a). This phenomenon provided an incentive for the government to implement old-age security schemes to ensure the economic well-being of elderly farmers. Accordingly, the Old Farmer Pension Program (OFP) was implemented in 1995 to improve the quality of life and the well-being of elderly farmers in Taiwan. Under this program, each eligible farmer (older than 65) can receive a pension payment of NTD 7,000 per month, which is equivalent to approximately USD 233.

This pension program provides lifelong income security for elderly farmers who qualify. However, the long-term operating costs of the OFP are high, and have an impact on government expenditure in other public sectors. For example, in 2008, 710,031 Taiwanese elderly farmers received an OFP allowance, costing the Taiwanese government USD 1.7 billion US (Chuang, 2011). This erosion of fiscal expenditure is expected to become progressively worse as the population of the agricultural sector is aging at a faster rate than other sectors. A further problem is that the productivity of the Taiwanese agricultural sector is decreasing. These concerns require a policy reform of the OFP program. Before any action can be taken to reform the policy, it is necessary to understand the current allocation of pensions to Taiwanese farmers. Also, it is important to know whether the OFP program affects choices for off-farm labor of the younger generation from farming households.

In many European and East Asian countries, there have been a number of studies about the quality of life and the well-being of the older farmers (e.g., Barrientos, Gorman, and Heslop, 2003; Chuang, 2011; Fan, 2010a; Monheit, Vistnes, and Eisenberg, 2001; Otomo and Oedl-Wieser, 2009). Moreover, many previous international studies have considered the effect of pensions for older farmers on productivity, private transfer, the propensity for increased consumption, off-farm employment, and farm succession (Lovo, 2011; Bertrand, Mullainathan, and Miller, 2003; Ranchhod, 2006; Jensen, 2004).

In a case study in South Africa, for example, Lovo (2011) investigated the effect of the government's old-age pension scheme on farmers with regard to household technical efficiency. He sought to obtain a broad understanding of whether the productivity of farm was associated with pension payments. The South Africa old-age pension program provides for all women over the age of 60 and men over 65. The author argued that the pension allows the household to be more productive both on and off the farm, so pensions improve the ability of farming households to make use of the best available technologies. In view of the South African old-age pension program and its influence on household behavior, other studies have contributed to the current debate. Bertrand, Mullainathan, and Miller (2003) and Ranchhod (2006) found that the pension payments had a negative effect on the labor output of adults living with a pensioner as well as the beneficiaries of the pension. However, Jensen (2004) found no evidence that there was a reduction in the labor output of those in the same household as a pension recipient.

Referring to the OFP in Taiwan, many studies indicate that the OFP lead to a reduction in private payments and farm succession (Biddlecom et al., 2001; Chang, 2013; Chuang, 2011; Fan, 2010a). For instance, Biddlecom et al. (2001) found that this pension program had a significant and positive effect on the likelihood that elderly people's main source of income changed from private payments to the pension allowance. Chuang (2011) argued that the impact of the OFP on private transfers to the recipients was significant; findings indicated that every NTD dollar of public payment, on average, has been met with an NTD 0.92 dollar reduction in private payments from the children of the elderly. Fan (2010a), using the annual Taiwan Household Income and Expenditure Survey data, indicated that every dollar paid for pensions decreases private payments by 0.30 to 0.39 (which is smaller than Chuang's (2011) results). Fan (2010a) found that the OFP had a positive and significant effect on recipients' household consumption, thus providing direct evidence of an improvement in the well-being of OFP recipients. Furthermore, Fan (2010b) suggested that the OFP pension leads to greater consumption (MPC, or marginal propensity to consume) in beneficiaries' households, although this was marginal. The estimated MPC portion of the pension income (0.43–0.70) is significantly larger than the corresponding estimate for private income (0.27–0.31). Chang (2013) considered the effect of a social security pension program for elderly farmers on family farm succession by examining the OFP program in Taiwan. The findings suggested that the OFP program significantly reduces the likelihood of farm succession. According to previous studies, the OFP program in Taiwan plays a critical role in the reduction on private payments and farm succession. However, to date, no study has investigated the effects of the OFP on the labor output of other family members. In addition, it is extremely important to examine the impact of the OFP on decisions to work off-farm made by the younger generations in farming households, because this issue affects farming household's economic behavior and family-farm succession.

This article contributes to the prevailing literature regarding the effect of a social pension program for older family members on the decisions of younger family members regarding their labor output. The main objective of this article is to measure the influence of the OFP program on family members' off-farm labor decisions. The study used a dataset of 7,270 farm households with 7,270 principle farm operators and 10,918 younger family members (excluding farm operators) aged 19–55. The sample was drawn from the 2011 Agricultural Household Survey in Taiwan. We estimated a mixture simultaneous equation system to investigate the effects of the receipts of the OFP pension on the off-farm labor output decisions of the family members aged 19–55. After controlling for the endogeneity of participation, our results suggested that the pension program increases the likelihood of other family members finding off-farm labor. This effect was more pronounced for the jobs in the service sector.

The Old Farmer Pension Program in Taiwan

The Old Farmer Pension Program (OFP) was implemented on May 31, 1995. According to the OFP, individuals who have received old-age benefits from other social insurance programs do not qualify for the OFP allowance (Bureau of Labor Insurance, Ministry of Labor, 2012). Therefore, eligible recipients were those who (1) were aged 65 or over, (2) had participated in the Farmers' Health Insurance program for at least six months, and (3) were not receiving any other pensions, social insurance, living allowances, or any kind of government assistance (Fan, 2010a). The OFP paid all eligible farmers a monthly pension of NTD 3,000 (equivalent to about USD 111, based on the exchange rate in 1995).

The Farmer Health Insurance program is a national social insurance system for agricultural workers in Taiwan. In order to assure that the Farmers' Health Insurance program adequately covers full-time farmers, it limits payment to those who (1) had reached the age of 15, (2) had worked in agriculture for at least 1 year, (3) had no other full-time off-farm work, (4) had at least 0.1 hectares of land and (5) worked on the farm for more than 90 days per year (Bureau of Labor Insurance, 2009). The eligibility rules give the OFP a unique opportunity to tackle the problem of endogeneity. Since the Farmers' Health Insurance coverage is a prerequisite for OFP consideration, the instrument variable selected was whether the farmer owned at least 0.1 hectares of farmland. In contrast to previous studies, we explicitly account for the potential endogeneity bias of elderly farm operators' pension income on the labor decisions of the younger adults.

During the period 2004–2012, the OFP allowance was increased four times, from NTD 3,000 per month (approximately USD 111) to NTD 7,000 per month (approximately USD 233) (Bureau of Labor Insurance, Ministry of Labor, 2012). Taiwan's OFP program is different from other countries' old-age security systems in that elderly farmers can receive a pension because there is no farmer retirement program in Taiwan.

Data

To examine the effect of the OFP on the decision of the younger members of farming households to work off-farm, we drew on the data from the 2011 Agricultural Household Survey in Taiwan, conducted by the Agriculture and Food Agency, Council of Agriculture in Taiwan (Council of Agriculture, 2012). The survey gathered the information of farm production practices, farm household activities and farm finances (income, expenses and assets). In face-to-face interviews with one principle farm operator identified for each farm, every farmer was asked to describe what was produced on the farm, family characteristics and his or her socio-demographic features. This large-scale dataset is nationally representative of farm households in Taiwan.

The Agricultural Household Survey includes a farm household level dataset and an individual profile for family members over age 15. We merged farm household information for each family member. After deleting a few observations due to missing values, we had a final sample of 7,270 farm households comprising 7,270 principle farm operators and 10,918 family members aged 19–55 (excluding farm operators). The principal farm operators' decision to participate in the OFP program is identified. Of the total, 38% farm operators participated in the OFP program.

Regarding the decisions of younger family members to work off-farm, family members over age 15 were asked to indicate any off-farm work in the survey. Accordingly, four categories were defined to demonstrate the off-farm work of the family members in 2011, including "without off-farm work", "with off-farm work in the agricultural sector", "with off-farm work in the industrial sector" and "with off-farm work in the service sector". According to the information given of family members' off-farm work, approximately 34% of the family members do not have off-farm work. Most family members (67%) have off-farm work; among them, only 3% work in the agricultural sector. Approximately 26% work in the industrial sector and 38% in the service sector.

This study agrees with the findings of previous studies of farming households' economic behavior. However, some independent variables showing the socioeconomic characteristics of farm operators and family members, farm and family structure, and geographic position are clearly delineated. In this dataset, the gender and the marital status of the farm operators and family members were represented by dummy variables. Some variables were created to control for family structure, including the number of household members aged 14 or under and aged 15 or over, and four dummy variables were used to indicate respondents' educational accomplishment as illiterate, primary school, junior high school, senior high school, and college or higher education levels. Several dummy variables for different farm types were also included: three dummy variables were used to indicate the geographical location of each farm, a dummy variable was used to define whether the farm was a full-time farm or not, and a continuing variable was used to indicate the farms' total land area. Detailed definitions and sample statistics of all selected variables are presented in Table 17.1.

Table 17.1 Sample statistics of the selected variables

Variable	Definition	Households Sample N = 7,270		Family Member Sample N = 10,918	
		Mean	S.D.	Mean	S.D
Dependent Variables					
Pension program	If the farm operator received old-age farmers' welfare allowance (= 1).	0.38	0.48	–	–
Without off-farm work	If the family member doesn't participated in off-farm work (= 1).	–	–	0.34	0.47
Off-farm work in agricultural sector	If the family member participated in off-farm work in agricultural sector (= 1).	–	–	0.03	0.16
Off-farm work in industrial sector	If the family member participated in off-farm work in industrial sector (= 1).	–	–	0.26	0.44
Off-farm work in service sector	If the family member participated in off-farm work in service sector (= 1).	–	–	0.38	0.49
Independent Variables					
HHsize_under15	Number of household members aged under 15.	0.44	0.91	0.69	1.13
HHsize_above15	Number of household members aged 15 or above.	3.25	1.60	4.60	1.57

Variable	Definition	Households Sample N = 7,270		Family Member Sample N = 10,918	
		Mean	S.D.	Mean	S.D
North	If the farm households located in northern area Taiwan (= 1).	0.24	0.43	0.25	0.43
Center	If the farm households located in central area (= 1).	0.32	0.47	0.35	0.48
South*	If the farm households located in southern area (= 1).	0.37	0.48	0.34	0.48
East	If the farm households located in eastern area (= 1).	0.07	0.25	0.05	0.23
Full-time farm	If a full-time farm (= 1).	0.31	0.46	0.08	0.28
Part-time farm*	If a part-time farm (= 1).	0.69	0.46	0.91	0.28
Farm size	Total land area (hectare).	0.74	1.33	0.79	1.53
At least 0.1 hectares of farmland	If the farmland per person is at least 0.1 hectares (= 1).	0.54	0.50	–	–
Rice	If rice farm (= 1).	0.24	0.43	0.27	0.45
Idle	If idle farm (= 1).	0.08	0.27	0.06	0.24
Grain	If grain farm (= 1).	0.06	0.23	0.05	0.22
Special	If special farm (= 1).	0.17	0.37	0.14	0.35
Vegetable	If vegetable farm (= 1).	0.20	0.40	0.21	0.41
Fruit	If fruit farm (= 1).	0.21	0.41	0.21	0.41
Mushroom	If mushroom farm (= 1).	0.01	0.09	0.01	0.10

(continued)

Table 17.1 Sample statistics of the selected variables *(continued)*

Variable	Definition	Households Sample N = 7,270		Family Member Sample N = 10,918	
		Mean	S.D.	Mean	S.D
Flower	If flower farm (= 1).	0.01	0.11	0.01	0.12
Other crops	If other crop farm (= 1).	0.01	0.09	0.01	0.08
Livestock*	If livestock farm (= 1).	0.02	0.14	0.02	0.15
Male	If the respondent is male (= 1).	0.80	0.40	0.48	0.50
Age	Age of the respondent (year).	64.38	11.99	36.43	10.17
Illiterate	If illiterate of the farm operator (= 1).	0.14	0.34	0.01	0.08
Elementary	If primal education of the operator (= 1).	0.43	0.49	0.05	0.21
Junior	If junior high school education of farm operator (= 1).	0.18	0.38	0.16	0.36
Senior	If senior high school education of farm operator (= 1).	0.18	0.38	0.36	0.48
College*	If college or higher education of farm operator (= 1).	0.08	0.27	0.43	0.50
Married	If the respondent is married (= 1).	0.74	0.44	0.53	0.50
Single*	If the respondent is single (= 1).	0.26	0.44	0.47	0.50

Notes: * indicate the reference group.

Econometric analysis

To examine the relationship between the OFP program and family members working off-farm, some econometric issues have to be considered. Firstly, it is necessary to control for self-selection bias in that the OFP program is not randomly distributed to eligible farmers. Secondly, it is necessary to consider the nature of the dependent variables. To address this, the mixture simultaneous equation system is estimated to investigate to what extent the OFP program farm affects the off-farm labor decisions of the adults aged 19–55. Empirical analysis is conducted in several steps. We first estimate a probit model for farm operators' participation in the pension program. The predicted probability of the program participation was then calculated. In the second stage of the analysis, we estimate a multinomial logit model for the off-farm work equations of younger family members. Details of the econometric model used in each step are described in the following two subsections.

First-stage analysis of the OFP participation

If Y_i^* is an unobservable latent variable of the OFP participation for the ith farm operator, Y_i is the observed participation decision, Z_i' is a vector of the covariates including socioeconomic characteristics of the farm operator, family and farm structure, β_1 is the vector of the associated unknown parameters, I_i is the instrumental variable (IV) that whether one has at least 0.1 hectares of farmland or not, and ε_i the random error, the probit model of the OFP participation equation can be defined as:

$$Y_i^* = I_i\alpha_0 + Z_i'\alpha_1 + \varepsilon_i = X'\beta_1 + \varepsilon_i, \varepsilon_i \sim N(0,1)$$
$$Y_i = 1, \text{ if } Y_i^* > 0; \qquad Y_i = 0, \text{ if } Y_i^* \leq 0 \tag{17.1}$$

The probability of the OFP participation ($P(Y_i = 1)$) can be presented as:

$$P(Y_i = 1) = P(\varepsilon_i > -X'\beta_1) = 1 - \Phi(X'\beta_1) \tag{17.2}$$

where $\Phi(.)$ is the cumulative density function of the standard normal distribution. The log-likelihood function of this probit model can be specified as:

$$L = \sum \left\{ Y_i \ln \Phi(X'\beta_1) + (1 - Y_i) \ln \left[1 - \Phi(X'\beta_1) \right] \right\} \tag{17.3}$$

With the estimates of the probit model, we compute the predicted probability of OFP participation for each farm operator to control the endogeneity of OFP participation.

Second-stage analysis for off-farm work of the younger family members

In the second-step analysis, the dependent variable had been divided into four categories to indicate younger family members' off-farm work, including "without off-farm work (j = 0)", "with off-farm work in the agricultural sector (j = 1)", "with off-farm work in the industrial sector (j = 2)" and "with off-farm work in the service sector (j = 3)". The probability that i^{th} family member chooses j^{th} type off-farm work ($P(y_i = j)$) can be shown as:

$$P(y_i = j) = \frac{\exp(\alpha_j \hat{y}_i + x_i\beta_j)}{\sum_{k=0}^{3} \exp(\alpha_k \hat{y}_i + x_i\beta_k)} \tag{17.4}$$

where $\hat{y}_i$ is the predicted value for the OFP participation of the farm operator calculated from the first-stage analysis. In Eq. (17.4), x_i is a vector of the covariates, including socioeconomic characteristics of the family members, family and farm structure etc.; β is the vector of the associated parameters. The maximum likelihood estimation method was used to estimate the model (Greene, 2008). In addition, we calculate the marginal effects (see Long and Freese, 2006).

$$\frac{\Delta P(y_i = j|x)}{\Delta x_i}\bigg|_{\text{all else constant}} = \frac{\partial p_j}{\partial x_i} = p_j \left[\beta_j - \sum_{k=0}^{3} p_k \beta_k \right] \tag{17.5}$$

$$\frac{\Delta P(y_i = j|x)}{\Delta x_i} = P(y_i = j|x, x_i = x_b) - P(y_i = j|x, x_i = x_a) \tag{17.6}$$

Empirical results

The estimated coefficients and the marginal effects of the exogenous variables on OFP participation are presented in Table 17.2. As shown in Table 17.2, the socioeconomic characteristics of the farm operator, the family and farm structure, and the geographic position are significantly associated with the likelihood of the farm operator to participate in the OFP program. The results indicated that one additional household member aged 15 or above will decrease the propensity of OFP participation by 1.90 percentage points. Moreover, compared to the part-time farmers, full-time farmers will increase the likelihood of OFP participation by 4.62 percentage points. Program enrollment also differs by farm types: Compared to farms producing livestock (the reference group), special and other crop farms have a higher probability of the OFP enrollment (7.81 and 14.91 percentage points, respectively).

Table 17.2 Estimation of the old farmers' pension program equation

Variable	Coefficient	SE	Marginal Effect
At least 0.1 hectares of farmland	0.2657***	0.0552	0.0583
HHsize_aged under15	0.0201	0.0273	0.0044
HHsize_aged 15 or above	0.0865***	0.0207	0.0190
Full-time farm	0.2104***	0.0617	0.0462

Variable	Coefficient	SE	Marginal Effect
Land_acre	−0.0018	0.0199	−0.0004
Rice	0.0888	0.1856	0.0195
Idle	0.0625	0.1993	0.0137
Grain	0.0233	0.2028	0.0051
Special	0.3560*	0.1897	0.0781
Vegetable	0.1290	0.1875	0.0283
Fruit	0.0613	0.1880	0.0134
Mushroom	0.1310	0.3555	0.0287
Flower	−0.1831	0.2884	−0.0402
Othercrop	0.6797*	0.4001	0.1491
Male	−0.0386	0.0706	−0.0085
Age	1.3868***	0.0585	0.0628
Age square	−0.0085***	0.0004	
Illiterate	1.3903***	0.1565	0.3050
Elementary	1.4338***	0.1482	0.3146
Junior	1.1819***	0.1618	0.2593
Senior	0.7519***	0.1685	0.1650
Married	0.0250	0.0658	0.0055
Northern_Taiwan	−0.4389***	0.0647	−0.0963
Central_Taiwan	−0.1475**	0.0611	−0.0324
Eastern_Taiwan	−0.3023***	0.1011	−0.0663
Constant	−56.5336***	2.1898	
Pseudo R2		0.6315	
Log likelihood		6,083.73	
Sample (# of farms)		7,270	

Note: ***, **, and * indicate significance at the 1%, 5%, and 10% levels, respectively.

The socioeconomic characteristics of the farm operators are also significantly associated with OFP participation. The results reveal that an additional year in a farm operator's age will increase OFP participation by 6.28 percentage points. The difference in farmers' education also affects the OFP participation. The results demonstrate that, compared to farm operators who finished college or higher education (the reference group), farm operators who were illiterate, finished elementary school, finished junior high school, and finished senior high school have a higher propensity to enroll in the OFP program, by 30.50, 31.46, 25.93 and 16.50 percentage points, respectively. The results seem to indicate that the more highly educated a farmer, the stronger the incentive to engage in off-farm work and the less likely to join the OFP program. Moreover, geographic location is also significantly associated with the OFP participation. The results show that farm operators living in northern, central, and eastern Taiwan are less likely to participate in the OFP program, by 9.63, 3.24, and 6.63 percentage points, respectively, than farmers living in the southern area (the reference group). Finally, in terms of the instrumental variable (ownership of at least 0.1 hectares of farmland), is also important to determine farmers' participation to the OFP program. The results show that the instrument is positively associated with the farmers' decision to enroll in the program. Compared to farm operators who don't own at least 0.1 hectares of farmland, those who have at least 0.1 hectares of farmland will increase OFP participation by 5.83 percentage points.

The OFP effect on younger family members' off-farm work

The estimated coefficients and the marginal effects of the exogenous variables of the multinomial logit model for the off-farm labor decision of family members aged 19–55 are presented in Tables 17.4 and 17.5, respectively. The dependent variable is an unordered variable of four categories: without off-farm works (the reference group), off-farm works in agricultural sector, off-farm works in industrial sector, and off-farm works in service sector. Since the OFP participation of the elderly farm operator will be affected by unobserved factors, it is necessary to correct for the self-selection bias. One of the critical eligibility rules of the Farmers' Health Insurance program is the ownership of farmland of at least 0.1 hectares. We use this information to define our instrumental variable (IV) to tackle the endogeneity problem of the OFP participation. Following the spirit of the two-stage estimation framework, we then calculate the predicted value ($yhat$) and use it to substitute the observed binary decision variable for elderly farmers' OFP participation in the estimation of the multinomial logit model.

As shown in Table 17.5, socioeconomic characteristics of the family members, family and farm structure, and geographic location are significantly associated with decisions of younger family members on off-farm work. The results show that males are less inclined to engage in off-farm work than females (11.31 percentage points). If they do work off the farm, males have a higher probability to work for the industrial sector by 15.38 percentage points, compared to female family members.

Family members aged 26–35 and 36–45 are less inclined to take off-farm work, and, if they do work off the farm, they are more likely to work in the industrial and service sectors. The educational level of the family members is also significantly correlated with family members' off-farm work participation. The results show that less educated younger family members are less likely to participate in off-farm work, and have a lower probability of participating in off-farm work in the service sector.

Among the other factors, family conditions also matter. Results indicated that an additional household member aged 15 or above will decrease the likelihood of the family members' working in service sector by 1.09 percentage points and increase the likelihood of not participating in off-farm work by 1.14 percentage points. This finding is consistent with the conclusions of the previous study (Mishra et al., 2012). Mishra et al. (2012) indicated that in the United States, operators of small- and medium-sized farms are more likely to have family members working off the farm, while operators and families associated with large farms whose main function is farming will be less likely to work off the farm. Furthermore, the family members of professional farmers have a lower probability of participating in off-farm work in the agricultural, industrial, and service sector by 2.68, 25.51 and 36.60 percentage points respectively. The results also show a positive connection between farm size and family members who do not work off the farm: an additional hectare of farmland decreases the probability of participating in off-farm work by 1.56 percentage points. The type of farm has an effect on family members' participation in off-farm work. Compared to people on farms producing livestock (the reference group), those on farms that are idle or produce rice, grain, special crops, vegetables and fruit are more likely to not participate in off-farm work by 8.09, 6.63, 10.17, 8.99, 8.03 and 8.47 percentage points, respectively. The geographic location can influence the propensity of participating in off-farm work. Compared to farms located in the southern part of Taiwan (the reference group), family members who live in the northern part of Taiwan have a lower propensity for participating in off-farm work in agricultural sector.

The results, most noticeably, indicated that the most important independent variable, "whether the operator receives OFP payments ($yhat$)", has a significant impact on the off-farm labor decisions of young adults. Moreover, a more pronounced effect is found for the jobs in the service sector. From the results, we find that the receipt of the OFP by the farm operator will increase the likelihood of family members have off-farm work in service sector by 6.8 percentage points, and also will decrease the propensity of not participating in off-farm works by 11.40 percentage points. Agreeing with the conclusions of Bertrand, Mullainathan, and Miller (2003) and Ranchhod (2006), a positive association was found between OFP participation and the likelihood of working off the farm. In addition, because OFP payments do not affect the likelihood of working off the farm in the agricultural sector, we can indicate that family members will choose to work on their own farm instead of others' farms, if they want to work in the agricultural sector.

Table 17.3 Marginal effect of old pension on the different groups of family members

	Marginal effect of without off-farm work		Marginal effect of with off-farm work in service work
	Male family member	*Female family member*	
Under 25	1.05%	7.36%	−4.24%
Age: 26–35	1.37%	7.68%	−6.76%
Age: 36–45	−9.20%	−2.89%	0.80%
Age: 46–55	−17.71%	−11.40%	6.80%

Furthermore, the interaction term of the predicted value (*yhat*) and gender, and the interaction terms of the predicted value (*yhat*) and age group have significant influences on family members' job allocations between on-farm and off-farm work in the service sector. Male family members are more likely to work off-farm compared to their female counterparts if the elderly farmer received the OFP allowance. Further, from those interaction terms, we can examine the marginal effect of the OFP on the different groups of family members. The calculations are presented in Table 17.3.

Since we are interested in the OFP effects on family members' labor allocation, we focus our discussion on the results presented in Table 17.3. It is evident that the OFP program has a significant effect on different groups of family members. When farm operators receive the OFP, the likelihood of family members aged 36–45 having off-farm work in the service sector increases by 0.8 percentage points. Similarly, it decreases the likelihood of male and female family members having no off-farm work by 9.20, and 2.89 percentage points, respectively. In addition, the results show that receipt of the OFP will decrease the likelihood of male and female family members aged 46–55 having no off-farm work by 17.71 and 11.40 percentage points, respectively. The OFP will decrease the likelihood of family members aged below 25 and 26–35 having off-farm work in the service sector by 4.24 and 6.76 percentage points respectively, and increase the propensity for male and female family members to have no off-farm work. Consequently, the OFP program will encourage a reduction in family members' labor output with more family members aged between 36 and 55 increasingly working off the farm in the service sector. These results are more significant among family members aged 46–55. Consequently, these results seem to indicate that the OFP pension plays a crucial role in determining the likelihood of family members participating in off-farm work, with effect that they are less likely to stay and work on their own farms.

Table 17.4 Estimation of the family members' off-farm works equation—coefficient

Variable	Off-farm work in agricultural sector		Off-farm work in industrial sector		Off-farm work in service sector	
	Coefficient	SE	Coefficient	SE	Coefficient	SE
Predicted value(yhat)	0.6734**	0.3236	0.7727***	0.1570	0.7632***	0.1387
Interaction term: yhat* male	0.6543*	0.3564	0.4467***	0.1619	0.3895***	0.1470
Interaction term:yhat*under25	−3.0003**	1.3147	−1.0780***	0.2576	−1.2276***	0.2077
Interaction term: yhat* 26-35	−1.2259**	0.5017	−1.1872***	0.2233	−1.3327***	0.2068
Interaction term: yhat* 36-45	−0.7929**	0.3973	−0.5051**	0.2105	−0.5901***	0.1941
HHsize_aged under15	−0.0543	0.0639	0.0546*	0.0286	-0.0312	0.0275
HHsize_aged 15 or above	−0.1276***	0.0448	−0.0527***	0.0199	−0.0861***	0.0185
Full-time farm	−4.2389***	0.5894	−4.4381***	0.2608	−4.2781***	0.2141
Land_acre	0.0438	0.0310	−0.1717***	0.0289	−0.0750***	0.0180
Rice	−0.0862	0.4599	0.7776***	0.2244	0.4478**	0.1890

(continued)

Table 17.4 Estimation of the family members' off-farm works equation—coefficient (continued)

Variable	Off-farm work in agricultural sector		Off-farm work in industrial sector		Off-farm work in service sector	
	Coefficient	SE	Coefficient	SE	Coefficient	SE
Idle	-0.6177	0.5610	0.6470***	0.2470	0.4023*	0.2099
Grain	0.3241	0.5029	0.8810***	0.2532	0.5872***	0.2194
Special	0.2053	0.4727	0.7950***	0.2317	0.5156***	0.1959
Vegetable	0.4928	0.4582	0.5473**	0.2278	0.5340***	0.1913
Fruit	0.2835	0.4569	0.7190***	0.2275	0.4972***	0.1913
Mushroom	0.9639	0.6639	0.6526*	0.3535	-0.3470	0.3505
Flower	-0.3653	0.8552	0.5272	0.3397	0.2994	0.2948
Othercrop	1.5466**	0.7286	0.5847	0.4417	0.0954	0.3840
Male	0.9727***	0.2039	1.2485***	0.0852	0.4469***	0.0753
Age 25 or under	-0.7764**	0.3733	-1.4776***	0.1540	-1.3204***	0.1277
Age 26 to 35	0.9493***	0.2718	1.1882***	0.1258	1.0626***	0.1120
Age 36 to 45	0.9766***	0.2574	0.7297***	0.1312	0.6921***	0.1162
Illiterate	1.9398***	0.4902	-1.5928***	0.5136	-2.6560***	0.4969
Elementary	1.7530***	0.2992	-0.2869*	0.1501	-1.6483***	0.1505

Variable	Off-farm work in agricultural sector		Off-farm work in industrial sector		Off-farm work in service sector	
	Coefficient	SE	Coefficient	SE	Coefficient	SE
Junior	1.4817***	0.2360	-0.1762*	0.0951	-1.1761***	0.0901
Senior	1.1932***	0.2171	0.1252*	0.0741	-0.4682***	0.0671
Married	0.0860	0.1710	-0.1508*	0.0812	-0.1372*	0.0759
Northern_Taiwan	-0.9791***	0.2101	0.0100	0.0807	-0.0115	0.0724
Central_Taiwan	-0.0580	0.1537	0.2342***	0.0738	0.0535	0.0676
Eastern_Taiwan	0.0119	0.2602	-0.6085***	0.1616	0.2616**	0.1242
Constant	-3.7140***	0.5667	-1.3388***	0.2689	0.4087*	0.2291
Pseudo R2			0.1861			
Log likelihood			-10,450.815			
Sample (# of persons)	10,918		10,918		10,918	

Notes: The reference group is the one who is without off-farm works. ***, **, and * indicate significance at the 1%, 5%, and 10% levels, respectively.

Table 17.5 Estimation of the family members' off-farm works equation—marginal effect

Variable	Without off-farm work		Off-farm work in agricultural sector		Off-farm work in industrial sector		Off-farm work in service sector	
	Marginal Effect	SE	Marginal Effect	SE	Marginal Effect	SE	Marginal Effect	SE
Predicted value (yhat)	-0.1140***	0.0185	0.0030	0.0073	0.0430*	0.0230	0.0680***	0.0248
Interaction term: yhat*male	-0.0631***	0.0204	0.0084	0.0080	0.0282	0.0213	0.0265	0.0236
Interaction term:yhat*under25	0.1876***	0.0284	-0.0511*	0.0309	-0.0261	0.0423	-0.1104**	0.0433
Interaction term: yhat*26-35	0.1908***	0.0284	-0.0077	0.0112	-0.0475	0.0291	-0.1356***	0.0329
Interaction term: yhat*36-45	0.0851***	0.0265	-0.0094	0.0088	-0.0156	0.0283	-0.0600*	0.0318
HHsize_aged under15	0.0003	0.0038	-0.0014	0.0014	0.0129***	0.0037	-0.0117***	0.0043
HHsize_aged 15 or above	0.0114***	0.0025	-0.0018*	0.0010	0.0013	0.0027	-0.0109***	0.0030
Full-time farm	0.6478***	0.0226	-0.0268**	0.0137	-0.2551***	0.0471	-0.3660***	0.0493
Land_acre	0.0156***	0.0026	0.0031***	0.0007	-0.0211***	0.0045	0.0025	0.0038

Variable	Without off-farm work		Off-farm work in agricultural sector		Off-farm work in industrial sector		Off-farm work in service sector	
	Marginal Effect	SE	Marginal Effect	SE	Marginal Effect	SE	Marginal Effect	SE
Rice	-0.0809***	0.0260	-0.0121	0.0105	0.0834***	0.0324	0.0097	0.0337
Idle	-0.0663**	0.0290	-0.0232*	0.0129	0.0706**	0.0353	0.0188	0.0369
Grain	-0.1017***	0.0301	-0.0046	0.0114	0.0826**	0.0358	0.0236	0.0380
Special	-0.0899***	0.0269	-0.0060	0.0108	0.0768**	0.0333	0.0191	0.0347
Vegetable	-0.0803***	0.0263	0.0025	0.0104	0.0310	0.0329	0.0467	0.0341
Fruit	-0.0847***	0.0263	-0.0034	0.0104	0.0653**	0.0329	0.0228	0.0341
Mushroom	-0.0103	0.0453	0.0204	0.0150	0.1384***	0.0514	-0.1484**	0.0616
Flower	-0.0524	0.0405	-0.0154	0.0197	0.0595	0.0485	0.0083	0.0517
Othercrop	-0.0502	0.0528	0.0308*	0.0163	0.0753	0.0616	-0.0559	0.0655
Male	-0.1131***	0.0103	0.0089*	0.0046	0.1538***	0.0109	-0.0496***	0.0119
Age 25 or under	0.2021***	0.0169	0.0051	0.0086	-0.1010***	0.0233	-0.1061***	0.0239
Age 26 to 35	-0.1648***	0.0150	0.0035	0.0061	0.0786***	0.0176	0.0827***	0.0191
Age 36 to 45	-0.1074***	0.0156	0.0111*	0.0058	0.0409**	0.0189	0.0555***	0.0204
Illiterate	0.3093***	0.0572	0.0813***	0.0120	-0.0005	0.0911	-0.3901***	0.1047

(continued)

Table 17.5 Estimation of the family members' off-farm works equation—marginal effect (continued)

Variable	Without off-farm work		Off-farm work in agricultural sector		Off-farm work in industrial sector		Off-farm work in service sector	
	Marginal Effect	SE	Marginal Effect	SE	Marginal Effect	SE	Marginal Effect	SE
Elementary	0.1508***	0.0185	0.0577***	0.0072	0.1128***	0.0229	-0.3213***	0.0271
Junior	0.1045***	0.0119	0.0463***	0.0058	0.0834***	0.0124	-0.2343***	0.0140
Senior	0.0271***	0.0094	0.0310***	0.0052	0.0611***	0.0093	-0.1192***	0.0101
Married	0.0197*	0.0106	0.0044	0.0038	-0.0114	0.0100	-0.0128	0.0115
Northern_Taiwan	0.0071	0.0101	-0.0230***	0.0049	0.0108	0.0108	0.0050	0.0118
Central_Taiwan	-0.0169*	0.0093	-0.0037	0.0034	0.0340***	0.0097	-0.0134	0.0109
Eastern_Taiwan	0.0089	0.0178	0.0029	0.0058	-0.1297***	0.0229	0.1179***	0.0217
Pseudo R2					0.1861			
Log likelihood					-10,450.815			
Sample (# of persons)	10,918		10,918		10,918		10,918	

Notes: The reference group is the one who is without off-farm works. ***, **, and * indicate significance at the 1%, 5%, and 10% levels, respectively.

Conclusions

The agricultural sector is ageing steadily. Determining how to maintain the well-being of the increasing number of elderly farmers has become a pivotal policy issue in many developed countries, because the operating costs of this welfare programs are increasing. To design a more effective pension program for elderly farmers, it is necessary to understand the effect of such a program on decisions made by the younger generation to work off the farm. This article examines the extent to which the OFP program may affect the decision to work off-farm of other family members, using a unique survey of farming households in Taiwan.

A mixed simultaneous equation system was estimated to explicitly account for the potential endogeneity of the OFP participation on the labor decisions of the young family members. The results show that socioeconomic characteristics, family and farm structure, and geographic position are significantly correlated with farm operators' participation in the OFP program. Moreover, OFP payments to the elderly farm operator have a significant impact on young adults' off-farm labor decisions. The OFP program significantly reduces the likelihood of family members' working off the farm in the service sector. A more pronounced effect is found for the jobs in the service section particularly for family members aged 46–55. These results assure us that the OFP program plays a crucial role in explaining the negative effect of the family members' on-farm work.

Despite some interesting findings in this study, there are some limitations. For instance, since a cross-sectional survey data set was used, we cannot comment on the long-term change of the OFP program on family members' off-farm work decisions. A panel data framework would be better to demonstrate this topic, and the robustness of our findings can be further confirmed if the panel data becomes obtainable. This could be the subject of future research.

References

Barrientos, A., Gorman, M., & Heslop, A. (2003). Old age poverty in developing countries contributions and dependence in later life. *World Development*, 31(3), 555–570.

Bertrand, M., Mullainathan, S., & Miller, D. (2003). Public policy and extended families: evidence from pensions in South Africa. *World Bank Economic Review*, 17(1), 27–49.

Biddlecom, A., Hermalin, A., Ofstedal, M., Chang, M., & Chuang, Y. (2001). Tradeoffs between public and private economic support of the elderly: results from a natural experiment in Taiwan. *Elderly in Asia Report*, No.01-58. Population Study Center, University of Michigan.

Bureau of Labor Insurance. (2009). *Farmers' Health Insurance Act*. Bureau of Labor Insurance, Taipei, Taiwan.

Bureau of Labor Insurance, Ministry of Labor. (2012). *Old Age Farmers Welfare Allowance Program*. Taipei, Taiwan: Executive Yuan.

Chang, H. (2013). Old farmer pension program and farm succession: evidence from a population-based survey of farm households in Taiwan. *American Journal of Agricultural Economics*, 95(4), 976–991.

Chuang, J. (2011). Do social allowance transfers crowd out private transfers? An analysis of responses among elderly households in Taiwan. *International Journal of Social Welfare*, 21(2), 194–202.

Council of Agriculture. (2012). *The Summary of Agricultural Household Survey in Taiwan in 2011*. Agriculture and Food Agency, Council of Agriculture, Taipei, Taiwan.

Fan, E. (2010a). Who benefits from public old age pensions? Evidence from a targeted program. *Economic Development and Cultural Change*, 58(2), 297–322.

Fan, E. (2010b). Does public income induce more consumption? *Economic Record*, 86(272), 15–27.

Greene, W. (2008). *Econometric Analysis*. 6th ed. New Jersey: Prentice-Hall, Inc.

Jensen, R. (2004). Do private transfers "displace" the benefit of public transfers? Evidence from South Africa. *Journal of Public Economics*, 88(1–2), 89–112.

Long, J., & Freese, J. (2006). *Regression Models for Categorical Dependent Variables Using Stata*, 2nd ed. Texas: Stata Press.

Lovo, S. (2011). Pension transfers and farm household technical efficiency: evidence from South Africa. *American Journal of Agricultural Economics*, 93(5), 1391–1405.

Mishra, A., El-Osta, H., & Ahearn, M. (2012). Health care expenditures of self-employed farm households in the United States. *Agricultural Economics*, 43(1), 75–88.

Monheit, A., Vistnes, J., & Eisenberg, J. (2001). Moving to Medicare: trends in the health insurance status of near-elderly workers, 1987–1996. *Health Affairs*, 20(2), 204–213.

Otomo, Y., & Oedl-Wieser, T. (2009). Comparative analysis of patterns in farm succession in Austria and Japan from a gender perspective. *Jahrbuch der Österreichische Gesellschaft für Agrarökonomie*, 18(2), 79–92.

Ranchhod, V. (2006). The effect of the South African old age pension on labour supply of the elderly. *South African Journal of Economics*, 74(4), 725–744.

Chapter 18

Succession decisions in family farms and public policies in developed countries

Alessandro Corsi

Introduction

Agriculture, both in developing and developed countries, is predominantly composed of family farms. The definition of family farming is debated, with some-one more inclined to stress the family links, others the economic dimension; the definition proposed by FAO (Garner and de la O Campos, 2014), encompasses both the labor contribution by family members and the role of the household:

> Family Farming (also Family Agriculture) is a means of organizing agricultural, forestry, fisheries, pastoral and aquaculture production which is managed and operated by a family and predominantly reliant on family labor, both women's and men's. The family and the farm are linked, coevolve and combine eco-nomic, environmental, reproductive, social and cultural functions.

The link between the economic unit (the farm firm) and the social unit (the house-hold) has several implications, one of which is the issue of succession. Actually, intrafamily transfer is predominant in many economies (Bryden et al., 1992; Perrier Cornet et al., 1991; Marsden et al., 1989) and farmers' children are more likely to follow their parents' employment than other profession's children (Laband and Lentz, 1983). Notwithstanding its relevance for the evolution of the agricultural sector, the issue of farm succession has not been analyzed intensively in the eco-nomic literature. We will present a review of the relevant literature with refer-ence to developed countries, starting with the theoretical models, then examining the empirical analyses of the determinants of family farm succession and its effect on farm behavior. Finally, we will discuss the policies that are relevant for farm succession.

Theoretical models of farm succession

Intrafamily transfer implies two separate issues. One is the transmission of the farm assets over generations (inheritance). The second is the transmission of the farm operation (succession). The issue of inheritance as such and is not specific for farms. The reasons for parents to leave their assets to the children, both during their life and through bequests, are largely debated in the economic literature (for a general review on the issue of intergenerational transfers see Laferrère (1999) and Schokkaert (2006)). There are different streams in the literature. Some economic models assume altruistic parents (e.g. Becker and Tomes, 1986), so that the motivation for leaving assets to the children rather than consuming them during lifetime is that children's welfare is an argument in parents' utility function. Other models consider intergenerational transfers as an old-age security: the parent loans to the child who will pay back in parent's old age (Samuelson, 1958; Shell, 1971; Hammond, 1972; Cigno, 1991 and 2000). Other models assume selfish behavior, thus implying that altruism towards the children is not required to explain bequests. According to Bernheim et al. (1985), intra-family transfer has strategic motives, and parents use bequests to induce care by their children by threatening them to otherwise be left with no inheritance. A further approach, still assuming selfish attitudes, is intrafamily transfers as an insurance against risk (Kotlikoff and Spivak, 1981). Individuals, when annuity markets are imperfect, insure themselves against the risk of running out of their resources if they live long by an implicit or formal contract with their children, benefitting from the risk-sharing.

Some of these general theories are adopted to analyze farm succession, with some specificities that intergenerational agricultural asset transfer raise. A stream of literature treats farm succession as in insurance problem. Pesquin et al. (1999) start from the consideration that individuals basing their consumption in retirement years enjoy greater consumption if they can rely on a actuarially fair annuity like a pension fund rather than on self-reliance on the wealth obtained selling the farm, since the probability of survival is averaged across all participants. A succeeding family receives the farm and takes on the obligation of providing the parents an income for the rest of their lives. Then family succession can be considered as a mutual insurance providing a fair annuity, and the family collectively enjoys the relevant economic surplus, which can be further increased by parents' contribution in labor and in farming experience. Additional benefits are a "smooth" transition, lower transaction costs, and possibly lower taxes. Unlike in Kotlikoff and Spivak (1981), Pesquin et al. assume an intergenerational cooperative behavior, since the division of the economic surplus is seen as the result of a bargaining process modelled as a Nash cooperative game. They do not test empirically the model, but rather simulate the outcomes based on the data of some Israeli farms. In this model, the reason for passing on the farm within the family is the additional benefits that family succession provides and, hence, the mutual interest in the collaboration.

Kimhi (1995) presents a theoretical model of farm succession based on the investment by the parent on sector-specific, farm and non-farm, human capital of two children, of which only one is going to succeed on the farm. Under the assumption that for an altruistic parent his descendants' utilities enter in his utility function, Kimhi derives the predicted investments in human capital for each sector without and with a constraint of equal welfare for the children. Uncertainty about future farm income of each potential successor implies decisions about the length of the period of delay of the succession decision, since delaying the decision allows accumulation of information on the potential successor's abilities in running the farm. However, this situation is prone to strategic behavior of both the parent and the child. A parent desiring to have a successor but wishing to delay as much as possible the succession will delay the decision until the child is about to give up and quit. A child knowing that a parent is extremely willing to have a successor can threaten to quit, forcing the operation to be transferred earlier.

Kimhi (1994) further offers a model of the timing of succession. The theoretical model assumes a family maximizing the present value of income streams from the parent and the child. Hence, if the transfer is made one year earlier, the family trades the loss of the income generated by the parent for the gain of the income generated by the child. The choice variable is therefore the time of transfer. The results, estimated on a sample of Israeli *moshavim*, suggest that transfer time decreases with the age of the parent and when he/she works off the farm, and increases with the child's education. The theoretical model is overall supported, thus suggesting an altruistic behavior of parents seeking to maximize family welfare.

A particular question is why the farm operation, and not only farm assets, are transferred within families. This is typical for farms much more than for other individual businesses. For instance, Blanc and Perrier-Cornet (1993) note than in France artisan bakers often sell to former bakery assistants who set up on their own account, rather than handing the bakery down to their children. The answer proposed by Rosenzweig and Wolpin (1985) is that the accumulation of farm-specific knowledge raises labor productivity, so that, if an offspring works on the farm and gains specific knowledge, he/she has an incentive to purchase the farm from his/her parents, since it is more profitable and the land is worth more than for anybody else. For the same reason, the offspring has an incentive to work for his/her parents at a young age for a lower cost than hired workers. The outcome is an implicit contract between generations involving transfer of land and use of family labor that is Pareto efficient compared to nonfamily sales of land and labor. The model does not require altruistic behavior, since both generations are better off with the arrangement. Rosenzweig and Wolpin test their model for a panel of Indian farms, taking experience on weather events as the indicator of specific knowledge, and find support to their thesis. They note that the effects of technological innovations reduce the value of accumulated knowledge. Hence, in developed countries, its effect should be weaker. Corsi (2009) investigates the determinants of succession for an Italian region and finds that variables proxies for specific knowledge do significantly affect the probability of intrafamily succession, though the effect is rather weak, and other determinants are also important.

In addition, the social science literature points to the farm cycle. The interest in this stream is not in explaining the reasons for succession, but rather in describing its different possible patterns. Errington (1998), in comparing research in France, UK, and Canada, depicts four different stylized paths: the "stand-by-holding", when the father sets up an independent farm for the child, which eventually can be amalgamated with the father's when he retires; the "separate enterprise", when the child develops his own enterprise, perhaps a pig unit or sheep flock; the "partnership", when the potential successor gradually acquires responsibility for particular aspects of the home farm; and the "farmer's boy" pattern, when the child spends many years working for the father, mainly in manual activities with little involvement in the management. Lobley et al. (2010) provide an international comparison of the modalities of succession, based on the results of coordinated enquiries in several countries. Other qualitative studies on the topic with similar approaches include Dumas et al., 1995; Keating and Little, 1997; and Otomo and Oedl-Wieser, 2009.

The determinants of succession

The issue is what favors and what impedes that the farm is handed on to some family member of the next generation, which is of interest to predict the evolution of the farm structure. Given that available agricultural land is virtually fixed, expansion of farm size is possible only if some farmers quit farm operation. This may happen because of economic reasons when the farmer is still active or because he/she retires without successors. Considering that most of the entry to farming is linked to intra-family succession, detecting under which conditions the intra-family transfer is easier is of interest also for policy makers. The lack of an agreed theoretical framework on which to base the empirical analyses pushes many researchers to analyze empirically what variables are influencing the succession, or its timing, regardless of the underlying theory. In some cases, the empirical analyses are presented as reduced forms of theoretical models, even though the estimates cannot discriminate among alternate theories. In other cases, the analyses give up the ambition of testing more structured theoretical predictions and simply assume that the choice is the outcome of some dynamic process within the family that produces the highest utility. Hence, they investigate which variables influence the outcome of succession, typically with logit or probit statistical methods.

However, the analysis of this issue is complicated by a set of empirical problems. First of all, the empirical definition itself of succession is not trivial. Since almost by definition intra-family succession happens at a generation time distance, to fully observe the entire process one should need very long panel data. This contrasts with the usually available data sets. In addition, even when data are periodically available for long periods, like for Agricultural Censuses, there is almost invariably a problem in matching the observations from one period to the other. Hence, it is often difficult to be sure that, e.g., a farm observed in one Census is the same farm in the following one. Moreover, it is not always possible to know with certainty, when the operator has changed, if the new operator is the child of the former one. As a result, most of the literature investigating the issue of succession is based on cross-sectional samples. Few exceptions are Weiss (1999) and Kimhi (1994), who utilize data matched from three and two Censuses, respectively, to build panel samples. The empirical identification itself of succession is diverse. Many studies use statements by farmers of having identified or designated a successor (Potter and Lobley, 1996; Hennessy, 2002; Viaggi et al., 2011; Calus et al., 2008; Kimhi and Nachlieli, 2001;

Mishra and El Hosta, 2008). However, Väre et al. (2010) warn that succession plans as stated by farmers may not be good predictors of actual following succession. Glauben et al. (2004) also stress the difference between the decision of a farm succession and the designation of a successor among the children. Weiss (1999) and Kimhi (1994) identify a change in operation by comparing the operator's age between two following periods. Corsi (2009) and Kimhi and Nachlieli (2001) use the presence of a younger household member working on the farm as an indicator of a likely successor.

Table 18.1 summarizes the main determinants found in the empirical studies, showing the sign of the estimates. A first group of explanatory variables concern the farmer's characteristics. Farmer's age is, quite obviously, included in almost all studies, and shows a positive effect on the probability of succession.[1] The approach to retirement age favors the definition of a succession plan.[2] Several studies also include a squared age variable, to represent a nonlinear effect. However, some found the age-squared variable not significant (Glauben et al., 2009; Kimhi and Nachlieli, 2001). Glauben et al. (2004) estimated that the probability of succession reached its maximum at the age of 53, while for Stiglbauer and Weiss (2000) it was at almost 70, well beyond retirement age, in line with Corsi (2009). The overall conclusion is that for all practical purposes, the probability of succession is strictly increasing with the operator's age. It should be noted that this variable presumably mainly affects the farmer's choice. The only possible effect on the potential successor's choice might be when he/she has another occupation, and the approaching retirement of the farmer is an inducement to accept the succession and go back to farming. A related determinant is the age difference between the farmer and the oldest child, which is estimated as significantly negative by Kimhi and Nachlieli (2001) and Glauben et al. (2009). The idea is that children, if much younger than their parents, can be still too young and unwilling to make a long-term decision like accepting the succession.

Some studies also include the farmer's education as an explanatory variable. Stiglbauer and Weiss (2000), Kimhi and Nachlieli (2001), Corsi (2009), and Mishra et al. (2010), all find a negative effect on succession of farmers' education, particularly for tertiary education, which is interpreted in several ways. Kimhi and Nachlieli (2001) argue that in the bargaining game their theoretical model assumes between parents and the potential successor, more educated parents are more able to postpone the solution; to this, Corsi (2009) and Mishra et al. (2010) add the consideration that, even if farmer's education usually raises farm income, thus increasing the child's willingness to take on the farm, it also raises the probability that the children receive a higher education, which in turn makes their potential off-farm wage higher, thus discouraging the farm continuity. However, for Mishra and El-Hosta (2008) the effect of education is positive, arguing for a prevalence of the effect of higher farm income, and for Glauben et al. (2009) it is nonsignificant.

The farmer being a woman raises the probability of succession (Stiglbauer and Weiss, 2000; Glauben et al., 2004; Corsi, 2009). There is here some suggestion of gender roles, and mothers apparently are more willing than fathers to hand over the farm operation to their children. Also, Glauben et al. (2004) find that the number

Table 18.1 Determinants of farm succession in the literature

	Sample type and size	Indicator of succession	Marginal effects included	Farmer's age	Farmer's age squared	Farm size	Owned land	Farm assets/ wealth	Debts
Aldonando Ochoa et al. (2007)	cross-section 61, grown-up children only	stated		–	+	+ (area, LU)			
Bertoni and Cavicchioli (2016)	cross-section 143 horticultural farms	stated	X	ns		(workdays)		+	
Calus et al. (2008)	panel 713 farms							+	
Corsi (2009)	cross-section 8,134	child working on the farm	X	+	–	+ (SGM)			
Glauben et al. (2009)	cross-section 233	stated		–		+ (profits)	+		
Glauben et al. (2004)	cross-section 1 650	stated		+	–	+ (SGM, LU)			–
Hennessy (2002)	cross-section 300	stated	X			+ (area & income)			ns
Kimhi and Nachlieli (2001)	cross-section 133	stated	X	+	ns	–			
Mishra et al. (2010)	cross-section 3,471	stated	X	+		ns (income)			
Mishra and El-Hosta (2008)	cross-section 4,161	stated	X	+				ns	
Stiglbauer and Weiss (2000)	panel 50,000	identified by age difference between 2 periods	X	+	–	+ (LU)			
Väre et al. (2010)	panel, 97	stated and realised		+		ns		ns	ns

Note: LU = Livestock Units; ns = not significant; SGM = Standard Gross Margin. + and − mean positive and negative effect, respectively

Farmer's education	Farmer's male gender	Farmer's part-time	Type of farming	Regional variables	Labor market conditions	N. children	Public policies	Child's education	Child-father age difference
ns		ns (+)	X	X		ns			ns
−	+			X	X	+		−	
−	−	− (minor PT); + (main PT)	X		X				
ns			X (dairy +)			ns (M); − (F)		+ (non-agric.)	−
+ (experience)	−	ns (+)	X (specialization +)	X		+ (M); ns (F)			
						ns		−	
−		ns (+)	X (fruitveg −; dairy +; poultry −)	X		ns + (M); ns − (F)			−
−		−		X		ns			
+		+		X		ns	+		
−	−	−	X (specialization −)	X (region and hardship zones)					
			ns	X					

of male children is significantly positively related to succession (the number of female children is negative but nonsignificant), and Glauben et al. (2004) have similar results (but the estimate is not significant for males). In the other studies, not distinguishing children's gender, the variable of the number of children is positive (Bertoni and Cavicchioli, 2016) or not significant (Hennessy, 2002; Mishra et al., 2010; Mishra and El-Hosta, 2008).

A second group of variables included in almost all studies comprises various indicators of farm income (Hennessy, 2002; Mishra et al., 2010), also including Standard Gross Margin (Glauben et al., 2004; Corsi, 2009), farm area (Kimhi and Nachlieli, 2001; Hennessy, 2002; Väre et al., 2010), livestock units (Stiglbauer and Weiss, 2000), and profits (Glauben et al., 2009). The majority of the studies find a significant and positive effect on succession (only for Mishra et al., 2010, and for Väre et al., 2010, the relevant estimate is not significant). An exception is Kimhi and Nachlieli (2001), who explain their finding with past lower investments in large farms, that therefore require less labor (resulting in a lower demand for successors) and provide less income (thus attracting less successors). Without any doubt, farm income mainly affects the potential successor's choice to take on the farm, making it more attractive relative to alternative occupations. It is much more uncertain how farm income can affect the farmer's willingness to hand on the farm to a child. The only link with theoretical models might be with Rosenzweig and Wolpin's argument of a higher productivity of the offspring, due to idiosyncratic knowledge. If this were the case, then the causality would be circular, with successors working on the farm and raising its income, thus making it more attractive for them.

Similar arguments apply to farm wealth, or assets. Mishra and El-Hosta (2008) find a positive relationship with succession, as well as Calus et al. (2008) and Glauben et al. (2009). Mishra and El-Hosta's interpretation of their finding is that a large farm capital stock is an indicator of a high farm income, making succession more attractive for the potential successor. To this, Glauben et al. (2009) add the consideration that farm assets, in particular owned land, help overcoming borrowing constraints for the successor. Calus et al.'s vision is more articulate, since they see large assets as conducive to a more likely family succession, but also as the result of good succession prospects.

The role of part-time farming for farm evolution has been a largely debated issue. Stiglbauer and Weiss (2000) find that if the farmer works off the farm the probability of family succession is significantly lower, a result consistent with Mishra et al. (2010). In other studies, though, the effect is positive (Mishra and El-Hosta, 2008), albeit nonsignificant (Kimhi and Nachlieli, 2001; Glauben et al., 2004). Corsi (2009) distinguishes between off-farm work as a minor occupation (that has a significant negative effect) and as the main occupation (with a positive significant effect). Overall, it seems that the relationship between off-farm work status of the farmer and the succession is unclear and might hide different phenomena. As noted by Kimhi and Nachlieli (2001), a successor is perhaps less needed in a part-time farm; on the other hand, Corsi (2009) argues that a parent with a successor might work off the farm exactly because he has someone substituting for him on the farm and wants to leave him more responsibility in running the farm, while an operator with no successor might work off the farm as a prelude to exiting from farming.

The type of farming is considered by some studies. Glauben et al. (2004) show that a farm specialization is more favorable to a family succession than diversification, quite the opposite of Stiglbauer and Weiss's (2000) findings. A specialization in dairy has a positive effect on succession for Kimhi and Nachlieli (2001) and Glauben et al. (2009), who argue that dairy allows an early division of labor and involvement of children in the farm operation and provides more stable income. Corsi (2009) interprets the positive effect of some specialized types of farming (cattle, dairy, quality viticulture) as those in which the accumulation of farm-specific knowledge creates an incentive for intra-family succession.

Almost all studies introduce some area dummies. The rationale behind these variables is not always clear. They can be interpreted as indicators of the type of production prevailing in specific areas or as indicators of the alternative local employment opportunities for the potential successor. Corsi (2009) explicitly introduces local labor market variables, finding that those implying more (and more attractive) employment opportunities do reduce succession prospects, a result opposite to the one of Bertoni and Cavicchioli (2016), who explain it on the base of the higher profitability of peri-urban, high-employment areas for their sample of horticultural farms. Aldanondo Ochoa et al. (2007) find that the distance of the farm from the main regional center is significantly negative, and argue that the lower opportunities of practicing part-time farming at longer distances discourage the children from taking on the farm.

Only one paper includes among the determinants a variable that could potentially be extremely important, that is, public policies. Mishra and El-Hosta (2008) model the factors affecting succession decision of a sample of US farmers and, conditional on the choice being made, its nature (family succession, non-family succession, and exit). They particularly include, among the explanatory variables of a multinomial logit, expected government payments, which turn out to have a (weakly) significant negative effect, even if they favor a succession plan. No study considers inheritance taxes or retirement schemes among the explanatory variables, probably because they are common for all observations at each national level.

A few considerations are in order. First, assessing the sign of the effect is often insufficient to really appreciate the effect of a variable. When the studies are based on logit or probit models, not all report the marginal effects, which give the actual importance of the variable. When evaluated quantitatively, the effects of some variables, though significant, become negligible: for instance, $100,000 more wealth, according to Mishra and El-Hosta (2008), increases the probability of succession by 2%, and according to Corsi (2009) a 10,000 Euro increase in the Standard Gross Margin raises the probability by 1%. Both effects are very weak in practical terms.

Second, the link of the variables to the theoretical models is somewhat weak, since they have a limited, if any, capacity to discriminate between alternative models. The above review is enough evidence that different interpretations can be given to the same results. Since both the farmer and the potential successor(s) are involved in the decision, given that the arguments in their utility functions can be different, and keeping in mind that farm stability can have culturally rooted meanings, it is very possible that different behaviors can coexist, so that the outcome is a weighted average of completely different mechanisms, altruistic and selfish, interested or indifferent to farm continuity in the family.

Third, as noted by Glauben et al. (2004), some of the variables considered as determinants of succession may pose a problem of causality. This is particularly the case of income and wealth variables. A lower farm income makes farming less attractive for a potential successor, hence decreasing the likelihood of succession. At the same time, the lack of a successor typically induces operators to reduce their enterprise, for lack of motivation (Marsden et al., 1989). This cause-or-effect puzzle may determine an endogeneity problem in the analyses, as observed by Mishra et al. (2010).

Finally, the succession can be analyzed strictly from the perspective of the potential successor. Hennessy and Rehman (2007) model the occupational choices of designated successors, as predicted by the farmers. The choices can be full-time farming, part-time farming, no farming or undecided. Their results suggest that the most likely outcome is part-time farming, and that the probability of working full-time on the farm increases with land and herd size and with a dairy type of farming and is lower when the farmer has an off-farm job and when the designated heir has a third-degree education. Aldanondo Ochoa et al. (2007) use a random parameter ordered probit to model the choice of farm children to work only, part-time or not at all on the farm, which they take as indicators of the children's willingness to succeed. They find that operator's and child's education, child's age, farm size and distance from urban centers all have a negative significant effect on the probability to work only on the farm. Cavicchioli et al. (2015) assess the willingness of children to take over the farm in a sample of Italian fruit growers; the number of children, the female gender, and education have a negative effect, while farmer's education and experience have a positive one.

The effect of prospected succession on farm behavior and performances

Not only the farm characteristics have an influence on the prospects of family succession, but also the opposite holds: having or not having prospects of succession can affect the way the farm is managed. Marsden et al. (1989) point to the influence of succession on farm operation, contingent on the income prospects: "the lack of a successor was a powerful variable in explaining the decline of farming operations. Alternatively, for many more, the existence of children was a major justification for the expansion of activities". Potter and Lobley (1996), perhaps the first to explicitly speak of a "succession effect", find that farms where a successor aged at least 18 has been identified and is currently working on the farm are significantly more likely to have expanded their farmed area, to have undertaken significant capital investments, and to have acquired land, than those in other succession situations. By contrast, farmers lacking successors are more inclined to disengage and to decrease the degree of intensification of their farms. They relate this behavior to the family cycle. Other qualitative studies (e.g., Inwood and Sharp, 2012) also suggest that the identification of an heir promotes farm expansion.

Among the quantitative studies, Calus et al. (2008) use Total Farm Assets (TFA) as a predictor for discriminating between farms with a high or low succession potential. They show, based on FADN data, that the designation of a successor results in an increase of TFAs. They also note that higher TFAs imply better succession prospects. This is consistent with the findings that more profitable farms make succession more likely, if TFAs are taken as indicators of the present value of future income streams, and suggests a circular causation, from succession perspectives to more investments to more prospective farm income, which makes succession more likely.

Viaggi et al. (2011), in a study on the determinants of investment reactions to the CAP reform, investigate stated investment intentions by farmers in several European countries. The results suggest that the choice of increasing the investment is made by a larger share of farmers who have a successor (27% versus 6% for those who do not have a successor). Sottomayor et al. (2011), in a comparative survey in Germany, UK, and Portugal, find that farmers with a successor are more likely to retire at the normal age, to adopt new farm activities (in Portugal only) and to intensify production (UK and Portugal). In general, the logic behind this observed behavior is that the existence of a successor extends the time horizon on which plans and investments are made and renders investments more likely. Hence, as already noted, many variables that are considered as determinants in models of succession probability might be viewed in the reverse causality. Just as an example, Stiglbauer and Weiss (2000) find that farm diversification is a significant explanatory variable of farm succession. However, one might argue that those farmers who have good perspectives of succession adopt a strategy of diversification, possibly to reduce risk in view of handing on the farm. The same argument might apply to the number of milk quotas included as determinants of the presence of a successor on the farm by Hennessy (2002). More generally, this applies to various types of income and wealth variables (farm size and proprietorship, farm assets, net worth, etc.).

A strictly related issue is whether farm succession has a positive impact on farm economic performances. Weiss (1999), analyzing farm growth between subsequent Censuses, finds that farms taken over by younger farm operators in the previous period are 9.29% more likely to survive in the subsequent period, but the effect is significant only for full-time farms. A slightly different issue is the performances of inherited versus non-inherited farms. The results are mixed, although predominantly for better performances of the former. Laband and Lentz (1983) use US data to show higher income of children following their parents in the farm business. The results by McNally (2001) on a sample of European farms are similar. They relate them to the transfer of human capital from father to son. By contrast, Carillo et al. (2013), using the FADN sample of Italian commercial farms, and taking Value Added per Work Unit as the measure of performance, conclude that non-inherited farms outperform inherited farms. The explanation they provide is drawn from the literature on industrial family firms, arguing that family transfer does not guarantee the choice of the best talent for managing the firm. However, one should note that, if the comparison is made between the performances of the farms with and without a successor, it is quite possible that a selection bias is at work: the most profitable farms are more likely to have a successor. Vice versa, in Carillo et al.'s interpretation, non-inherited farms are more profitable because non-inheriting farmers choose to operate the most profitable farms. The selection bias problem is addressed by Bertoni et al. (2016) using a Propensity Score Matching technique on a panel of Italian farms. Their results indicate that the performance per ha of UAA (Utilized Agricultural Area) is lower for farms with succession, though it is higher if measured per labor unit, and no effect of succession is discernible in the most recent years. This suggest that the apparent superior performances of farms after succession is actually due to self-selection: it is the most profitable farms that have more likelihood of a successor.

Policies affecting intrafamily farm succession

Looking at policies influencing farm succession, the questions are the rationale behind the relevant policies, and their effect. It is useful to divide the policies between (1) inheritance laws and regulations, (2) general agricultural policies, (3) fiscal and retirement policies and (4) policies directly concerning farm transfers. Inheritance laws affect the transfer of farm assets, along with all other assets composing the estate. There is a large diversity in rules regarding farm inheritance. In some countries, the testator has little or no discretion as to the distribution of his property, while in others the testator has much more discretion as to whom to leave the land (Baker and Miceli, 2005). OECD (1998) distinguishes three group of countries in this respect: (1) those with a preference for a single-heir inheritance (Germany, Austria, Switzerland, Greece, Denmark, Sweden, Norway and Finland), where the legislation allows one single heir to inherit the whole farm, in return for monetary compensation for the co-heirs; (2) those based on the Principle of Egalitarianism, mainly influenced by the 1804 French Civil Code (France, Belgium, Luxembourg, the Netherlands, Italy, Spain and Portugal), where the principle is to ensure equal treatment to all heirs; (3) those following freedom of will, and referring to Common Law (UK, Australia, Canada, Ireland, New Zealand and the United States), where an heir can be designated as a single farm successor by testator's will and inherit a whole farm without any obligation to pay monetary compensation to other co-heirs.

The rules are mostly relevant in determining the evolution of farm structures when there are several claimants to the farm estate. Laws giving the right to descendants (and spouse) to a share of the estate tend to favor the fragmentation of farms, which leads to a lower efficiency if economies of scale exist. This is the case of France and the other countries of the second group, as opposed to the countries of the first and third groups. In France, for instance, children have the right to equal shares to the heritage. At present, the surviving spouse has the right to the usufruct of the estate or to one-fourth of its value, while the descendants have the right to equal shares of the rest, or to the entire estate, if there is no surviving spouse. In Italy, the law prescribes the shares of the estate that are reserved to the children and the spouse, and the share (a minor part) of which the testator can freely choose the beneficiary. The countries where the one-heir principle dominates avoid the problem of fragmentation, but at the cost of charging the sole heir with the obligation of monetary compensation to the other ones. By contrast, in the UK, Ireland and the USA, the spouse has in some cases a right to a share of the estate, but the children do not, so that the assets can be transferred according to the testator's will.

The rationale behind the French approach is linked to equity motivations, not to discriminate among children. Historically, the equal rights for the children were created in France by the *Code Napoléon*, and also responded to the goal of breaking the power of the aristocracy and the inefficiency of the system of *majorat*, according to which the whole property went to the oldest son and the land could not be divided nor sold. Nevertheless, both the primogeniture rule (like in Norway) and the equal share rule prevent the possibility of the testator's choosing the best fit heir, even if both rules eliminate rent-seeking by the potential heirs. This decreases the farmer's utility if ensuring the continuity and the profitability of the farm are arguments in his/her utility function.

The equity and rent-seeking elimination reasons for equal shares among children may nevertheless contrast with efficiency issues when there are economies of scale in farming and when the potential heirs have different farming skills. A material division of the farm among different heirs can decrease its efficiency. Hence, different mechanisms have been created to cope with this issue in the countries where the equal-shares rule dominates. For instance, in France the law envisages the possibility of a preferential allotment (*attribution préférentielle*) of the totality of a good to a co-heir, while the others are awarded a monetary compensation, or are even compelled to rent their shares on a long-term basis to the co-heir who is continuing the farm operation. In a similar way, the Italian law prescribes that if an heir is operating the farm, the other co-heirs have to rent him/her their shares of the relevant land. On the opposite side, in the UK it is possible to introduce limitations on the destination of land by creating trusts, though the law tends to limit the extent of the disposition (Commission of the European Communities, 1980). A final remark on this issue concerns the demographic and employment variables. The problem of the fragmentation of farms was more serious when the average number of children was high, but has been alleviated by the decrease in fertility, and by the increasing job opportunities in other economic sectors that induced many farm children to leave agriculture.

General agricultural policies may influence farm income and/or land value. Without going into details, most agricultural policies in developed countries have the goal of raising farm income, though in different ways and with different effect by type and size of farms. Regardless, the effect of farm income for the potential successor is clear, inasmuch it renders farming more attractive relative to other jobs and makes succession acceptance more likely. It is nevertheless unclear whether it makes intra-family transfer more likely from the parent's perspective. From this point of view, the crucial points are whether the farm value is higher if sold to the child than to anyone else, and whether the parent cares for the child or not. If the value of the farm is higher if passed on to the child, then the intra-family succession is of mutual interest, and any policy increasing farm income and farmland value will encourage it. Provided that some form of informal or formal agreement between the parties can be reached, parent's altruism or selfish attitude will not matter, though it obviously would affect the distribution of the benefits. The value of the farm, and the effect of agricultural policies affecting it, may be ambiguous in other cases. A parent interested in the child's utility will encourage him/her to take on the farm if the parent thinks that this is in the child's best interest and, hence, if it provides a good income. In this case, parent's concern goes in the same direction as the child's (which would explain the common finding that farm income favors family succession), and policies enhancing farm income should favor family succession. On the other hand, even altruistic parents are constrained in their generosity towards their children by the necessity of having an old-age income. In countries where public welfare system are widespread, old farmers can count on pensions, which should make them more willing to leave the farm to a child, as they do not need make their living in old age only from the farm asset. However, Mishra and El-Hosta (2008) note, with reference to the US, that for many farmers the farm is the only source of income for retirement, but they also find that passive income like Social Security, income from disability, and other public retirement programs and assistance, as well as government payments, have a negative effect on family succession. Their explanation about the effect of government payments is that they are capitalized into higher rents and/or higher land values. This seems to suggest a non-altruistic attitude, since if the transfer of farm assets to the children were constrained only by the retirement income needs of the parents, then both passive income and government payments should relieve the constraint and have a positive effect on succession. However, Pietola et al. (2003) have showed that farmers do respond to early retirement programs that favor both the exit from farming and the transfer to a new entrant (which can be the child). Mishra et al. (2014) have shown that the intensity of government payments decreases the intention of exiting farming, hence implying more likelihood of an intrafamily succession. Overall, the evidence for a selfish attitude of parents is not strong, and cultural values concerning the intergenerational transfer can differ among countries and, in each country, among individuals. The discrepancy between the finding of a negative effect of government payments in favor of agriculture and the general finding of a positive effect of farm income calls for more research on the issue.

Among policies directly affecting farm succession, fiscal and retirement policies are also relevant. However, this issue has not been investigated, probably for the reason that in studies concerning the same country the legislation is the same, which prevents detecting the effect of different rules. Only Glauben et al. (2009) assess the subjective importance of tax and pension consideration for the timing of succession, since they note,

In Germany, there are various ways in which farm succession can lead to tax benefits for the family of the farm owner [...]. Furthermore, there is a highly subsidized old age pension system for German farmers. Apart from age requirements, one of the conditions for receiving benefits from this system is that the farm was transferred to the successor.

Copus et al. (2006) ascribe to this rule the low share of farmers over 65 in Germany.

Policies potentially affecting farm succession also comprise Early Retirement Schemes (ERSs) and New Entrants Schemes (NESs). Such programs have operated for a long time in the European Union (they started with the so-called Structural Directives in the 1970s), and are typically implemented together; they are now under the general framework of Rural Development Programmes (RDPs, i.e., in the EU jargon, the second pillar of the Common Agricultural Policy (CAP)), but a direct payment for young farmers is also given under the first pillar. ERSs aim at incentivizing the exit of older farmers, NESs at supporting the entry of new ones. In this case, the rationale is that substituting younger farmers for older ones should enhance the efficiency of the sector. Basically, the issue is one of timing of succession, since the argument for adopting such schemes is that younger farmers are more efficient, and that a delay in the older farmer's retirement might reduce the opportunities for the successor or for the new entrant (Davis et al., 2009). Notice that this goal is based on the assumption of a higher productivity of younger farmers, which, though commonly retained (see the discussion on p. 339), has also been questioned (Davis et al. 2009). Also social objectives, such as guaranteeing a sufficient income to low-income farmers, are at the origin of some national schemes, like the ones adopted in France (Allaire and Daucé, 1996). The related NESs, in addition to the efficiency issue, are motivated by the concern for the aging of the farm population and by the risk of desertification in disadvantaged areas (European Parliament, 2008).

The effectiveness of such schemes as to the desired goals has been largely questioned. Examining the French Early Retirement Scheme 1995–97, Daucé et al. (1999) conclude that it encouraged farmers to accelerate their retirement decision, but in the following period the number of retirements was lower. Bika (2007) concludes that ERS did not change retirement rates on the long term. Actually, ERSs have little uptake: Regidor (2012), in a study for the European Parliament, reports that "in 2007–2010, the number of beneficiaries (some 19,200) and of applications approved (around 19,800) in the EU-27, 80% of whom were in the EU-12, was negligible". Copus et al. (2006) also state that "early retirement schemes have had relatively little effect" on the age structures. Among the factors that, in the survey done by Davis et al. (2009), farmers stated as important for their willingness to participate in an ERS, the value of pension and health considerations were rated first, while the desire to establish a successor on the farm was far less important, even if the majority intended to transfer the farm to their children. Apparently, the ERSs have little impact in general on the age structure and little impact on farm succession, too.

The uptake of EU NES schemes has been higher. Under RDPs, beneficiaries less than 40 years of age setting up for the first time as head of an agricultural holding could receive a support up to 50,000 euro (70,000 after 2009). In 2007–2013 around 126 thousand young farmers were assisted in the whole EU-27, with a total expenditure of 3.65 billion Euro, or 75.8% of the programmed expenditure (ENRD, 2014). However, the effects have not been the actual entry of new young farmers. Rather, the general view is that the scheme has been mainly utilized to pass on the farm to a young family member. Carbone and Subioli (2011) document with data from some Italian regions that the large majority of applications concerns transfer within the family, which is confirmed by INEA-OIGA (2005). The measure is subject to a strong risk of deadweight losses, as young farmers who would otherwise self-finance investments or use commercial loans can use the support as an alternative source of finance (Davis et al., 2013). As to its effect on succession, the measure can, in the best case, accelerate it, and in the worst determine only a formal transfer, directed to get the subsidy but with no real effect on the management of the farm.

Conclusions

The theoretical models concerning succession are quite varied and conflicting, since the basic assumptions are much different. Altruistic versus selfish parents is a crucial assumption, since motivation for succession from the parents' side is a prerequisite for the conceptually following choice by the child to take on the farm. But there is another possible component in the interplay, i.e., utility stemming from farm continuity. In some cultures, this can be a powerful motivation, especially where the tradition of farming is deeply rooted in a community, and is a value transmitted from father to son. Regardless, the diversity of theoretical models might also be explained with the coexistence in the real world of different attitudes. After all, it is realistic to imagine that there are parents caring for their children as well as indifferent ones and, on the other side, children caring for their parents as well as selfish ones. The models can therefore correctly represent different behaviors, of which the results are a weighted average. It would then be unfeasible to check the theoretical models on the basis of their predictions, unless one is able to divide a priori the population between the different attitudes.

These considerations might help explain why the empirical studies do not find many clear-cut determinants of succession. The only two that are significant in virtually the totality of the papers are the farmer's age, and some measure of farm income or wealth. It should nevertheless be added that another potentially important determinant, retirement rules and provisions, has not been investigated, and would require a comparative analysis across countries. The effects of policies concerning farmers' pensions have not been investigated in depth, even if they might be important determinants of succession choices. More information is available on the impact of Early Retirement Schemes and New Entrant Schemes that is apparently modest, being limited, at best, to accelerating the intrafamily succession where it has already been envisaged. Also general agricultural policies have arguably an impact on the evolution of the industry through their effect on farm succession, but this issue has not been much studied, though it would deserve the effort.

The most important policy variable concerning succession is probably inheritance laws. They respond, in different group of countries, to different policy goals and principles, among which equity, freedom of will and productive efficiency are the main ones. Some compromise among the different goals is visible in some legislation, mainly in the sense that egalitarian rules tend to have an impact in terms of farm fragmentation, so that various mechanisms have been envisaged to cope with this drawback. More research would nevertheless be needed on the effect of inheritance rules on farm structures, since the effect of fragmentation is not homogeneous among countries with similar rules, as shown by the diversity of average farm sizes in Italy and France, both adopting the egalitarian rule. It is a long-term effect, so detecting the implications of different inheritance rules and disentangling them from the ones of other policies and from changing economic and demographic conditions is not a trivial task, but it is an import issue for the long-term future of the industry.

Notes

1 Only Aldanondo Ochoa et al. (2007) find a negative effect of age, that they attribute to the sample of only farms with grown-up children. The probability decreases up to the age of 59, then increases.
2 Mishra and El-Hosta (2008) find a positive relationship with the definition of a succession plan, but a negative one with family succession.

References

Aldanondo Ochoa, A.M., Casanovas Olivy, V., Valmansa Sáez, C. (2007), Explaining farm succession: the impact of farm location and off-farm employment opportunities, *Spanish Journal of Agricultural Research*, 5 (2): 214–225.
Allaire, G., Daucé, P. (1996), La préretraite en agriculture 1992–1994. Premier bilan et éléments d'impact structurel, *Économie rurale*, 232: 3–12.
Baker, M., Miceli, T.J. (2005), Land inheritance rules: theory and cross-cultural analysis, *Journal of Economic Behavior and Organization*, 56: 77–102.
Becker G., Tomes N. (1986), Human Capital and the Rise and Fall of Families, *Journal of Labor Economics*, 4, S1–S39.
Bernheim, B.D., Shleifer A., Summers L.H. (1985), The Strategic Bequest Motive, *Journal of Political Economy*, 93:1045-76.
Bertoni, D., Cavicchioli D. (2016), Farm succession, occupational choice and farm adaptation at the rural-urban interface: The case of Italian horticultural farms, *Land Use Policy*, 57: 739–748.
Bertoni, D., Cavicchioli, D., Latruffe, L. (2016), *Impact of succession on performance: The case of the Italian family farms*, Paper prepared at the 149th EAAE Seminar 'Structural change in agrifood chains: new relations between farm sector, food industry and retail sector' Rennes, France, October 27–28, 2016, available at: http://ageconsearch.umn.edu/bitstream/245166/2/Bertoni%20et%20al_149EAAE_Rennes.pdf

Bika, Z. (2007), The territorial impact of the farmers' early retirement scheme, *Sociologia Ruralis*, 47: 246–272.

Blanc, M., Perrier-Cornet, P. (1993), Farm transfer and farm entry in the European community, *Sociologia Ruralis*, 33(3–4): 319–335.

Bryden, J., Bell, C., Gilliatt, J., Hawkins, E., MacKinnon, N. (1992). *Farm Household Adjustment in Western Europe, 1987–91*. Commission of European Communities, Brussels.

Calus, M., Van Huylenbroeck, G., Van Lierde, D. (2008), The relationship between farm succession and farm assets on Belgian farms, *Sociologia Ruralis*, 48: 38–56.

Carbone, A., Subioli, G. (2011), The Generational Turnover In Agriculture: The Ageing Dynamics And The EU Support Policies To Young Farmers, in Sorrentino, A. Henke R., Severini S. (eds.) *The Common Agricultural Policy after the Fischler Reform: National Implementations, Impact Assessment and the Agenda for the Future Reforms*, Ashgate, Farnham.

Carillo, F., Carillo, M.R., Venittelli, T., Zazzaro, A. (2013), Aging and Succession on Italian Farms, *PAGRI – International Agricultural Policy*, 1: 39–45.

Cavicchioli, D., Bertoni, D., Tesser, F., Frisio, D.G. (2015), What factors encourage intrafamily farm succession in mountain areas? Evidence from an alpine valley in Italy, *Mountain Research and Development*, 35(2): 152–160.

Cigno, A. (1991), *Economics of the family*, Oxford University Press, New York.

Cigno, A., (2000), Saving, Fertility and Social Security in the Presence of Self-enforcing Intra-family Deals, in Mason A. and Tapinos G. (eds.), *Sharing the wealth*, Oxford University Press, New York.

Commission of the European Communities (1980), Factors influencing ownership, tenancy, mobility and use of farmland in the United Kingdom, *Information on agriculture*, n. 74.

Copus, A., Hall, C., Barnes, A., Dalton, G., Cook, P., Weingarten, P., Baum, S., Stange, H., Lindner, C., Hill, A., Eiden, G., McQuaid, R., Grieg, M., Johansson, M. (2006), *Study on Employment in Rural Areas*. Final Deliverable, a Study Commissioned by: European Commission, Directorate General for Agriculture, Unit F.3. Consistency of Rural Development, Contract No. 30-CE-0009640/00-32, May 2006, available at: http://researchrepository.napier.ac.uk/2865/, last accessed 10/1/2016

Corsi, A. (2009), Family farm succession and specific knowledge in Italy, *Rivista di economia agraria*, 64(1–2): 13–30.

Daucé, P., Leturcq, F., Quinqu, M. (1999), L'impact du deuxième dispositif de préretraite agricole sur l'installation des jeunes agriculteurs, *Économie rurale*. 253: 51–57.

Davis, J., Caskie, P., Wallace, M. (2009), Economics of farmer early retirement policy, *Applied Economics*, 41(1): 35–43.

Davis, J., Caskie P., Wallace M. (2013), Promoting structural adjustment in agriculture: the economics of New Entrant Schemes for farmers, *Food Policy*, 40: 90–96.

Dumas, C., Dupuis, J.P., Richer, F., St-Cyr, L. (1995), Factors that influence the next generation's decision to take over the family farm, *Family Business Review*, 8: 99–120.

ENRD (European Network for Rural Developmen.)t (2014), Measure 112 – Setting up of young farmers, Rural Development Programmes 2007–2013. Progress Snapshot 2013 / updated May 2014, available at: http://enrd.ec.europa.eu/enrd-static/app_templates/enrd_assets/pdf/measure-information-sheets/C_Infosheet_112.pdf, last accessed 10/1/2016.

Errington, A. (1998), The intergenerational transfer of managerial control in the farm-family business: a comparative study of England, France and Canada, *Journal of Agricultural Extension*, 5(2): 123–136.

European Parliament (2008), *European Parliament resolution of 5 June 2008 on the future for young farmers under the ongoing reform of the CAP*, (2007/2194(INI)).

Garner, E., de la O Campos, A.P. (2014), *Identifying the "family farm": an informal discussion of the concepts and definitions*. ESA Working Paper No. 14-10. FAO, Rome

Glauben, T., Petrik, M., Tietje, T., Weiss, C.R. (2009), Probability and timing of succession or closure in family firms: a switching regression analysis of farm households in Germany, *Applied Economics*, 41: 45–54.

Glauben, T., Tietje, H., Weiss, C. (2004), Intergenerational succession in farm households: evidence from Upper Austria, *Review of Economics of the Household*, 2: 443–461.

Hammond, P. (1972), Charity: altruism or cooperative egoism?, in E.S. Phelps (ed.), *Altruism, Morality and Economic Theory*, Russel Sage Foundation, New York, pp. 115–131.

Hennessy, T.C. (2002), *Modeling Succession on Irish Dairy Farms*, Paper prepared for presentation at the Xth EAAE Congress 'Exploring Diversity in the European Agri-Food System', Zaragoza (Spain), 28–31 August 2002.

Hennessy, T.C., Rehman, T. (2007), Factors affecting occupational choice of farm heirs, *Journal of Agricultural Economics*, 58: 61–75.

INEA-OIGA (2005), *Insediamento e permanenza dei giovani in agricoltura*. Rapporto 2003/2004, Roma.

Inwood, S.M., Sharp, J.S. (2012), Farm persistence and adaptation at the rural-urban interface: succession and farm adjustment, *Journal of Rural Studies*, 28: 107–117.

Keating, C.N., Little, H.M. (1997), Choosing the successor in New Zealand family farms, *Family Business Review*, 10:157–171.

Kimhi, A. (1994), Optimal timing of farm transferal from parent to child, *American Journal of Agricultural Economics*, 76(2): 228–236

Kimhi, A. (1995), Differential human capital investments and the choice of successor in family farms, *American Journal of Agricultural Economics*, 77(3): 719–724.

Kimhi, A., Nachlieli N. (2001), Inter-generational succession on Israeli family farms, *Journal of Agricultural Economics*, 52: 42–58.

Kotlikoff, L.J., Spivak A. (1981), The family as an incomplete annuities market, *Journal of Political Economy*, 89: 372–391

Laband, D., Lentz, B. (1983), Occupational inheritance in agriculture, *American Journal of Agricultural Economics*, 65: 311–314.

Laferrère, A. (1999), Intergenerational transmission models: a survey, *The Geneva Papers on Risk and Insurance*, 24: 2–26.

Lobley, M., Baker, J.R., Whitehead, I. (2010), Farm succession and retirement: some international comparisons, *Journal of Agriculture, Food Systems, and Community Development*, 1(1): 49–64.

Marsden, T., Munton, R., Whatmore, S., Little, J. (1989), Strategies for coping in capitalist agriculture: an examination of the response of farm families in British agriculture, *Geoforum*, 20: 1–14.

McNally, S. (2001), *Intergenerational Succession on European Farms*, Paper presented to the 15th General Assembly of the European Society for Population Economics (June 16), Athens, Greece.

Mishra, A.K., El-Osta, H.S. (2008), Effect of agricultural policy on succession decisions of farm households, *Review of Economics of the Household*, 6: 285–307.

Mishra, A.K., El-Osta, H.S., Shaik S. (2010), Succession decisions in U.S. family farm businesses, *Journal of Agricultural and Resource Economics*, 35(1):133–152.

Mishra, A.K., Fannin, J.M., Joo, H. (2014), Off-farm work, intensity of government payments, and farm exits: evidence from a national survey in the United States, *Canadian Journal of Agricultural Economics*, 62: 283–306.

OECD (1998), *Adjustment in OECD agriculture: reforming farmland policies*, OECD, Paris.

Otomo, Y., Oedl-Wieser, T. (2009), Comparative analysis of patterns in farm succession in Austria and Japan from a gender perspective, *Jahrbuch der Österreichischen Gesellschaft für Agrarökonomie*, 18 (2): 79–92.

Perrier-Cornet, P., Blanc, M., Cavailhes, J., Daucé, P., Le Hy, A. (1991), *Farm Take-Over and Farm Entrance within the EEC*, Luxembourg: Office for Official Publications of the European Communities.

Pesquin, C., Kimhi, A., Kislev, Y. (1999), Old age security and inter-generational transfer of family farms, *European Review of Agricultural Economics*, 26: 19–37.

Pietola, K., Väre, M., Lansink, A.O. (2003), Timing and type of exit from farming: farmers' early retirement programmes in Finland, *European Review of Agricultural Economics*, 30 (1): 99–116.

Potter, C., Lobley, M. (1996), The farm family life cycle, succession paths and environmental change in Britain's countryside, *Journal of Agricultural Economics*, 47: 172–190.

Regidor, J.G. (2012), *EU measures to encourage and support new entrants*, European Parliament Directorate-General for Internal Policies, Policy Department B: Structural and Cohesion Policies, Agriculture and Rural Development, IP/B/AGRI/CEI/2011-097/E008/SC01.

Rosenzweig, M.R., Wolpin, K.I. (1985), Specific experience, household structure, and inter-generational transfers: farm family land and labour arrangements in developing countries, *The Quarterly Journal of Economics*, 100 (supplement).

Samuelson, P.A. (1958), An exact consumption loan model of interest with or without the social contrivance of money, *The Journal of Political Economy*, 66: 467–482.

Schokkaert, E., (2006), The empirical analysis of transfer motives, in Kolm S.C, Ythier J.M. (eds), *Handbook of the Economics of Giving, Altruism and Reciprocity: Foundations*, Elsevier, Amsterdam.

Shell, K. (1971), Notes on the economics of infinity, *Journal of Political Economy*, 79, pp. 1002–1011.

Sottomayor, M., Tranter, R., Costa, L. (2011), Likelihood of succession and farmers' attitudes towards their future behaviour: evidence from a survey in Germany, the United Kingdom and Portugal, *International Journal of Sociology of Agriculture and Food*, 18(2): 121–133.

Stiglbauer, A.M., Weiss, C. (2000): Family and non-family succession in the Upper-Austrian farm sector, *Cahiers d'économie et de sociologie rurales*, 54: 6–26.

Väre, M., Pietola, K., Weiss, C.R. (2010), The irrelevance of stated plans in predicting farm successions in Finland, *Agricultural and Food Science*, 19: 81–95.

Viaggi, D., Raggi, M., Gomez y Paloma, S. (2011), Understanding the determinants of invest-ment reactions to decoupling of the Common Agricultural Policy, *Land Use Policy*, 28: 495–505.

Weiss, C.R. (1999), Farm growth and survival: econometric evidence for individual farms in Upper Austria, *American Journal of Agricultural Economics*, 81(1): 103–116.

Chapter 19

Concluding remarks

Davide Viaggi, Sergio Gomez y Paloma, and Ashok K. Mishra

This book has investigated policy impacts under a number of different perspectives and in different countries. The background of the book is clearly characterised by a number of dramatic changes occurring in the context of future scenarios. Among several others, two major issues are in the spotlight. First, the need for further increase in food production brought in by rising world population. Second, climate changes affecting most of the world. This is accompanied by major technological changes, push towards a more bio-based economy, globalisation of markets and agricultural production. Some of these phenomena are only at their inception. Following the development of electronics and informatics, the current focus is on the digitalisation of agriculture, which is only at its initial stage and probably one of the key issues for the future. The same applies to technologies linked to genomics and materials. This book investigates agricultural policy in a changing environment. This concluding section draws from selected findings of chapters comprised in the book. We deal with this using the following main reading keys: changing agricultural structures and actors, the multiple roles and impacts of policy, the evolving policy instruments, different contexts leading to impacts and the needs for adapting methods. We conclude with some outlook considerations with focus on current trends and implications for further research.

Changing agriculture

The changing pattern of farming is the basis for understanding policy impact and for establishing the background of policy action in general, including policy-making and the political economy of agricultural policies. Agriculture is changing over time and the same applies to its actors, under a number of major drivers (Chapter 2). Agricultural structures have shown major changes over time. This has been especially true in transition economies, such as in the Balkan region (Chapter 4), but also in the Western EU and in the United States. Classic measures of structural change, such as farm size, remain key indicators. However, a number of more functional issues have become predominant over time.

First of all, we address the link between land and rural households. Farm households remain a key actor, representing the basis of farms and the medium for social impacts of agricultural policy. On the other hand, off-farm income has increased (in the United States, the EU and elsewhere, especially in industrialised and in service-based economies) as well as part-time farming, changing the reactivity to agricultural policy and the needs for more household-level income diversification strategies. This is studied, for example, with reference to Norway (Chapter 9). In parallel, move from household to legal entities is under way in many areas. This is accompanied by hybrid forms, in which household members are in the background of new legal entities. Farm succession is also considered a key issue and evolving feature in agriculture, as cross-generation interrelationships still determine a lot of the ways agricultural structures actually change over time (Chapter 18). Several areas are characterised by high rates of younger populations abandoning farming while the number of farms is decreasing, yet lack of succession is a problem, which, however, goes in the direction of encouraging structural change. At the same time, new entrants in the farming sector are more and more relevant, and their profile is changing due to migration in many areas. In order to look at the new dimensions of these social dynamics, attention needs to be shifted to the transfer of farming knowledge and how this occurs (Chapter 16).

Third, agricultural technology has changed dramatically in the last 80 years. As a result, agriculture has been characterised by an important increase of productivity. This has been more evident in the third quarter of the last century, emphasised by the increase of land productivity in industrialised countries, but it has continued even in recent decades, more focused on developing countries and on productivity of factors other than land (labour, fertilisers). As a result of these changes, presently, on average, the farming households do not have lower income compared to non-farming household; yet, incomes are more heterogeneously distributed and poverty is more relevant in rural areas (Chapter 8). This questions the rationale for generic income support to agriculture and rural areas, while highlights the need of more and more targeted policies even within the rural target population. The characterisation of this changing pattern is also linked to appropriate definitions and adaptation of statistical systems. However, statistical systems often adapt slowly, after changes occur and altogether are lagging behind, remaining mostly focused on a model of agriculture of the past (e.g., Canada) (Chapter 5). On the other hand, when systems have changed, it takes time before satisfactory time series are available for researchers and analysts.

Multiple roles and objectives of policy

The role of agricultural policy in the latest 80 years has moved from reducing risks and ensuring food production and income to farmers to a variety of aims largely related to rural dynamism and public good provision in rural areas (environmental, social). This can be seen in the changing objectives of policy and implied changing focuses of policy evaluation. In particular, it means that an increasingly wide set of impacts needs to be investigated. In recent years, due to markets liberalisation, climate change and prices volatility, risk reduction has again become a major policy focus.

Not only "flow" indicators, such as income and use of polluting input, are relevant to assess policies, but also "stock" values. An example is the impact of recent programs on farm real estate. This aspect has a prominent role in several papers in this book and is usually one of major concerns of policymakers when designing agricultural policies. Examples in this book confirm that the impact of policy on real estate values are very relevant (Chapter 12, Chapter 15). Policy impacts are also strictly connected to land tenure institutions (Chapter 14). The chapter reviews the variety of tenure institutions in Europe using different keys of classification; also interconnection with environmental regulation is a key concept in a property right perspective. The explicit attention to development and social issues has also shifted attention to new impacts, which also requires appropriate indicators (Chapter 3). This is in turn an evolving and diverse theme, ranging from more traditional employment measurement issues, to gender, equality, social inclusion and opportunities for youths, which are at the core of more recent policy and academic concerns.

Policy instruments and impacts

In order to meet the evolving objectives illustrated above, policy instruments have also evolved. On the one hand emphasis has been given to instruments less distorting markets and minimising barriers to trade, by focusing on decoupled policies. On the other hand, more budget has been devoted to actions related to provisions of public goods related to the environment and to the improvement of social aspects of rural life. One important issue is that these more target-oriented actions also require monitoring and sanctioning, with implications in terms of organisation and administrative burden. Finally, more complex mechanisms intervene on different entry points of agriculture and the food system in order to promote collaboration and innovation, especially towards chain coordination. More recently, innovation has become again a major focus of policy.

An example of the policy changes recalled above is the recent EU Common Agricultural Policy (CAP) reform, with its new instruments and their articulated application patterns in different countries. One major point is the new structure for the distribution of the basic payment (Chapter 10). Further characterising the evolutions outlined above is the current ongoing debate about the "greening" of the CAP, which is related to both the introduction of cross-compliance and more environmental friendly policy measures in the first CAP pillar, and also to the potential move of increasing financial resources to the second CAP pillar (Chapter 11).

Classical policy impacts concern income and farm structure. This connection is actually part of a loop between institutions, needs-policy design and impacts (Chapter 13). Farm succession is also a concern directly addressed by policy with both general income support (and stabilisation) and dedicated measures. The impact of different policies is also relevant; e.g. the impact of pensions on the youngest generations. The example of Taiwan shows how these different aspects are interlinked (Chapter 17). The adaptation of policies to evolution of actors is also an issue. An example is the tension between policies mostly designed for full-time farmers, and the economic and social reality, which is more and more marked by part-time farmers (Chapter 7). Another example is how agricultural policies in the United States affect household income for farmers and labour, and how labour policies affect farmers and labour income (Chapter 6).

Different contexts

One key issue in policy impacts is the context of implementation. It means caring for institutional settings, enabling factors and surrounding market parameters. In the process of market liberalisation and market globalisation, however, this is now only a part of the story. The real point is the interplay between policy in different areas and the role of local policies when stimuli are connected to world-trade issues. Migration has become a key factor in the policy context, with relevant hints on different aspects of the labour market, but also of the changing consumption patterns. Finally, land markets are not anymore local and closed markets, but rather connected by investments undertaken from one sector to another, and in different, sometimes far geographic areas. In general, land markets in a given area are the results of economic and monetary conditions which relate to that area to others, e.g. the exchange rate between the currency of that area and other currencies, which may make attractive the previous for investors coming from the latter; such has been (and to partially it is still) the case for investors from the British Pound (at least up to 2016) and Swiss Franc areas willing to invest in the Euro area – being the previous currencies stronger relative to the latter. Also, for several decades before the establishing of the Euro, it has been the case for investors from the Deutsche Mark and Dutch Guilder areas willing to invest in Southern Europe (Italy, Spain, Portugal, Greece, and to a certain extent France) – the latter having currencies weaker compared to the previous.

Outlook

The issue of assessing the impacts of agricultural policy is a growing subject. The issue is boosted by the increasing focus on agriculture as a producer of food and agricultural commodities to meet the demand of ever growing world population, while at the same time, to meet the needs of feedstock for the bio-economy and the expected provision of public goods. These interconnected tasks will give a prominent role to policy for the future, as it is maybe today evident that, in the agriculture and food sectors, it is hard to expect that the optimal mix of goods will be produced by the market forces alone.

On the other hand, the evolution of policy intervention has gone in the direction of much more complex instruments, more oriented than in the past towards the aim of favouring the enabling conditions for markets to operate, rather than providing direct incentives to actors. The main example is the move away from price regulation instruments, towards a mix of market stabilisation, income support, incentives to innovation and investment and compensation for the provision of public goods by agriculture in the EU.

In this context, policy evaluation has become over time a more and more pressing concern, especially under tighter budget constraints by most of the countries. The more and more articulated mix of different potential impacts, instruments and rapidly evolving contexts also brings with it the use of multiple methods for monitoring and evaluation, and most likely demands an evolution of methods researchers use for this purpose. Two interesting pathways in this direction are those offered, on the one hand, by the higher availability of interconnected data (big data) and, on the other, the need of integration of qualitative and quantitative instruments into consistent evaluation approaches.

Index

For Product Safety Concerns and Information please contact our EU
representative GPSR@taylorandfrancis.com
Taylor & Francis Verlag GmbH, Kaufingerstraße 24, 80331 München, Germany

www.ingramcontent.com/pod-product-compliance
Ingram Content Group UK Ltd.
Pitfield, Milton Keynes, MK11 3LW, UK
UKHW021022180425
457613UK00020B/1022